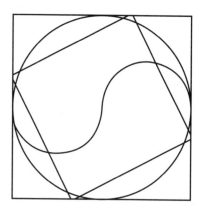

Human Systems Management

HSM

Integrating Knowledge, Management and Systems

Milan Zeleny
Fordham University, USA

World Scientific

NEW JERSEY · LONDON · SINGAPORE · BEIJING · SHANGHAI · HONG KONG · TAIPEI · CHENNAI

Published by

World Scientific Publishing Co. Pte. Ltd.

5 Toh Tuck Link, Singapore 596224

USA office: 27 Warren Street, Suite 401-402, Hackensack, NJ 07601

UK office: 57 Shelton Street, Covent Garden, London WC2H 9HE

Library of Congress Cataloging-in-Publication Data
Zeleny, Milan, 1942–
    Human systems management : integrating knowledge, management and systems / by
Milan Zeleny.
      p. cm.
    Includes bibliographical references and index.
    ISBN 981-02-4913-6
    1. Knowledge management. 2. System theory. 3. Organizational effectiveness. I. Title.

HD30.2.Z45 2005
658.4'038--dc22

                                2005048143

British Library Cataloguing-in-Publication Data
A catalogue record for this book is available from the British Library.

Printed in Singapore by World Scientific Printers (S) Pte Ltd

To Olga

To every thing there is a season, and a time to every purpose under the heaven:

A time to be born, a time to die; a time to plant, and a time to harvest that which was planted;

A time to kill, and a time to heal; a time to break down, and a time to build up;

A time to weep, and a time to laugh; a time to mourn, and a time to dance;

A time to cast away stones, and a time to gather stones together; a time to embrace, and a time to refrain from embracing;

A time to get, and a time to lose; a time to keep, and a time to cast away;

A time to rend, and a time to sew; a time to keep silence, and a time to speak;

A time to love, and a time to hate; a time of war, and a time of peace;

A time to ...

To Olga

Foreword

Human Systems Management (HSM) refers to the integration of three basic dimensions of modern business: knowledge, management, and systems. Increasingly, humans contribute knowledge rather than labor, energy or information. Knowledge is purposeful coordination of action and coordination is management. Systems, rather than specialized subdivisions, functions or departments, are increasingly the object of coordination and management.

The scope of Human Systems Management has evolved and its three main components, Human – Systems – Management, have been meshed and integrated to form a unified organism of thought. Human systems are systems with significant or dominant human contents or interactions. Humans are the source of systems interactions. Systems refer to an integrated whole rather than a separate functioning of separate, specialized parts. It is inadequate to manage human business *per partes*. Management refers to human coordination of human action in all their effective modes and forms. None of the three components can be reduced or omitted without degrading the whole. In the following table we list typical concerns of each of the three HSM components:

HUMAN	SYSTEMS	MANAGEMENT
knowledge	information	goal setting
intelligence	data	coordination
creativity	optimization	teamwork
innovation	organization	strategy
brainware	structure	tradeoffs
decision making	communications	self-management
judgment	reengineering	knowledgement
intuition	resource allocation	leadership
human capital	information technology	motivation

The above scheme provides a framework for HSM. None of the concerns can be isolated or applied in isolation.

All chapter themes are characterized by an integrative, systems oriented and knowledge-based way of thinking, which transcends the boundaries between social and biological sciences. They are providing the ideas needed for understanding networks, knowledge, self-management and self-production, as well as multiple criteria, conflicts and reintegration of labor, task and knowledge.

Even a headline in *The Wall Street Journal* refers to "A New Model for the Nature of Business: It's Alive!" and exclaims: "Forget the Mechanical – Today's Leaders Embrace the Biological." The time of the corporate organism and biological economics has arrived.

Networks are replacing corporate hierarchies as models for both inter- and intra-organizational arrangements. Many speak of the Network economy; corporate networks, cooperative networks, small-business networks, networking, intranets and extranets, network society, *keiretsu*, the age of the network, virtual networks, etc., all are entering the new vocabulary of networks.

Networks behave differently. People in networks behave differently. Technology in networks functions differently. Networks are different from hierarchies. We cannot use the old hierarchical thinking, practice and experience and transfer it into the network era by replacing a few well chosen words with "network."

Most of our current models are *static*. Both nodes and the linkages between nodes are predefined, fixed and often "hard-wired." Whether visible or not, real or virtual, the linkages are static.

In the Network economy we have to deal with *dynamic networks*: strategic alliances, supply chains and value networks, cooperative arrangements, customer and consumer communities, intracorporate markets, global markets, open-source networks, small-business networks, operations networks, etc. Their dynamics are essential: both nodes and linkages (relationships) are being continually and cyclically *generated, interconnected and dissolved*, or *produced, assembled and dismantled* – all according to the changing external and internal signals, conditions and contexts.

To put it differently, while the material and information flowing through networks is continually changing, in terms of quantity, quality and context, the networks themselves are being reshaped, reconstructed, reconnected and redefined at the same time.

"Information superhighway" with the highways continually dismantled and rebuilt.

New concepts of self-management, self-coordination and self-organization, rather than command, order or directive, are appropriate for networks rather than hierarchies.

Imagine a factory where machines transform a variety of inputs into a variety of outputs while they themselves are being redesigned, dismantled, reconfigured and reconstituted, in a dynamic and flexible fashion, in the process.

Modern production and service delivery systems are networks that produce not only products (goods, information and services), but also themselves and their own ability to produce (corporate knowledge): they are both *producing and self-producing networks*.

M. Z.

Acknowledgments

This book has been a long time in the making. Its completion was significantly affected by the horrors of 9/11. It has survived.

In writing *Human Systems Management* I have drawn on the information, knowledge and wisdom of quite a few people. It all started with the founding of a journal of the same title, some 25 years ago. The journal of Human Systems Management still exists, entering its twenty-fifth volume of global outreach, now being stronger than ever. At its beginning, there were just three people: Manfred Kochen, Erik Johnsen and Igor Ansoff – my thanks go to them.

Then there were the scores of excellent authors, contributors, collaborators, colleagues and friends who have all participated in the formation of Human Systems Management. Their thoughts are embedded not only in the text, but also in my mind and heart. They have all been excellent teachers throughout the decades of searching, learning and doing. Among them, I am privileged to acknowledge at least some, more personal mentors, teachers and friends: Erich Jantsch, C. West Churchman, Anatol Rapoport, Oskar Morgenstern, F.A. Hayek, Humberto Maturana, Francisco Varela, Stafford Beer, George Katona, Peter Drucker, Ilya Prigogine, Heinz von Foerster, Lotfi Zadeh, Thomas J. Bata, W. Edwards Deming, Joseph Juran, Myron Tribus, Homer Sarasohn, Nicholas Georgescu-Roegen, Kenneth Boulding, Ernest von Glasersfeld, Arthur Koestler, Yoshio Kondo, Leon Festinger, Paul A.Weiss, and P.L. Yu.

There have been many others, who worked with me or supported me throughout the Human Systems Management project: Christer Carlsson, Marek Hessel, Luigi Fusco-Girard, Yong Shi, Alan Singer, Malcolm Warner, Jeffrey Grau, John P. van Gigch, and Frank-Juergen Richter.

Then there were the most helpful "doers": Peter Djanev and Maximilian Zeleny, who worked tirelessly to see this project through. I remain indebted to Olga for her support, faith and encouragement. Without the patience and encouragement of Juliet Lee Ley Chin of WSP, this book would never see the light of the day. The trauma of 9/11 in New York has been just too much for me.

I had to get off my intellectualizing fence and choose my side: I did it, free, and once and for all.

Milan Zeleny
At "Castanea," January 22, 2005

Introduction

Human Systems Management consists of synergistically interacting components of human knowledge, its production and use, management systems conceptual development and technical modeling, and the management itself: as rules and principles of decision making, coordination and evaluation.

Human societies and institutions can maintain their cohesiveness and unity through their "rules of conduct." The order of social events, although it is the result of human action, has not been entirely created by men deliberately arranging the elements in a preconceived pattern. If the forces or rules that bring about self-organizing orders were understood, then such knowledge could be used to produce orders of greater complexity and effectiveness than those attempted by deliberately designing all the action and activities of a society. We shall show that if a social institution is self-producing (or autopoietic) then it is also necessarily "alive," i.e., it maintains its identity in a biological sense.

The task of human management is to stimulate growth of a network of decision processes, systems, programs and rules, i.e., an organization, which would be effective in attaining institutional objectives.

Humans *live* their lives through human systems – they do not "just go to work." Rather, they shape the institutions through their individual aspirations, goals, norms and action, creating a set of systemic aspirations, goals, norms and behavior, which could be quite different and independent of the individual ones. Humans are in turn continuously being shaped by such self-organized entities, their spatial and temporal arrangement evolving through a succession of interrelated, state determined structures.

A new mode of inquiry into such complex human systems is being evolved – Human Systems Management. It is based on a set of observations and experiences:

1) Human systems are to be managed more than analyzed or designed. HSM is not systems analysis or design.

2) Management of human systems is a process of catalytic reinforcement of organization, communication and bonding of individuals. HSM does not design a hierarchy of command and control.

3) The components of human systems are humans. HSM is not a general systems theory but an experience-derived theory of human organizations.

4) The inherent complexity of human systems can be lost through the process of mathematical simplification. They can be studied through a relatively simple set of semantic rules, governing the self-organization of their complexity. HSM is not operations research, econometrics or applied mathematics.

5) The interactions among individuals are not those of electronic circuitry, communication channels, or feedback loop mechanisms – they are action-based. HSM is not cybernetics or information theory of communication.

6) The order of human organizations is maintained through their structural adaptations under the conditions of successive environmental disequilibria. HSM is not a theory of general equilibrium.

7) The concepts of optimization and optimal control are not meaningful in a general theory of human systems. Human aspirations and goals are dynamic, multiple and in evolving, continuous conflict. Such multiple criteria conflict is the very source of their catalysis. HSM is not an optimal control theory or a theory of conflict resolution.

8) The inquiry into human systems is trans-disciplinary by definition. Human systems encompass the entire hierarchy of natural systems: physical, biological, social and spiritual. HSM is not interdisciplinary or multidisciplinary, it does not attempt to conciliate scientific disciplines, and it transcends them.

The way a self-producing, autopoietic system will respond to a gross environmental challenge or fluctuation can be highly predictable – once *the nature of its autopoiesis* is understood. Good managers and politicians intuit such adaptations naturally. They can be helped by good scientists using human system management concepts and models. Not so good managers and politicians fail to grasp why corporations and social institutions do not lose their identities overnight when they are presented with perfectly logical reasons why they should. And not so good scientists devote their lives and efforts to developing such irrelevant logic of strategy, design and change.

Human Systems Management (HSM) has two inseparable, conjoint ying and yang aspects:

Management of human systems – the science and technology of management, striving for productivity, efficiency, and competitive competence through innovation.

Human management of systems – the art of management, linking human beings into teams and networks, catalyzes their full creative potentials through enterprise and leadership.

In this book we try to start our walk along the above outlined path. The contours of the goal – an effective Human Systems Management – are only slowly emerging from the fogs of habits and experience. We do not pretend to achieve such goals through sharper and sharper defining and redefining the target. We sense it is there and we can see it come forth by thinning the fogs.

Contents

CHAPTER 2 MANAGEMENT OF SYSTEMS:
Global Management Paradigm

CHAPTER 3 PRODUCING NETWORKS:
Management and Self-Production in Networks

CHAPTER 4 PRODUCING DECISIONS:
Multiple Criteria, Tradeoffs and Conflicts

CHAPTER 5 ATTAINING WISDOM:
Wisdom of Management Systems

Chapter 1

PRODUCTION OF KNOWLEDGE: Moving From Data and Information to Knowledge and Wisdom

1.1 Information is Not Knowledge

In the Information era and its IT/S enablers, it is clearly important to establish essential differences between information and knowledge, information and data, and knowledge and wisdom. Without such distinctions and definitions, both the practice and theory of IT/S would remain plagued by interchangeable usage of terms like data, information and knowledge, often even within the same body of argument. Such ambiguity could be quite "deadly" as, for example, the undefined "intelligence" was for Artificial Intelligence (AI) or the undefined "life" has been for Artificial Life (AL).

The so called New Economy has already started using "knowledge" as its keyword, yet it still supports itself with Information Technology (IT) and not Knowledge Technology (KT). There are many fashionable fields and areas of research and practice which proceed without seriously defining their fundamental terms and concepts, and rely instead on a common or habitual usage of linguistic labels and their meanings, often dating hundreds of years back. Not surprisingly, they are often forced to face a speedy demise because their fuzziness and ambiguity broadens the realm of irrelevance and invites critical masses of shoddy work and thought. Recalling the fate of the once promising fields of Cybernetics and General Systems, among others, should be educational in this context.

The issue of distinction and definition is not resolved by engaging in hasty classifications. For example, dividing knowledge into the tacit and explicit without defining "knowledge" and without distinguishing it from information is simply curious. Here we attempt to offer some coherent and fundamental lines of reasoning which will provide the distinctions necessary for further effective development of IT/S, KM and emerging Wisdom systems.

1.1.1 Knowledge Era

"Knowledge" is rapidly becoming a new keyword of the New Economy, global hypercompetition and the Global Management Paradigm (GMP). It appears that the "Information age" has not lasted all that long. Management information systems (MIS) are already passé and Information technology and systems (IT/S) are often being referred to as Knowledge Technology. We are all starting to have quite a lot of information available worldwide and worry about Information overload and information irrelevance. Yet, we all seem to be increasingly aware of being short of knowledge.

So, the knowledge era appears to be settling in: knowledge industries, knowledge workers, knowledge as capital, knowledge support systems, chief knowledge officers (CKO), knowledge production, organizational learning, and so on.

Companies are investing in knowledge, nations are building knowledge infrastructures, and economies are thriving on brains and becoming increasingly indifferent to muscle. We are working smarter, not harder. Is having more information the same as having more knowledge, the same as knowing more? Is knowledge just a more complex form of information, tacit or otherwise?

The change from the Information Society to the Knowledge era is rapid, powerful and real. It is accompanied and supported by an equally swift change from information processing to knowledge production and management. At the core of the change is the fundamental shift from information to knowledge as a strategic foundation of business management, decision making and judgment.

That *information is not knowledge* is intuitively understood and evidenced by the shift in labels and vocabulary: "Knowledge" has quickly become a new keyword and yet "Knowledge management" has first emerged quite recently (Zeleny, 1987). The so called "Information age" is all but over. We are starting to have quite a lot of information available worldwide and worry about information overload or information irrelevance. Yet, we all seem to be increasingly aware of being short of knowledge, with no "knowledge overload" entering our vocabulary.

L. Prusak (1999) recently reflected on the status of KM as being "…much more focused on explicit, articulated knowledge (or data), which is really another way to say information. Now, there is nothing wrong with managing information." Indeed, nothing. What is wrong (and rather hopeless for the future of KM) is calling *that* managing knowledge.

1.1.2 Knowledge versus Information

"It is the greatest truth of our age: Information is not knowledge"[1]

It can be demonstrated that the richest nations are those well equipped in knowledge and human capital, while the poorest countries have and rely only on natural resources. But natural resources are not resources without knowledge, as witnessed by the "richest" country in the world, Russia. Also, the man-made capital of buildings, roads and bridges is useless without knowledge. Money can not do a thing without knowledge – it can only pay for it. Countries can be resource rich, information rich and still knowledge poor.

Only a few would argue against increasing knowledge, living in a knowledge society or continually striving for knowledge enhancement. Yet, many have already argued against information, especially wrong information or too much information.

Although it is quite natural to say that there is too much information, it would be rather difficult to even imply that there could be too much knowledge. Just try to say it aloud: "I know too much" or "there should be less knowledge" or "too much knowledge is bad." Compared to data or information, knowledge has a much more positive connotation. Knowledge is good. So what is bad about it?

The only bad thing about knowledge is that many people, experts and laymen alike, treat knowledge as some sort of higher-level information: extended, synthetic, advanced, complex, etc., but still information.

Although information is an enhanced form of data, knowledge is not an enhanced form of information.

It is quite clear, even on an intuitive level, that knowledge is not and cannot be the same as information, not even a special form of information. It cannot be handled as information, does not have the same uses and will resist any simplistic and expedient methodological transitions from information systems to "knowledge systems." Having information is not the same as knowing: not every well-read collector of cookbooks is necessarily a great chef.

Human language is not very precise on this matter because there was never before such a great need for drawing the distinction. We may even characterize a piece of information, like "the productivity at Toyota is 132 cars per employee per year," as knowledge. Witness: do you *know* it, do you *know* of it, how do you

---

[1] Caleb Carr, *Killing Time: A Novel of the Future*. 2000.

know it, he *has* that *knowledge*, she does not *know* it, and so on. Such language does not by any means transform that piece of information into knowledge.

We can also memorize or "learn" that piece of information; we can become quite *knowledgeable* about vast amounts of information – or even *have knowledge* of or *know* how to bake bread or milk cows.

Here, the last two examples do not fit. Baking bread and milking cows is not information but "true" knowledge. *Knowing* is what we mean and understand by knowledge in the modern sense. Knowledge is not a thing to be possessed, like information or money, but a process to be learned, mastered and carried out, like baking and milking. One can have information, one cannot have knowledge, one only knows.

Linguistic "knowledge" of information can be demonstrated through a statement, recall or display. Knowledge itself, i.e. *knowing*, can only be demonstrated through action, only through doing.

There is no way of demonstrating my knowledge of baking bread other than baking it. I know how to write books because I do write them. I cannot claim to know how to milk cows by a mere statement or by writing a book. I do not know how to manage a company, but I can provide you with plenty of information on that subject.

The expression "he wrote the book" does not prove knowledge of anything other than writing books and processing plenty of information. That does not mean that a good milkmaid cannot write a book on milking cows. In many areas they often do.

We can summarize our intuitive distinctions between information and knowledge in the following table:

Table 1 Intuitive distinctions.

Information	Knowledge
can be too much	is never enough
is a thing	is a process
one can have it	one must demonstrate it
Piece by piece	always a whole
Right or wrong	More or less
individually confirmed	socially approved

"To reach decisions, a President needs more than data and information. A President needs real and current knowledge and analysis of the plans, intentions, and capabilities of our enemies."[2]

It was Albert Einstein who cautioned our world that: "Information is not knowledge." Einstein also asserted that: "Knowledge is experience. Everything else is information." This was some time before the Information theory, MIS, IT and KM, before many world cultures started treating knowledge *as* information. As "Knowledge Management (KM)" got carelessly reduced to information and data manipulation and processing, and the oxymoron of "explicit knowledge" started making broad rounds, Einstein's wisdom (but not knowledge) became all but forgotten.

In the rapidly unfolding "Post 9/11" times of the 21st century, it has again become clearly insufficient to rely on our vast depositories of data and information. It has become quite unsatisfactory to rely on our information technologies. In this new world of new action we need to focus on continually produced, improved and shared knowledge and on new Knowledge Technology (KT) designed to support and expand the processes of knowledge formation, enhancement and transfer.

We shall argue that while information is a *symbolic description* of action, knowledge refers to the *action itself*, more precisely to its *purposeful coordination*. No amount of data or information will replace our coordination abilities, our knowing. In our view, information and data are mere inputs into the activity of coordinating production and generating processes towards achieving objectives or goals. When we know we do – and when we do we know. Being informed or having the information is necessary but not sufficient for a successful action in the knowledge era.

Relying only on data and information is already "so 9/10."

1.2 Knowledge as Capital

Most importantly, *knowledge is the primary form of capital*. All other forms are dependent and derived, only secondary to knowledge. Without knowledge, money is just a pile of paper, machines just a concoction of metals, buildings just a heap of bricks and concrete, and raw materials remain just that: raw materials. Knowledge gives life to it all.

---

[2] George W. Bush, At the Citadel, December 11, 2001.

Capital is characterized by the three requisite properties[3]:

1. It is capable of being bought, sold, transferred, and held
2. It is capable of being used, deployed, and consumed
3. It must remain available for the next production cycle

Many *capital assets* possess these properties and are therefore differentiated forms or components of capital. Capital is that part of the proceeds of production that has to be produced, maintained or reproduced in order to realize the next production cycle. The capital asset is that part of the proceeds that is set aside for the next cycle. Knowledge can be stored and consumed and still remain available for future use. Capital is therefore a self-renewing *knowledge matrix* that is to be continually regenerated so that the individual capital assets are properly embedded and coordinated in the matrix. Even if individual components (capital assets) are replaced, the knowledge matrix remains and retains its character. Knowledge is the "glue" that holds all forms of capital together. *Capital is the catalyst of production*:

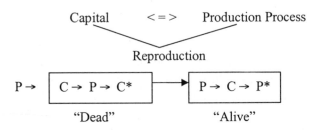

Figure 1.1 The two roles of capital.

Capital is the catalyst of production, yet, for some, production is the catalyst of capital. If the only purpose of capital is more capital, then production is just the means: such capital is "dead." Capital becomes a catalyst only if the purpose of production is to achieve more or better production: such capital is "alive." The purpose of knowledge can never be just more knowledge: such knowledge would be "dead." The purpose of knowledge is to achieve better or more action (production): then knowledge *is* a catalyst of production.

---

[3] Donald Dewey, *Modern Capital Theory*, Columbia University Press, New York, 1965.

1.2.1 Knowledge and the Prosperity of Nations

It can be demonstrated that the prosperous and richest nations are those well equipped in knowledge and human capital, while the poorest countries have and rely only on their natural resources and labor. Man-made, built capital is quite useless without knowledge. Bags of money cannot become productive capital without knowledge. Countries and cultures can be resource rich, even information rich, and yet remain knowledge poor.

Knowledge, defined as the ability to coordinate one's actions, alone and with others, effectively and purposefully, is embedded within and activated by human, social and cultural *institutions*.

Learning to coordinate one's actions, i.e., producing, maintaining and sustaining human capital, can only take place within a requisite social infrastructure: cultural and educational institutions, family-based kinship systems and shared experiences of history, habits, values, beliefs and aspirations.

A functioning democracy is based on respect and free-market behavior is based on trust. This is why democracy and markets are to a large extent learned behaviors, brought forth by strong cultures and social infrastructures. Without the learned and deeply habituated respect and trust, both democracy and markets become merely gaudy and often cruel caricatures of themselves. Russia and Eastern Europe are the prime examples of today.

Only socially and culturally strong nations, rich in human capital, family values, respect and trust, can ever become prosperous – regardless of their natural, physical or financial endowments. Only the learning nations, evolving their human and social capital continually and reliably, can ever taste truly sustainable prosperity.

A wealthy nation, like a wealthy farmer, must be able to continue increasing its stock of capital. Such accumulation of the capital stock enlarges the set of alternatives and opportunities for subsequent generations, thus making current wealth sustainable.

Increased wealth also helps to generate higher income, although higher income can also be temporarily created through decreasing one's wealth and reducing the capital.

Only poor countries, like poor individuals, live mostly from their income while only maintaining or even dipping into its capital stock. Income based on the depletion of capital is not sustainable and should not be accepted as income, but only as a consumption of capital. Only the poorest of the poor consume their own substance: they eat up their own capital endowments.

It is therefore the charge and challenge of current generations to leave future generations with more capital per capita.

There are at least four basic forms of capital:

1. Man-made capital, produced physical assets of infrastructures, technologies, buildings and means of transportation. This is the manufactured "hardware" of nations. This national hardware must be continually maintained, renewed and modernized to assure its continued productivity, efficiency and effectiveness.
2. Natural capital, i.e., nature-produced, renewed and reproduced "inputs" of land, water, air, raw materials, biomass and organisms. Natural capital is subject to both renewable and non-renewable depletion, degradation, cultivation, recycling and reuse.
3. Human capital (or human resources) refers to the continued investment in people's skills, knowledge, education, health & nutrition, abilities, motivation and effort. This is the "software" and "brainware" of a nation, perhaps the most important form of capital for rapidly developing nations.
4. Social capital is the enabling infrastructure of institutions, civic communities, cultural and national cohesion, collective and family values, trust, traditions, respect and the sense of belonging. This is the voluntary, spontaneous "social order" which cannot be engineered, but its self-production (autopoiesis) can be nurtured, supported and cultivated.

All of the above capitals must be developed in a balanced, harmonious ways. The last two forms are currently the most significant and effective in wealth and prosperity creation. The vector or portfolio of capitals, its structure and profile, is more significant than its overall aggregate sum. A country that has all or most of its wealth in natural resources might become an international supplier, but it will not progress *per se*. Although the tradeoffs among the capitals are often necessary, and sometimes wise and strategically desirable, they are rarely sustainable. The optimal capital portfolio could be negatively affected by irreversible or too frequent tradeoffs and substitutions.

In the long run, it appears to be the social capital which provides the necessary supportive infrastructure for human capital to manifest itself effectively. Through renewing primarily both social and human capital, and consequently also man-made and natural capitals, the set of opportunities is being widened for future generations.

Social capital is clearly critical, although one of the most neglected and ignored. Social capital is a spontaneous social order (an uncoerced and unforced civil society and culture), which defines people's abilities to work towards common goals and objectives in groups and organizations, form new associations and cooperative networks, and dismantle and slough off the old institutions without conflict or violence. It is the enabling environment for human capital to become effective.

Social capital not only includes business, but also voluntary and not-for-profit associations, educational institutions, clubs, unions, media, charities and churches. A strong civic community is characterized by a preponderance of horizontal organizations, self-reliance, self-organization and self-management. On the other hand, autocratic, centralized and hierarchically vertical organizations are found in societies of lesser trust, lower spontaneous sociability and thus of lower economic performance. The State then has to compensate for the lack of reciprocity, moral obligation, duty toward the community, and trust – a role for which the State is the least equipped and the least reliable to undertake.

Strong cultures, strong spontaneous social orders, and strong levels of civic trust tend to produce higher economic performance and generate wealth, not the other way around. Strong economic performance and wealth creation are not precursors or prerequisites to strong civil societies.

Nations with weak cultural and civic traditions will generally be poorer, saddled with "strong" governments, relying crucially on their natural resources and man-made capital, and neglecting the social and human spheres of existence. Wealthier and high-performing economies will typically be engendered by nations characterized by strong, dense and horizontally structured cultures of trust, cooperation and voluntary associations.

One would therefore expect the wealthiest nations to have most of their wealth embodied in social and human capital, only a lesser part in man-made or natural capital. For example, the wealthiest and highest income countries have, on average, only 16% of their total wealth in produced assets and 17% in natural capital, but some 67% in human resources.

The poorest countries are raw material exporters, having 20% of their wealth in produced assets, but 44% in natural capital and a meager 36% in human resources.

If we look at the U.S. dollar *wealth per capita* and the percentages lodged in *human/social*, *man-made* and *natural* capital respectively, we find, for example, the following "wealthy" portfolio profiles:

Italy	($373,000; 82, 15, 3)
Belgium	($384,000; 83, 16, 2)
Netherlands	($379,000; 80, 18, 2)
Japan	($565,000; 81, 18, 2)
Switzerland	($647,000; 78, 19, 3)
Luxembourg	($658,000; 83, 12, 4)

Japan has virtually no natural resources. The accumulated wealth is virtually all due to human and social capital investments. These can be compared with some selected "poor" country's portfolios:

Ethiopia	($1,400; 40, 21, 39)
Sierra Leone	($2, 900; 14, 18, 68)
Bhutan	($6,500; 8, 7, 85)
Zambia	($13,000; 9, 18, 73)

The above capital portfolios have so little investment in human and social capital that their future prospects are quite discouraging indeed. On the other hand, there are some poor and developing countries which seem to have the right "mix" of capitals, indicating a possible economic takeoff in the future:

Viet Nam	($2,600; 74, 15, 11)
Slovakia	($33,000; 78, 17, 5)
Czech Republic	($50,000; 66, 15, 19)
Mexico	($74,000; 73, 11, 16)
Slovenia	($111,000; 67, 16, 17)

Richer countries are generally those which invest more in their human capital, education, nutrition, health care, etc., over longer periods of time.

Some poor countries have relatively high incomes because they do not invest enough into renewing their capital portfolio, but actually consume their capital (consume their next-year plant seed). Especially Sub-Saharan countries have recently registered very high levels of disinvestment, negative savings and capital depletion. Most countries of Eastern Europe are artificially increasing their current incomes for political reasons, but at the cost of depleting their long-term wealth. It is quite discouraging to see many of such countries rapidly disinvesting their educational, health care, nutritional and cultural endowments, nurturing corruption and the anything-goes culture, being culturally blind to "dirty money" and fashionably myopic about their future.

This adds up to very short-sighted and nation-damaging policies, destroying nations' social capital and wealth, virtually irreversibly.

Many World Bank studies have confirmed the leading role of human capital in economic development. With the exception of some raw material exporters, human capital exceeds both natural capital and produced assets combined: sustainable development is best achieved by investing in people. Yet, the bulk of current economic policies remains focused on man-made capital, i.e. on the less than one fifth of total wealth formation. The World Bank and similar institutions have so far emphasized building assorted "Aswan dams" rather than founding technology institutes and enterprise foundations, educating people and expanding their self-reliance and self-managing opportunities and abilities. That is why most of the world still remains poor after some 50 years of misplaced efforts.

Many of the misguided policies are the result of naive beliefs and neo-pagan market worshipping, especially in Russia and Eastern Europe. Free-market efficiency is only one of the many by-products of preexisting moral communities.

Without such moral communities, the unfettered free market is neither conservative nor constructive but a most radically disruptive force, relentlessly dissolving the loyalty of corporations to their communities, customers to their neighborhood merchants, athletes to their teams and nations, teams to their cities, and so on. Without the culturally preformed, spontaneous social orders of trust, loyalty and reciprocity, a nation cannot achieve and maintain sustainable wealth.

America's human capital (Capital portfolio profile: $421,000; 59, 16, 25) accounts for some 60 percent – compared to only 15 percent for the produced capital – of the productive capital stock. Developing America's human capital is therefore by far the most important factor in maintaining its global competitiveness.

Lowering taxes for speculators in used cars, used goods, used stocks and used bonds cannot compare to the importance of giving the tax incentives to teachers and educational institutions, thus encouraging more and better people to educate their nation's children. The payoffs would be incommensurable.

Buying and selling used cars is no different from buying and selling used stocks for gain: no tax incentives are needed for speculation. Also, the wave of mechanically and politically motivated deficit-cutting efforts appears to be similarly short-sighted. Deficit-cutting could turn into a useless political exercise if the creation of crucial social and human capitals is undermined and their accumulation stunted.

Contrariwise, creating a reasonable deficit by investing in the most productive, non-speculative forms of capital and assets could be a safer way towards prosperity. Politicians often argue how they, as individuals, have to balance their budget. It is typical, especially in the United States, that individuals take out home mortgages that are up to 300 percent of their incomes – and these are clearly the richer, not the poorer segments of the population. The poor only have very little or no debt.

In other words, it is not how much to invest or how far to go into debt, but where and how and to what productive, non-productive or speculative purposes is investment deficit or debt applied to. This holds true for individuals, companies, economies, and nations.

1.3 Definition and Taxonomy of Knowledge

What is knowledge?

Knowledge is the *purposeful coordination of action*. Achieving an intended purpose is the sole proof or demonstration of knowledge. Its quality can be judged from the quality of the outcome (product) or even from the quality of the coordination (process).

If we can engage in any activity in a purposeful and coherent way, then we demonstrate knowledge or *we know*. Such purposeful action can be both physical and mental, ranging from doing and behaving to speaking and thinking.

The keywords are purpose and coordination (or coherence). In order to coordinate our action, we have to embody certain enabling structures, like neural patterns, physical and mental dexterities, appropriate concepts, distinctions and guiding images, and so on. All such enabling structures can be embodied though inheritance, learning, training or similar processes. A more comprehensive definition of knowledge would then read as follows:

Knowledge is an embodied complex of action enabling structures, externalized through a purposeful coordination of requisite activities.

Such a definition includes not only action itself (we do no act all the time) but also potential action through the embodiment of enabling structures, purpose driven coordination and a selection of activities. The nature of the purpose itself is unimportant and the efficacy of its attainment (or non-attainment) does not have to be explicitly mentioned. Knowledge is gradual, ranging from non-achievement, through partial achievement to perfect achievement and overachievement.

We naturally exclude incoherent and purposeless "trashing around," fumbling and disoriented action. We also exclude automated coordinations by instincts, physiological controls, reflexes and all machine-embodied coordinations. Although often powerful enablers, we do not typically refer to them as knowledgeable.

In this sense, any notion of "computer-based knowledge management" must be an oxymoron. Only data and information management and processing can be computer-based.

Similarly, the information management profession can never bootstrap itself into knowledge management without abandoning the computer's (information) storage paradigm and accepting the manager's (knowledge) action coordination viewpoint. Knowledge management is about managing people, not about managing data or information. It belongs in the areas of management and organizational behavior, not in management information systems or information technology. KM is not about data mining, databases, information warehousing, storage or exchange. KM is about strategy and organization for learning, training, developing, sharing and coaching processes and mechanisms in a corporation.

Instead of the comprehensive definition above, we shall characterize knowledge simply as a purposeful coordination of action.

In Table 1.2, the taxonomy of knowledge is outlined. Its logical progression is from top to bottom, increasingly enfolding more and more context of a purpose or purposes. For example, data are very simple elements, their purpose still unclear and ambiguous, with many degrees of freedom (Many different things can be "baked" from the elements, not only bread).

Table 1.2 Taxonomy of knowledge.

	TECHNOLOGY	ANALOGY (Baking bread)	EFFECT	PURPOSE
DATA	EDP	Elements: H_2O, yeast, bacteria, starch molecules	Muddling through	Know- Nothing
INFORMATION	MIS	Ingredients: flour, water, sugar, spices + recipe	Efficiency	Know-What
KNOWLEDGE	DSS, ES, AI	Coordination of the baking, *process – result, product*	Effectiveness	Know-How
WISDOM	WS, MSS	Why bread? Why this way?	Explicability	Know-Why
ENLIGHTENMENT		Bread, clearly	Truth	Know-For-Sure

Information is more purpose-specific, involving data aggregates plus their formulas and procedures. The ingredients plus the recipe do not lend themselves to baking many things other than bread. Once we turn data into information, it becomes hard to deconstruct back into its elements (it is impossible to reconstruct individual observations from their average or to reconstitute eggs from an omelet).

Knowledge refers to the actual processing of inputs (data, information, recipes, etc.), involving the coordination of action to achieve results, products or purposes. The rules, sequences and patterns of action coordination determine further *forms of knowledge* with respect to the internal or external validation of rules, procedures and outcomes.

1.3.1 Forms of Knowledge

We speak of *skills* when the rules are *internally* established and controlled by the subject. We speak of *knowledge* when the rules of coordination are established *externally*, by a social context, with expected outcomes being validated socially.

Skills are validated by the action itself. When he chops wood or types on a typewriter, the actor can evaluate his own action and judge whether it has been successful or not. A fallen tree or a typed page is the proof.

Knowledge can only be validated as an act in social context of peer or professional institutions which, not the actors, establish the rules. One cannot claim knowledge without a social validation; one can only claim internally validated skills.

Expertise is socially sanctioned knowledge (coordination of action) combined with the attained ability to reflect upon a relationship between the actor and the requisite *social system of rules*. One can master the rules of the profession, peer group or culture so well that they no longer need to be obeyed. Experts thus gain power over the rules and criteria that decide quality standards. Expertise just amounts to being able to (and being allowed to) change the rules. *The system (of rules) is based on learning from the individual.*

Observed or postulated modalities of knowledge (like implicit, explicit, tacit, objective, subjective, etc.) are exercises that are only secondary to the success of the achieved goals. If I can consistently bake good bread then I *know* how to bake bread – regardless whether it has been acquired or "learned" from cookbooks, training or experience.

Wisdom refers to explicability: If I also know why – not just what and how – then I am also wise, not just knowledgeable. Many can use information and follow the recipes efficiently: they possess dexterity and are specialists. They do not choose their goals, let alone knowing why they follow them. Only the master-chef knows how to coordinate action towards chosen goals. But only the wise man knows why such goals should be chosen and others rejected.

1.3.2 DIKW Chain

The progression from data and information through knowledge to wisdom forms the *DIKW chain* from which all our searches for a competitive advantage are an integral part. Progressing from information to knowledge is as unstoppable and irreversible as the future transition from knowledge to wisdom and the past shift from data to information. The DIKW chain provides a framework for evaluating and forecasting our efforts. We are entering (reluctantly) its "K" stage.

The current "K" stage is characterized by coordination of action. *What is coordination of action?*

Coordination of action involves identification of objectives and goals, selection of inputs (both quantities and qualities), establishing the sequences, stages and progressions, assigning responsibilities, delegating the tasks, carrying out the processes, and submitting the outcomes for evaluation.

Coordination of action involves not just Know-how but a whole range of other knowledge components which must be woven into a coherent whole.

For example, *Know-what* refers to the knowledge of objects, facts, components and goals. This involves either information (what to have or to possess) or wisdom (what to do, act or carry out).

Know-why refers to the explicability of action, relationship or causality. This can either be information (why is) or wisdom (why do). Wisdom always involves the explicability of choice and presumes selection.

Know-how refers to skills and capabilities to act or to do something. This is knowledge.

Know-who becomes increasingly important. Who knows what and who knows how to do what is a critical resource. It involves the formation of special social relationships to gain access to external knowledge.

Know-when is also a part of coordination. In fact, timing of efforts is crucial to achieving stated purposes.

Know-what and know-why can be obtained through reading books, attending lectures and accessing databases; the other components of knowledge are rooted primarily in practical experience. Know-how will typically be learned in situations where an apprentice follows a master and relies upon him as the authority. Know-who is learned in social practice and sometimes in a specialized educational environment. Know-when generally follows from one's own experience and acquired sense of timing.

1.3.3 Tacit and Explicit Knowledge?

There is an academic fashion to classify knowledge into categories, like tacit and explicit, without attempting to define knowledge. Expanding such classifications is the safest way for novices to enter the KM field. It is fast, cheap and pointless: it has no practical import. The only practical or operational contribution is that it draws a strong and useful distinction between information and knowledge and knowledge and wisdom.

All knowledge is tacit, in the sense of not being symbolically captured or described. As soon as it becomes recorded, made explicit through symbols or otherwise "captured," it becomes information. *Knowledge is action, not a description of action*. However, action is not really tacit in the sense of being implied, abstract or esoteric. Knowledge is fundamentally real and explicit. Although reading a book (information) on milking cows can be quite esoteric and intangible, there is nothing intangible or esoteric about actually milking cows and getting some milk from them.

So called *codified (explicit) knowledge* is therefore a symbolic description of action, which is *information*. So called tacit knowledge is action itself, i.e. the process of *knowing* rather than knowledge as subject or object. Knowledge (knowing) is purposeful coordination of action. Symbolic description of action is information. In other words, "All doing is knowing and all knowing is doing" as Maturana and Varela assert.

K.E. Sveiby (1999) supports this understanding quite clearly: "All knowledge is either tacit or rooted in tacit knowledge. All our knowledge therefore rests in the tacit dimension." Yet, the KM field itself is all about the explicit (capturable and transferable) knowledge, i.e., about information. This view comes from M. Polanyi's *Tacit Dimension*, asserting that "Knowledge is an activity which would be better described as a process of knowing." *To know is to do*, according to Sveiby.

It remains difficult to explain why so much KM effort has been expended on manipulating simple information under the oxymoronic banner of "explicit knowledge."

The very roots of the label "information" (symbolic description or codification of action) come from the original meaning of "in-formation": i.e., a physical deformation of the object or environment caused by the action itself.

Can information alone be used to coordinate action? Yes, but the knower still must impose or inform the purpose. Automated (symbolically captured) instructions, rules and recipes are information. They can coordinate action but cannot impute purposes. Purposeful coordination of action is *human* knowledge. When knowledge becomes automated (turned into information), wisdom and the explicability of objectives becomes the new frontier. This is already happening: as companies are becoming more informed and more knowledgeable, they – the best ones – are searching to become wise.

1.3.4 Measuring Knowledge

It is an often perpetuated myth that knowledge is somehow intangible or abstract, not really "real," and therefore difficult to measure. Nothing can be further from the truth.

Knowledge is very *real* and very *tangible*. What can be more tangible than an automobile we have produced, bread that I have baked or milk that I have brought from the stable? Knowledge *produces* very tangible things and very tangible things are the measuring rods of human knowledge. The value of money is intangible, especially during the periods of hyperinflation. The value of information is intangible, unless it is translated into knowledge and thus into measurable action.

Because knowledge is so intimately related to action and the products of action, it is also eminently and simply *measurable.* My knowledge of skiing is well and precisely measured by how well I negotiate a slope (speed, style, grace), as is my knowledge of bread making, measured by the bread itself (taste, price, quality, appearance).

Knowledge is measured by the value our coordination of effort, action and process adds to materials, technology, energy, services, information, time and other inputs used or consumed in the process. *Knowledge is measured by added value.*

What is added value?

It is the value of shipped (sold) products or services, corrected by subtracting all internal and external purchases (or the market value of) of inputs, operating costs, and general administrative costs (supplies, lighting, heating, transportation, traveling expenses, rent, depreciation, etc.). The total deduction of shipments is then divided by the hours worked:

$$\text{Total Deduction/Total Hours} = \textit{Added Value/Hour}$$

Observe that all salaries and wages can only be covered from the added value. If no value is added, no useful competitive knowledge has been applied, and no payment for successful coordination of action (knowledge) is sustainable.

Current knowledge indicators are primarily measures of knowledge *inputs* or codified knowledge – i.e. of information. Stocks and flows of *tacit knowledge*, such as learning that depends on conversation, demonstration and observation, cannot be measured by currently prevalent indicators. New indicators are needed to evaluate the *process of coordination* itself.

In the end however, it is not the measurement that is the most important part of knowledge management, *it is the process.* If the process of knowledge production, use and enhancement is well designed and organizationally embedded, then its measurement will be safely provided by the market.

1.3.5 Value of Knowledge: An Example

It is clear that the *value of knowledge* can only be measured by its specific contribution to the institution, market, company, department or individual in terms of its *added value*.

Knowledge is not abstract, intangible or esoteric. It is a most concrete, real and tangible process, the action itself, with a clearly defined purpose and criteria for its attainment. It is not intangible as all the symbolic descriptions of information, money, exchange rates or stock market valuations. Knowledge must be useful and its usefulness tested by an institution.

Useless knowledge is no knowledge at all.

All knowledge is action and so it can only be manifested in a specific, individual microcontext of space and time. Knowledge in the U.S.A. is not the same as that knowledge in Iraq; the knowledge of today is not the same as the knowledge of tomorrow.

Knowledge is part of human capital and as such it needs social capital (institutional infrastructure) for its embedding and manifestation. Knowledge, being a coordination of action, is *embodied* in the sensorimotor structures of the organism and *embedded* in the circumstance of its situational microcontext.

Descriptions and representations are just information and so they can be relatively context-free, neither embodied nor embedded. They can be "measured" in a *default context*, outside of action and situation.

Thus, the measurement of the value of knowledge must take into account both the individual (embodiment) and his circumstance (embedding).

Let us use a simple example which demonstrates the natural simplicity of measuring knowledge, regardless of the complexity or scale that could be brought into consideration.

The Iron Chef has invented a rather attractive *foie gras* based dish. He has mastered its preparation and is now offering it in his two restaurants in Manhattan and Paris. The dish went for $100 in Manhattan, but it pulled in $120 in his Paris establishment.

The calculations in Manhattan showed the following items:

Fresh ingredients	...	$50
Use of equipment	...	$10
Fuel & energy	...	$6
Information	...	$10
Time	...	20 min

It was the same in Paris, except $60 was needed for the fresh ingredients.

The information download included analysis of daily clientele, their preferences and the preparation adjustments. The Iron Chef served the dish himself.

The typical questions could be: What is the value of his cooking knowledge, in Paris and in Manhattan? How much should he be paid for his knowledge, per hour? How much can he be paid?

Clearly, we subtract the costs of all the inputs from the received price (market valuation of his product, based on supply and demand):

In Manhattan $100 – $76 = $24
In Paris $120 – $86 = $34

This is the *added value* due to the Chef's coordination of action, his knowledge of cooking the *foie gras* dish.

Observe that added value is different from profit. Wage or salary paid does not enter as costs, nor should it. Added value is the only legitimate source of wages and salaries. A business cannot and should not pay more than the added value of the knowledge services. Because the Iron Chef is directly exposed to the market, his added value is correctly and fairly measured. He should receive:

In Manhattan $24 × 3 = $72/hour
In Paris $34 × 3 = $102/hour

Observe that the Iron Chef's knowledge is clearly worth more in Paris than in Manhattan. The same knowledge would probably not add much value in Harare or Mogadishu. Its proper embedding is crucial. Also, a different chef or, God forbid, this author, would most likely not add much value even in *La Coupole* on Montparnass: the proper embodiment of knowledge is equally crucial.

The subject of Knowledge Management (KM) is the proper embodiment and optimal embedding of individual knowledge.

We should note that in traditional companies people are not being paid according to their added value, but according to their position and performance as evaluated by their superiors. They are not exposed to the market, but shielded from it. So, the evaluation of their knowledge is difficult, if not impossible. It is easier to pay them for position or performance, then for knowledge or added value. The danger is that some would be paid more than their added value and others less than the value they added through their knowledge. This is the price we pay for not letting the market forces penetrate beyond the factory gates: significant inefficiency and gross unfairness.

The only way we can realign the pay with the added value is through letting the market in – exposing the employees to the market valuation of their skills, knowledge and expertise. The Bata System of Management did that in the past and the Amoeba System of Kyocera Corp. is doing it today. Needless to say, both used *intracompany markets* with great success.

1.3.6 Knowledge-Information Cycle: ECIS

It is important that knowledge (process, action) and information (input) become interconnected in an integrated, mutually reinforcing system of a self-enhancing cycle. A process cannot be carried out effectively without the proper inputs. But managing inputs, such as information or data, autonomously and separated from action, decision making and judgment, would amount to self-inflicted corporate defect.

Clearly, there is a useful connection between action and its description, between knowledge and information. While knowledge management should and does include information management, information management, being an input component, cannot include knowledge management. The process can include its inputs, but no single input can include its process. Knowledge produces more knowledge with the help of intermediate information.

The purpose of knowledge management is to produce more knowledge, not more information.

In order to do that effectively, we have to concatenate knowledge and information flows into a *unified human system of transformations*. It is insufficient, although necessary, to manage, manipulate, mine and manage data and information. It is incomplete and inadequate to manage knowledge without also managing its descriptions. It is both necessary and sufficient to manage integrated and interdependent flows of knowledge and information.

Useful knowledge is codified into its recording or description. Obtained information is combined and adjusted to yield *actionable* information. Actionable information forms an input into *effective* coordination of action (knowledge). Effective knowledge is then socialized and shared, transformed into *useful* knowledge. In short, the cycle <Knowledge → Information → Knowledge> can be broken into its constituent transformations:

- Externalization: knowledge → information
- Combination: information → information
- Internalization: information → knowledge
- Socialization: knowledge → knowledge

These labels are due to Nonaka (1991) exploring transitions of knowledge: tacit to explicit, Externalization; explicit to explicit, Combination; explicit to tacit, Internalization; and tacit to tacit, Socialization. However, they are not separate dimensions and should not be treated separately.

The above sequence *E-C-I-S* of knowledge and information flows is recursively in a circular organization of *knowledge production*.

Every enterprise, individual or collective, is engaged in two types of production:

- Production of the other (products, services), heteropoiesis.
- Production of itself (ability to produce, knowledge), autopoiesis.

Production of the other is dependent on the production of itself. Any successful, sustainable enterprise must continually produce itself, its own ability to produce, in order to produce the other, i.e. its products and services. Production, renewal and improvement of knowledge to produce are necessary for producing anything.

Knowledge production (production of itself) has traditionally been left unmanaged and uncoordinated. The focus used to be on the product or service, on "one or the other." In the era of global competition, the omission of knowledge management is no longer affordable. Knowledge production leads to sustained competitive products and services, but not the other way around. Even the most successful products do not guarantee a sustained knowledge base and competitiveness of the enterprise.

The E-C-I-S cycle is concerned with *autopoiesis* (Zeleny, 1980), the production of itself. Traditional management is focused on its products and services, while neglecting its own continued ability to produce requisite knowledge for their production. Therein lies the imperative of knowledge management in the global era: information is becoming abundant, more accessible and cheaper, while knowledge is increasingly scarce, a valued and more expensive commodity. There are too many people with a lot of information, but too few with useful and effective knowledge.

The E-C-I-S cycle. We can now characterize all four essential transformations in greater detail:

- Externalization: transformation (knowledge → information) is designed to describe, record, and preserve the acquired, tested and proven-only, effective knowledge and experience in a symbolic form of description. All such symbolic descriptions, like records, manuals, recipes, databases, graphs, diagrams, digital captures and expert systems, and also books, "cookbooks" and procedures, help to create the symbolic memory of the enterprise. This phase creates the information necessary for its subsequent combination and recombination into forms suitable for a new and more effective action.
- Combination: transformation (information → information) is the simplest as it is the only one taking place entirely within the symbolic domain. This is the content of the traditional information management and technology (IT). It transforms one symbolic description into another, more suitable (more actionable?) symbolic description. It involves data and information processing, data mining, data warehousing, documentation, databases and other combinations. The purpose is to make information actionable: a useful input into the process of coordination of action.
- Internalization: transformation (information → knowledge) is the most important and demanding phase of the cycle: how to use information for effective action and for useful knowledge. Symbolic memory should not be passive information, just lying about in libraries, databases, computers and networks. Information has to be actively internalized in human abilities, coordination, activities, operations and decisions – in human action. Only through action does information attain value, gain context and interpretation and – integrated with the experience of the actor – become reflected in the quality of the achieved results.
- Socialization: transformation (knowledge → knowledge) is related to sharing, propagating, learning and transferring the knowledge among various actors, coordinators and decision makers. Without such sharing through the community of action, knowledge loses its social dimension and becomes ineffective. Through intra- and inter-company communities, markets, fairs and incubators, we connect experts with novices, customers with specialists, and employees with management for the purpose of learning through example, practice, training, instruction and conversation. The learning organization can emerge and become effective only through the socialization of knowledge.

The E-C-I-S cycle is continually repeated and renewed on improved, more effective levels through each iteration. All phases, not just the traditional combination of IT, have to be managed and coordinated *as a human system*.

Circular knowledge and information flows are stimulated, coordinated and maintained by a *catalytic function* of the Knowledge Exchange Hub (KEH). The KEH functions under the supervision of the KM Coordinator who is responsible for maintaining all four transformations of E-C-I-S.

For the first two transformations, Tuggle and Goldfinger (2004) developed a partial methodology for externalizing (or articulating) knowledge embedded in organizational processes. Any such externalization produces useful information (Desouza, 2003).

It consists of four steps.

- A process important to the organization is selected.
- A map of the selected process is produced (by specifying its steps and operations and identifying who is involved in executing the process, what are the inputs and the outputs).
- The accuracy of the process map needs to be verified.
- We examine the process map for extracting the embedded information: What does the process reveal about the characteristics of the person executing the process? What about the nature of the work performed? What about the organization in which this process occurs? Why is this process important to the organization in question?

What benefit (added value) does the process contribute to the organization?

There are two forms of information extracted from process mapping. The first extraction produces information about process structure while the second extraction produces information about process coordination. By producing a map of the process, a symbolic description of action, one extracts information about the process. The second extraction works with the process map directly (extracting information from information), i.e., shifting into Combination of E-C-I-S. It describes properties about the agent conducting the process; insights regarding the steps carried out in executing the process, and reveals comprehension about the communications going on during the execution of the process.

This methodology involves only the E-C portion of the E-C-I-S cycle. The all-important stages of Internalization and Socialization are not yet addressed. This incompleteness is probably due to widespread habit of treating the dimensions of E-C-I-S as separate, autonomous and independent. *Yet, they form a self-enhancing cycle and should not be separated.*

1.3.7 Theory of knowledge

A useful theory of knowledge comes from C.I. Lewis's system of conceptualistic pragmatism, rooted in the thoughts of Peirce, James and Dewey. Both knowledge and "truth" are necessarily social phenomena. We are able to bring our world forth only through the operations of separation and integration of sensory data. Knowledge, in order to be shared and validated through a social intercourse, must be expressed in words, which are further interrelated in language. We use language to coordinate our action in a social domain.

Because knowledge coordinates human action, socially divided or distributed knowledge can fulfill its coordinating function only through some form of language.

Especially John Dewey, through a thoroughly American philosophy of *pragmatism*, understood that action is internal and integral to knowledge. Action is not some tool for knowledge "acquisition" or belief "beholding": action is integral to whatever we claim to know. The process of knowing helps to constitute what is known: *inquiry is action*. Reciprocally, what is known by the knower is not stored as data or information, independently of the process of knowing: *action is inquiry*.

This simple, effective and powerful American philosophy of knowledge has been abandoned by American proponents of knowledge management: they proceed without definition, on the basis of a vague concept of "justified belief" (totally devoid of action), and with the mechanistic but void differentiation between explicit and tacit "knowledge." Why would Americans abandon pragmatism and action and substitute a simple, computer-powered manipulation of symbolic data and information, even renaming it knowledge management, remains a perplexing mystery.

Lewis captured the social dimension of knowledge through his term *community of action*. Congruity of behavior and consensual human cooperation are the ultimate tests of shared knowledge.

We as humans not only think (interpret) but also act (behave) and so we are part of a temporal *process*: the prediction or forecast of action shapes our present as much as our past experience. There is no knowledge of external reality without the anticipation of future action (experience).

It is proper to emphasize that thought or reflection can do only two things: (1) to *separate* (by analysis) entities which in their temporal or spatial existence are not separated; (2) to *integrate* (by synthesis) entities which in their existence are disjoined and distinct. Humans can either *divide* or *integrate* (more precisely *reintegrate*) *their* world. The nature of human knowledge must be correspondingly twofold: either analytic or synthetic. One can argue that we cannot integrate what has not been previously divided: any reintegration necessarily follows its preceding division. So, the early division and specialization of knowledge must be later followed by *knowledge reintegration*.

1.3.8 Language

Knowledge, in order to be shared and validated through social intercourse, must be expressed in words which are further interrelated in language. We use language to coordinate our actions in a social domain.

In addition, any coordinative language must display a sufficient degree of ambiguity, i.e., the same "word" conveys a more or less restricted meaning (or even different concepts) on different occasions; words must exhibit *degrees* of clearness about their meaning; and the identity of meaning is derived from implied modes of behavior (action).

Fuzzy labels divide the field of experience into classes with overlapping qualitative ranges of denotation. Without such an exquisite device, the human mind could not succeed in imparting order onto a given experience.

For the purposes of bringing forth relationships among concepts and thus fostering consensual communication among coordinators of action, meanings and their linguistic labels have to be "fuzzified" so that they become "common to different minds." To reduce such a powerful knowledge-building strategy to simple notions of imprecision, lack of information or vagueness would be self-limiting.

C.I. Lewis (1929) offers the following useful summary:

"In experience, mind is confronted with the chaos of the given. In the interest of adaptation and control, it seeks to discover within or impose upon this chaos some kind of stable order, through which distinguishable items may become the signs of future possibilities. Those patterns of distinction and relationship which we thus seek to establish are our concepts. These must be determined in advance

of the particular experience to which they apply in order that what is given may have meaning."

A large part of science is therefore searching (and re-searching) for things worth naming within a given consensual model of experience. All empirical knowledge of objects is only probable and all human judgments remain forever at the mercy of future experience.

1.3.9 Community of Action

Lewis also captured the social dimension of knowledge through his term community of action. Congruity of behavior and consensual human cooperation are the ultimate tests of shared knowledge.

Consensual cooperation of human beings does not stem from some vague identity of their psychological perception, experience or compatible worldviews. It stems from their inherent propensity toward action, their basic similarity of needs, and their shared physiological structure. The wonder of consensual cooperation is that it can take place within the realm of vast diversity of sensual and social experiences.

Human beings possess a strong natural tendency toward explicit and implicit cooperation. Socially engineered destruction of their consensually shared concepts and common actions – like the social isolation stemming from the extreme specialization and division of task, labor and knowledge – reduces human consensual communication to a minimum and replaces it with man-designed non-consensual communication "bypass": an externally imposed and enforced form of coordination of action. The purpose of communication is the coordination of behavior: it is therefore essential that all of its aspects remain consensual.

1.3.10 Knowledge as a Process

Human knowledge cannot refer to simple static descriptions or "captures" of facts, things or objects, that is data and information "out there" that is outside us, in the "objective world." Such "captures" and "codifications" could only be labeled as data or information, but they cannot constitute knowledge because they describe separate objects and not their *relationships*. Knowledge is about *coordinating* and *relating* descriptions of objects into coherent complexes. The relationships among objects are not simply "out there," to be captured, but are being continually produced, constructed, deconstructed and re-established by the knower, the agent of action.

Knowledge thus cannot be separated from the process of knowing (establishing and coordinating relationships). Knowledge and knowing are identical: *knowledge is a process.*

What is meant when we say that somebody knows or possesses knowledge? We imply that we expect one to be capable of *coordinated action* towards some goals and objectives. Coordinated action is the test of possessing knowledge. Knowledge without action reduces to simple information or data: *All doing is knowing, and all knowing is doing.*

Vast repositories of data and information (data banks, warehouses, info marts, encyclopedias) are only passive recordings of the "raw material" of knowledge. Only coordinated human action, i.e., the process of relating such components into coherent patterns, which turn out to be successful in achieving goals and purposes, qualifies as knowledge.

Among the myriads of possible relationships among objects, only some result in a successful coordinated action. Every such act of knowing brings forth a world of action.

Bringing forth a world of coordinated action is human knowledge.

Bringing forth such a world manifests itself in all our action and all our being. *Knowing is effective* [i.e., coordinated and "successful"] *action.*

Knowledge as an effective action enables a living (human) being to persist in his coordinated existence in a specific environment from which he continually brings forth his own world of action. All knowing is coordinated action by the knower and therefore depends on the "structure" of the knower. The way knowledge can be brought forth in doing depends on the nature of "doing" as it is implied by the organization of the knower and his circumstances (working environment).

1.3.11 Uses and Users of Knowledge

Knowledge is an effective coordination of action. For example, a baker coordinates his actions so effectively that the result is not only edible but also "good" and generally desirable. He *knows* how to make bread.

A successful baker can also share his knowledge: he can teach others how to make bread that is "good." He can also share his knowledge *by parts,* instructing others how to perform smaller parts of the entire task and retaining only the overall coordinative function. Ultimately, he might lose the detailed knowledge of all the subtasks and thus of the integrated knowledge of making bread. At such point, no single individual would know the entire task. Such is the situation present after the millennia of progressive division of task, labor and knowledge.

According to F.A. von Hayek, the central question of all social sciences is precisely that: how combining the *fragments of knowledge*, residing in different minds, can bring about results which, if they were to be brought about deliberately, would require knowledge on the part of the directing mind which no single person can possess. No single individual or even group of individuals can know how to build a space shuttle and yet space shuttles get built.

Most human knowledge has been dispersed into the bits and pieces of specialization, into all the incomplete and contradictory information possessed by separate individuals.

There are at least two essential modes of approaching this dilemma:

All local knowledge is conveyed to the central authority, integrated and used to form plans which are then communicated down to the local agents for the purposes of coordinating their action by command and order.
Central or strategic knowledge is supplied to individuals and their localities as an additional knowledge, needed by them in order to coordinate their own plans and actions with those of other similar localities (self-coordination).

The first mode (centralized planning) prevails in traditional corporations and separates coordination from action, limiting the value of local knowledge and ultimately transforming local agents into executors with substantially constrained freedom to act and accept responsibility. The second mode (decentralized planning) enriches local knowledge and enhances agents' responsibility for the purposes and execution of their own autonomous coordination of action.

Local agents (workers and employees) possess crucial and irreplaceable knowledge of the particular context and circumstance of time and place. Each individual agent thus possesses knowledge that is *unique*. We can treat this unique knowledge of people, local conditions and special circumstances, as an asset to be enhanced and enriched, or we can treat this unique knowledge (and its possessors) with contempt and replace it with context-free and locally useless directives of specialist expert coordinators.

What is the strategic frame to be communicated to the possessors of local knowledge? Do they need to know all the reasons why the quantities or qualities of particular items have changed? Certainly not. They need a simple information index which would reliably indicate how scarce or abundant a particular item or its attribute is at any given moment. Such a numerical index should not be derived from any intrinsic properties of things, because it has to be continually adjustable and changeable in order to reflect *immediate relationships* of the relative scarcity of things. In other words, a *system of free prices* is what is needed for the *effective* coordination of action *within a corporation*.

Prices are the necessary informational "glue" that allow free agents to coordinate action even under conditions of significant division of knowledge. Free market prices are the most effective telecommunication system of broadcasting and circulating relevant information among economic agents and thus assuring their explicit (and implicit) cooperation.

1.4 Division and Reintegration of Knowledge

There is a wealth of economically and socially valuable concepts hidden in the now overused and overrated notion of the "division of labor." Today it is the *division of knowledge,* rather than the division of labor, that determines the limits and potential competitiveness and productivity of an enterprise. As usual, it is still Friedrich von Hayek who was "there already":

"Clearly there is here a problem of the division of knowledge, which is quite analogous to, and at least as important as, the problem of the division of labor. But, while the latter has been one of the main subjects of investigation ever since the beginning of our science, the former has been as completely neglected, although it seems to me to be the really central problem of economics as a social science."

Division of knowledge *is* the central problem of economics as a social science. Especially today, when neither traditional economics or knowledge management address the issues of the division of knowledge, important insights and opportunities continue being lost to the business and management community.

One important exception is the current thought of Joseph Stiglitz who appears to understand von Hayek's insights and restates them in the modern language of knowledge economy:

"The information transmitted upwards in a hierarchy to inform decisions is explicit codified information, so decisions are made in a hierarchical structure without lower level uncodified tacit knowledge. Better decisions might be made lower in the hierarchy closer to the source of the knowledge. Decentralized authority also partly unifies principal and agent to mitigate agency problems. When these local decisions require informational inputs from various different job categories, it is best for the decision-makers to have rotated through those job categories to have acquired their tacit components. These arguments for fuzzy job boundaries and job rotation cut against the traditional arguments for specialization and division of labor."

The fuzzy job boundaries are represented in the following Figure 1.2. Many arguments against the specialization, division of labor and division of knowledge have accumulated.

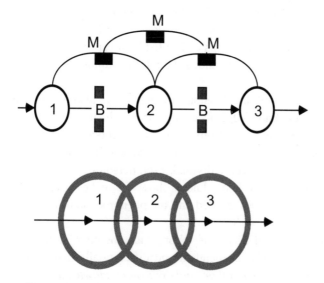

Figure 1.2 Fuzzy job boundaries as an enabler of knowledge.

Division of knowledge needs a hierarchy of coordination – layers upon layers of bureaucracy. Division of knowledge does not promote cooperation but rather separates the agents through barriers and buffers interlaced throughout the process. Reintegration of knowledge enables the agents in cooperation, innovation, and coordination of their efforts.

How has the fragmentation of knowledge, task and labor surpassed its natural and economic limits?

First, any task can be broken into a large number of subtasks and operations. Such task disaggregation then allows parallel processing and could translate directly into increased productivity. This kind of division is directly related to the *number of parts* constituting the product. As long as such tasks are performed either by a single worker or by a number of automated machines, there is no reason to talk about the division of labor, but only about the *division of task*. Some products consist of thousands of parts, including all sorts of accessible or less accessible screws, nuts, washers, bolts, caps and pins. This type of "medieval" product design is bound to be of a low quality and reliability.

Second, in order to realize the *parallel processing* of thousands of specialized tasks, different tasks have to be performed and controlled by *different workers*: labor itself has to be appropriately divided. Only in this sense can we talk about the *division of labor* properly. Division of task may or may not be followed by the division of labor. If a hundred workers, coordinated by a supervisor, were replaced by a hundred machines controlled by a supervisor, the division of labor would be reduced to a 100:1 ratio, although the number of subtasks remained the same.

Third, together with the division of labor we are also disaggregating, dividing and dispersing the knowledge necessary for coordination of the entire task. When one person makes a chair, from cutting the proper wood to selling it at the market, such a person commands a full package of the chair-making knowledge. As the task and labor become divided, each person can claim only a part of that overall knowledge: "Nobody knows how to make a chair anymore." The knowledge itself becomes divided and the phenomenon of *division of knowledge* must be considered.

The concept of "division of labor" thus includes at least three separate, separable and relatively independent and differentially manageable phenomena: *division of task, division of labor, and division of knowledge.*

Originally, one person would perform the entire task: he would make his own clothes, starting from hunting for the animal and ending with the sewing and decorating. As the process of division of labor advances, more and more people become involved and their subtasks become more specialized. Coordinative agents and leaders (precursors of today's management) soon emerged. As markets grew, the division of labor and specialization expanded correspondingly.

In Figure 1.3, we show how the division of labor leads to the emergence of coordinating agents (M1, M2 and M) organized properly in a coordinative hierarchy, because of the individually limited *span of control* (Urwick's old dictum that no human brain should attempt to supervise more than five or six other individuals). Although the productivity increases, the complexity and the cost of coordination increase even faster. Division of labor is limited by its own requisite cost and complexity of coordination, *not* solely by the Smithian extent of the market.

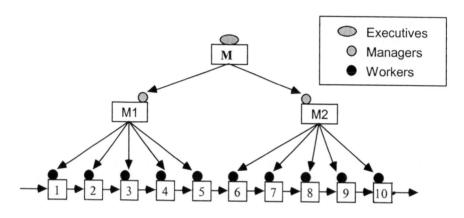

Figure 1.3 Division of labor.

Every subsequent doubling of the number of specialized subtasks (and laborers) leads to more than double the requisite number of coordinators (managers). Coordinative hierarchy is bound to grow in size, complexity and costs.

Ultimately the cost and complexity of requisite coordination, accompanied by frequent breaks in communication and increases in misinformation, make further division of labor less and less attractive.

Coordinative hierarchies and bureaucracies can be viewed as representing a form of *social memory*. Since nobody knows how to make a space shuttle and yet space shuttles get built, coordinative hierarchies are a way of *preserving and storing societal knowledge*. The more splintered the task, labor and knowledge, the larger and more complex the coordinative hierarchies must be.

Only a purposeful reintegration of task, labor and knowledge reduces bureaucratic hierarchies permanently.

the desired schedule programmed. At a pre-selected hour Auto Bakery starts mixing, kneading, yeasting, punching and shaping the dough, with sensitive microprocessors monitoring the room temperature and continually optimizing the process. Similarly controlled is the actual baking so that every single product is perfect. The whole automated process takes 3-4 hours and the system can be "primed" up to 12 hours ahead of time.

More importantly, large number of tested recipes is now available and unlimited number of recipes can be introduced and experimented with by the consumer. From beer bread and cheese bread to rolls, bagels and croissants, every morning freshly baked on a kitchen table for the whole family and by one person. The whole process is directly observable through a clear dome cover.

3. Knowledge Reintegration

Any reintegration of labor must be accompanied by the corresponding reintegration of knowledge. As the task is performed by a smaller number of persons, the originally scattered knowledge has to be brought together and concentrated. Reintegrated knowledge, being a process of coordination of action, can be stored either in human brain or in the technology itself.

Both processes are taking place: workers are mastering broader and multiple functions, engaging in job rotation and enhancing their own flexibility. At the same time, technologies are absorbing larger number of steps of task coordination and thus more knowledge is being embedded in them. Both examples presented above demonstrate a high degree of such knowledge reintegration.

To provide a different example, not so excessively dependent on technology, we note the reintegration of knowledge (coordination of action) at one of the best run ranches in the U.S.: Pitchfork Ranch (Meeteetse, Wyoming), established in 1878. In 1986 Pitchfork had more than 120,000 acres and employed only ten rather than hundreds of cowboys of the earlier times.

On most classical ranches different people do different jobs. At Pitchfork, *whatever the job is* – farming, calving, plumbing, or irrigating the fields – the same and any cowboy does it. Current manager Jack Turnell hires only the best multitalented people he can find. Then the simple management rule is: "pay them well and treat them well."

One is here reminded of the entrepreneur Ross Perot, who expressed the need for integrated-knowledge systems through the following metaphor: *If you are the first to see a snake, kill it.* At most mass-production bureaucracies, if you see a snake, the first thing you do is go and hire a consultant on snakes. Then you get a committee on snakes, and then you discuss it for a couple of years. The most likely course of action is nothing. There is a need for management system where the first person who encounters a problem is also able to take care of it.

As labor becomes work again, meaning is replacing alienation, professionalism and craftsmanship are replacing expertism and specialization. The basic coordinative mechanisms of traditional administrative management of labor-performing operators are being replaced by the self-coordinative systems of *mutual adjustment* and by the *consensual reciprocity* of modern "craftsmen."

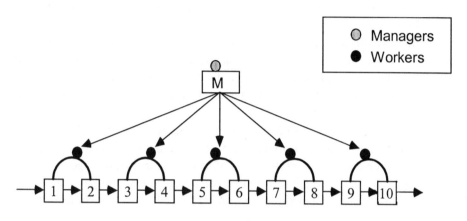

Figure 1.4 Reintegration of labor.

In Figure 1.4 we present the three kinds of reintegration schematically. Compared to Figure 1.3, if each worker now performs two instead of one task (with the aid of the requisite technology), task productivity would be maintained, the number of workers cut in half, and the number of managers cut by two-thirds, making the whole operation simpler, more streamlined, cheaper, more flexible and of higher quality. Knowledge is being recovered from the splinters and knowledge management grows in importance.

1.4.1 Process of Reintegration

There are internal *systemic* limits to the old processes of task, labor and knowledge division. Coordination becomes more difficult, more costly and more complex. Although markets continue to grow and are in fact becoming global, processes of the division of labor do not keep pace, slow down and ultimately reverse towards the opposite direction of reintegration. One person performs the tasks previously carried out by two people; one person controls two instead of one machine; a group of workers manage themselves, without managers or supervisors; and so on. These reintegrative processes continue to gather momentum.

These processes (division and reintegration) cannot be characterized as a "cycle" or "wave," or as a "revolution" or "transformation," and not even as a "metamorphosis" or "growth." The closest label seems to be Vico's concept of *corsi e ricorsi* in the evolution of social systems.

Any real origin in human affairs – and the process of division of labor *certainly is* of real origin – ultimately meets with a real end. After each *corso* there follows a different and yet organically related *ricorso*. There is a course and recourse, outswing and rebound, disaggregation and reaggregation. The processes of *corso* and *ricorso* cannot be divided or taken apart. Every *corso* in human affairs is internally self-binding and self-limiting, transforming itself into its inevitable *ricorso*.

Processes of the *division* of task, labor and knowledge, through their own internal dynamics and self-organization, transform spontaneously into the subsequent processes of the *reintegration* of task, labor and knowledge.

A good description of the self-limited corso-ricorso cycle in physical, social and human affairs can be borrowed from an MIT metallurgist C.S. Smith:

"A new thing of any kind whatsoever begins as a local anomaly, a region of misfit within the preexisting structure. The first nucleus is indistinguishable from the few fluctuations whose time has not yet come and the innumerable fluctuations which the future will merely erase. Once growth from an effective nucleus is well under way, however, it is then driven by the very type of interlock that at first opposed it: it has become the new orthodoxy. In crystals undergoing transformation, a region having an interaction pattern suggesting the new structure, once it is big enough, grows by demanding and rewarding conformity. With ideas or with technical or social inventions, people eventually come to accept the new as unthinkingly as they had first opposed it, and they modify their lives, interactions and investments accordingly. But the growth too has its limits. Eventually the new structure will have grown to its proper size in relation to the things with which it interacts, and a new balance must be established. The end of growth, like its beginning, is within a structure that is unpredictable in advance."

1.5 Knowledge Management

The "field" of Knowledge Management (KM) is suffering not only from the lack of distinction between data, information and knowledge (and wisdom), but also from the lack of definition and lack of action or process orientation.

KM should be less about managing "something" (like an object of knowledge) and more about the process of management *infused* with production, improvement and sharing of knowledge through action and interaction. KM is therefore more about *"knowledgement"* (the processes of knowing and doing) than about knowledge management. Knowledge is not a thing.

Traditionally, KM is roughly concerned about the following:

1. Producing (creating) new knowledge internally, within a corporation.
2. Improving formal and informal flows of knowledge among individuals and teams.
3. Codifying knowledge to facilitate its transfer, learning and sharing.
4. Tapping into external sources of new knowledge.

One can readily see that all such efforts are about generating data and information transfers, or about turning knowledge into information (codifying). All these efforts could very well be carried under the banner of data and information management.

Why has traditional KM been failing so often?

Knowledge is not "stuff." It is not an input or resource to be treated like other organizational resources (money, raw materials, technology, information, land, and labor) have been treated in the past. Knowledge is the process of coordinating all other resources and inputs in the most effective way. Knowledge is not information.

Thus, it was a costly error to confuse knowledge with information. It was even costlier to approach knowledge with MIS conceptual toolbox and confound it with computerized databases, their construction, management, mining and warehousing. It led to the centralization and disbursement of available organizational "knowledge" and the development of instruments to prevent the "loss of knowledge." Huge amounts of resources were invested in the acquisition and internalization of systems dealing with the retrieval of information. The false identification of "information" with "knowledge" also led to an artificial resuscitation of traditional strategy, focusing on "empirical data" and attempting to improve on the forecasting of future market trends.

This dead-end path of KM has caused unnecessary delays in the much needed global paradigm change. It has postponed mastering corporate foresight and flexible response, building up effective process knowledge and led to prolonging the data & information stage. Most companies have thus ended their KM phase with a reduced ability to recognize fundamental changes and trends in the global environment. They have failed to understand that it is impossible to discern such changes from mining the organizational information itself. A well developed and effective organizational information system could become an impediment to such recognition. The information supplied by corporate information systems has been accumulated according to outdated and often irrelevant models of the preceding era.

Resulting strategic plans are conceived as *status quo*, preserving exercises in drastic cost reduction – closing plants, cutting down manpower, canceling and redirecting investment plans. Such changes preserve the failing way of doing business and simply prescribe doing more (or less) of the same. Such "strategy" will only enhance the slide towards organizational demise.

But the real problem lies elsewhere: in the global era the *organizations themselves must change*. The knowledge produced by them must also serve their own coping with change: with the new problems in the evolution of the organization, and not just with the issues of preserving the *status quo*.

There are many specific, "local" reasons for KM failures, but among the more general culprits we can list at least the following:

Definition of operational knowledge is not well established. Distinctions of information and data are weak, implying *information management* (processing and use of symbolic descriptions), leading to no perceptible competitive advantage and a sense of disappointment.

Firms are already managing knowledge, even if not very well. They act, produce, coordinate, and make decisions. KM is an ongoing and all-involving process, albeit unrecognized and out of focus. It cannot be all tucked under the convenient labels of KM department or CKO.

Information technology (IT) cannot be a substitute for social interaction. Description of action cannot replace action itself ("It doesn't matter what they say, what matters is what they do"). Knowledge Technology (KT), even where undeveloped, cannot be simulated by IT.

Traditional KM concentrates on sharing, storing and recycling existing knowledge, while the real game is in producing new knowledge, continuously.

Most KM techniques are just traditional IT techniques, explicitly avoiding action and its coordination, manipulating symbolic descriptions.

Mediocre or worst practice is the easiest to codify, share and transfer, while the best coordination of action is necessarily tacit and should be handled as such.

All knowledge that can be codified and so reduced to information can be transmitted over long distances at small costs. It is the increasing codification of certain elements of knowledge that has led the current era to be characterized as *"The Information Society."* However, our society in the 21st century is *"The Knowledge Society"* and it is the knowledge, not the information, which is going to come to dominate it. It is the Knowledge Technology (KT), rather than the Information Technology (IT), which is going to enable it.

Thus, *tacit knowledge*, in the form of skills and capabilities needed to handle codified knowledge (information), is more important than ever. Codified knowledge (information) might be considered as inputs to be transformed, while tacit knowledge, particularly the know-how and know-why, is the demonstrated capability for coordinating information with all other inputs.

The real purpose of knowledge management is *not* transforming knowledge into information (there is a plenty of that) but the very opposite: *transforming information into effective action* – there is always too little of that.

1.6 Wisdom and Strategy

The motto of my university is *Sapientia et doctrina*, expressing the commitment to the discovery and diffusion of *wisdom and learning*.

Wisdom does not have to remain a vague philosophical or theological construct. It can be reframed and become, like knowledge, a well defined, pragmatic concept, object of study and the aspiration of practice of informed, knowledgeable and inquiring, self-aware enterprises.

Management systems have witnessed cumulative progression from *data* processing, through *information* technology, to current *knowledge* management (see Table 1.2).

The next step is wisdom.

1.6.1 Definition

In the global era, corporations are usually *informed*, some become *knowledgeable*, but the best ones seek *wisdom*. *Wisdom of enterprise* goes beyond data, information, learning and knowledge.

Because of the global economy, corporate wisdom itself is emerging as a global concern. We want wisdom to become – like knowledge and information before – a manageable resource for rooting corporate *efficiency* and *effectiveness* in the realm of *explicability* and *ethics*.

What is wisdom?

One can clearly be knowledgeable without being wise. (One can also be well informed without knowing much.) Many use information and follow prescribed rules efficiently: they acquire dexterity and become *specialists*. Others choose their goals and change the rules, with the approval of others – and become *experts*. But even the very masters of rules and purposes cannot be wise if they cannot satisfactorily explain *why* particular purposes, rules or courses of action *should* be chosen or rejected.

Inquiring into the nature of our own actions and being able to respond satisfactorily to the inquiries of others, to justify and explain our actions as well as theirs, brings us to the gates of the realm of wisdom.

Wisdom is socially accepted or experience-validated explication of purpose.

Enhancing human wisdom, pursuing practices and systems that are not only efficient or effective, but also wise, i.e., building wisdom systems is the next frontier of the long and tortuous progression from data and information to knowledge and wisdom.

As the global economy shows its maturation, the search for a competitive advantage moves from efficiency and effectiveness to strategic wisdom and ethics. Moral and ethical behavior is an integral part of wise behavior. Without the ethical dimension one could perhaps be clever or astute, but not wise.

As with knowledge, wisdom has to be reflected in action. Isolated, purposeless and passive "wisdom" of philosophizing hermits, autodidacts and social recluses is not the wisdom we seek and admire – it does not translate into action. Wisdom has to be communicated.

But what is communication?

We expand on communication in the next section. Although communication is closely related to knowledge and information, simple conventional wisdom would weaken the usefulness of the concept by including any information transfer within its domain. An exchange of information or messages is not necessarily communication.

In exchanging symbolic or linguistic labels (information) we strive to coordinate action and modify behavior. Only when such coordination or modification occurs, we communicate. When it does not, we simply broadcast, transfer or exchange information.

Communication takes place when the result of a particular exchange of information is coordination of action or modification of decision making and behavior.

What is the difference between *action and behavior*?

Action is the result of deliberate decision making within a novel context or circumstances. *Behavior* is an embodied, habitual or automated response to repeating circumstances of a familiar context. Both carry purpose and are affected by communication.

Communication is an action-enabling exchange of information.

1.6.2 On the Art of Asking Why

Wisdom is therefore akin to the *knowing why* things should or should not be done – locally, regionally and globally – and wisdom remains in a short supply.

The art of asking "why" (inquiry into causes, motives and purposes) has fundamentally different effects than the more customary asking of "how" (inquiry into processes, means and ways). Why is asking "why" more important?

Whenever we explore a coordinated process in the sense of asking "what" or "how" (what is to be done, how sequenced, how performed, etc.) we have already accepted or conserved the process. The process is *a given*, subject to improvement, learning or mastering, but not subject to rejection or change.

It is only when we start asking "why" (why should we do it this way, why do it at all, why this operation and not another, why this sequence, etc.) we question the very structure of knowledge (coordination of action) and introduce the *possibility of change*.

In the global economy, frequent or continuous strategic changes are becoming the norm of competitiveness. Doing the same, given thing better and better (continuous improvement) will be inadequate for strategic success. We increasingly have to *do things differently* (not just better) and *do different things*, not just the same ones.

The idea of *continuous improvement*, i.e., asking how things can be done better and better, will not lead to new things but only to the old things improved. Continually improving horse carriage will only fixate it and make it less capable of change; the process of continuous improvement would not "stumble" into an internal combustion engine. The *discontinuous improvement* is needed.

Only when we start asking "why," can the old processes be replaced with different ones or abandoned altogether.

1.6.3 Wisdom and Ethics

Wisdom and ethics are obviously closely related, often being indistinguishable and inseparable. Both are related to strategy and strategic action.

While knowledge is related to know-how, i.e. the more rational and technical part of action coordination, being wise is also related to being good (being ethical) not only in the sense of "knowing," in terms of description and recognition, but primarily in the sense of *doing*.

We know only through doing. Popular "knowledge" *of* or *about* things is not of interest here; it being in the realm of descriptions and representations, i.e., information.

Truly ethical behavior does not come from deliberate judgment, decision making and reasoning, but from human coping with immediate circumstances, from being and acting good, not just describing what "good" means, out of context and devoid of action.

The most remarkable lapses in ethical behavior have occurred at companies with admirable ethical rules and covenants, stunning ethical vision statements and other elaborate props that simulate and substitute for ethical know-how. The problem with corporate ethics is not with "knowing" what is right, but with doing right and being good.

Teaching ethics, i.e., providing descriptions, does not necessarily lead to ethical behavior and deeds, to being good and wise.

The differences and interactions among know-how, know-what and know-why form the substance for integrating knowledge, ethics and wisdom.

Ethics, more than anything else, is about what one does, not just about what one says.

All action takes place within individual action microcontext, the individual or personal context of space, time and circumstance. Many of these contexts are recurrent – we learn them, master them and feel good within them. Other contexts are novel, unfamiliar and demanding, we do not feel "at home." It is through action that we get to understand our microcontext, and only through action can we construct it. It is not perceived through descriptions and representations, but our action, our knowledge of it, becomes embodied within us. We become masters and experts of the microcontext we have created through our *embodied action.*

Only when our microcontext breaks down (through the unusual or the unexpected) or when we enter unfamiliar and novel territory, our ability to act is challenged. Instead of embodied action we have to rely on analysis, deliberation and rules of behavior.

It is the embodied action, which is the result of mastering our constructed microcontext, which leads to ethical behavior. Such ethical know-how is a spontaneous and internal inclination, and stems from a desire for gain. Actions that are habitual arise from following the rules or come from the extension of other experiences that are external to us, disembodied.

There is a difference from reading or learning an ethical rule, then from putting it into action consciously and purposefully, or acting ethically through mastering one's microcontext, i.e. acting ethically through one's own internal self-interest. In order to be truly ethical, one cannot be consciously and intentionally "ethical."

1.6.4 Wisdom Based Strategy

One of the main implications of the wisdom focus is the realization that corporate strategy – the art of inquiry and knowing why – should be based on knowledge rather than information, rooted in action rather than its symbolic description, and supported by the recursive *wisdom cycle* of inquiry: exploration, action and explication.

Strategy is not about statements but about action.

Traditionally, organization executives prepare a set of statements, symbolic descriptions of future action: mission, vision, and set of goals (strategic, tactical operational), plan of ways and means for action, and so on. All such statements are simply information. It all has to be translated into action. That is where most strategists and organization executives stumble.

Most "strategists" are conditioned to ask "what" to do and "how" to do it. They rarely exhibit the wisdom of asking "why." Why should this or that statement be translated into action? Even more importantly: Why should not it be? What should not be changed and why? Only then can an effective strategy emerge from realizing what is conserved and unchangeable, and from what is already being done.

Corporate strategy is not just about writing a plan, derived top down from the mission-vision hierarchy of symbolic descriptions. It is a way of managing the entire organization in order to create a *coherent pattern of action*.

All executives can write statements, but they cannot "do" them. The action itself is elsewhere, down in the operational action space, carried out by others. All the descriptive statements, from mission to plan are hovering "above the cloud line" separating them from the reality of coordinated action. It is hard to see from the high clear skies of information into the chaotic and confusing reality of knowledge down below. One can only look.

There was some justification for fixed mission-vision statements in the slow-changing competitive environment of the past. In rapidly changing environments of the global economy and emerging markets (especially in the areas of information, technology, entertainment, telecommunications and consumer electronics) relying on long-term visions of corporate writers can quickly translate into the "tunnel-vision trap," distracting executives from newly emerging opportunities and threats.

We do not live in a predictable world anymore. We cannot invest too heavily and too early into visions. We cannot crave certainty in a sea of change and demand ever clearer visions from the top. The "vision thing" ultimately outdid CEO Pfeiffer at Compaq: while he was crafting clear visions, Dell simply pulled ahead by doing its mass customization worldwide. The HP takeover of Compaq continued with the vision, totally disconnected from reality, and had done in also Ms. C. Fiorina. The same can be said about the "corporate dreamers" at Mercedes Benz. The last thing IBM needed in 1993, the year of profound crisis, was a vision. The action was needed and CEO Gerstner delivered it: integrated customer solutions. It is better to be hazily and ambiguously right than to be precisely and clearly wrong.

Precise wording of an admirable mission statement may appeal to stockholders, careless investors and uninformed stakeholders, but only the doing, quick execution of competent action, will impress competitors and customers.

Strategy is about what you do, not about what you say you do. Strategy is about action, not about description of action. Strategy is about doing, not about talking. All organizations have strategy, whether they know it or not: it is embedded in their doing.

Strategy is what you **do**. What you do **is** your strategy.

All the rest is words.

A good example of the failure to grasp such a simple truth is the so called "Lisbon Strategy" of the European Union. Hammered out in 2000 by EU bureaucrats and political wordsmiths, this hugely expensive document – with an already misplaced goal of catching up and surpassing the U.S. by 2010 – has never amounted to anything else but a heap of ill-chosen words. It has been all but abandoned in 2005 with an even more expensive display of restatements, corrections, reductions and reformulations. One cannot engage in strategic planning without knowing what strategy is. Again, strategy is what you do, not what you say.

Because all organizations do something, all organizations already have a strategy. Their executives should stop managing information by issuing statements and start managing knowledge by coordinating action.

Even though in this book we do not deal with the details of effective strategy for the global era and its Global Management Paradigm (see Part II), let us at least outline the steps and proper sequencing of the strategic process:

First, we have to create a detailed map of key corporate activities to find out what company is doing – to reveal its actual strategy that is embedded in action. Remarkably, many corporations do not know their own processes, what they are doing; do not know their own strategy. They only know what they say, through their mission statements.

Second, after creating coherent *activity map*, one has to analyze the activities by comparing them to benchmarks of competitors, industry standards or stated aspirations.

Third, so called *value-curve maps* are produced in order to differentiate one's activities from those of the competition. *Differentiation, not "catching up" or imitation* is the key to effective competitiveness and strategy.

Fourth, identified selected activities are changed – in order to fill the opportunity spaces revealed by value-curve maps – as being most effective for successful differentiation. The rest of action space is conserved.

Fifth, after a newly changed action space (and its activity map) has emerged and become reliably functional, the descriptive mission and vision statement can be drawn for the purposes of communication. The description now actually describes the action and the action reflects the description.

Through the *wisdom systems*, through exploring corporate action via wisdom cycle of inquiry, we can effectively change the action, and consequently the strategy, without ever leaving the action domain. Corporate strategy remains the doing, even though we are doing something else. No need to implement or execute the "strategy" (set of statements) – it has already been enacted.

Executives are supposed to "execute" their strategic statements. Traditional strategies are hard to execute as they are probably created "above the cloud line," far removed from the corporate doing. Often they should not be executed at all. Effective (forced) execution of incorrect or impossible to implement strategies is likely to damage the corporation and its strategic resilience.

1.7 Human Systems Management

Living in the age of telecommunications, global markets and socio-economic turbulence demands deeper individual and corporate attention to the basics of humans systems – to the fundamental underpinnings of human communication, conversation and attitudes towards change.

It is also necessary to revisit these foundations from an organismic vantage point: viewing basic categories as involving organisms rather than machines, as living systems rather than artificial constructs, learning more from biology than from mechanical engineering.

Arie de Geus, the businessman (Shell Oil), introduced the idea of the living company, viewing it and living it as an organism, not as a machine. Humberto Maturana, the biologist, has taught how the principles of self-production (autopoiesis) apply also to social systems, management and business. Drawing on their wealth of experience and brilliant thought is a privilege and pleasure for any management scientist.

Human Systems Management is primarily about living beings, their learning and action, their networks, orders and systems, and interaction and communication.

Human systems evolve and change – they have a history.

1.7.1 The Notion of Change

Individuals, groups and corporations exist in the continuous present. We can only act *now* – in a continually shifting present, from the previous second to the next, from yesterday to tomorrow. All we can ever do, all our action, occurs now. All the rest is description. We describe the past, we describe the future, but we act and live now.

Our access to the future and the past is only through information, while our action and existence is enabled by knowledge.

We have to invent (describe) history and forecast (describe) the future in order to explain (gain knowledge) and enable our action in the present.

Imagine a wave front moving through the ocean: it exists only on the "wave front," only now, not before and not after. All life, all living action exists on a wave front. It is the intersecting wave fronts of many histories that form the interlinked contexts of life. The only thing to remember is that both history and future are only propositions and descriptions – the only real action is now.

Most of the emphasis in biological evolution is on what has changed. What is central in evolution or any history is not what has changed, but what has been *conserved*. The study of change in human systems cannot be about what changes but what persists unchanged and remains conserved.

Take a person. His body grows and withers, his hair falls out, his teeth loosen, and muscles slacken. However, what is central, important and mysterious is that which is conserved: the man is still of the same identity, basic organization, and character, still a unique, recognizable individual. That is his real story, the story of his existence, the story of what has been preserved. The same is with human systems, the same with corporations.

The structures change, the organization remains. Some life forms disappear but living systems go on. Companies go bankrupt but business continues. Departments are cancelled and formed but corporations live on. Individuals come and go but institutions persist.

The conservation of system organization is the true contents of history. There are some systemic rules which are implied:

When some pattern of relations is being conserved, there is a space opened for all other relations to change around that which is conserved. There is no change without conservation.

When we say that a particular company, like the Bata Co., has existed since 1894, we mean that something has been conserved – that which we perceive as constituting the *identity of the company*. Because of that preserved pattern, the company has a history. All the rest could and did change.

In this sense, what can change is determined, specified and defined by what is conserved. We are so preoccupied with change that we do not notice that what is important is what remains unchanged. That is why enthusiastic newcomer managers who want to "change everything" fail so often: they do not understand what must be conserved; they do not grasp the identity of a corporation. All human systems exist only as long as there is conservation of that which defines them. There would be no culture without conservation.

We shall deal with the issues of organizational stability and structural flux and change in the sections dealing with autopoiesis. We shall examine the Bata Co. and its preserved system of corporate wisdom in the last sections.

While *information* describes the past and proposes the future, and *knowledge* guides the action of the present, it is that what has been unchanged and conserved through the system history that represents its *wisdom*.

The second systemic rule pertains to humans and their role in human systems:

Human history is not a history of resources and opportunities, but of wants and desires.

There are no resources and opportunities *per se*. Something becomes a resource or opportunity if somebody wants it or desires it. Resources and opportunities are created by human wants. If we do not want, if we do not desire, then there are no resources for us and there are no opportunities open to us.

Why are you reading this sentence today? It was your destiny, the result of the history of your wants and desires. Since the time you were born – and therefore also even before that – every turn, every decision, every action leads you precisely to this very moment. But this compelling but naive "destiny" emerges only when we look backwards, when we describe our own past. The real action was lived through a series of now-moments and each such moment was guided by your wants and desires. And it is our needs, wants and desires that define what we choose to conserve. So, nothing is predetermined, it only appears that way.

When we are concerned about our action, we are concerned about conserving what we desire. Finally, the third rule:

When a pattern of relations is conserved, then it can be connected with other such conserved patterns and this new configuration of connections may be also conserved.

This is how complex, interconnected and intersecting networks of systems embedded in other systems emerge. All individuals are embedded in a community, or a family, or an organization in which they work. Human systems are not hierarchies of containment or control, but interconnected embeddings of individuals, groups, teams, departments and companies... within companies, within networks of companies, within the global economy.

Any human system must be "closed" in terms of its conserved organization and "open" with respect to its changing structure. It would dissipate into chaos otherwise. A human system is a network of individuals and their embeddings that interact in such a way that through their interactions they produce the same kinds of individuals as the network that produced them – so they conserve the network and its organization, and so are entitled to their history. We call this process self-production or autopoiesis.

1.7.2 The Impact of Communication

The human interactions described above take place in language and take the form of communication through coordination of action.

Language is a system of symbolic descriptions of action, but its true purpose is to help coordinate action itself. *If we coordinate our actions we communicate.*

Communication is therefore a form of human interaction.

If two parties exchange symbolic descriptions (i.e., information), mostly in language, they do not have to communicate. A simple exchange of information is not necessarily communication; it must lead to coordinated action for communication to occur.

So, we can talk for hours on a phone without communicating. A professor can transfer large amounts of information without communicating. People can engage in intensive and protracted dialogues without communicating. Or, we can communicate strongly and lastingly without uttering a word. It is all in the coordination of action we elicit through our interaction. We engage in communication when the result of a particular interaction is the coordination of behavior, doings, and operations – coordination of action. Language itself is *not* a system of communication, yet communication in humans does occur through language.

Because human knowledge is a purposeful coordination of action, human communication, not mere exchange of information, produces human knowledge.

Human knowledge allows us to coordinate individual coordinations of action. It puts the "management" in Human Systems Management. It allows us to purposefully coordinate, i.e. manage, other human beings.

Language, as knowledge itself, is not abstract or intangible. Both relate to the concreteness of doings, to the coordination of actions. Symbolic descriptions or information are mere commentaries about what is happening.

Human systems do not have fixed structures. They have flexible structures that are continually changing, never returning back to the same structure. But they change only around that which has been conserved – i.e., their organization, the source of their identity. So we maintain a sense of continuous being, of fundamental sameness, without becoming suddenly alien to ourselves; all this in spite of rather radical changes in our structures.

1.7.3 The Nature of Love and Respect

We shall see in the last sections on wisdom that Tomas Bata, the entrepreneur extraordinaire, manager, executive and businessman, often talked in his business speeches about love.

What does love have to do with it? What does it have to do with human systems and their management? Humans do not only kill, compete, fight and hate, but also cooperate, play, trust – and love. Humans coordinate their action, less or more effectively, less or more intensely.

In the business of human systems we get angry, revengeful and hateful, but we also enjoy and establish friendships, likings and loves. Sometimes we destroy, degrade and damage our coordination of action – and sometimes justifiably, if it threatens the things we have conserved in the corporation. But mostly we want to create and promote coordination of action, produce knowledge and build relationships.

In human systems, love (or respect) refers to those actions through which another person, being, process or thing enters into a legitimate, conserved coexistence with us. Love is a form of (often unpurposeful but voluntary) coordination of action which creates a desired pattern of coexistence with somebody or something.

Friendship is living in mutual respect and love. There is no demand, no expectation – you put in a demand or an expectation, and the friendship comes to an end. With friends you can talk about anything. A friend knows that whatever you say is in the acceptance of his or her legitimacy. Friendship emerges in human systems as a conservation of coexistence, conservation strong enough to persist beyond its original circumstance.

One cannot use aggression, degradation or neglect within a desired pattern of coexistence. It negates it, destroys it, and cancels its conservation and thus its history. One cannot conserve what one does not respect, i.e., love, in human systems.

So, the nature of love in human systems is a form of relation forming behavior, the expression of our longing for coexistence and poverty of loneliness. We learn this as children, spontaneously and automatically, as a great foundation for our human systems... until we lose it in our latter years because of the neglect of what we desired to preserve.

1.7.4 The Role of Conversation

Markets are really human conversations.

The word conversation comes from the Latin con, which means "with," and versare, which means "turning around." So conversation is turning around together with others. It is through conversation that we coordinate the respective coordinations of behavior and action.

Through conversation, which takes place in language (i.e., languaging), we bring forth objects into their existence. The objects, like resources or opportunities, do not exist unless we desire, describe and label them by shared symbols of language. The only way of confirming and conserving such symbols – and thus the objects themselves – is through conversation. I cannot evolve a language if I have nobody to talk to, nobody to converse with.

Through conversation we continually create new labels and through them new objects. The entire vocabulary of management has emerged from conversations. Firms, companies, profits, incomes, etc., did not exist a priori and then receive their names and labels. Their very existence was brought forth through conversation, intimately integrated with the process of labeling. Then we conserved them.

As you read these sentences, we are engaged in conversation. That relationship, or coordination of action, is different with each reader – and so we are engaged in multiple, parallel conversations. If intelligent, we can create new objects, new meanings and new labels, or destroy the old ones – thus we communicate. This is a powerful means of knowledge production.

1.7.5 Purpose and Identity

Purposes, goals, objectives and tradeoffs are all in the realm of human interpretations and descriptions. *Per se*, human systems have no other purpose than the one ascribed to them.

While the purpose of a corporation to one person is to make money and to another to serve the public – there is always that one person for whom the real purpose is an opportunity for robbery.

When we see a purpose in a system, it is just that and nothing more: we see a purpose in a system. But the system itself doesn't have a purpose. Corporations do not have objectives, people do. Human systems can serve individuals, groups, nations or mankind – depending on the purposes we impute to them.

Even if we create a system with an explicit purpose and design, its operations according to the criteria that define the purpose, the system itself still operates according to its internal organization of processes. That's how living systems operate. Human systems are living systems.

Yet, through human systems we derive our identity as humans. Human identity is a systemic phenomenon. Our identity stems from our basic organization as human beings, from that which is preserved in the chain of structural adaptations. We continually change our structure while maintaining our identity, our organization. The same is with human systems. Harvard remains Harvard in spite of its structural changes and constant churning of its human contents: students and faculty come and go, the identity remains. So it is with all living systems.

The mystery is that I remain myself and maintain my identity even at Harvard. Humans maintain their identity in and through human systems. And, yet Harvard maintains *its* identity.

The mystery is solved by differentiating between the organization and the structure of a system. More on this can be found in our sections on autopoiesis. I maintain my identity at Harvard because my *organization* is being conserved. Yet I am significantly influenced and transformed by Harvard, because of my *structural* adaptations and change. And Harvard can maintain its identity because of the structural plasticity and adaptations of its faculty and students.

The identities of a human being or system persist because of conservation of a particular way of living. If this way of living is not conserved, then the identity disintegrates. Through living, through action and doing, we create the conditions that conserve our way of living. This is why knowledge as coordination of action, not mere information of its symbolic descriptions, is so fundamental and important for the management of human systems.

1.7.6 Human Systems

In human systems we often speak of power and control, commands and orders. There are some who still confuse that with management.

Yet, power is only constituted, maintained and conserved *by obedience*. Without obedience there is no power. Power arises in obedience. Hierarchical systems take place under power relations and so are rooted in obedience brought forth by fear. When there is fear and obedience there is no cooperation. Without cooperation there can be no human systems, just hierarchies of command.

In a human system one cannot replace people with robots or robot-like humans, because they require the particular kind of beings that humans are, with the particular kinds of emotions humans have, so that humans can participate in the particular kinds of conversations that constitute collaboratively doing things humans are good at. In a hierarchy, replacing humans with robots or robot-like humans would lead, undoubtedly, to higher efficiency and performance.

Technology is only a tool, only an instrument in human systems. It becomes an end in itself in a hierarchy. So we have to view technology as a form of social relationships, view its support network of human interactions as a constitutive component, not just as a piece of hardware. More about this and the support network in our sections on technology.

Just because something is possible, does not mean we have to do it. What defines a healthy and mature person is not controlling what we think and feel, but controlling what we *do* with our thoughts and feelings. Our thoughts and feelings do not have to be politically correct or morally pure. It is the loss of awareness of, or worse, indifference to, the impact of our acts on others that produces social misfits. Controlling symbolic description of action degrades freedom; failing to control irresponsible action kills freedom.

Responsibility takes place as an experience when one is aware, of the possible consequences of what one does in relation to other human beings or other circumstances, and one acts according to whether one wants or does not want those consequences. Human systems are based on mutual, reciprocated responsibility. Responsibility does not mean goodness, it does not mean compliance with agreements, it simply means that you act with awareness of your wanting and being, *willing to live the consequences of what you do* – not just running away, committing suicide or "Enronizing" your environment with lies...

And so in human systems one must be free and *freedom* is what human systems are based on. People accepting responsibilities in human systems are free. People avoiding and escaping responsibilities in hierarchies can never be free.

If one is aware of one's responsibilities, accepts them voluntarily and without coercion, wants to live with the consequences of one's actions and wants and accepts the wanting itself enough to act – then one is free.

Free people can say "I want it, but do not like it and will not act on it" or "I want it, like it and will act." Freedom is all about the willingness to accept responsibility for one's actions. *Freedom is responsible action,* the experience of being responsible for one's own responsibility.

If you act and then accept the social consequences, you are responsible. If you want and choose to act, and accept the consequences, then you are free. (This is why terrorists are neither responsible nor free.)

Freedom is a systemic experience of responsible action and it can only be attained through human systems. Freedom is negated by obedience and fear, by power and control, by hierarchy of command.

1.8 Fuzzines, Ambiguity and Imprecision

"A 'concept' is not merely its clear luminous centre, but embraces a surrounding sphere of meaning or influence of smaller or larger dimensions, in which the luminosity tails off and grows fainter until it disappears. The hard abrupt contours of our ordinary conceptual system do not apply to reality and make reality inexplicable."

Jan Christiaan Smuts

Fuzziness, ambiguity, and imprecision are integral to the human production of decisions and knowledge. Fuzziness cannot be separated from knowledge or studied independently of knowledge. A viable theory of linguistic fuzziness should be properly embedded in its own requisite theory of knowledge.

Human mind is not an information-processing machine or a computer program computing symbolic representations. Computer does not "understand" anything, can have no knowledge of anything, even if it can pass the Turing test (machine's outputs indistinguishable by humans from human's outputs). Machines just work with substitutable strings of symbols, processed according to computational rules – and that is all. Turing test is irrelevant to both human and machine "intelligence."

Without a proper theory of knowledge production or construction, no phenomena of fuzziness can be explained and no theory of artificial knowledge (or intelligence) can properly approximate or model natural knowledge, decisions and intelligence production.

One cannot interpret human preferences in a default context. If no context is specified, I can list tea or coffee as my *typical* beverage, but in the context of watching Super Bowl I choose beer, at a dinner party wine, and with my love I drink champagne. Therefore, my linguistic labels for objects of knowledge do change and are created and reinterpreted again and again, with every whim of circumstance. The graded structures cannot be manipulated by fuzzy sets logic due to Zadeh. A *guppy* is a good example of *pet fish*. Yet, it is neither a good example of the category *fish* nor of the category *pet*. Fuzzy-sets approach cannot derive the label *pet fish* by any intelligent manipulation of the component labels *pet* and *fish*. Fuzzy or graded labels are being continually produced *de novo*, and their meaning negotiated with respect to changing contexts. Computers are and shall remain helpless with respect to fuzzy labels of human communication.

There exist at least two interpretations (and uses) of fuzziness, ambiguity and approximateness in human natural languages:

- Expressing lack of information and thus capturing a human sense of imprecision and uncertainty about a given concept, object or system. For example: "I don't know her age, but she is *still young;*" or, "We predict our sales to be *very high,* possibly close to 500." All sorts of "fuzzy labels," like *very old, very young, red* and *thirtyish,* are appropriate here.
- Expressing the knowledge-constructive intent of human exploration, communication or conversation by allowing a distinction between the generic and the specific in human discourse. For example, "She's thirty-one today, but she is *still young,*" or, "Our sales are exactly 500; that is *very high.*" All sorts of "fuzzy labels," like *very old, very young, red* and *thirtyish,* are appropriate here.

The unresolved dilemma of "fuzziness" is quite apparent in the above dichotomy. While the first interpretation has received most of the attention, the second, more fundamental interpretation of fuzziness has been judiciously avoided. We therefore devote this paper to the second, knowledge-constructive interpretation and use of fuzziness in human natural languages.

The traditional ("Zadehian") theory of fuzzy sets deals explicitly with the first interpretation introduced above. It has its roots in the classical utility theory which associates a "utility function," defined on the interval [0, 1], with the fuzzy concept or label *prefer.* Ranging from *do not prefer at all* (0 degree of utility) to *prefer very much* (1 degree of utility), any utility function expresses the degrees of preference or utilities assignable to various interpretations or "intensities" of the linguistic label *prefer,* including the inflection point of *indifference.*

The vast mathematical and conceptual formalism of the classical utility theory has thus been used and applied in the fuzzy sets theory. "Zadehian" fuzziness satisfies most of the axioms and assumptions of the utility theory, especially the independence of "ends and means" (context-free treatment of utility), relative stability (transferability) of "preferences," as well as nontransitivity, quantifiability, unidimensionality and separability. Instead of "utility function," a label of "membership function" has been appropriated.

Such direct transfer and use of the already existing mathematical apparatus could explain the explosive voluminosity of fuzzy sets publications. Most of them stress formalism at the expense of inquiry and insight into the very nature of knowledge, languages, linguistics, judgment and decision making.

Reflecting upon the motto of this section, we observe that Smuts stressed that the lack of ambiguity and fuzziness would "make reality inexplicable." That is, he believed the fuzziness and ambiguity in natural languages are not simple expressions of imprecision and uncertainty, i.e., something to be reduced, improved or corrected, but quite the opposite: fuzziness and ambiguity are the very foundation of the human biological ability to make sense of perceptions, to produce knowledge, to communicate and to coordinate action.

There can be no theory of fuzziness without requisite theories of knowledge, language and human communication. Any theory of fuzziness must be implied by and emerge from such supportive theories – it cannot be constructed *a priori* and *per se.* Fuzziness is a function of a system of knowledge production.

1.8.1 Language and Fuzzy Labels

The important questions in the study of fuzziness are related to when and why humans choose to use fuzzy labels (instead of using precise numerical measurements) and less so to how should a given fuzzy label be modeled through existing mathematical formalism.

What could be the purpose and intent in characterizing my mother's age as *still young,* either to her or to others, on the occasion of her birthday? Why do I describe a given color as *red* instead of looking up its precise wavelength measurement in Angstroms? Why do Japanese managers leave job descriptions ambiguous and overlapping while Americans managers continue to elaborate them with as much precision as they can? Why can I refer to my little son as being *very tall* while at the same time point to that *tall* basketball player on the court? What is meant by *hot* superconductors?

Answering such questions is not trivial. Does it say anything useful about the fuzziness of human language? Does it say anything useful about language?

What is language?

Is language an iconic system of separate labels and names which are to be attached to equally separate things, events and concepts floating "out there"? If we say "that boy is *tall,*" is it permissible and useful to concentrate on the label *tall,* study it as such, extract it from its cozy embedding and transfer it unchanged to other utterances, like "Bill is also *tall*" or "Shorty was *tall*"?

Recalling Bill Clinton's infamous discourse on what the meaning of "is" is. Is not the verb "is" really fuzzy and ambiguous? Do we mean "it appears to us," or "was declared by others," or "it is a fact that"?

Is not that *boy* we are pointing too an equally fuzzy designation? Is this *boy* a three-year old, or twenty-year old, or "one of the boys," or an "old boy"?

Are not concepts like *dog, chair,* and *automobile,* or *hit, prefer, like* and *is* at least as fuzzy as *tall, red* and *old?* Of course they are. If I say, "I prefer the *red* automobile," what do I mean? What kind of automobile? And what is meant by *automobile* anyway? Can it have three wheels? What kind of *red?* And how much do I *prefer* it and to what? To single out the label *red,* which could actually be the least fuzzy of all the characteristics involved, and ignore all other fuzzy components – is that justified?

While the concepts conveyed by nouns or adjectives can be fairly described by a simple paraphrase, the conceptual situations designated by verbs, like *hit, like, is* or *means,* have structural complexity that defies simple paraphrasing: verbs designate action, process or change and derive their meaning only from being part of a sequence of discrete operational steps.

Is not language primarily about the situations and contexts which give meanings to words and their sequences? Language is a social skill about creating contextually determined *sequences of words and gestures,* concatenated together for the purposes of coordinating human action.

So, the meaning of *tall* cannot be understood without the meaning of *is,* and that cannot be derived without knowing the meaning of *boy* and *tall,* which cannot be understood without knowing the meaning of *Boy is tall* in a given context: who is telling all this to whom, when and why.

Language is closely associated with human socialization, communication, division of labor, specialization of task and the distribution of knowledge. Not only do different individuals coordinate different tasks, but the tasks themselves are performed in different sequences and different patterns of knowledge emerge at different times. In order to purposefully coordinate individuals and the sequencing of their tasks we need to act in language.

The origin of language is rooted in action, gestures and communication. To paraphrase Malinovski, in its primitive uses, language functions as a link in coordinated human activity, as a piece of human behavior. It is a mode of action and not an instrument of reflection.

This communicatory (community-forming) behavior (i.e., language) could evolve in situations where cooperation requires not only coordinated activity of different individuals but also some form of sequencing, or organization, in the sense of division of task, labor and knowledge. The seeds of language are therefore present in the consensual (non-instinctive) parts of coordinating the very act of human procreation.

Individuals can coordinate sequences of task or action separately or in isolation, or so that they interact or interlock with the sequences of task or action coordinated by other individuals. Such coordination can be consciously selected or chosen, i.e., consensual, or it can remain subconscious and instinctive. In the first, consensual case, both types of coordination of action (individual and social) take place in language and are distinguished in language.

Instinctive, i.e., "hard-wired" or preprogrammed coordination of action is not consensual and does not require language for its coordination. Observe that animal and human behavior are mixtures of both instinctive and consensual action, the difference being in the relative proportions and preponderance of both action modes, as it is reflected in relative language complexity and its efficacy for action coordination.

Maturana defined language as a consensual coordination of consensual coordinations of action. This should be understood that *language* is consensual coordination, not the (possibly instinctive or forced) action itself. Language must be consensual, agreed upon and understood, not necessarily the coordinated action itself. Commands and orders do not necessarily induce *consensual* coordination of action, nor do the triggers of involuntary instinctual responses. Yet, in order to be effective, the language used must be consensual.

1.8.2 Fuzziness and Interpretation

"When I use a word," Humpty Dumpty said, in rather a scornful tone, "it means just what I choose it to mean – neither more nor less."
"The question is," said Alice, "whether you can make words mean so many different things."
"The question is," said Humpty Dumpty, "which is to be master – that's all."

Lewis Carroll

It is inadequate to study fuzziness by analyzing linguistic utterances like "John is tall." In fact, very little can be learned from such isolated utterances. Everything important is missing and thus furnishing the adjective tall with some sort of "membership function" is a bit rash and not scientifically convincing.

The *information* transmitted is not derived from the meaning of words or utterances. Information is a result of the interpretation by the listener. The listener always interprets the linguistic cues within a given context of a number of extralinguistic cues.

Who said that "John is *tall*"? Why was it said? In response to what? In response to whose question or inquiry? What is meant by "is"? Why is not "John's height precisely 6'1" an equally acceptable substitute? Why are we not sharing with each other our precise heights, weights and ages when they are undoubtedly known (or at least knowable) to most of us? If a label *tall* is a result of my interpretation, how does it differ from its intended meaning (what *you* wanted to hear)? Can we utter the same statement about John in a different context, at a different place, in a different group or at a different time? That is, is John's "tallness" his own, relatively stable attribute, or is it an imputation of the interpreter or observer? If it is context dependent, as our empirical experience seems to suggest, how can we assign a one-to-one matching (or a membership function) to it?

One could go on with posing questions about the specifications of what could be meant by "John is *tall*." Such statements do not cause us great difficulties in practice, because they are always uttered within a specific frame or context. This should not mean that we are justified to study them in a default context, *as if* no context specification was necessary.

The utterance "John is *tall*" is actually much more complex and represents an *interpretation* of John by an observer. That is, "John is *tall*, Bill replied," is a more complete example of a possible embedding of the utterance in question. So, Bill "interprets" John and *tall* is the result of his interpretation.

Humans search for the "acceptable" or "compatible" equilibrium meaning or fuzzy label definition (interpretation) through communication, conversation, negotiation or argumentation. Useful or operational meaning of the fuzzy concept is therefore *negotiated by the users of language who wish to coordinate their action.*

In fact, this meaning or definition (the results of interpretation) has to be negotiated *de novo* in every new context or circumstance. Although we do rely on recurrence, replication and habit in our social intercourse, thus affirming the relative permanency of previously negotiated meanings, we have to test the compatibility of meanings, no matter how implicitly or tacitly.

1.8.3 Negotiated Meaning

"What's the use of their having names," the Gnat said, "if they won't answer to them?"
"No use to them," said Alice, "but it's useful to the people that name them, I suppose. If not, why do things have names at all?"

Lewis Carroll

The meaning of tall is not fixed in an interactive (cooperative or competitive) society and it cannot be mapped onto a numerical scale of measured height. The meaning of tall is negotiated and renegotiated in different social contexts and can refer to all or any portion of the scale. One person's circumstance – purposes, intentions, experiences, thoughts, concepts, sensations, emotions – cannot be directly compared with another person's circumstance. There is no "true picture" of the world "as it is" to be found.

The only thing we can aspire for is a revealed compatibility or acceptability of meaning in a given context. This can only be revealed via communication or conversation, it can only be negotiated. People will engage in such negotiation only if they intend to cooperate, if they wish to coordinate their action. So, in order to study fuzziness and ambiguity of human language we have to study human cooperation in coordinating their task, labor and knowledge activities.

If I do not wish to coordinate my action with yours (but competition or even fighting is a form of coordination), it does not matter to me what you mean by *red, tall* or *important.* Your words mean, and properly so, what you choose them to mean, in your own circumstance. As long as your circumstance is operationally *non-intersecting* with mine, there is no need for the negotiation of meaning.

In Figure 1.5, observe that John's height is known precisely, but it is interpreted differently by observers, author *A* or interpreter *S*. In *A*'s context, John occupies the upper part of the height scale and is therefore being interpreted as *tall.* In *S*'s context, John occupies the lower part of the height scale and is therefore interpreted as *not tall.* As long as the two contexts remain separated, i.e., *A* and *S* do not wish to communicate or coordinate their action, both interpretative results are correct in their respective domains and there is little need for language to emerge: we simply "pin" the labels to concepts as we find them useful in our own isolated circumstance.

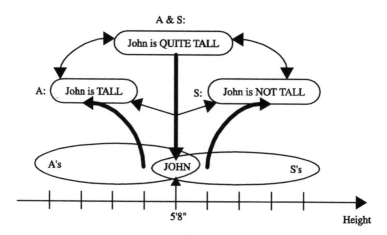

Figure 1.5 Negotiated meaning of fuzzy concepts, arising from confrontation of separate constructs or interpretations of different individuals.

However, if *S* and *A* wish to communicate about John, for the purposes of action coordination or cooperation, the discrepancy in interpretation must be addressed through some sort of negotiation or testing of compatibility and viability of meaning. It can perhaps be found that interpreting John as being quite tall is an acceptable interpretation of his height 5'8" for cooperation between A and S to take place. This does not exclude the possibility that either A's or S's original interpretation prevails and is accepted by the other party as viable. The negotiated meaning is then imputed to John by both parties involved in the social intercourse: language, or at least its new capacity, has emerged.

The imputation *quite tall* could mean that John has been recognized as being part of the *intersection* of the originally separate contexts and that this contextual intersection constitutes a viable domain for cooperation or coordination. John could also have been recognized as being part of the *union* of originally separate contexts and this contextual union considered a viable domain for cooperation: perhaps the imputation *medium height* would have resulted.

In Figure 1.5 we can distinguish two separate contexts *(A*'s and *S*'s), their union, their intersection or any other *context formulation* considered viable or necessary for cooperation of the parties involved. All these different contexts lead to different interpretations of John: *tall, not tall, quite tall, medium height,* and so on, *ad infinitum*.

When such connections between different contexts and corresponding viable (action – tested or accepted) fuzzy concepts are agreed upon within a particular family of contexts (groups, places, times, cultures, etc.), then the choice of a particular fuzzy label evokes or brings forth its corresponding context. (For example, *quite tall* implies intersection, *medium height* implies union, etc.)

One of the reasons why humans choose to employ one or another fuzzy label (when precise measurement is available) is to propose, define, reframe or impose a particular context within which coordination of action (cooperation or competition) is intended to take place. Fuzzy labels allow the necessary extension of meaning, induced overlaps, intersections or unions of contexts, while precise measurement (being a "point") allows nothing of the sorts.

In verbal communication, as in any other coordination of action, speakers and listeners must cooperate. But this cooperation is not symmetrical: speakers have no means of guaranteeing that their utterances will be understood as intended. Ultimately, any transmission of information depends on the action of the listener. Words, phrases and sentences uttered by the speaker do not have meaning *per se* and should not be studied in isolation. The listener, with his contextual construction of meaning, is the decisive side of the speaker-listener relationship.

Information to be transmitted must be possessed by the speaker and not by the listener: verbal communication is the result of the *difference in knowledge* between the participating individuals. Some common knowledge must be shared by both as a medium of transmission. The richer and more reliable is the shared knowledge and experience, the less precise (and more "fuzzy") the information transmitting utterance can be. Much more complicated and much more precise utterances have to be constructed when there is little or no preexisting knowledge shared or assumed. Taken in its requisite context, a fuzzy utterance can therefore be as or even more precise than a "precise" utterance. An ambiguous wink of the eye, "uttered" in its proper context, can transmit more information, more reliably and more precisely, than a mathematically reasoned discourse on the desirability of certain knowledge.

1.8.4 Meaning from Imprecision: Fuzzy Sets

In Figure 1.6, observe that the fuzzy-sets approach of Zadeh is quite different. Its basis is that we do not know John's height or know it only approximately. There are then two ways of proceeding. First, we assess the extent of our ignorance (the range of viable heights) and attach a label tall to it. Or we proceed in reverse: characterize John as being tall first, and only then continue to identify the range of heights corresponding to the label. In either case, because there are no explicit contexts considered, there is no need for language (as a coordinator of action) and distinct participants, we can concentrate on characterizing the label tall through the context-free device of the membership function.

Why should the scheme in Figure 1.6 be preferred to the scheme in Figure 1.5? After some reflection, we see that even if we start from the assumption of ignorance (knowing John's height only approximately), we still have to negotiate the label, propose the context and coordinate the interpretations: A's extent of ignorance about John's height can be quite different from S's extent of ignorance about John. So, even the traditional approach to fuzzy sets would have to adopt the Figure 1.4 approach if it would take itself seriously as a study of language rather than a mere study of labels.

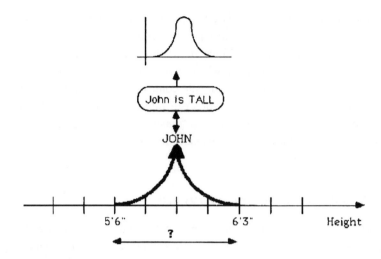

Figure 1.6 Traditional fuzzy-sets approach to *a priori* fixed meaning of fuzzy labels as descriptions of uncertainty or imprecision.

What then does Figure 1.6 represent? What *is* being studied here? Is it a context-free and language-free functional correspondence between ranges of values and their linguistic labels? We have a mimicry of a "smooth" response (via the continuous membership function) applicable to *control systems:* accelerating and decelerating subway trains, warming and cooling of a jacuzzi's water temperature, smoothing the movement of cranes, elevators and nuclear fuel insertions, selling smooth automobile cruise control systems, air-conditioner controls of temperature and humidity, spacecraft docking, submarine detection, and so on, improving on the traditional thermostat-like control devices.

Such an approach must come from engineers and engineering, not from linguists, cognitive scientists or practitioners of human systems management. It is devoid of the concepts of human cognition, like context, knowledge, wisdom and communication. It describes machines, not organisms.

In all such examples, the membership-function control can and does provide a smoother, more gradual and thus safer response than the human hand or human use of a mechanical device can provide. So, we have fuzzy logic, fuzzy control, fuzzy mathematics, fuzzy computers and fuzzy data bases, i.e., anything that does not explicitly deal with *human* judgment, knowledge, decision making, natural language, perception and social coordination of action.

The problem with traditional fuzzy sets theories is that they have been presented as something different than they actually are. They are *not* theories of human language, linguistic coordination or knowledge production, but are studies of smooth machine responses, potentially far exceeding human abilities in this area. Therefore, engineering and machine-oriented societies and cultures will more readily accept the self-imposed limits of fuzzy logic, while more human, social and knowledge-oriented societies and cultures will continue to express dissatisfaction and push beyond the mechanistic contrivances of "smooth" response. Fuzziness of language is more about human beings and less about human contrivances.

1.8.5 Production of Knowledge

Language is the necessary ambient or milieu in which human coordination of action takes place. Maturana and Varela speak about "languaging" rather than "language," emphasizing the process rather than the tool quality of natural language. Similarly, it would be more precise to talk about "knowing" rather than "knowledge."

Knowledge refers to an observer's ability to bring forth from the background of experience a coherent and self consistent sequence or network of coordinated action.

Knowledge therefore is not a passive reflection of the structure of external "reality," nor is it a simple coherent concatenation of concepts. Knowledge is a particular distinction, selection and organization of objects (things, concepts, events) which *brings forth a coordinated action*. Active "knowing" (rather than static "knowledge") is the process of coordination of action: knowing is doing, and doing is knowing.

So, a predator "knows" how to hunt because it coordinates its own action with that of the prey and that of other hunters in a viable fashion, i.e., more or less successfully in terms of its own survival. A bird "knows" how to build a nest because it is able to bring forth, from all possible sequences of activities, that sequence of coordinated action which leads to a "success" or fit in the particular eco-niche. An animal "knows" how to copulate because it can successfully coordinate not only its own action, but also the action of its mate.

One can claim to possess all kinds of pieces of data and information, and demonstrate such possession without resorting to action, but in order to claim knowledge at all (and of anything), one has to be able to coordinate action successfully.

1.8.5.1 Knowledge of the Constructed

Successful consensual coordination of action is brought forth by selecting a goal or purpose, choosing a particular sequence or network of activities, and carrying them out in an acceptable or fitting way in terms of the eco-niche result.

Such coordination or structure must be the outcome of the observer's or the coordinator's activities, it is of his own production or construction. Successful coordinative structures are not "out there," ready made, waiting to be discovered by us: they have to be produced or *constructed*.

In fact, we can only know in depth, that is understand, what we ourselves have constructed (consensually, not instinctively), either as individuals or as a species. We know our machines and we know how to make things, organize our activities, and so on. We cannot know life and the functioning of the living beyond what can be learned by exploiting some analogy with machines. We cannot know the physics beyond what our own constructs (mathematics, statistics and machines) allow us to comprehend. We cannot know spontaneous social orders (markets, language, money, etc.) beyond what we can glimpse by exploiting machine analogies again: *we cannot go beyond our own constructs.*

Our progress in learning about things we have not constructed is limited by our progress in things we construct. The more things and structures we construct ourselves, the more we can learn about things and structures we have not constructed. In order to understand life, we would have to construct life. Perhaps Vico understood this human predicament best: *Verum ipsum factum* – the truth is the same as the made. According to Vico, the only way of knowing a thing is to have made it, for only then do we know what its components are and how they were put together.

Vico, in the year 1710, already knew that:

"As God's truth is what God comes to know as he creates and assembles it, so human truth is what man comes to know as he builds it, shaping it by his actions. Therefore science (scientia) is the knowledge (cognitio) of origins, of the ways and the manner how things are made."

Knowledge does not refer to a reflection or photographic snapshot of a somehow pre-ordered reality, but to an individually and socially tested construct that orders reality in a particularly viable human way. In fact, there are as many human ways (as many constructed realities) as there are humans. Frogs and dogs also order the same reality in their own ways and so does God. There is no universe, but only a multiverse – and to realize this is liberating.

1.8.5.2 Construction of the Fuzzy

The *objects of knowledge,* concepts, things, events, items, etc., are not given, fixed and pre-structured *a priori*, but are repeatedly brought forth, configured and re-configured into networks by the ongoing operation of human distinction and concatenation. Objects are brought forth in terms of their "organization" as members of definite categories or families (common names) and not in the form of their "structure" as specific particulars (proper names). Knowledge refers to the overall network configuration of these concepts, not to any of its particular components.

Common names are defined by their reference to the *characteristic* or concept which determines membership in a certain category. Proper names are defined by their reference to specific, *particular members* of a category.

Common names, based on characteristics like *color, sweetness* and *warmth,* derive from the nature and structure of human sensory perception, i.e., sensory verbs like *see, taste* or *feel*. They can be further differentiated, *(colored* into *black, red* and *deep red)*. All such common names must be "fuzzy" by definition, regardless the information transmitted. Proper names have as referents specific members of specific categories, like *Mary, my car, this tree*. They are not "fuzzy" by definition. Some "continuous" categories are not labeled by attaching proper names: we do not name a specific color or a specific tone (although we do name a specific height or weight). This perhaps explains the attractiveness of using "color" in favorite examples of fuzzy sets theories.

The old idea of symbolic computation of reality assumes that the objects of reality can be simply "captured" and their "causal" relationships learned via computation of symbols and transformations of symbolic expressions.

In Figure 1.7 we present such an observer-as-computer C: he computes his way through a given objective world and his goal is to uncover its pre-given structures. If the world "out there" is clearly delineated or "crisp," he neatly represents it by a crisp symbolism (Figure 1.7a), preserving the sharp boundaries of individual concepts. He feels entitled to deal with separate concepts individually because that is how he uncovers them "out there."

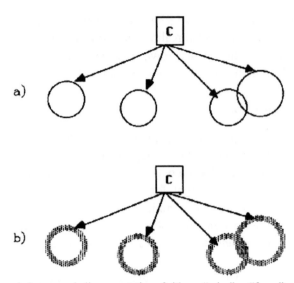

Figure 1.7 Knowledge as symbolic computation of either a "crisp" or "fuzzy" environment "out there."

If a human "computer" C discovers or assumes that some (or even all) of the objects "out there" are somehow imprecise or fuzzy, he then ploughs through the world of fuzzy concepts and computes their fuzzy relationships, replacing the crisp formalism by a more suitable fuzzy formalism. Accordingly, concepts, things and events have to be modeled as fuzzy because they are fuzzy.

The world "out there" is of course neither crisp nor fuzzy. We cannot even know that because we have not constructed it. It is our carefully crafted tools that are either crisp or fuzzy (mathematical formalisms) and they determine how we "read" *the world: as crisp if we have "crisp" tools to apply,* or *as* fuzzy if we have "fuzzy" *tools to* sharpen. The (crisp or fuzzy) capturing of the crisp or fuzzy world "out there" allows treating knowledge through symbolic rules of manipulation of separate components in an essentially context-free fashion.

In Figure 1.8 we represent the constructivist viewpoint: our "computer" has now become the observer-as-constructor C. His operations of distinction and concatenation bring forth concepts from the essentially unordered flux of the background. The structure is not "out there," but it is constructed "up here," in the human "noodle." Infinitely many constructs are possible, but only some are viable: only some coordinate human action successfully.

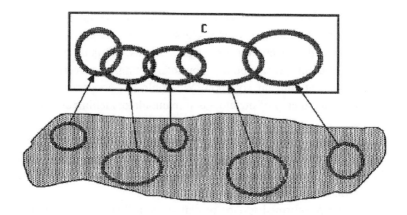

Figure 1.8 Knowledge as construction: "things" or "events" are brought forth, categorized and concatenated by the observer – constructor and their fuzziness imputed to them according to purposes and context.

As we bring forth the concepts from the background, their definitional boundaries cannot be crisp: they must come out imprecise or fuzzy by definition. Whether or not the reality out there is crisp or fuzzy is irrelevant: *we* cleave it out from the background in a fuzzy way. We can *then* artificially deemphasize this fuzziness by applying the crisp tools of mathematics and logic. Or we can re-emphasize the fuzziness by applying the fuzzy tools of mathematics and logic: i.e., by re-fuzzifying (what has been previously de-fuzzified) via a broadly popular and highly efficient process of Goguen's "fuzzification."

In Figure 1.8, the reality is constructed in C's head and only that reality can be understood – because it has been constructed. Any particular construct can then be tested for its viability: how well does it coordinate individual action? Does this construct lead to tasty bread? Do I survive by avoiding lions?

But most human action, starting with procreation, is not individual but social. None of us is a Robinson Crusoe and we need to coordinate our action with other individuals. Unfortunately, different individuals end up with different constructs of reality and therefore coordination of action would be almost impassable. So, the constructs must be confronted, shared through community (communicated), socially tested and their meanings negotiated. Social coordination of action can only take place through language. Fuzzy language allows separate and distinct constructs to be reconciled, made compatible and acquire community viability.

Without fuzzy language we would never be able to classify ourselves and our things into groups, categories and classes – the necessary condition for communication and cooperation. Our ages, heights, weights, perceptions, etc., would all be different, precise points, non-intersecting, non-overlapping, forever separated, having nothing in common. We could not cooperate spontaneously. We would be at the mercy of dictators and manipulators telling us what to do and where to go.

The fuzzy label like *thirtyish* does not mean that we do not know our or somebody else's age (although perhaps we do not), but it is our way of finding something that we have in common, a group concept we have constructed for the purposes of viable coordination of action.

There are no pre-formed groups or classes "out there" in nature; they are all our constructions, helping us to make some sense of our world. There is no *thirtyish* "out there," to be captured and modeled by membership function formalism. We construct it, we negotiate its meaning and we also change its meaning as we see fit in the ever-changing context of human social intercourse.

1.8.6 Cognitive Equilibrium

Decision production should be recognized as an emergent "harmonious" pattern or equilibrium, properly balancing all decisional components. Conventional wisdom of so called "rationality" is not correct. Human decision making and the problem solving process is determined by the way neural networks are structured as a whole: as a spontaneously wired and re-wired self-organizing "free market" of repeatedly propagated patterns of formulation, re-formulation of re-formulation and so on and so forth.

Humans do not maximize functions, but search for recognizable patterns. Decision making is not about maximizing some components subject to given levels of some other components, but about relatively stable patterns of harmony and equilibria among all components.

Most if not all thinking and judgment can be related to pattern recognition. Human thinking is not to be modeled by logical rules and calculations, but through application (or even matching) of "habits of mind" (patterns) prompted by specific contexts.

Humans *create* or *construct* both information and decisions. All important aspects of decision making: *criteria, alternatives, representations* and *evaluations* are maintained in a constructive flux of mutual adjustment and interdependent co-determination. *Nothing* is to be fixed *a priori*. Figure 1.9 shows a scheme of a minimal decision production network of components and their interconnections.

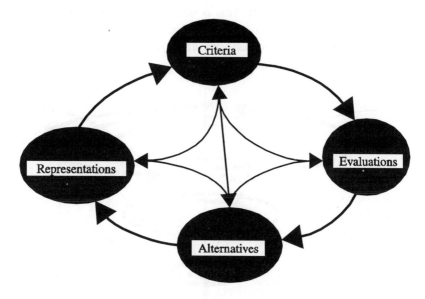

Figure 1.9 Decision-producing network of basic decisional components and their languages.

The human decision-making process is a complex, organizationally closed search for *internal consistency*, passing through interrelated layers of definitions and redefinitions of the *problem*. A problem has been fully formulated only after it has been solved. All aspects of decision making are ever-changing and mutually adjusting until a relatively *stable pattern* or *cognitive equilibrium* among them has been reached. The problem is then temporarily *dissolved*, the harmony achieved and recognized; there remains no other "choice" possibility than that of the accepted pattern (ideal solution, dominant option, prominent alternative).

Nappelbaum based his choice-producing networks on the interconnections between the respective *languages* of (1) option descriptions, (2) instrumental intentions and (3) value judgments. Decision making cannot be separated from the production of knowledge and thus from the construction of individual local worlds. Any "large" world (universe) consists of a variety of cognitively closed and essentially unmergeable "small" local worlds (multiverses).

In Figure 1.10 we provide a metaphoric sketch of the self-producing *(autopoietic)* process of decision making. Observe that all aspects (criteria, alternatives, representations and evaluations) are continually re-examined and re-adjusted throughout the process. This is not pointless "muddling through" or a chaotic whirlpool. It is a purposeful and often masterful *search for harmony:* a stable pattern which would (at least temporarily) dissolve the tension (or conflict) between what is and what remains desirable.

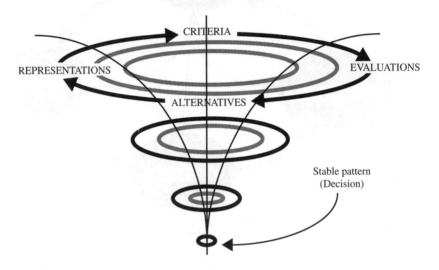

Figure 1.10 Recursive search for the cognitive equilibrium (→ decision).

Following Fuller, knowledge production can be viewed from two essential vantage points of a production designer:

Assuming that he already knows the purpose of producing knowledge, he can then determine how and whether the parts of the knowledge production process function to realize that purpose. This is the view of classical epistemology.

Assuming that he already knows that the parts of the knowledge production process function optimally to realize some purpose, he can determine what that purpose could and could not be. This is *panglossian* design: knowledge production process works optimally towards some ends, but it is a matter of empirical determination what the ends are. *What sorts of goals can be realized given the actual structural constraints on knowledge production?* This is one of the fundamental questions of the CE (cognitive equilibrium) paradigm.

Under the CE paradigm, each problem must be initially ill-structured. Yet, each solution is the solution to a well-structured problem, i.e., a problem in cognitive equilibrium. So, each ill-structured problem is a problem well structured towards its cognitive equilibrium.

There is therefore a sort of *cognitive economy* of a community of knowledge negotiating agents: objects are regularly passed from being represented to being themselves representatives, back and forth, so as to maintain a *cognitive equilibrium*. The word *table* is not as clear and distinct a representation of the table as the table itself.

Balancing of representational gains and losses is equilibrium in a cognitive economy.

For the first time in history we are posed to understand decision making not merely as computation of the world given "out there," but as the very way of constructing our local world, ordering our individual and collective experience, making sense of the "chaos" of reality. Making decisions does not mean finding our way through a fixed maze of given structures. Problem solving and decision making refer to the very construction of that maze: decision-making structures – i.e. our own ordering of nature so that we ourselves can find our way through *it*.

A more formal analysis of non Zadehian fuzziness of human language is presented in Appendix 8: Formal Analysis of Fuzziness.

The presented view refers only to the first level of modeling: that of the individual and *his* context. The next level refers to matching different individuals and their respective contexts through negotiating process by which the socially acceptable meaning of fuzzy language is derived and the proper context for cooperation (intersection, union, or other reformulation) is proposed.

It is also clear that fuzziness is not only brought about by multiple participants communicating in language, but by their purposes or goals. Multiple Criteria Decision Making (MCDM), weighing and balancing competing multiple dimensions, is also at the core of language fuzziness. In the same way as modern MCDM theory and methodology overcame the context-free, single-dimensionality of the utility theory or multi-attribute utility theory, so the knowledge-based contextual theory of fuzziness can overcome the context-free, functionalistic single-dimensionality of the traditional fuzzy sets theory.

MCDM's current experiences with holistic simulations of interactive systems, their increasing reliance on displacement of ideal or reference points, and the increasingly graphical mode of analysis provide a whole new set of tools and methodologies which are eminently suitable for the study of fuzziness.

Points of reference are necessary for expressing at least basic shifts in the contexts of decision making, communication and action. The world appears to us as a seamless web or continuum. Even perceiving our location, knowing where we are, is impossible without relevant reference points. Remove the reference points, like in the sea or in the desert, and we are lost, clueless in an impoverished informational field.

Similarly with the preferences or fuzzy linguistic labels: without reference points and their displacement we would be incapable of forming contextual preferences or discerning the meaning of fuzzy labels. We would not know where we are. There is *no preference without reference*: the context effects are crucial in the studies in psychology, economics, decision making, communication, marketing, cognition, knowledge management and, of course, human language and its fuzzy categories.

The concept *big* has meaning only if we know *small*.

The constructivist's view of knowledge, as presented in this and other papers, is based on distinction, selection, choice, judgment and decision making being the forces behind fuzziness of language. Without a theory of knowledge, multiple criteria decision making, negotiation and human coordination of action there could be only a very limited understanding or analysis of fuzziness.

We should not define fuzziness so that it is compatible with the tools of fuzzy sets currently available to us. Adjusting and "correcting" our reality to the tools available is an old expediency of very limited import (The human brain has often been "modeled" as a mechanical contrivance, electric switchboard, input-output computer, or massively-parallel computer, etc., by whatever tool is available at the time).

A more useful approach would be reversed: first, study the fuzziness of natural languages and how it relates to human knowledge construction and coordination of action. *Then* decide which tools and formalisms are suitable for dealing with the challenges of agreed upon goals.

If the second approach were taken, we would know more about the fuzziness of language, even though perhaps less about the membership functions and their formal properties.

Fuzzy sets theories should not limit themselves to the study of "smooth," gradual or continuous response in control systems and electronic contrivances. They should also embrace the questions of cognitive sciences, neuroscience, neurolinguistics, evolutionary epistemology, radical constructivism, general systems theory, autopoiesis, and other related areas.

The world with its "objects" is an unlabeled place – the number of ways in which macroscopic boundaries can be partitioned by an animal in an eco-niche is very large, perhaps infinite. Any satisfactory theory must account for object definition and generalization from a world whose events and "objects" are not pre-labeled by any *a priori* scheme. Again, the study of fuzziness can and should contribute to these fundamental questions of human existence, not only to the "smooth response" of thermostat servomechanisms.

We owe it to ourselves as scientists and to others as the intended users and beneficiaries of our efforts: it is time to learn and pass beyond a context-free treatment of social reality. Nothing ever takes place out of context – and all our analytical efforts most reflect that simple truth.

One is reminded of the exquisite insight of the equally exquisite Spanish philosopher, Jose Ortega y Gasset:

"I am myself and my circumstance."

Chapter 2

MANAGEMENT OF SYSTEMS:
Global Management Paradigm

With the emergence of the global economy and its *global customer*, it is self-evident that a globally effective management system must emerge as well. In order to satisfy global customers, companies must adopt transnational and transcultural production and marketing systems in order to effectively address the global customer's craving for low price, high quality and high speed of delivery. Global customers want things *cheaper, better and faster*, year after year, with no end in sight. In fact, they want it all: Free, Perfect and Now.

Even though the elimination of tradeoffs flies in the face of traditional proponents of tradeoffs and specialization, there is no turning back. The new strategy has to deliver it all, without tradeoffs, with multidimensional differentiation and utmost flexibility. The global customer does not want anything lesser, and things will not get any better for tradeoffs-bound local producers. Globally competitive companies have no choice and fundamental realignment of their practices has been long overdue.

Satisfying the global customer is not easy. Delivering low cost, high quality and impressive speed requires new, globally effective management systems. We refer to them as the *Global Management Paradigm* (GMP). GMP is capable of delivering tradeoff-free products and services in at least three dimensions: cost, quality and speed. GMP consists of 10 essential dimensions which have to form a *system*.

Each of these ten dimensions refers to a specific strategic realignment of the organization, its knowledge and skills, technology and product/service design. Without their effective realignment, a company would be doomed to deliver *either* low cost *or* high quality *or* high speed, but never all the requisite dimensions together, forever. Yet, what is needed in the global economy is to deliver *both* low cost *and* high quality *and* high speed. The need for a shift from Strategy OR to Strategy AND is palpable.

The ten dimensions of GMP are as follows:

1. Horizontal Corporation
2. Reengineering of the Process
3. Mass Customization
4. Autonomous Teams or Cells
5. Customer integration
6. Intracompany Markets
7. Supplier Integration & Co-location
8. Elimination of Tradeoffs
9. Open-Book Management
10. Corporate Kinetics

We shall shortly characterize all ten dimensions of GMP and elaborate on several of them in more detail in the following sections and chapters.

2.1 Managing in the Global Era: GMP

Individual components of the GMP have been coming steadily during the last decade, in different countries, different corporations and under different conditions. Only in recent years they have started to come together, vigorously integrated by a small but fast growing subset of world-class corporations, forming a new management system.

A management system is not just a collection of techniques, methods and approaches, but a *coherent complex* – a system of interdependent practices in the spheres of organization, management, decision making and motivation.

A new management system is brought about *not* by the continuous improvement of the old, but by the changes in external conditions and forces – making the new system natural, spontaneous and inevitable.

The newly emerging GMP is bound to be globally dominant and widespread, at least among the actively competitive, industrialized and increasingly knowledge-based economies. Overall, national and cultural differences increasingly constitute only a thin overlay and "coloring" of the style, but do not affect the foundations of GMP. Global competition and its intensification require not only the same ballgame, but also the same ballpark.

It is becoming virtually impossible for world-class companies to continue competing while preserving, enhancing or even improving the traditional management paradigm of hierarchy, mass production and specialization, both in manufacturing and services. Working harder *and* working smarter within the confines of the given traditional system is not sufficient any longer. One has to start working differently: working wiser.

Components of GMP

Let us take a closer look at the individual components of GMP:

1. **The Horizontal Corporation**. The layers of the command hierarchy are disappearing. Vertical pyramids of the functional organization are flattening out and the horizontally organized corporation is emerging. The process or portfolio of processes represents the organizational focus, not the divisions, functions, departments or staff specialists and experts. The transitional hybrids, combining the best of both paradigms, are temporarily effective and even necessary, but the trend is inescapably accelerating towards the uncompromised and undiluted Horizontal Corporation.
2. **Reengineering of the Process**. Production and service-delivery processes are being reengineered in the sense of reintegration. The essence of reengineering has very little to do with being fundamental, radical or dramatic; it has everything to do with reintegrating the process: its tasks, labor and knowledge. Tasks, operations, functions, responsibilities and skills are combined and unified into larger coherent wholes. That in itself is the major cause of the flattening of the hierarchies, not the artificial and politically motivated downsizing, "cutting the fat" or debureaucratization.
3. **Mass Customization**. Instead of statistically defined and behaved "mass markets", each individual customer or group of customers has now become the market. "Markets do not buy anything, individuals do," captures the shift quite succinctly. Individually customized products, customer-controlled completion of the production and service-delivery process, self-service and do-it-yourself – all such phenomena represent not only a change in the strategic focus, but a fundamental restructuring of the traditional ends and means of production. New technological platforms support the newly found economies of scope.
4. **Autonomous Teams or Cells**. Horizontal organizations of reintegrated processes represent networks of interacting teams, cells or amoebas: highly integrated, small teams of employees who "own" the production process. Process ownership, responsibility, creativity and self-management are the main characteristics of teams. Teams can be closer to the customer, can mass-customize, and can respond flexibly and behave responsibly. They assure higher productivity and quality while allowing the cost to decrease.

5. **Customer integration**. The customer has become a part of the production process, a part of the purpose of the enterprise, a driving force of the strategy and the final arbiter of product and service quality, variety and cost. The customer provides crucial input into product design, production scheduling and post-purchase maintenance, recovery and recycling. The customer has become the major corporate stakeholder and investor and customer satisfaction has become the primary measure of corporate performance.

6. **Intracompany Markets**. Autonomous teams in a Horizontal Corporation are organized, coordinated and synchronized with the help of an internal market economy. This is based on external market prices, free contractual agents, internal competition and continuous formation, re-formation and dissolution of teams and networks of teams in order to fit the business environment and circumstances most effectively. Corporate boundaries become semipermeable to physical and informational fluctuations. The external suppliers and customers are drawn into direct interaction with corporate internal customers.

7. **Supplier Integration**. Also known as Co-location, it reaches well beyond Lean Production and JIT by bringing the suppliers directly and physically within and inside the production or assembly plant. Supplier Integration also differs from classical vertical integration in that the co-located suppliers are physically integrated, but do remain autonomous and independent in terms of management and performance.

8. **Elimination of Tradeoffs**. Also known as Tradeoff-Free Management, the Elimination of Tradeoffs allows for the improvement in quality, cost, flexibility, productivity and timeliness – all at the same time. The portfolio of corporate resources and its optimization (or optimal design) is the key towards tradeoffs elimination. Managing any given system optimally is fundamentally different from and vastly inferior to managing an optimally designed system.

9. **Open-Book Management**. Corporate information is not a secret or privilege, but an increasingly important management tool. All employees must know not only what to do and when, but mainly why. Information has to be shared, propagated and broadcast throughout the company: only then can employees share directly in the company's success or failure. Employees cease being hired hands and start thinking like owners.

10. **Corporate Kinetics**. Even seemingly insignificant market events could produce information and knowledge that could lead to new products, improvement of processes or satisfying the customers. A *kinetic company* is agile in ferreting out, extracting and mining innovation leads from the daily plethora of all corporate and market events.

The introduced dimensions of GMP could be too few or too many – it is still too early in its evolution to predict them with full confidence. Some dimensions will be fused, others added or dropped over time. However, in its broad outlines, this is what the new management paradigm contours are and they are unlikely to change fundamentally.

Consumers and customers will change their behavior and preferences accordingly, together with the producers of goods and services. The differences between producers and consumers will ultimately disappear and Toffler's "prosumers" will become an integral part of new economic reality. The differences between production (and products) and services are already disappearing quite rapidly: producers offer fundamental services and services market new and innovative products. The term "service industry" captures it too.

Let us take a closer look at some other GMP components.

2.1.1 Business Process Reengineering (BPR)

For the entire history of business, management and economics, the *production process* was considered "given," fixed and unchangeable. It was the product, the final outcome, not the process leading to it, was the legitimate concern of business managers. Business as "core competencies" was unknown. *What* companies were producing mattered more than what they were *doing*. The process itself was in the domain of engineers, technologists and technicians. Consequently, influential management figures of the pre-BPR era were engineers (Taylor, Gilbreth, Deming, Juran, and so on).

Until very recently, production processes were designed by engineers and accepted *as given* by managers. While the product was a competitive tool, the process was not. Nobody wondered why the processes were composed of thousands of operations, producing countless parts and subparts, assemblies and subassemblies, ultimately held together by a striking variety of bolts, screws, washers and the like.

Naturally, the quality, reliability and usability of such products were low, suffered from the constant need for specialized attention and repair, and had a short product life with frequent breakdowns. The nature of the process determines the nature and quality of the product, but not *vice versa*.

Global competition has brought change. The very architecture, the technological sequencing and time-honored partitioning of processes, is being redesigned, i.e., reengineered. Technological processes are not "given" anymore, but are to be optimized, streamlined, reduced and integrated. Reengineering, i.e., reintegration and streamlining of the process, has also engaged the latest advances in IT/S in order to achieve its competitive objectives: minimize the number of operations and parts, minimize costs and non-value adding activities, minimize division of labor and specialization, and minimize time to delivery and time to cash – in short, maximize value.

2.1.1.1 What is BPR?

Reengineering does not ask "how do we improve this operation?" but rather "why do we have to perform this operation?" While a cartoon may show a worker, spanner in hand, asleep with his feet up (*Economist*, Oct. 31st, 1998) – in order to describe the British productivity gap – it is more accurate to show a British worker busily tightening up nuts with a spanner, while evoking the thought of a Japanese worker using a robot to do it five times faster and a German worker redesigning a product that eliminates the need for nuts and bolts altogether.

American businesses, led by Ford, Texas Instruments and Taco Bell in the 1980s, went even further and introduced the reengineering of the entire process – after experiencing failures with Japanese-style robotization or German-style product redesign with their traditional production lines intact. The rest is history.

Reengineering itself has become a much overused word, often with even negative connotations. This unfortunate technocratic label does not even begin to suggest what BPR is all about. The BPR label is neutral, directionless, purposeless and thus misleading. The authors of "Reengineering the Corporation" were, in its later edition (Hammer, Champy 1994), compelled to add the chapter "What Reengineering Isn't" – a clear sign of careless definition, little theory and hasty practices.

Reengineering is not downsizing. Reengineering also is not automation or autonomation. It is not restructuring, reorganization, debureaucratization, delayering or flattening of an organization. It is not "New architecture" or "New Economy."

Reengineering also is not TQM or any other manifestation of the quality and productivity improvement practices. Nor is reengineering an expression of continuous improvement, incremental management or kaizen. Reengineering is not Mass Customization.

The essence of the phenomenon of BPR is *process reintegration*. Process reintegration is partially a spontaneous process of responding to the extremes of *specialization and division of labor.* Reengineering represents the overcoming of the increasingly negative effects of the time-weathered Smith-Marx-Gilbrethian strategies.

In Figure 2.1, the main distinctions between process and operations are presented. Clearly, a process consists of at least two (related) operations. The process is the totality of operations *and* their relationships. Viewing production as a network of processes and operations is due to Shigeo Shingo, the Japanese "father" of reengineering of the 40s and 50s (Shingo, Robinson 1990). Improving individual operations while conserving their relationships (process architecture) may rise to process improvement but it is not process reengineering.

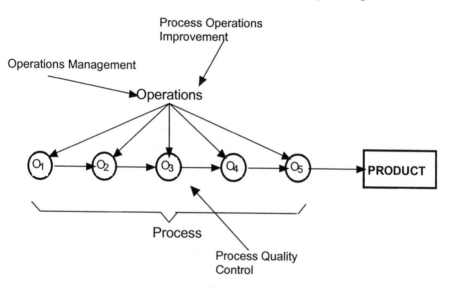

Figure 2.1 Process and operations.

The authors (Hammer, Champy 1994) are aware of the distinction and they do describe BPR correctly, as the "idea of reunifying those [previously broken down] tasks into coherent business processes."

They also write that BPR rejects the assumptions inherent in Adam Smith's industrial paradigm: the division of labor, economies of scale, hierarchical control, etc. Specifically: "The old ways of doing business – the division of labor around which companies have been organized since Adam Smith first articulated that principle – simply don't work anymore."

Yet, inexplicably, when they attempt a formal definition, in "Reengineering Formally Defined," the authors offer the following cliché:

"Reengineering is the fundamental rethinking and radical redesign of business process to achieve dramatic improvements in critical contemporary measures of performance, such as cost, quality, service, and speed."

"This definition contains four key words," they add.

Yet, in defining BPR there can only be one keyword: *process*. The other keywords, like fundamental, radical and dramatic could be keywords in revolutionary politics or show business, not in business management of the 21st century.

2.1.1.2 Reengineering as Reintegration

The essence of BPR has very little to do with being fundamental, radical or dramatic. It has everything to do with reintegrating the process: its tasks, labor and knowledge. *Reengineering is the reintegration of the process.*

There are three basic domains where this reintegration takes place:

***Reintegrating the task*:** Combine smaller process subtasks and subactivities into larger, integrated units and packages. Reduce the number of parts, components, segments and constituents comprising products and processes. This is a clear and unambiguous charge: reduce the number of parts in products and processes (fundamentally, radically and dramatically, if you wish).

***Reintegrating the labor*:** Allow workers to perform and coordinate larger rather than smaller portions of the process. Encourage multifunctionality, job rotation, despecialization and process ownership. This is a clear and unambiguous charge: let people work in autonomous teams and coordinate an integrated process rather than laboring individually on atomized and linear mass-production assembly lines. The results are bound to be fundamental, radical and dramatic.

***Reintegrating the knowledge*:** Workers must *know* (i.e., be able to coordinate successfully) larger and larger sections of the process and product, not smaller and smaller portions. Knowledge is the ability to coordinate one's action purposefully. If one is specialized, atomized and reduced to a machine appendage, one cannot coordinate action, but only carry out single and simple commands. The charge is clear and unambiguous: the integrated rather than specialized education, training and skills acquisition – quite fundamental, radical and dramatic, by definition.

What makes the mislabeling of BPR (and the associated high cost of executive confusion and misinterpretation) more remarkable is the authors' expressed understanding of the underlying problem:

"Today's airlines, steel mills, accounting firms, and computer chip makers have all been built around Smith's central idea: the division or specialization of labor and the consequent fragmentation of work. The larger the organization, the more specialized is the worker and the more separate steps into which the work is fragmented. This rule applies not only to manufacturing jobs. Insurance companies, for instance, typically assign separate clerks to process each line of a standardized form. Then they pass the form to another clerk, who processes the next line. These workers never complete a job; they just perform piecemeal tasks."

Hammer, Champy 1994

The above refers to the key and still unresolved problem within the traditional US management paradigm: centralized command system, division of labor, overspecialization, assembly line mentality, lack of mass customization, and too many uninvolved, non owning and non entrepreneurial employees.

Adam Smith's and Karl Marx's concept of the "division of labor" has been overcome. The phenomenon in question actually includes at least three separate, separable and relatively independent and differentially manageable aspects: division of task, division of labor, and division of knowledge (Zeleny 1989, 1990).

We have discussed the division and reintegration of task, labor and knowledge in section 1.4, on Division and Reintegration of Knowledge. The reader can review this section and see how it applies to reengineering.

2.1.1.3 Continuous Improvement

Improving the existing systems, continually – incessantly, piecemeal or incrementally – will not do the trick. For example, one cannot "continually" improve the horse carriage and create internal combustion engine. Improving the quality of a horse carriage and breeding the horses according to the latest standards will not bring forth automobiles. Horses and carriages of the highest and continually improving quality are of little use when facing the "horses" of Henry Ford. Quality and continuous improvement are slogans which may be used to improve or preserve the status quo, not bring about a breakthrough.

Reengineering the horse carriage, fundamentally, radically and dramatically, could produce white Arabian steeds, aluminum wheels, laser guided whips, computerized brakes or train cabbies to wear white gloves. Customers might even flock in for the ride. Yet, it is not good enough: a sputtering, smelly little gas engine will do them in every time.

Reengineering *per se* is not enough: one also has to know how (in which direction) and why to carry out BPR. Not every dramatic change is really dramatic: some are just showy. One has to work one's way to the internal combustion engine and beyond. This requires creativity, competence, courage and conviction. It has nothing to do with quality focus, reengineering or continuous improvement. It has everything to do with reintegrating the task, labor and knowledge of production and service.

The same applies to management systems. Why should one improve (even if continually) a hierarchical, centralized command system with extreme division of labor? Of course it can be done. Should it be done?

The new millennium is not the 1960s, and appearances and lifestyles do not matter anymore, no matter how radical. What matters is a management system which takes us from the horse carriage to the automobile: from the specialized assembly lines of hirelings to the reintegrated processes of autonomous process owners.

2.1.1.4 The "10-90 Rule"

In the 1990s, during the widespread BPR efforts, it has been empirically established that only some 10 percent of potential process improvements were found in process operations, while the bulk 90 percent of such improvements were hidden in process relationships, depicted by the arrows in Figure 2.1.

One does not see the relationships, one only sees the operations. When a consultant observes the process *in situ*, he notices when something is being done, when activities are carried out, when there is a movement. His natural tendency is to take measures to improve these "visible" operations. Yet, the problem of improvement lies precisely in the things we do not see, when nothing is going on or when there is no movement. These are the regions of the process where some 90 percent of the improvement is hidden.

In the language of Figure 2.1, the devil is in the arrows, not in the circles. There are simply *too many arrows* in traditional processes. The process is broken down into a large number of operations (due to the extremes of division of labor and specialization) and their coordination requires too many relationships.

It certainly amounts to misplaced underachievement when managers try to improve operations, O_1 through O_5, while maintaining the process architecture (the number and sequencing of arrows), which is fixed and unchanged. In BPR, it is primary and paramount to attack the arrows, the invisible parts of the process, first and foremost.

In BPR, we do not ask "How can we improve this operation?" We ask: "Should we perform this operation at all?" Before considering improving any operation, we must be absolutely sure that such an operation must be performed. The largest possible improvement to any operation – in terms of time, cost and reliability – must be its elimination.

Before we improve, streamline or computerize the operations of supplied parts billing, checking and warehousing, we have to ask whether we should perform them at all, whether we should not co-locate our supplier and let him own his parts until he installs them in our product.

The reengineered process should not only have the minimum architecture (smallest number of operations and relationships), but also add maximum value to the product. First, we have to eliminate all operations that do not add value. Second, we have to integrate those operations that add little value separately, but would add much more jointly. Whenever we integrate two or more operations, we also eliminate at least one arrow (relationship) in the architecture. Thus, improving operations attacks only 10 percent of the problem, while integrating operations attacks the entire 90 percent of the problem. Of course, eliminating operations attacks the full 100 percent of the problem.

2.1.1.5 The Process of BPR

When Compaq shifted from the 140-person assembly lines of the Smith-Marx division of labor paradigm to the 3-person cells responsible for the entire PC assembly, there was a lot of integration and elimination of traditional operations carried out. Effective integration of operations requires a creative approach, product redesign, process redesign, skills realignment and knowledge enhancement. Reengineered processes require people to widen their expertise, not limit it; to expand their knowledge, not specialize it; to broaden their task, not narrow it. Workers are becoming modern craftsmen and artisans, capable of micro-managing the subprocesses they own or should own.

The pinnacle of the BPR process is full integration, like in Figure 2.2, where all six original operations are ultimately integrated and performed by a single worker, manager or employee. Such a fully integrated operation, like O_{123456}

can be further improved by traditional means, in terms of its time, cost, quality and reliability – continuously.

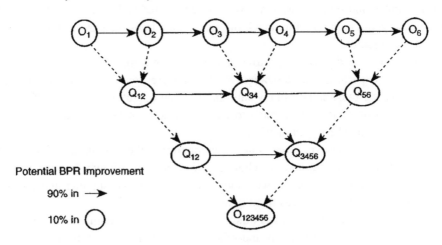

Figure 2.2 Integration of operations in the BPR process.

The outlined scheme of the process of BPR captures the direction and purpose of reengineering, not just its effects. Reengineering refers to changing the architecture of production and service delivery processes towards reintegrating previously atomized task, labor and knowledge. In this sense, BPR reflects a full reversal of trends brought forth by the Industrial Revolution: the division of labor and specialization.

The famous theorem of Adam Smith – that the extent of the division of labor is limited only by the size of the market – ceases to be valid in the modern era. In the era of unprecedented global markets and global demand we do not see meaningful expansion or intensification of specialization and division of labor. Instead, we are witnesses to the proliferation of the opposite phenomena: multifunctional workers, reprogrammable robots, multipurpose machinery, disintermediation, pay for knowledge, integrated teams or cells, parts minimization, compact and "weightless" redesign, self-service and do-it-yourself, etc.

2.1.1.6 Reengineering and Strategy

BPR and its reliance on core competencies and process ownership has brought forth fundamental changes in strategy and strategic planning.

		GOALS	
		Same	Different
MEANS	Same	Efficiency	Strategy Formation
	Different	Effectiveness (BPR)	Strategic Reengineering

Figure 2.3 Classification of strategic modes.

In the era of hypercompetition, it is inadequate to pursue the same or different goals via the same means (processes and resources) as competitors. The focus has shifted towards pursuing the same goals through different means (BPR) or pursuing different goals by different means: doing different things differently.

In Figure 2.3, strategic positions are classified in terms of a means-goals framework and the shift towards Strategic reengineering is noted. In fact, the shift is even more fundamental: rather than searching for adequate means to reach given goals, as in traditional strategic planning, one has to search for the right goals to validate and enhance the existing means (core competencies, key processes, knowledge abilities).

This reversal in strategic thinking, focusing on the process (doing, action) rather than on the product (outcome, purpose) is increasingly forced by global hypercompetition.

Many would argue that the extensive reengineering of U.S. corporations in the 90s lies at the core of the robust economic performance of the U.S. economy. Indeed, having "lean and mean" production processes, downsized bureaucracies and aggressive global competitive strategies assures products and services which are characterized by high quality, low cost and rapid delivery. Yet, reengineering is only one necessary condition and by no means a sufficient one. Successful, economy-wide completion of corporate reengineering is only the first step towards global competitiveness.

The reengineering of processes must be supported by the corresponding requisite corporate organization, right information technology and modern strategic considerations. BPR cannot stand alone.

2.1.2 Customer Integration (IPM)

New global management principles related to customers, consumers and suppliers are being synthesized into the management system approach, identified as *Integrated Process Management (IPM)*. Its major characteristic is customer (and supplier) integration into the production process.

To increase the productivity of the work and quality of the product, we have to aim to increase the quality of the process. Increasing the quality of the process means *integrating the process* through BPR (Business Process Reengineering), which assures a higher-quality product at lower cost, larger added-value and faster response/delivery time.

The product and its process should be integrated for as long and as far as possible. The product in the hands of the customer is still a part of the production cycle. That implies *integrating the customer* – and (at the other end of value chain) also the supplier – into the production process. Modern production process is thus doubly integrated: 1. *per se*, in terms of the minimal number of operations performed by the minimal number of workers, and 2. in terms of indirect or direct customer/supplier involvement.

Finally: our customer, our master. The integrated customer becomes the source and main purpose of the firm's strategy, tactics and operations. Only the customers know what they prefer and why. The producers supply the how. *Integrating the knowledge* of the customer into the enterprise, letting them trigger, schedule, coordinate and manage the process itself, is the third main integration needed for Integrated Process Management (IPM).

2.1.2.1 Roots of IPM

The emphasis is clear: the customer is the purpose and driving force of the enterprise; he must therefore be integrated into the process of production or service delivery. Improving the quality of such a customer integrated process then becomes a tool by which customer satisfaction is achieved, and thus his role as a driving force both amplified and maintained.

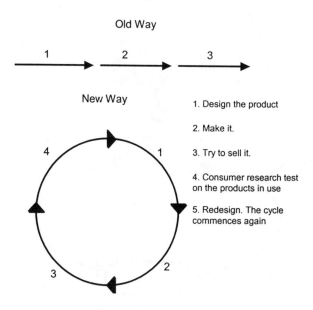

Figure 2.4 The Deming cycle.

One can concentrate on the management of inputs (human, financial and material resources); or on the management of outputs (product or service characteristics, advertisement, selling); or even on the management of the production transformation itself (process). All these separate components have received their due and mostly separate attention in the history of management.

In reality, business production is not a linear transformation of inputs into outputs. Most practitioners and theorists of management are familiar with the original summary of the new philosophy by W. Edwards Deming; we reproduce its version in Figure 2.4.

The difficulty is not with any of the above components themselves, but with their interconnecting system: the customer remains an object, isolated "out there," in the environment. The product is allowed to leave the production system and "in the hands" of the customer it is "gone." No matter how loudly we proclaim our concerns for the customer or how elaborate are the institutions we establish (return policies, warranties, questionnaires, recalls), the customer remains an external object.

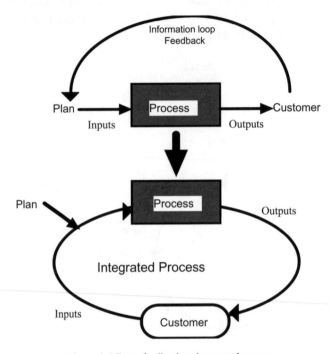

Figure 2.5 From feedback to integrated process.

This amounts to a loss. A very important "real" linkage has been lost and replaced by a "symbolic" information feedback loop of data gathering, market and consumer research, and forecasting and information processing (in order to learn about the customer and his environment). This is graphically represented in the upper portion of Figure 2.5. The loop is an *information feedback loop*: It further separates the "real" world from the "symbolic" one; it does not involve the customer in the real process but has him just "feeding info" into the symbolic loop.

2.1.2.2 Role of Feedback

If we view the customer only as part of the environment and not of enterprise, being an object rather than subject of production, being anonymous rather than individually addressable, his remoteness and isolation become fundamental and definitional.

Still, companies have to modify, correct and adjust their production according to their customers' wishes and preferences, at least in capitalistic systems. They need to learn their customers' preferences via gathering information about them. An information feedback loop must be set up.

This need for feedback distinguishes capitalism from socialism (where no feedback is needed: customers' needs are determined by the plan and the plan is produced by the Central Planning Committee.).

But feedback does not end the customer's separation. Feedback is dependent on what consumers say (express, describe, evaluate), only *ex post* on what they do. Feedback carries symbolic information, description of action (words, numbers, pictures), but not real "in-formation," i.e., action itself.

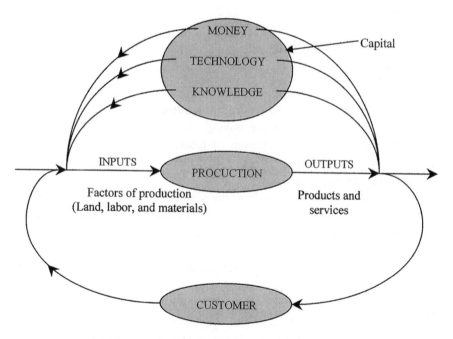

Figure 2.6 Customer integration into the production process.

It is more important in business to rely on what people do (choose, decide, and act) and not just on what they say they'd do. Symbolic feedback must be replaced by "action feedback," the description of an action by an action.

Traditionally, we have perceived the production process as simply a transformation of inputs into outputs. Such a linear scheme is being replaced by the circularly integrated process, as portrayed in Figure 2.6. The customer becomes both the purpose and the driving force of an enterprise.

In Figure 2.6 we observe the multidimensional "capital loop," the continuous self-renewal of the portfolio of *money, technology and knowledge*, which helps to "produce," over and over, the enterprise itself.

It is increasingly realized that any modern enterprise is engaged in *two types of production*: 1. *heteropoiesis*, producing "the other" than itself (i.e., goods and services), and 2. *autopoiesis*, producing itself, i.e., its own production *process*, its own ability to produce.

Self-sustainability of systems is crucially dependent on the efficacy of the second type of production, autopoiesis. Only systems that can continually "produce themselves" under changing environmental conditions can become self-sustainable.

2.1.2.3 The Role of Knowledge

Managing labor, land, money or technology is *fundamentally different* from *managing knowledge*: coordinating knowledge of workers, suppliers and customers into the integrated and coherent enterprise.

If it is only the labor we are buying, as in the industrial era of mass production, specialization and division of labor, we can afford to manage by order and command. We say, "Do this!" and then reward the doer according to how the command was carried out.

If it is knowledge we have to buy, the whole situation changes. We cannot command "Think this!" or "Solve this!" or "Be creative!" Extracting knowledge from employees, suppliers and customers requires entirely different skills than getting their labor, supplies or purchases.

To engage and utilize knowledge, one has to "get" the *whole person*. Only the whole person can be a source of knowledge.

Who are the possessors of needed knowledge? Clearly, they are the customers, employees, managers and suppliers: customers, because of the sovereignty of their needs and preferences and employees because of their unique command of the local process environments and contexts. Both customers and employees must be fully integrated into the enterprise.

The same goes for suppliers and managers. Suppliers *supply* the process (with parts, inputs and services), affect its quality and are integrated to share their responsibility for it. Managers should *manage the process*, not just its separate functional "silos," via orders and directives.

Customers are also primary *investors* in the enterprise. Through *their* purchases and loyalty, they finance and sustain most of the firm's activities, supply it with knowledge and purpose, and provide its justification. This is a more valuable service to the firm than putting in short-term money on risky stocks. Customers become partners and participants of the process, no longer detained in the anonymous mass consumer status of the past.

Employees and managers are also internal *customers* and investors *vis à vis* each other. *Customer integration* must refer to integrating both external and internal customers into the process.

2.1.2.4 Prosumer

In Figure 2.7, the integrated customer becomes a part of the production process and serves not only as a consumer but also as a producer (or "prosumer" in Toffler's terms).

The most significant inputs into the production process are not raw materials, machines, money or buildings, but information and knowledge. Knowing what to do, how, when and why is the most important input. Without knowledge, money could never become capital and raw material would stay raw. In Figure 2.7, this input is called Control information. Whoever controls Control information controls the process. Traditionally, it was the producers, employees and managers, but increasingly it is the customers, consumers and suppliers who directly trigger "the controls." They become producers in the sense of controlling the information and knowledge of the enterprise.

PROSUMER

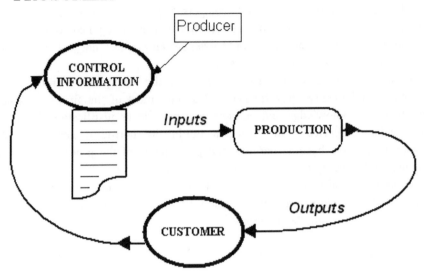

Figure 2.7 Production is information processing by the consumer → "prosumer."

2.1.2.5 Summary of IPM

We can summarize the major principles of IPM as follows:

1. Knowledge – defined as the "purposeful coordination of action" – has become the most productive form of capital. *Knowing* how to employ resources (information, money, technology, materials, skills, etc.) towards achieving desired purposes is more important than just having them. Labor (performing operations) has become work (coordinating operations), and work has turned into knowledge work, best performed by independent, self-managing and directly rewarded individuals.
2. To be effective, knowledge must be primarily produced, enhanced and embodied in people. Employees should be empowered and responsible for coordinating requisite action (process) in their own business or entrepreneurial microspace. Subsets of routine knowledge (repetitive coordination of tasks) can be embodied in technology and thus free humans to perform unique coordinative and managerial tasks.
3. Reintegration of task, labor and knowledge is accomplished in an integrative horizontal organization through individualized reward systems, integrative IT/S and continuous education of individuals.

4. Customers are the primary stakeholders of the enterprise: its purpose and its driving force. They pay all the current and future costs, taxes and profits. Their satisfaction comes first – through a continually improved product at continually declining prices. It is what consumers do and not what consumers say they do that matters in business.

5. All employees are autonomous agents and act as customers to each other. They enter into contractual agreements to deliver their products and services reliably, on time, at the best quality and at the lowest price – most effectively through the intracompany competitive markets.

6. The gap between owners (external stockholders) and employees (managers and workers) must be reduced just as the gap between coordinators (managers) and operators (workers) is being reduced. Hierarchical coordination is replaced by self-coordination of the process through mutual market adaptation.

7. Continuous support and improvement of employees' total quality of life (not only the quality of their work life) is the responsibility of the modern enterprise and its employees.

8. Continuous broadening and expansion of flexibility, adaptability and responsiveness is the major aspect of strategy formation.

9. Continuous knowledge expansion is accomplished through education, training, job rotation and the creative experimentation of all employees.

10. All management principles are rooted in and derived from treating others, through mutual consent, as we would wish to be treated by them.

2.1.2.6 Process Ownership

Transferring work processes and work places to line employee self-management, responsibility and control raises the question of ownership: who owns the vital processes and workplaces? Impressive business successes (when and if tried) of such modern arrangements as "process ownership," "workplace ownership," "entrepreneurial microspace ownership" or "equipment ownership" provide persuasive argument.

The future needs of the global economy will require:

1) Reducing overspecialization in work organization and work structures.
2) Increasing and sustaining teamwork and cooperation across functional work units and between labor and management.
3) Integrating the introduction of new technology with human resources innovations.

4) Encouraging business strategies that support and reinforce adaptation and flexibility in the workplace.

Employees' self-management is an important requirement of social justice. Even papal encyclicals tend to pose the issue of social justice in terms of the socialism-capitalism dichotomy without addressing the "conflict" between capitalists and workers. Supporting systems of employee participation dissolves the "conflict" by making all employees capitalists.

Employees' self-management and co-ownership, free-market institution within firms, distribution of income according to individual contribution and long-term community needs are principles applicable not only to business, but also to institutions of social, political and cultural life.

2.1.2.7 Planning and Strategy Formation

Through IPM, internal functions of planning can be viewed as purposeful perturbations to the enterprise interflow. Such perturbations form process "deformations" (in-formation) to be propagated along the entire "loop" of the enterprise. The process becomes self-managing and self-maintaining, but subject to managerial and even environmental perturbations. Any locus of the interflow loop can be perturbed by purposeful in-formation.

In terms of external planning, there is a shift away from traditional planning as forecasting and prediction.

In Figure 2.8, the traditional, prediction and feedback based concept of planning is contrasted with the modern concept of planning as flexibility enhancement. Rather than estimating probabilities of future states, one builds up a response (technological) platform which would allow the appropriate and profitable response under any conceivable circumstances of the states of Nature.

Instead of computing the environment "out there" (long-range planning of centralized hierarchies), the IPM emphasis is on the continuous buildup of the internal and autonomous response flexibility. To become sufficiently flexible in technology, labor and knowledge, to attain the capability of responding "just-in-time," rather than hedging "just-in-case," is the only true long-term strategy for the global era of turbulence, unpredictability and constant change. The time of educated guesses and "crystal balls" has passed.

The declining role of traditional forecasting affects traditional corporate and strategic planning. Instead of forming goals based on predicting the future environment, and *then* mobilizing the ways and resources for reaching them, the process of strategy formation is increasingly being reversed by practice.

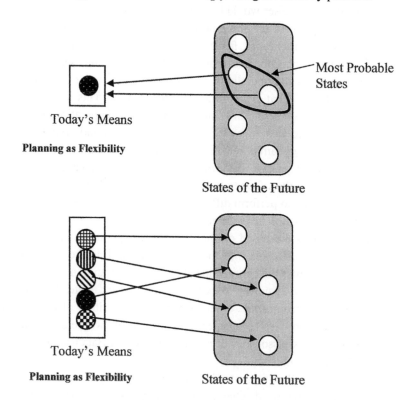

Figure 2.8 Planning versus flexibility.

First, one enhances current processes and resources into core competencies. *Then* one formulates the goals for the most effective utilization and further enhancement of these competencies to satisfy the customer. Instead of the *goals* → *ways* → *resources* dogma-sequence of forecasting-based strategy, modern and flexible corporations are exploiting the *resources* → *ways* → *goals* sequence of strategy formation, rooted more firmly in the organization's abilities, competencies and knowledge, not in increasingly blurred and expensive dreams of stability and predictability.

There are many businessmen and managers who still fail to distinguish between operational effectiveness and strategy. People still fail to distinguish between the two. The goals must be an integral part of any strategy formation, whether they enter *a priori* or *ex post*. Discussing business strategy without mentioning goals or processes would be a strange exercise.

Companies can perform *the same* processes and activities in order to attain *the same* goals, but do it cheaper, faster, and more reliably – simply better. That is *operational efficiency*. Other companies could aim for the same goals, but perform their processes and operations in *different ways* in order to achieve their goals more effectively. That is *operational effectiveness*. This strategy is best exemplified by the reengineering of business processes and operations (BPR).

Many companies are also engaging the same processes and operations (core competencies) in the dynamic pursuit of different, multiple and frequently changing goals. They engage in *strategy formation*, moving beyond the efficiency or effectiveness of operational pursuits. Yet other companies have found it quite beneficial to perform different processes and operations in order to attain different goals. That is *strategic reengineering*.

Integrated processes are based on the minimizing operations and integrating external and internal customers into the process, as well as the key suppliers. This is to add value across the entire value chain. Any operation not adding value is to be eliminated. The customer loses his anonymity and instead of being an object of "sales" he becomes an "order provider." Acquisition of orders rather than "selling" is what modern companies seek. Instead of "workers" we speak of process owners, business associates or partners, as Tomas Bata used to do in the 1920s and Jan Bata in 1930s.

Functional barriers that separate departments and internal customers from each other are being removed. One cannot manage the process without team work. Teams cannot exist if there are functional and departmental barriers. The process cuts across these barriers and therefore becomes a new ordering principle in the modern corporation.

2.1.3 Mass Customization

Mass Customization (MC) represents a new way of designing, producing, selling and distributing goods and services: individualized, fitted and customized for individual customers, yet provided at the cost of mass-produced, standardized, off-the-shelf items. In this sense MC emerges from a special fusion of two traditional approaches: mass production and custom made modes. MC retains the best features of both: low cost and high (perfectly fitted) quality.

Mass production offers poor-fit, low-quality items at low cost. Poor fit and lack of individualization is tackled by sorting and classifying, usually by size, but also by color, style, taste, ingredients, etc. This sorting into classes reduces the poor-fit, but increases the proliferation of variety (and numerosity) at the same time – leading again to the higher cost of warehousing, displaying and selling.

At the other end of the traditional spectrum of choices is the "custom made" or "made to order" mode of production. This offers a much better or even individually perfect fit, but at a much higher cost. Traditional consumers are thus forced into tradeoffs they would not normally care to make: you can have either a good fit at high cost, or a poor fit at low cost. Such forced tradeoffs are the heritage of the industrial era's mass production and mass consumption.

The global consumer wants to have it all, good fit and low cost, and Mass Customization has started respecting such deeply seated, natural wants and needs. Unnecessary tradeoffs are not suitable for consumers and producers of the global era.

IT/S is the enabler of MC. IT/S provides computers, scanners, bar coding, telecommunications, CAD/CAM, etc., necessary to design and produce the right fit and individualization.

Mass Customization is unavoidable in global hypercompetition. Customers everywhere prefer custom fit *and* low cost at the same time, without tradeoffs. Producers traditionally (and even by definition) prefer custom fit *or* low cost (and mass produced *or* high cost). During the times of producer domination, that is how it was: "You can have a car of any color, as long as it is black." Now we have entered, quite irreversibly, the era of customer domination: The customer is king and our customer, our master. Producers have to adjust to their customers, not vice versa.

This is important to realize, because any IT/S designed to maintain and strengthen traditional mass production or custom made modes has very little or no future. IT/S that enhances MC are the wave of the future.

MC allows companies to disintermediate, to communicate directly with their customers without the expensive and slow interlinks of assorted agents, intermediaries, dealers and other "facilitators." Such direct contact makes the customer real and specific, not anonymous anymore. Masses of anonymous customers cannot be as effective and loyal as masses of specific individuals. Markets do not buy anything, individuals do, insists Tom Peters.

So, this entry is important in that it establishes the concept and provides numerous examples of Mass Customization – a wave of today, not of the future.

Mass Customization is a new mode of production and service delivery that has become an integral part of the Global Management Paradigm (GMP). The term itself was first coined by S. Davis back in 1987 (in his book "Future Perfect"). We should emphasize the *customer-unique value chain* (CSVC), relating it to the effort to overcome the "mass-oriented" thinking and behavior which appears to be dominant in the mass-production era. Mass production was predicated upon – and could not have survived without – mass consumption.

The American "Keeping up with the Joneses" was prototypical of the mass consumption era: I want to have what the Joneses have. The modern consumer does not want "what the Joneses have" but wants to have it his way: "Have it your way" is the metaphor of Mass Customization, of being different from the Joneses. With the curious exception of the last jerk of mass behavior and uniformity – the SHUV, "Suburban Housewife Utility Vehicle," i.e., the irrational fashion of suburban pick-up trucks – most Americans have entered the era of Mass Customization and have-it-your-way era with vengeance.

Producers have to reengineer their production processes, in fact their entire value chains, from the first inputs to the final consumer, to fit the needs of their unique customers.

2.1.3.1 Customizing Value Chain

The customer-unique value chain (CSVC) is a part of customer-integration efforts within the Global Management Paradigm (GMP) that consists of a number of interdependent and mutually enhancing practices which increasingly characterize corporate management systems emerging in the theater of global competition.

Globally competitive companies are now less likely to differentiate between their domestic and international operations. For example, Coca-Cola has officially dropped its international and domestic divisions. In 1994, T. Turner banned the use of labels like "foreign" or "domestic" in describing the activities of TBS and CNN. Some institutions are belatedly discovering the bandwagon of "international" orientation – at a time when emphasizing such a distinction is starting to sound flat, if not meaningless.

As we can recall, there are ten major dimensions of GMP, all of which are currently making significant headways in high-competition economies: 1. The Horizontal Corporation; 2. Business Process Reengineering; 3. Mass Customization; 4. Autonomous Teams or Cells; 5. Customer integration;

6. Intracompany Market; 7. Supplier Integration; 8. Elimination of Tradeoffs; 9. Open-Book Management and 10. Business Kinetics.

The components of GMP are often treated as separately functioning concepts, implementable individually and without regard to their mutually supportive properties and benefits derivable from their synergy. Their systemic effects are qualitatively higher than the individually selective "cherry picking" on the fertile mountain of GMP.

The experience shows that one cannot isolate and transplant an organic item into a hostile organizational environment and still hope for success. The fiasco of Quality Circles within traditional hierarchies or the failure of robotics in un-reengineered processes would be good examples.

Mass Customization (MC) represents one of the most potent components of GMP, deriving its strength directly from the customer, agile manufacturing, and horizontal organization. It strives for no tradeoffs among variety, delivery time and costs. However, even MC cannot stand alone and must have its own support net (or infrastructure) reliably co-established. MC can succeed only as an integral part of GMP: it resists uprooting.

2.1.3.2 New Realities

Producing goods and services that are perfectly and continuously fitted to the individual customer without any significant cost, quality or time tradeoffs is among the newly acquired technological and cognitive abilities of the producers. It is also a long-time cherished and often subconscious desire of the majority of customers.

These new realities toll final bells for a number of holdovers from the Jurassic period of business and economics: mass production and mass consumption, of-the-rack/off-the shelf shopping, standard sizes and measures, alterations, returns and complaints departments and services, division of labor and specialization, "It ain't my job" attitudes, business forecasting, inventories and warehousing – all rapidly disappearing from the New Economy business experience.

They are being replaced by more agile, newer concepts and practices: database marketing, self-customization, self-service, high-velocity delivery, Integrated Process Management(IPM), Global Management Paradigm (GMP), Mass Customization (MC), flexibility enhancement, teleshopping, telemanufacturing, customer-triggered production, customer-specific value chain (CSVC), and so on.

Take traditional marketing – producing ahead of time for the shelf or inventory – which relies on expensive selling, promotion and advertising efforts of mass marketing. Over the years, mass marketing was replaced by market segmentation, then by niche marketing and micromarketing, and now database marketing. Ultimately, traditional post-production marketing of goods and services will be replaced by a pre-production *marketing of capabilities*. The real challenge is not in selling what you have in the inventories (what you produced), but how to develop, build and deliver what has already been ordered (purchased) by the individual customer: producing what you have already sold.

One thing should become clear, although it still might be puzzling to some: consumers do not want extensive choice and selection; they do not want variety and endless options. *Consumers want what they want.* If I want ivory-grey paint then the mere fact that the retailer stocks 1,500 other paint colors is of no consolation to me. I am much better off having my colors mixed right there, on the premises, preferably through self-service, according to the producer-furnished mixing recipes and store-provided mixers.

2.1.3.3 Customer-Triggered Production

Customizing and tailoring to measure is becoming easy and affordable. In the garment and apparel industries, now all it takes is a *three-dimensional body scan*, developed for example by TC^2 Co. Within two seconds, precise body measurements and shapes are captured, embedded in a Personal Profile Card and mapped directly onto a cutting pattern of a laser-gun cutting machine in a remote factory. The garment is manufactured within hours and the custom-made clothing delivered to customer's home within days.

Levi Strauss & Co. was the first major producer to introduce (back in 1994) a computer-assisted measuring system for mass-customized women's jeans. This MC pioneering system (Levi's "Personal Pair") now appears to be quite cumbersome, customer-annoying and even obsolete: women still have to try on several pairs of stock jeans with clumsily built-in measure tapes, the customized pair costs $15 more, the time of delivery is often more than 3-5 days, etc. Also, men were (and still are) "out of the loop" (even though men abhor off-the-rack shopping much more intensely). The TC^2 body-scan system shall displace such tentative, half-baked pioneering efforts quite rapidly. The Personal Profile Card (PPC) will become the reverse side of all major credit cards for most goods and services.

It is estimated that about 50 percent of Americans still buy and wear the ill-fitting, off-the rack clothing, even underwear, swimming suits and bras. The advancement of MC promotes not only a more stylish nation but could help to preserve and even revive a rapidly disappearing domestic apparel industry which is likely to fall victim to protectionism and tariff-based political "solutions." The only long-term solution is via increased competitiveness: MC could certainly propel not only the garment and shoe industries, but all U.S. industries in the right competitive direction.

There are still unionists and politicians pretending to care about the U.S. garment industry and its workers. Yet, direct labor is only 11 percent of the cost of the garment delivered to customers. Fighting against the "cheap" foreign labor fixates these 11 percent as the main "playing field" where nobody fights for the MC and the customer. Non-value-added handling *after* manufacturing accounts for 27 percent of the cost: that is where the name of the game is.

The U.S. is about the only country with sufficient rapid-mail and computer-network infrastructures to support reliable MC transformation on a large scale. Federal Express, UPS and even the U.S. Post Office are the backbone of MC, providing the necessary infrastructure and encouraging both customers and producers to "Have it their way."

2.1.3.4 Examples of MC

Andersen Windows' "Window of Knowledge" system offers about 50,000 varieties of their custom-made windows. Motorola is capable of delivering over 29 million different versions of its personal pager. These are only the beginnings: *continuous variety* of sizes, styles and patterns is the ultimate goal.

How does it work? Sales representatives of Motorola use Macintosh laptops to help customers co-design the pager features they want. The laptop software allows the design module to be electronically transmitted (via EDI) to the Motorola plant in Boynton Beach, Florida. *Within 20 minutes*, an individual customer order is launched down Motorola production lines. Within an hour, it is completed and ready for shipment. The originally mass-produced item has now become fully customized, on a worldwide basis, with no extra costs.

Custom Foot used electronic scanners to produce custom-made shoes – in northern Italy. Fast response capability is obvious: from new fashion-style design to production – within weeks (traditionally and currently – up to 18 months). Lutron Electronics makes custom lighting systems of all shapes, colors and sizes. Individual, Inc. scans 600 news sources to compile a different report for each individual customer. Paris Miki (Japanese company) in Bellevue, Wash., uses a digital scan of a customer's face to produce a customized eyeglass lens shape to enhance the wearer's appearance. BMW is planning to offer virtual reality "test drives" (with all possible engine combinations over all kinds of terrain, worldwide) while the customers design their custom-made vehicle.

Dell Computer Corp. offers more than 14,000 different configurations of personal computer systems whose production is *triggered after* a customer-specific order has been received.

McGraw-Hill, Inc. custom-produces specialized college textbooks, composed by professors from their own sources or from the publisher's menu of modules, even in small batches of less than 100 copies. A growing number of progressive publishers now offer similarly customized textbooks. The days of nationwide mass-produced and uniformly-consumed textbooks, suitable for the mass consumption/production era of mass thinking, are over: each instructor now has a different, custom-made book for his students.

In March 1995, The Wall Street Journal introduced the first newspaper ever published for a circulation of one.

In the hotel services business, Ritz-Carlton has advanced the farthest on the road to MC. Personalized, customer-driven delivery of both service and quality utilizes an international reservation system and total employee participation to customize according to individual guest's needs and desires. A *Customer Preference Profile* is formed and shared worldwide, updated immediately after each checkout, translated into "guest preference pads" and made available to all staff employees.

Ritz's employee empowerment is based on two rules: 1. *The "1-10-100" rule* – what costs you $1 to fix today will cost $10 to fix tomorrow and $100 to fix later on – gives employees the authority to identify and solve customer problems *on the spot.* No more calling for the supervisor and "Waiting for Godot." 2. *The"24-48-30" rule* – any reported problem will be acknowledged within 24 hours, assigned within 48 hours and resolved within 30 days – enables employees to make changes in the process and "normal" procedures in order to resolve a guest's complaints. The list goes on: ITT Hartford customizes insurance policies; John Deere Harvester Works customizes planters via its "Vision 21" project; etc.

Virtually *all* products and services can and will be mass-customized. Even so called commodities, although more or less uniform, are differentially delivered, put to alternative uses, individually paid for and consumed in diametrically opposed patterns. What is defined as "commodities" by speculators, are not necessarily commodities for actual producers and actual consumers. Every product, no matter how uniform, is a part of a product package (product + service) and that package can be endlessly customized.

Take milk and dairy products. Rather than being commodities with artificially induced price wars based on quantity and market shares (forced mass production), dairy products present an infinite variety of flavors, contents, textures and packagings. How do containers stack? How to customize mixed flavors to local habits? Delivery times? Factory price pre-labeling? The opportunities for Mass Customization are limitless – if we know who our customers are and break out of the mass-production mindset.

Consider the flavors: hours of blueberry flavor production runs, followed by the production runs of strawberry, peach, and all other flavors. Then follow the days of storing, refrigerating, promoting, and stretching the "shelf life." Why not introduce the flavoring at the point of purchase – letting the customer customize? This is called *point-of-delivery customization*.

Consider banking, insurance and similar service "commodities." Mass Customization means taking a "product" (product/service package) and molding it to *any* individual. Mortgage and bank loans present a good example: rather than prefixing a package and then spending all the time, money and effort for screening and sorting those who do or do not qualify, why not customize these loans to fit each individual's circumstances *precisely*? Like performing a financial "body scan." Then every loan would be different, everybody qualifies and – as Wells Fargo Bank is proving – the cost plummets and competitive performance soars at the same time.

2.1.3.5 Discarding the Old, Learning the New

Customers are no longer an anonymous mass of statistically measurable entities with homogeneous desires, but are uniquely distinguishable individuals, forming "markets of one," whose needs and desires must be satisfied. Markets do not buy anything, individuals do. There are no markets anymore, only individual customers. It is therefore imperative that companies embrace efficiency, effectiveness, low costs, and customization at the same time, with no tradeoffs forced.

Traditional concepts of *Continuous improvement* and *Total Quality Management* (TQM) also do not amount to Mass Customization, the Customer-specific value chain or the Global Management Paradigm. They do not explicitly recognize the need for high-technology enablers (like computers and telecommunications), a mandatory horizontal organization (and Intracompany Markets of autonomous agents), a shift from markets to individual customers (individuals rather than the statistical "mass"), individually customized products (treating products as the statistical "mass"), linking defect elimination with process reengineering and establishing permanent, cross-functional cooperation around markets rather than products.

Continuous improvement should organically include the concept of radical and discontinuous change. One cannot continually improve mass production, command hierarchy and statistical forecasting while hoping to stumble somehow into Mass Customization. One cannot continually improve an oxcart and expect to be ready and fit for the internal combustion engine. Some things and processes, at certain stages, should not be improved at all – least of all continually – rather they should be discarded, like horsewhips.

Mass-production techniques have pushed companies into standardized, one-size-fits-all design, long product cycles, automated but inflexible manufacturing, and the MRPII-style of planning. *Traditional forecasting* is also losing its role in MC. Producers do not have to forecast market demand if they produce only what has already been purchased. Forecasting (like inventory management and buffer hedging) is necessary only in mass production, i.e., when producing standard and other ill-fitting sizes or configurations for the warehouse or shelf, ahead of the purchase, in a "just in case" fashion. All mass producers remain obsessed with market forecasts.

2.1.3.6 Knowledge Beyond Information

It is therefore not the information (or access to it) that will differentiate individuals, nations and economies in their competitive strivings. It is the *knowledge as purposeful coordination of action,* the ability to translate information into action. Many display the best cookbooks on their shelves, but only a few can cook. Countless companies have all the information there is and possess all the books ever written on JIT, GMP and MC, but only a self-selected few know how to apply it in practice – only a few *know* "how to cook." Multitudes worldwide are soon going to have all the information at their fingertips – only a few will ever achieve the knowledge.

Some more progressive companies have already recognized the need for knowledge and its management. For example, CLO (*Chief Learning Officer*) is the new executive function and title overseeing the mechanisms of corporate knowledge production, acquisition, sharing and usage. This function has very little in common with the CIO (Chief Information Officer) or any other MIS or IT/S related functions. The CLO is in charge of action, not of a description of action; he is concerned about doing and coordination, not about symbolic records, encryption or alphanumerical entombment of corporate experience.

Mass Customization still represents mostly the producer's view, the production side and the supply-chain vantage point. However, the customer does not care about the "mass" at all: he simply wants what he wants. So, from the customer's viewpoint there is a desire to pull out or bring forth an entire *customer-specific value chain* (CSVC) out of the many demand chains constituting the fully reengineered network of production processes. Both sides are equally important and both have to be developed.

The Personal Profile Card will unlock and trigger the production process by bringing forth a customer-specific value chain in order to realize the product or service according to the customer's specifications. Only the knowledge-intensive companies will be able to customize – not just their products and services, but also the processes leading to them. The goal is not to customize goods and services, but to *customize the value* to specific individuals. Customer-specific value chains and customer-triggered production schemes are the right tools.

2.1.4 Elimination of Tradeoffs

Technological change essentially rewrites the notion and management of tradeoffs that underpin established business in all sectors. Global customers do not want tradeoffs between price, quality, speed, customization, reliability, etc. – they want it *all*. Global producers are thus forced to adjust and *eliminate the tradeoffs*. Not all customers want "the mix" but specific, item-by-item, individual customer-focused bundling. Another tradeoff: offering a wider range of products to the same customers, or exploiting the value-added reserves through seeking a larger share of each customer's purchases. Digital business changes it all: disintermediation, vertical disintegration, direct customizing – industry value chains have to be redefined.

A new, somewhat discomforting, possibly radical and certainly challenging idea has started making rounds in better business management literature: *"Are tradeoffs really necessary?"*

The answer is no: *tradeoffs are not necessary.* Pursuing and achieving lower cost, higher quality (and improved flexibility), all at the same time, is not only possible but clearly desirable and – within a New Economy – also necessary.

Tradeoffs can be postulated among different, conflicting objectives or criteria. Conventional wisdom recommends dealing with such conflicts via "tough choices" and a "careful analysis" of the tradeoffs. Yet, many Japanese factories have achieved lower cost, higher quality, faster product introductions, and greater flexibility, all at the same time: Lean manufacturing has apparently eliminated the tradeoffs among productivity, investment, and variety.

"Quality and low cost" and "customization and low cost" were long assumed to be tradeoffs, but companies are forced to overcome these traditional tradeoffs.

There is a *basic asymmetry* between the producer's and customer's view of tradeoffs. The producer wants to produce either low-cost *or* high-quality *or* high-speed delivery products. The customer wants to purchase both low-cost *and* high-quality *and* high-speed delivery products – all at the same time. These two traditionally opposing vantage points are being reconciled and matched with the help of IT/S.

Turning to more professional literature (Anderson et al., 1988), in "The Need to Make Tradeoffs," the authors concluded:

"Recently, tradeoffs have been called into question as operations are being designed which have better quality, lower cost and faster delivery than the competitors. These operations have moved to a new level of performance rather than making tradeoffs on an existing level. Because of these new insights, the exact nature of tradeoffs is no longer clearly understood."

How can traditional tradeoffs be "eliminated" or "overcome"? Are not tradeoffs generic to multiple-criteria conflicts? Can we have it both ways? Can one decrease cost and increase quality at the same time – and continue doing so? The answer is yes: tradeoffs are properties of badly designed systems and thus can be eliminated by designing better, preferably optimal, systems. Tradeoff-free (TOF) management and design of resources is the key. Enterprise Resource Planning (ERP) systems have to include the notion of the optimal *portfolio of corporate resources*.

2.1.4.1 Multiple Objectives and Tradeoffs

Consider the following quote (Zeleny, 1982):

"There are no conflicting objectives per se. No human objectives are in conflict by definition, that is, inherently conflicting. Everything depends on the given

situation, the historical state of affairs, the reigning paradigm, or the lack of imagination.

We often hear that one cannot minimize unemployment and inflation at the same time. We are used to the notion that maximizing quality precludes minimizing costs, that safety conflicts with profits, Arabs with Jews, and industry with the environment. Although these generalizations may be true, they are only conditionally true. Usually inadequate means or technology, insufficient exploration of new alternatives, or the lacks of innovation – not the objectives or criteria themselves – are the causes of apparent conflict."

Tradeoffs among multiple objectives (there can be no tradeoffs when only a single objective is considered) are *not* properties of the objectives themselves, but of the set of alternatives or options they are engaged to measure.

For example, tradeoffs between cost and quality have little if anything to do with the criteria of cost and quality themselves: rather, they are implied by the limits and constraints on the characteristics of available vehicles they measure. Measuring sticks are neutral and any apparent relations (like tradeoffs) are only induced by the objects measured.

2.1.4.2 Tradeoffs Graphics

Suppose that objectives f_1 = Profit and f_2 = Quality. Both of these objectives are to be maximized with respect to given resource constraints (feasible options).

In Figure 2.9, the polyhedron of system-feasible options is a well-defined System I. Maximizing functions f_1 and f_2 separately leads to two different optimal solutions and levels of criteria performance (designated as *max*). If System I remains fixed, observe that the maximal, separately attainable levels of both objectives lead to an *infeasible* "ideal" option. The tradeoffs between quality and profits are explicit and must be dealt with (selecting from the heavy boundary, i.e., non-dominated solutions, of System I).

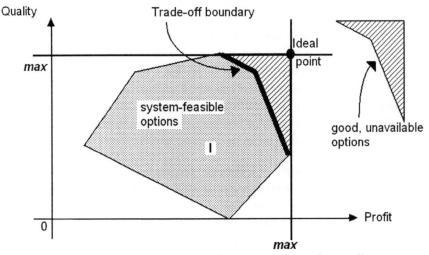

Figure 2.9 System I: given design with natural quality-profit tradeoffs.

In Figure 2.9, System I is poorly designed because there exists a set of good, currently unavailable options which would make the "ideal" point feasible and thus would allow the maxima of f_1 and f_2 (Profits and Quality) to be attained both at the same time.

Any manager's lifetime of work in System I shall unfailingly yield the following wisdom: There is always a trade-off between profits (or costs) and quality, one cannot have both ways – one has to pay for quality. As more and more managers derive (from their own experience) the same wisdom, textbook writers and instructors accept the wisdom as conventional, embed it in their own educational efforts and teach it to multitudes who had no such prior experience.

In other words, reshaping the feasible set (reconfiguring resource constraints), in order to include the "missing" alternatives, would lead to a superior system design with higher levels of criteria performance.

Such a desirable "reshaping" of the feasible set is represented in Figure 2.10, where System II of system-feasible options is sketched. Given System II, both objectives are maximized at the same point (or option): System II is superior in design to System I.

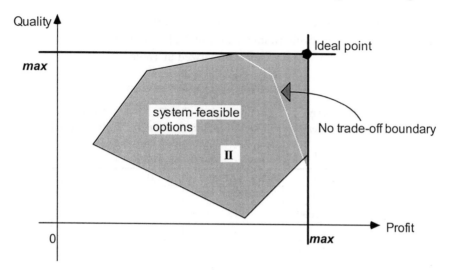

Figure 2.10 System II: optimal design with no apparent quality-profit tradeoffs.

There is one system configuration, given some cost or effort constraint, which yields the best possible performance. Such a system (like System II in Figure 2.10) will be superior with respect to both profit and quality and no tradeoffs between them are possible. Tradeoffs have been eliminated through optimal system design.

In Figure 2.10, a system with no quality-profit tradeoffs is presented. Observe that the maximal separately attainable levels of both criteria now form a feasible ideal option. Consequently, the tradeoffs between quality and profit cease to exist (the heavy trade-off boundary of System I has disappeared in System II).

Any manager's lifetime of work in System II shall unfailingly yield the following wisdom: There is no trade-off between profits (or costs) and quality, one cannot have one without the other, quality pays for itself. As more and more managers derive (from their own experience) the same wisdom, textbook writers and instructors accept the wisdom as conventional, embed it in their own educational efforts and teach it to multitudes who had no such prior experience.

2.1.4.3 Numerical Tradeoffs

Let us consider a simple production problem involving two different products, say suits and dresses, in quantities x and y, each of them consuming five different resources (nylon through golden thread), according to technologically determined requirements (technological coefficients). Unit market prices of resources are also given, as are the levels (number of units) of resources currently available (portfolio of resources). The data are summarized in Table 2.1.

Table 2.1 Original data for the production example.

Unit Price ($)	Resource (Raw Material)	Technological Coefficients (Resource Requirements)		Number of units (Resource Portfolio)
$x = 1$	$y = 1$			
30	Nylon	4	0	20
40	Velvet	2	6	24
9.5	Silver thread	12	4	60
20	Silk	0	3	10.5
10	Golden thread	4	4	26

In the above example, observe that producing one unit of each product x and y (x = 1 and y = 1) requires 4 units of nylon (4×1 + 0×1), 8 units of velvet (2×1 + 6×1), etc. The total number of available units of each material (given resource portfolio) is given in the last column of Table 2.1.

Current market prices of resources (first column) allow us to calculate the costs of the given resource portfolio:

$$(30×20) + (40×24) + (9.5×60) + (20×10.5) + (10×26) = \$2600$$

The same prices can be used to compute unit costs of producing one unit of each of the two products:

$$x = 1: (30×4) + (40×2) + (9.5×12) + (20×0) + (10×4) = \$354$$
$$y = 1: (30×0) + (40×6) + (9.5 × 4) + (20×3) + (10×4) = \$378$$

In other words, it costs $354 to produce one suit and $378 to produce one dress. Suppose that we can sell all we produce at the current market prices of $754/unit of x and $678/unit of y.

Expected profit margins (price-cost) are:

$$x: 754-354 = \$400/unit \qquad y: 678-378 = \$300/unit$$

As profit maximizers, we are interested in maximizing the total value of function $f_1 = 400x + 300y$.

As a second criterion let us consider some quality index: say 6 points per x and 8 points per y (scale from 0 to 10), so that we can maximize the total quality index or function $f_2 = 6x + 8y$.

We are now in a position to analyze the above outlined production system with respect to profits and quality. Maximizing levels of x and y (best product mix) can be easily calculated by techniques of mathematical programming (here we need only the results).

1) Function f_1 is maximized at x = 4.25 and y = 2.25, achieving a maximum of $(400 \times 4.25) + (300 \times 2.25) = \$2375$ in profits.
2) Function f_2 is maximized at x = 3.75 and y = 2.75, achieving a maximum of $(6 \times 3.75) + (8 \times 2.75) = 44.5$ in the total quality index.

This situation corresponds to the situation in Figure 2.9. The two maximizing points are the endpoints of the trade-off boundary. One can trade-off quality for profits by moving from (x = 3.75, y = 2.75) to (x = 4.25, y = 2.25) and back again, trading profits for quality. Because we can produce only one product mix at a time, we can choose to either maximize profits (x = 4.25, y = 2.25) or maximize quality (x = 3.75, y = 2.75), but *not both*. The choice is difficult because of the tradeoffs between profits and quality. Their importance is difficult to evaluate.

Let us heed the productivity consultant's advice and purchase a portfolio of resources different from that in Table 2.1, other things being equal.

We keep this new production system comparable and compatible in all respects, except the last column of Table 2.1. The new portfolio of resources in Table 2.2 has been proposed by the consultant.

We are now in a position to analyze the newly proposed production system under the same conditions.

Table 2.2 New data for production example.

Unit Price (\$)	Resource (Raw Material)	Technological Coefficients (Resource Requirements)		Number of units (Resource Portfolio)
$x = 1$	$y = 1$			
30	Nylon	4	0	16.12
40	Velvet	2	6	23.3
9.5	Silver thread	12	4	58.52
20	Silk	0	3	7.62
10	Golden thread	4	4	26.28

1) Function f_1 is now maximized at $x = 4.03$ and $y = 2.54$, achieving a maximum of $(400 \times 4.03) + (300 \times 2.54) = \$2375$ in profits.
2) Function f_2 is maximized at $x = 4.03$ and $y = 2.54$, achieving a maximum of $(6 \times 4.03) + (8 \times 2.54) = 44.5$ in the total quality index.

Both previously achieved maximum values of f_1 and f_2 have been matched. More importantly, *both* maximum profits (\$2375) and maximum quality index (44.5) are achieved through a single product mix: $x = 4.03$ and $y = 2.54$. This particular product mix, or ideal point in Figures 2.9 and 2.10, was infeasible in the previous system. By allowing its feasibility now, we have eliminated all and any tradeoffs between the criteria of profits and quality.

The previous tradeoffs-based system (Table 2.1) was operated at the cost of \$2600. The newly designed tradeoffs-free system (Table 2. 2) is realizable at the following cost:

$$(30 \times 16.12) + (40 \times 23.3) + (9.5 \times 58.52) + (20 \times 7.62) + (10 \times 26.28) = \$2386.74$$

The superior performance of the newly designed system comes at \$213.26 cheaper than the suboptimal performance of the original system.

2.1.4.4 Optimal Portfolio of Resources

The above example demonstrates that the chosen portfolio of resources is crucial for assessing maximum achievable levels of profits, costs, quality, flexibility, etc., at which the corresponding production system can be operated, other things being equal.

In our example, should any company choose to operate *any other* resource portfolio (at cost $\leq\$2600$) than that of Table 2.2, other things being equal, then its performance with respect to f_1 and f_2 would be necessarily inferior. A simple rearrangement of resource levels (Comparing Table 2.1 with Table 2.2) "reshapes" the management system (of feasible opportunities) From Figure 2.9 to Figure 2.10 and provides superior performance at the same or even lower costs.

The explanation is simple. Productive resources should not be engaged individually and separately because they do not contribute one by one according to their marginal productivities. Productive resources perform best as a whole system: they should be determined and engaged jointly as a portfolio and in an optimal fashion.

Consequently, any company running any other than the optimal portfolio of resources cannot outperform a company running the optimal portfolio, *ceteris paribus*. A company of Figure 2.9 has, under these conditions, no chance of successfully competing with the company of Figure 2.10. Regardless of its product-mix positioning along its trade-off boundary, the tradeoff-free company is bound to *always* do better.

We have identified the portfolio of resources to be the key to the system's potential performance and maximum productivity. The issues of technology, education, skills, work intensity, innovation, flexibility, quality, etc., are all very important in business, but they could only come to their full fruition if applied to an optimally designed, tradeoff-free system.

Profit Maximization. Free market systems are rooted in the assumption of profit maximization by individuals and their corporations.

This time-honored premise is usually not further specified or elaborated, as if there was only a single form of profit maximization.

Yet, rational economic agents can maximize profits in *at least two* fundamentally different – often mutually exclusive – ways:

1. Manage (operate) a *given* system so that a profit function is maximized.
2. *Design* a system so that its management (operation) would result in maximal profits.

These two forms of profit maximization are not the same.

In the first case, we are doing our best to squeeze maximum profits from a *given* system. This is known as profit maximization.

In the second case, we design (re-engineer) a profit-maximizing system: by doing our best we achieve maximum profits. This is, undoubtedly, also profit maximization.

The two modes are mutually exclusive because one cannot follow the second without first dismantling the first. It is not sufficient to (continually) improve the given system: because there is *only one* optimally designed system, all *other* systems must be suboptimal by definition.

One mode of profit maximization leads to consistently lower profits than the other, other things being equal. This could not have been intended by Adam Smith.

Because the second case is, *ceteris paribus*, always superior to the first case, we are facing two strategically different concepts of profit maximization. It *does* matter – in business, economics and management – which particular mode of profit maximization the individuals, corporations or cultures mostly adhere to: free markets are committed to reward those who consistently adhere to *the second* mode of operation.

The race is on towards transforming production and management systems from tradeoff-based to tradeoff-free. This race moves well beyond the assorted world-class, TQM, lean production or Mass Customization labels. Corporate portfolios of resources will have to be optimized before all other relevant efforts could become effective.

There are two fundamental dimensions to management: *what* is your system and *how* do you operate it. One can operate a bad system well or a good system quite badly. The main competitive challenge, yet to be recognized and achieved, is to *operate good systems very well*. Global managers may operate well, often performing virtual miracles with inadequate and outdated systems. But running optimally designed, high-performance tradeoff-free systems would return the joy, pride and self-confidence into business and management endeavors of the IT/S era.

2.1.5 Intracompany Markets and Amoeba Systems

The self-sustaining organization has found its corporate embodiment in the "amoeba system" of Kyocera Corporation. The "amoebas" are independent, profit sharing and semi-autonomous teams or departments of three to fifty employees. Each amoeba performs its own statistical control, profit system, cost accounting and personnel management. Amoebas compete, subcontract, and cooperate among themselves on the basis of the intracompany market, characterized by real market-derived transfer prices.

Depending on the demand and amount of work, amoebas can divide into smaller units or integrate with other amoebas into larger wholes. All amoebas are continually on the lookout for a better buyer for their intermediate products. Some amoebas can even produce the same or similar products or services. They are authorized, as in the famous Bata-system, to trade intermediate products with outside companies. If the internal supplier is unreasonable, the buying amoeba will search for a satisfactory supplier outside the company.

The most remarkable feature in the amoeba autonomy is personnel trading. Heads of amoebas form alliances, lend and borrow team members, compete for experts and human resources, and so eliminate the losses caused by surplus labor. Kyocera's amoebas multiply, disband, and form new units according to the autopoiesis (self-production) of the enterprise. Amoeba division and breakup are frequent occurrences and are guided by the criteria of output and added value per hour and worker.

This concept of ultimate flexibility is best summed up by Kyocera's founding President Inamori: "Development is the continued repetition of construction and destruction," an insight extracted directly from the systems theories of autopoietic self-organization. Neither age nor training is essential for becoming the head of an amoeba – only the competence to do the job within current context. If unsuitable, amoeba heads are replaced immediately.

The amoeba system represents quite a revolutionary step beyond the traditional Toyota "just-in-time" philosophy. At Kyocera, orders received by the sales department are passed directly to the amoeba of the final process. The rest of the amoebas in the preceding processes are then given a free rein in working out mutual contracts: the intracompany market takes over. Kyocera Corporation remains one of the most profitable companies in Japan.

2.1.5.1 Biotic Amoeba Analogy

It is instructive to invoke biotic amoebae as a useful analogy to the corporate amoebas described above. Amoebae or Cellular Slime Mold is a good example of autopoietic social system. The slime molds (Gymnomycota) are an example of a fungus-like protist. They are decidedly fungus-like at some stages and animal-like at others. Their life cycle includes an amoeboid stage and a sedentary stage in which a fruiting body develops and produces spores.

In *Dictyostelium discoideum*, the vegetative cell is amoeboid. Amoebas are individual cells moving around in search for bacteria to feed on. They will grow and divide indefinitely. Often they digest so much and produce new amoebas so rapidly that their food supply has no chance to replenish itself. When the food supply has been exhausted, they move rapidly to a central point, collecting themselves into a well-differentiated spontaneous aggregation (center cells, boundary cells, etc.) – a pseudoplasmodium. The aggregation is triggered by the production of cyclic adenosine monophosphate (AMP) which attracts other amoebas in a chemotactic fashion.

The group then assumes the shape of a "slug" with a head, tail, and an apparent "purpose": searching collectively for a new, potential source of food. Around the outside is secreted a mucoid sheath (aggregate boundary). It migrates as a unit across the substratum as a result of the collective action of the amoebas. The changing of the roles of individual amoebas is prevalent; the original leaders who formed the center of attraction are dispersed throughout the "slug," and new leaders emerge, forming the "goal-seeking" head.

The head of the target-homing "slug" is formed from the fastest-moving amoebas. The "slug" is just a spontaneous temporary metaorganism, preserving each amoeba as a separate individual. The slug is positively phototactic (migrating toward light), and it usually migrates for a period of hours. Its behavioral responses are essential "to ensure" that the spores will be borne in the air and so can be effectively dispersed.

Fruiting body formation begins when the slug ceases to migrate and becomes vertically oriented. The amoebas change quickly from the first to the last. The head of the slug forms the base of a stalk which follower-amoebas continue to build (they secrete cellulose to provide rigidity) up into a mushroom-like metaorganism. At its top, hundreds of thousands of amoebas transform into spores that are embedded in slime and, after the mushroom "head" matures, burst. It disperses the spores to new and potentially nourishing environments. When they fall to earth, they change once again into individual amoebas, which reproduce by cell division. This ecological cycle is then repeated.

2.1.6 Business Kinetics

The Kinetic Enterprise (also Business or Corporate Kinetics) is a set of practices that are part of the Global Management Paradigm (GMP).

Small-sized, non-statistical markets require the handling of each business, market or customer event on its own, as a unique business opportunity. Events are unpredictable, but each can be converted into myriads of business opportunities by sufficiently motivated and properly organized kinetic workers and employees.

In Figure 2.11 we compare the traditional statistical-market approach with the new Business Kinetics.

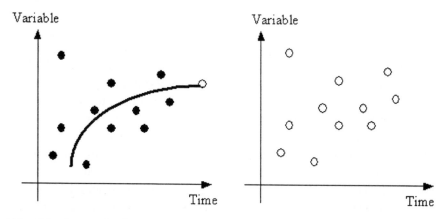

(a) Traditional approach: all events (observations) are inputs into creating business opportunities.

(b) Kinetic approach: all events (observations) are business opportunities of their own.

Figure 2.11 Comparing traditional regression with kinetics.

Observe that in the old paradigm not all events were exploited but served as mere observations or inputs into the regression-based establishment of trends, predictions, aggregates, averages and best-fit curves. New opportunities were created rarely and sparsely, most promising opportunities were often excluded as "outliers," everything was pulled down to the safest medium (often mediocre) level. This approach is represented in Figure 2.11 (a).

In Figure 2.11 (b) we can see that no averaging or "fitting" is used to reduce the number of opportunities, no "outliers" are excluded. Each and every event is a singular trigger and is considered for conversion into an opportunity. There are no unimportant, too small, too risky or "untypical" events: all events constitute the opportunity space of business, not just their aggregate or average.

Forecasting usually means extrapolating past trends and thus cannot predict *critical discontinuities* – that is precisely what needs forecasting and where the real money can be made or lost. Forecasting "things as usual," trends, averages, most probable expectations, etc., is the least needed exercise – businesses do not have to forecast that. So, the only way to move from continuities to discontinuities is through exploring all business events kinetically.

Just imagine Seiko, producing 5,000 separate and distinct watch models, relying on executives predicting customer demand, scale manufacturing facilities to accommodate those unsure and imprecise forecasts, and meeting revenue and cost estimates for all 5,000 models – they would not get too far with such a monumental task without kinetics.

Responding to a customer event means engaging all the necessary processes of the entire enterprise – selling, marketing, new product development, billing and knowledge management – all carried out for a single customer. Business Kinetics is a natural outgrowth of system-wide successful Mass Customization.

IC3D Jeans is already beating mass-customizing Levi Strauss by offering online ordering for do-it-yourself designers. Also Sui Generis Co. is ready to produce a unique jacket, shirt, suit, or slacks to online customers.

Business Kinetics grows out of biology, not from physics. Informal knowledge-networks are continually reshaped and realigned to maintain innovative ferment, to keep a company alive, to keep it "disorganized." The point is not to empower workers, but to make them kinetic: take charge in exploiting business events and pulling everybody, including the bosses, along with them into satisfying individual customers.

Business Kinetics means that one cannot hire purely on the basis of skills and expertise – they will be obsolete within 5 years. Are the kinetic prospects capable of interdisciplinarity, connecting seemingly disparate domains of knowledge? Can they ask the right questions? Can they collaborate effectively? Are they capable of learning to learn? Are they risk takers, willing to bet on the company's future through stock options? So, one searches for innate talent, attitude and abilities, systems thinking, resilience, transdisciplinary consilience and plain brain power – all the rest can and will be learned.

Business Kinetics has no use for people who have no opinion, "do not know," have to "think about it," do not listen to others or "have to read more on it" – such people are far better suited for the traditional, non-kinetic enterprise.

With the right people, the Kinetic Enterprise is on its way: embed strategic purpose in all employees; let the customer drive the enterprise; train workers to play any role, any time; manage the transfer of control; build vehicles for knowledge transfer; allow workers to chart their own course and use projects to train for spotting and exploiting business events.

In terms of rewards, forget climbing the ladder to get pay raises. Instead, reward enterprise-wide performance (profit sharing, stock options); reward behavior, not just results (the means are more important than the ends); and reward with more than money (grants, study time, peer recognition).

The Kinetic Enterprise is based on the following *kinetic infrastructure* elements:

1. *Design protocols for simultaneous work.* Instead of step-by-step rules, shared protocols allow workers to address a challenge simultaneously, shifting roles, changing sequences, reassigning tasks. All the parts have to fit each other, seamlessly. Linear sequences of processing tasks are ineffective. IT/S support is crucial for creating a virtual workspace across time and distance.
2. *Networks for spontaneous collaboration and learning.* Spontaneous arrangements and communication are enabled through networks. Old LANs are replaced by a single enterprise-wide network accessible by all employees, allowing them to communicate with "anyone, anytime, anywhere."
3. *Information technology for zero-time transactions.* All employees must be able to access accurate, up-to-the-second information when, where and how they want it. Customer transactions are continually and instantly handled one at a time, not in "batches," not once a week. No central MIS department is needed.
4. *Process technology to serve single customers.* Respond to individual customer demand: master Mass Customization. This includes installing sophisticated IT/S technology, but it pays off.
5. *Facilities for adaptability.* Facilities of the Kinetic Enterprise cannot be "built to last." In order to respond to the infinity of events, they must be infinitely flexible, stretchable and reshapable. Adaptability, not just flexibility, is the key.

Examples of Andersen Windows (virtual-design software, automated order entry), Haworth, Inc. (just-in-time system for customized office furniture), Volkswagen-Resende (supplier Co-location from start to finish) and Solutia (customer driven production of nylon fibers) are among the best Kinetic Enterprise infrastructures to follow.

A different but very good example of kinetics is the Open-source software development project (called Darwin) by Apple, inspired by the experience of

Linux. The source code is placed on Apple's Website for free downloading in order to create a network community of developers, users and customers – generating a virtually boundless space of customer events.

Like in IPM (Integrated Process Management), customers (more precisely, customer events) drive the kinetic enterprise. Customers design their own sales relationships, products, and services. Financial advisers, insurance agents, real-estate agents, and other intermediaries cease to be the only source of information. Now only customer advocates are needed. In a kinetic enterprise, all access channels are open to all customers and all resources of the enterprise are accessible to a single customer. *Corporate memory* has to be created and maintained. Every employee is a customer advocate and customer advocates control all necessary resources.

2.2 Forecasting and Foresight

Modern corporations are facing unprecedented challenges in the New Economy: predictability is dead, flexibility provides strategic advantage, markets are shrinking to the size of 1, yet there are myriads of them, each one different; Mass Customization is *de rigueur*, from designing your own jeans and pop CDs, to custom made drugs, investment portfolios and computers. There are fundamental discontinuities in modern business and management, the very notion of continuous improvement is an oxymoron in the age of discontinuous innovation. How can businesses cope – and on a global scale at that? The answer is: forget long-range planning, strategy and prediction, create a *kinetic enterprise*, a self-adapting, self-renewing, and instant-acting network enterprise.

We cannot predict the future, but we can be ready for whatever the future brings. Predictability is out and flexibility is in – at least in business. All business is necessarily global: as soon as we use the Internet, for whatever purpose, we go global. Global business is unpredictable: it mandates speed, flexibility and innovation.

Markets do not buy anything, individuals do. Each individual customer is a market. Every consumer is a single customer. Every employee or department is a customer of another employee or department. They all have to be engaged and satisfied fast, online and preferably at "zero-time." The customers' time is of the essence in the New Economy.

Customer sovereignty and customer-generated events are becoming the driving force of the global economy. This is not meant to be some recent cliché about "responding to the customer," "customer intimacy" or the "customer service department." What is emerging is a customer strategic focus *as an organizational principle.* Instead of organizing corporations by functional departments, by products or by production processes, we have to *organize by customers.*

For example, Microsoft Corp. has reorganized itself according to four groups of customers rather than the previous three groups based on technology. The four customer groups are 1. Consumers; 2. Enterprises or corporate customers; 3. Software developers; and 4. Knowledge workers. The last group includes telecommuters and work-at-home or self-service customers. The old-fashioned product-based organization at Microsoft was: 1. Computer operating systems; 2. Applications; and 3. On-line business.

IT/S therefore does not enable only the customers and networks-markets: it changes fundamentally the way companies operate internally. Companies are forced to put all of their processes on a common footing, with the help of ERP systems, and bring the external networks and markets inside.

Companies must think of their internal processes and their reengineering *first* and specify the computer system only *afterwards.* Blindly applying IT/S habitually misfires when purchased *per se*, without deeper restructuring and reengineering of the company and its processes. In such cases, only the software providers benefit.

2.2.1 Decline of Forecasting

Forecasting of the future has become less reliable in both business and political environments. A number of major corporations have recently dissolved their traditional economic and econometric departments and professionals. The cost of forecasting has skyrocketed while its precision and reliability has either stagnated or declined.

The cause is quite obvious and mostly irreversible: the ever decreasing sample size of the corporate "market." While it is fairly easy to predict behavior of statistically large mass markets, with rapidly narrowing market niches, small groups and individual customers and consumers, predicting has become virtually impossible.

Tom Peters's famous "Markets don't buy anything, individuals do" refers to the same trend that has become a curse of forecasters: they can predict what ten thousand people will do, but not what one person might. From a corporate viewpoint, markets will never become mass markets again and the days of statistical forecasting are inevitably numbered. Familiar chapters on statistical forecasting, econometrics, "exponential smoothing" and economic forecasting are rapidly disappearing from the more up-to-date MBA textbooks.

Instead of forecasting the future states of nature (and their probabilities of occurrence), companies are opting towards increasing their flexibility and responsiveness in order to cover *all possible* states of nature, regardless their probabilities. Planning is finally becoming the *true planning*, based not on forecasts and predictions but on building up an ever-widening portfolio of response capabilities. Planning for the future is no longer based on educated guesses – which can obviously fail – but on being prepared for all and any circumstances.

Even if the state of "total preparedness" is still an ideal state for most companies, far from being reliably and timely achieved, the direction of improvement has been set and the competitive race has begun.

This powerful shift also implies, at least in business and management, that the era of symbolic information is virtually over. For companies, in dealing with their customers, increasingly it matters less "what they say they'll do" and more "what they actually do."

There are two significant forms of information and communication: *information* as a symbolic description of action, and *in-formation* as the action itself. Both forms "inform" and communicate important messages – the latter form is now increasing in importance, fitting into the era of knowledge as action and its coordination.

There is a significant and irreducible difference between saying "I'll knock your teeth out" and actually knocking somebody's teeth out. Action itself cannot be approximated or replaced by its symbolic description.

What matters most is what consumers do, not what they say they will or would do on assorted polls or questionnaires. Consumers have a complete freedom to say as they please and to do as they please; they do not have to do what they say or say what they do; they can change their minds, preferences and reasoning as many times as they want and they do not have to explain it; they do not have to be transitive or consistent in their preferences.

The reason for the growing discrepancy between saying and doing or description and action is quite simple and fundamental: while all and any decision making has to take place in a given context and under specific circumstances, any symbolic inquiry or description of intent has to be – by definition – context free. It is a miracle that the two modes sometimes match, especially when the mass, statistically behaving markets are shrinking so rapidly and their forecasting becoming an astute guesswork or educated guess.

Economic Forecasting. The worst "hit" area of forecasting is not only consumer forecasting but so called *economic forecasting*, a part of econometrics.

In 1999, economic forecasters and analysts were setting historic benchmarks for inaccuracy. In the U.S., for the fourth consecutive year, economic analysts have underestimated economic growth so markedly that the rush to revise predictions started in parallel with the forecasts being released.

Forecasters did not predict the Network Economy and its reversals of economic "laws." Instead, they remained trapped in the model that their education and training drilled into them. One of their major errors was underestimating the impact of technology, especially high technology and IT/S. They are also baffled by consumer behavior, never grasping its fundamental and irreversible changes. They still have not grasped deflationary pressures of the New Economy.

Early in 1996, *The New York Times* ran a story "Economic Forecasting Is Just a Sideshow Now," documenting the virtually free fall of forecasting and (economic) forecasters. Most corporations cannot afford forecasting services that damage their global competitiveness. They are focusing on reducing their exposure to risk via strategic flexibility, IT/S technology, kinetics, responsiveness and Mass Customization.

For example, IBM – which counted more than two dozen in-house economists in the early 1970s – no longer employs a single professional to estimate key numbers like interest rates, capital spending and inflation. Similarly GE has no in-house economist.

IBM used to employ twenty six PhDs and near PhDs to run their own macro model. Big forecasting firms like Wharton Econometrics (long ago renamed WEFA) and Data Resources (renamed DRI/McGraw-Hill) provided expensive retail services to companies that could not afford IBM's wholesale route. IBM could not either and in the 1980s it retired its entire forecasting staff.

The inexorable decline started when The President's Council of Economic Advisers' forecast for 1974 overestimated economic growth by a whopping three percentage points and underestimated inflation by the same figure. Nobody explained, nobody apologized – and so the forecasting era has ended.

Even Citibank has virtually abandoned in-house forecasting in favor of risk management. Citibank, after McGraw-Hill the very "hotbed" of forecasting, now matches liabilities against assets in ways intended to protect the bottom line *no matter what* happens to interest rates.

Corporate America's faith in computer-model economic forecasting, already eroded by its failure to signal the stagflation of the late 1970s or the economic turnaround of the early 1980s, has been further shaken by recent research on the complexities of the buying habits of households and businesses. Rather than pouring numbers into computers, companies are using financial derivatives to hedge against price and interest rate fluctuations, minimizing inventories via just-in-time systems, employing temporary workers and expanding to offer Mass Customization of their products and services.

The so called "models" of the economy – series of statistically estimated equations that describe the determinants of consumption and investment – were first brought forth in the 1930s. Their failure is not so much a failure of mathematics or statistics, but a result of a rather rapid change in market behavior and the rise of global economy.

Of course, forecasting would be helpful in principle if it could predict big turnarounds and shocks, unexpected changes and out-of-the ordinary ups and downs. If it would not treat significant changes as "aberrations" and "outliers" and keep predicting averages, normal situations and "things as usual" – SNAFU might work in the military, but not in econometrics and economic forecasting. DRI/McGraw-Hill can forecast "virtually unchanged revenue – right on the nose," provided there is no change. Nobody is interested in that.

When companies stop relying on forecasting, they are forced to redesign their processes and activities in order to reduce time and increase flexibility. Companies that increase their dependency on forecasting – through investing in it and improving it – become even more strongly bonded to their traditional, inflexible and costly ways and means. Global competition and its customers favor the former and make things so much more difficult for the latter.

After experiencing the general doldrums and declining sales in the personal computer business, some companies have chucked forecasting and market directly to customers and most importantly deliver their products built to order, i.e., mass customized. If you produce for the shelves, you must forecast; if you produce for the customer, you do not have to.

In the personal computer business, shifting to a build-to-order system reduces how much companies have to depend on market forecasts. Errant market forecasts have been the bugbear of the PC industry. In a business with six-month product cycles, market forecasting amounts to trying to hit a fast-moving target of customer demand twice a year for desktops, notebooks and servers. Compaq, Dell and even IBM do not want to be enslaved to astute guesswork. Compaq stopped relying on forecasts, switched mainly to three-person assembly cells that produce *only* what customers order, and introduced direct links with the customer.

The need for forecasting is undoubtedly a function of the time difference between an event and our ability to respond to it. As this "lead time to satisfaction" is reduced to a blur, corporate reliance on forecasting grows weaker. Competing for the compression of the "lead time to satisfaction" is intensifying and the achievements are often starting to border on "instantaneous" or "zero time."

If I can instantaneously satisfy my need for food every time I feel hungry, then my need to predict the periods and occurrences of hunger is very small. If it takes me two hours to prepare or get food every time I feel hungry, my need for planning, predicting and forecasting such events becomes crucial. If your lead time to react, to produce or to deliver is substantial, you have only two options: forecast or compress the time. It is the second strategy that modern businesses are increasingly pursuing.

2.2.2 Reframing Strategy and Knowledge

It has become clear that the very concept of strategy is about to change.

Strategy is increasingly about what a company is *doing*, much less so about what a company is *saying. Strategy is action, not a description of action.*

This is fairly self-evident and few would choose to argue for words rather than acts. Strategy is not information to be trickled down from the top to the bottom, below the "cloud line" of the *mission-vision-goals* statements and restatements of corporate wordsmiths. Strategy is the knowledge embodied in the actions, decisions and behaviors of corporate employees at the operational level. The network and coordination of corporate activities – what the company actually does – *is* its strategy.

Traditionally, "strategy" is a concept derived from military context. The thinking and ideas about the goals and plans of the higher echelons of the army are instructing and commanding the troops in order to win a war. "Strategy" is also used to denote thought processes about long-term aims and plans meant to be carried out by the people at the top of public and business institutions.

The "forecasting assumption" is justified only if there is a steady, identifiable and predictable tendency or trend, i.e., as long as no fundamental or unexpected changes occur in the business environment.

Similarly, the "control assumption," according to which there is a direct and predictable relation between strategic planning and the organization's activities, similar to the engineer's planning and design of a production process and the activity on the production floor, was relevant to the industrial age, but is irrelevant, if not harmful, for the knowledge age. During the industrial age, it was believed that the top management could achieve full knowledge of occurrences on all levels of the organization, and thus could control it fully "from the top." Today, it is understood that organizations are complex *human systems* in which self-evolving and self-organizing processes occur in the middle and operational echelons, connected with a knowledge-producing environment.

In view of the rapid changes in the global environment and the need for greater flexibility and foresight of thought and action, strategy itself has to be reframed.

New conceptions and conceptualizations, in order to increase organizational differentiation, must be evolved. A new organizational mindset is needed. It must be infused with knowledge.

Broader scope of vision and analysis requires extending corporate cognitive "systemic boundaries," becoming more systems oriented. A system view, rather than a *per partes* functional view of a corporation is necessary.

Strategy is not a product, but a continuous *process* of systemic reframing. Strategy must be an ongoing process because it is all about action, not about statements and descriptions. It is never finalized and it cannot be carried out intermittently.

Strategy is not about formulating a document of recommendations for others to implement and carry out. The organization itself (all levels of its management) must engage in strategic "doing" as an integral part of the ongoing organizational process. They have to produce and live in a *strategic environment*.

Organizational theory can no longer ignore the fact that every process of strategic decision making requires a much deeper process of thinking, conceptualizing and doing. One can not rely on the widely shared, fixed templates for the analysis of aspects and dimensions of the activities of the organization, and simply classifying them into future "opportunities" and "threats" (like the SWOT model of Strengths, Weaknesses, Opportunities and

Threats). Such things look good only on paper (and make great bullets in power-point presentations) but rarely lead to action.

In my view, the product of the strategic process should not be a thick document presented to the board of directors for a decision. The goal is to produce a strategic environment within which each individual can effectively *do* the strategy, not just read about it.

Modern strategic thinking views the reality as a series of rapidly evolving, interrelated contexts for action. There is no time to formulate a new strategy for each emerging context, especially not through the clumsy and long-winded *mission-vision-goals* template. Strategic environment allows the organization to recognize, interpret and adapt to emerging contexts in a spontaneous, self-organizing fashion.

Strategy cannot respond to each context separately, by formulating its requisite "vision," but must encompass responding to the entire string of contexts. Modern strategy is a *strategy of response.*

The question is how do we *respond* to whatever comes our way, not how do we *forecast* what may come our way? That is the difference between strategic environment and strategy, as well as between foresight and forecasting. The concern is therefore more about *how* rather than *what*; more about knowledge, less about information.

Rather than periodically responding to perceived revolutionary shifts, a modern strategic environment enables continuous evolutionary transformation and adaptation, so it is not too early or too late, but always there, just in time, because it lets the external environment influence its internal strategic environment.

2.3 Self-Service and Do-It-Yourself

Self-service and do-it-yourself modes are asserting themselves all around us. They have become part of our everyday experience. Producers and providers are outsourcing their production and service processes to customers.

Outsourcing to customers is a natural and necessary accompanying process to disintermediation, customer integration and Mass Customization, all driven the by global productivity growth race, competing for a global customer. In order to get what he wants, the global customer must learn and accept doing many things for himself, engaging in self-service. Service jobs are not being outsourced just to India; they are being outsourced to customers worldwide.

Instead of the information society, we have a knowledge society. Instead of the service society, we have a self-service society.

This shift towards self-service is a part of the natural, spontaneous evolution of human and economic systems. It is as necessary and inevitable as the agricultural, industrial and services eras before. Its "seeds" have been visible for more than a century. But the self-service mode cannot fully assert itself until the service mode has run its course. No economy can "freeze" at the services stage, with some 80 percent of the workforce employed in services. No "new jobs" can be generated in the service sector, as they cannot be generated in the agriculture or manufacturing sectors any more.

Service work first got outsourced, then it got offshored, and now it is getting passed on for the last time – to the customer. New jobs in the knowledge era will be self-service jobs.

Human work and leisure are being radically redefined. The key words are empowerment, self-reliance, autonomy and self-service, replacing the more traditional notions of division of labor, specialization, manual work and the physically remote workplace of the mass production, mass assembly and mass consumption era. Most human activities – work, labor, jobs, leisure, recreation and the overall ways and quality of life – have changed and are going to change further before the first decade of this millennium is over.

2.3.1 Key Concepts

Human action can be loosely differentiated into work (creation) and leisure (recreation) activities. This is not an exhaustive distinction – there could also be non-voluntary human activities that are neither work nor leisure (like breathing, eating, sleeping), or either work or leisure depending on the person (sex, escort or companionship for money), or even mixtures of work and leisure (hobbies such as gardening and do-it-yourself).

The key to any useful differentiation of this kind must be the *purpose*, the why, the motivation of the activities being carried out. If the purpose is a direct or indirect economic exchange – for money, goods, time or any other reciprocity of economic value – then humans engage in work. If the purpose of such activities is not directly economic or exchange motivated, then we can speak of leisure. That is why somebody doing 'absolutely nothing' in exchange for money would be working, while somebody sweating in the garden for their own pleasure and satisfaction would be at leisure – and, if sufficiently "deranged," having a "good time" at it. Professional sports are work, amateur sports could be a mixture of leisure and work, and recreational sports activities are leisure.

Also, domestic, household and at-home work or chores, as well as all forms of do-it-yourself and self-service, represent *bona fide* work because their purpose is substituting for an exchange or economic alternative, like having such in-house work performed by paid (external, for exchange) help or professionals. The purpose of a given activity provides the key. Yet, some governments still consider taking care of one's own children as leisure and taking care of someone else's children as highly taxable work – with the obvious societal impacts. The sheer exertion of neuro-muscular energy does not necessarily amount to work if it is not economically motivated and cannot or would not be exchanged. An individual going out to plant some tulips, for relaxation and enjoyment, is at leisure. An individual going out to plant the same tulips in order to avoid the high costs of landscaping services, is working.

Leisure activities must be chosen, voluntary, non-contractual and unforced, seeking recreation rather than economic gain or exchange of value. Forced unemployment or serving a jail term are not leisure as there is no immediate alternative to them. Forced labor is work only if remunerated, at least partially. Work and leisure are not mutually exclusive or exhaustive categories.

"Work" can be defined as an economically purposeful activity requiring requisite human coordination of task and action. "Job" designates the kind of work that is performed contractually, that is, explicitly for remuneration and in the employ by others.

"Labor" (often used as a synonym for hard work or toil) can more properly be related to performing simplified work-components or tasks without engaging in their substantial coordination towards given purposes. Work often involves labor but not vice versa. Work involves coordination of tasks while labor relates only to their performance. Building a fish pond is work, digging a hole is labor.

"Leisure" and activities of leisure are motivated by non-economic and non-exchange purposes, like relaxation, pleasure, joy, recreation, satisfaction and so forth.

Through the reintegration of task, labor and knowledge, labor is again becoming work, meaning is replacing alienation, professionalism and skill are replacing narrow specialization. Basic coordinative mechanisms of the traditional administrative management of labor-performing operators are being replaced by the self-coordinative systems of mutual adjustment and consensual reciprocity of teams of empowered skilled workers.

2.3.2 Evolution of Sectors of Employment

Reintegration of work is accompanied by very strong co-trends towards self-service and do-it-yourself modes of work activities. Mature economies, especially in the U.S.A., are characterized by a large percentage of people working in the service sector. Some 80 percent of the total U.S. workforce is in the services. However, the service sector is no different from any other economic sector, for example agriculture or manufacturing, that all went through irreversible loss of employment decades ago. The accelerating productivity growth rates in those sectors have caused a steady decline in their job-generating capacity. The service sector is simply following the same pattern: increasing automation, increasing productivity, global competitive pressures, high relative costs and overgrown hierarchies are annihilating its own employment opportunities.

In Figure 2.12 we display the general sectoral dynamics that all economies, slowly or rapidly, sooner or later, are bound to follow.

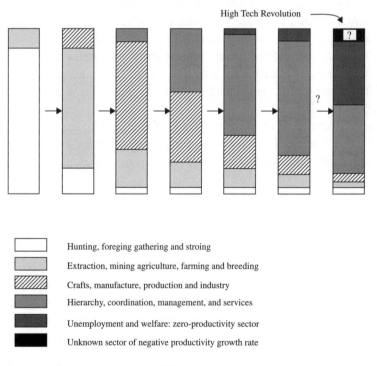

Hunting, foreging gathering and stroing

Extraction, mining agriculture, farming and breeding

Crafts, manufacture, production and industry

Hierarchy, coordination, management, and services

Unemployment and welfare: zero-productivity sector

Unknown sector of negative productivity growth rate

Figure 2.12 Sectoral evolution and differentiation (in a rapidly maturing economy).

Due to its productivity growth rates, each sector has to emerge, grow, persist, stagnate, decline and dissipate in terms of its employment-generating capacity.

The high-productivity growth sectors are emerging and dissipating first, the low-productivity growth sectors (like services) are completing their cycle only now. Different productivity growth rates in different sectors are accompanied by virtually *uniform* growth rates in wages and salaries across all sectors (Figure 2.13).

In third world nations this may still be the other way around: food and manufactured goods are most expensive, while services remain relatively cheap. That is, in developed countries, chicken, bread, computers and cars are getting cheaper, while insurance, healthcare and education costs are skyrocketing without adequate quality, productivity or availability improvements. In Figure 2.13 we represent this phenomenon.

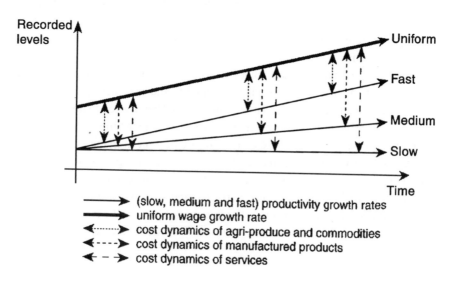

Figure 2.13 Price gap: differential productivity and uniform wage growth rates cause price to grow faster in low-productivity sectors.

2.3.3 Towards Self-Service

The fundamental systemic disharmony of Figure 2.13, that is, between differential productivity growth rates and the uniform wage/salary growth rates across sectors, points to a self-organizing, spontaneous mode of resolving the tension.

Rational economic agents will exhibit and support the tendency towards substituting relatively cheap capital-intensive manufactured goods for relatively dear labor-intensive services. Consumers will tend to use goods instead of services wherever economical and possible, while the producers will tend to respond by supplying them with goods instead of services wherever economical and possible. As a collective result of this individually rational decision making, one shall observe the emergence of automated teller machines instead of bank tellers, self-service gas stations instead of full-serve stations (except where prohibited by law), self-driving instead of chauffeurs, do-it-yourself pregnancy kits rather than hospital test services, self-handled optical scanners rather than cashier-handled services, and personal computers instead of centralized mainframes. In other words, self-service and do-it-yourself activities are replacing the traditional, other-person-delivered services at an increasingly accelerating rate. Mature economies are entering the era of self-service and do-it-yourself societies.

Self-service activities are characterized by high efficiency: they can be delivered when, where and at whatever quality the user desires, at lower costs and in a shorter time periods. They require user-friendly requisite products with easy-to-use, reliable instructions and support, sufficient time and the high costs of alternative services. All these conditions are present in mature economies. The self-service society is characterized here by an increasing autonomy of workers and consumers, growth of work-at-home, telecommuting, self-employment, community self-help, home office, part-time and seasonal work, early retirement, barter and exchanges, networking, flexible work hours, self-management, decline in supervisory and administrative "services," decentralized self-reliance and so on.

2.3.4 Work and Leisure

There is no conspicuous increase in leisure and leisure-related activities perceived in the modern economy: the traditional leisure activities are themselves becoming overpriced services and thus being substituted by self-service. There is a tendency for job-holders to work even longer hours, although the overall amount of time worked per person is declining. The time spent for self-service and do-it-yourself activity is one of the few expanding categories of economic activities, as sketched in Figure 2.14.

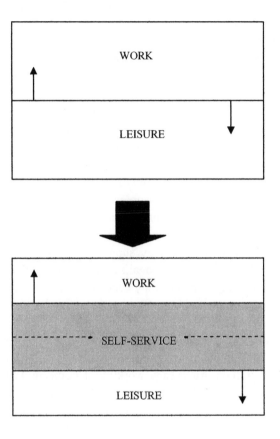

Figure 2.14. Work and leisure.

Households are again becoming primary investment/production units, producers and consumers are merging into "prosumers." One of the fastest-growing sectors in developed industrial economies, especially in the U.S.A., is "work at home." Work at home relates to self-employment, part-time self-employment, work after regular office hours, work instead of regular office hours, self-service and do-it-yourself, typically relying on a home office, telecommuting, neighborhood networks, virtual office, personal computers, modem, fax, multiple and cellular telephone lines and similar technologies. Work at home is the most potent job-generating sector, moving the self-reliant population towards more productive and efficient self-service activities, reducing the pressures on energy, ecology, human stress, traffic congestion and the cost-intensive physical commuting inherited from factories from the turn of the century. Clearly, individual or corporate telecommuting presents a powerful alternative to the traditional emphasis on "railroads, highways and bridges."

Modern production is primarily based on the processing of information, not on the hauling of goods, humans and machinery over large distances. One can more effectively "haul the information," to produce goods and provide services locally. Information and knowledge travel effortlessly through electronic superhighways, through telecommunications networks and the World Wide Web. Citizens and employees working at home are now in control of their time, can take care of their own children, can invest in home technologies; they do not have to pay excessively for petrol, insurance, childcare and waste most of their precious off-work hours on commuting to work. Temporary, freelance, contingent and interim workers are increasingly forced into or voluntarily choose new modes of economic action. They support and accompany empowerment, autonomy, self-reliance and professionalization – main attributes of the future work and jobs. Knowledge, enhanced by education and training, is taking over as the main form of capital. Self-employed people (in the U.S.) earn about 40 percent more hourly than those employed by others. Hired operators, laborers and farmhands are rapidly declining in their importance as well as pay.

In spite of the continued governmental obstacles and barriers, there were already about 40 million Americans working at home in 1992. This is to be compared with only some 25 million in 1988. From these 40 million home workers, there are 12.1 million self-employed, 11.7 million part-time self-employed, 8.6 million working at home after regular office hours, and 6.6 million working at home instead of regular office hours. High technologies – e-mail, computer teleconferencing, real-time teleconferencing, and video teleconferencing – are all helping to create the electronic networks necessary for self-help and work-at-home business styles. The U.S. economy appears to serve as an experimental laboratory for many new forms of work and leisure, from work at home and telecommuting to self-employment and virtual offices. Spending on home improvement products by individuals was about $25 billion in 1980, but has reached about $95 billion in 1995, and the trend is accelerating rather rapidly.

2.3.5 Telepresence and Telework

Remote handling of objects, remote work or sensory experience, remote "presence" or telepresence: Can one be at one place and transmit not only symbolic information, voice, sound or pictures, but also action itself (or work) to another place? Programming a computer to control a distant sojourner's movement and activities is one thing; transforming one's immediate and unique action directly into the same or enhanced remote action is another and more desirable thing.

The action of one's organs, limbs and hands can be "captured," transcribed, transmitted and the action reconstituted at a remote location(s). The action of one person can thus be multiplied into a thousand actions at different destinations. Telework technology is the next frontier.

One person performing different jobs at different places represents work cloning more desirable and less objectionable than any other kind of "cloning," with potentially vast gains in productivity. Broadcast telework, combined with distributed robotics, spells the manufacturing mode of the not too distant future. It is a matter of focus and vision: it is being done today, albeit with very crude and clumsy devices and machines. Yet, their improvement and refinement could bring forth strong and functional telework technology within a decade.

Humans have always appreciated all forms of action at and from a distance. From the primitive "telekinesis" – eliciting distant action by throwing rocks and yodel-hollering across mountain summits, to controlling Mars sojourners and having remote cybersex, they increasingly choose to spend their free time clicking away with TV remotes, chatting on their mobile telephones, teleworking from their homes. The world of IT/S is already bristling with dynamic networks, hotelling, mobile work, virtual corporations and everything "tele," from telecenters and telecottages to telework and teleexperience. The age of teleaction has arrived.

Doing things at a distance... is it the next best thing to actually being there? Can it be better than being there? Why is it economically and psychologically so attractive?

Is it simply due to economic tradeoffs or is it part of a deeper, more intuitive longing of humankind? Is it just a "male thing" – as the infatuation with teleexperiencing appears to be – or is it part of an all-encompassing (fe)male kind transformation?

The notion of tradeoffs seems to be ancient and fundamental: Do you want to go there in person or send a messenger? Whisper in the ear or write a letter? Go and talk in person or use a phone? Go out or listen to the radio or watch TV? Go to browse the local bookstore or browse Amazon.com"? Go shopping or use mail-order? Send a human crew or dispatch a robot? Make a speech in Peoria or put an ad on local TV? Or get your ad into their telephones? Go and "shoot it out" personally or launch a guided missile? Do it only here or do it also there and elsewhere and everywhere? These are all real tradeoffs and people make them all the time. The remote-site, teleoperator-based economy was first conceived by Robert A. Heinlein in his 1940 novel, *Waldo*. The first crude sci-fi-derived teleinstruments were constructed in 1947. The functioning electric force-reflecting teleoperator was developed by Ray Goertz in 1954. The idea of telework was revived by Marvin Minsky in 1979. Now is the time to bring telework to both the virtual and the "real" reality of human action.

2.3.6 What is Telework?

Imagine a person wearing a comfortable jacket (and gloves, a cap, shoes, etc.), lined with tiny sensors and muscle-like motors. Each motion of the arm, hand, and finger is reproduced at a distant location by mobile, mechanical hands, fingers, feet or other organs. Distant mechanical hands have their own sensors through which the operator can see, hear and feel what is happening, what he is tele-doing. Heat, pain, electric impulses or chemical surges are digitized and fed back at appropriate (i.e., enhanced or reduced) levels of sensation.

Programming of robots for operating in distant and dangerous environments – dismantling of explosives, roaming Mars, penetrating narrow tunnels, pruning trees, etc. – is becoming quite common. Programming robots through expert guidance and tracing is also on the rise. But still missing is the capability of simply working and having the action directly reproduced and carried out at remote or dangerous locations.

Telework allows performing not just routine, repetitive and simple programmable tasks, but enables the highly skilled, unique and even artistic action performed, perhaps by a unique individual, yet multiplied a thousand times and performed virtually anywhere.

Telework is remote action guided by human action (in-formation) rather than by symbolic instruction or information.

Today's handling of radioactive materials with mechanical gloves and other instruments comes perhaps the closest to telework. But the areas of application are virtually unlimited. Remotely controlled surgical procedures, even across the

Atlantic, have been enabled. Nuclear power generation and waste processing, land and sea mining, low-cost space station construction are among the obvious examples. Multiplied and enhanced fabrication, inspection and maintenance could take the notion of work productivity to the next qualitative level. Chemical and physical work hazards can be reduced or eliminated. Nuclear accidents could be handled directly, without the fear of absorbing lethal doses of radioactivity. Most importantly, telework allows one person to perform the job of many.

Even an artist's special brushstroke can be simultaneously applied to hundreds of canvases simultaneously. One special human can provide his or her special touch or service at a distance – to one or to many. The only thing needed is to improve telework instruments so that they start feeling and working like our own hands or organs: a task well within the realm of today's technological and scientific capabilities.

2.3.7 Applications of Telework

Some of the areas of applied telework have been outlined more than a decade ago (Minsky 1985).

- *Mining and petrology.* Remote-controlled mining combines high productivity with human safety – we can have it both ways and tradeoffs free. Miners work on the outside, in simulated virtual environments, while telework robots work down below. Thin mineral deposits, underground combustion and gasification and other risky technologies can be reconsidered.
- *Nuclear technology.* Human-free plants allow for much more vigorous safety and maintenance procedures. No stealing of sensitive and dangerous materials is possible. Breeder technology can be reconsidered.
- *Undersea exploration and mining.* Remotely manned sea-floor exploration, construction and mining are possible. telework in sea-floor mines allows opening up of vast fuel and mineral deposits. Tunneling through sewers, pipelines, wires, etc., can be done from within, internally, not through the traditional "digging up the city."

In addition to obvious industrial and business applications, there are many high-return applications, like nuclear safety and security, where great losses and suffering have occurred in the past, simply because telework was not present.

One could place teleoperators within the nuclear core itself, handle waste processing, allow public monitoring, develop automatic detectors and integrate all operations, without transfers.

Semi-automation of surgical procedures, micro-surgery, vessels repair, deep-brain access, cerebral circulation monitoring and repair, etc., all can be enhanced remotely. Operating sealed laboratories would remove the dangers of hazardous microbiology.

The best example is the *da Vinci* system, made by Intuitive Surgical of California. It allows performing remote operations from heart surgery to prostatectomy and mitral valves repair. The doctor works at a computer console and coordinates surgical action remotely by guiding robotic arms with uncanny precision. The computer filters out minute hand tremors, scales down movements when tinier cuts are needed.

That means no more "open" surgery, sawing through rib cages and profuse bleeding. Robotic hands are guided through small incisions; there is less blood loss, less pain and shorter recovery times. The patient derives the benefits of virtually tradeoffs-free treatment.

Modern surgeons are learning to operate with their brains rather than with their hands. Knowledge is coordination of action and the doctor can sit in the next room as well as on the other side of the world. Outsourcing to the best surgical brains worldwide is in the offing.

In the U.S. alone, about 20 thousand telesurgeries were performed in 2004.

Mass transit is not capable of solving traffic problems and congestion. It moves masses of people through places they do not want to go to or pass through. It is much better to operate ultra-efficient, semi-automatic and totally safe hybrid automobiles. If gasoline is so much less expensive than bottled water (in the U.S. at least) and if Japanese hybrids can go up to 870 miles per tank, why not increase automobile safety through telework and discard the mass transport of the industrial era? In addition, telework reduces much of the traffic due to enhanced telecommuting and teleworking. Not only white-collar infoprocessing, but also manual and "dirty" work could be teleperformed and thus become prestigious, interesting and "clean."

Work cloning will allow the formation of true work communities of geographically and culturally different peers: something sorely needed in the global era.

2.3.8 Technical Challenges

Teleoperator instruments require enhanced force reflection (action feedback) and also information and sensory feedbacks to achieve full and reliable telework. Where human action is not mainly physical or neuromuscular but based on cognition and intelligence, telework can be carried out through voice-command supervisory control. Robotics has achieved high and reliable levels of performance within one decade: it now stands ready as a technological platform for telework.

The mechanical clumsiness of instruments is being rapidly overcome. Successful sensory and "feeling" transfers have been recorded. The senses of touch, texture and vibrations are being simulated in virtual environments. Systems reliability through responsible software has been further enhanced. One can simply compare action with its description: what program actually does what the explicit statements of its intentions are?

Multi-arm, multi-finger, multi-leg systems are needed to complement or replace traditional levers and wheels. The wheel is not the greatest invention of man, legs are.

The telework project, being non-military in its intent, could be carried out openly, through self-organizing, internet-based efforts of many individuals of many nations. Distributed networking of effort, based on the Linux-type model experience, would provide the most efficient organization. No "Manhattan Project"-type, centrally located "Lab" would do.

The government did not take any leadership in the area of telework, concentrating instead on politically and strategically "sexy," but technologically expensive, risky and morally indefensible human presence. So, telework will have to be developed by the private sector with university-business collaboration, emphasizing the profits rather than the military-political dimension, which could be the best mixture for technological innovation anyway: free of governmental bureaucracy and political interference.

The U.S. especially should not lose the opportunity of becoming the leader in telework technology: the new era is not so much about information superhighway as about action on innovation superhighway. Current teleoperator and robotic technology is clumsy, crude, immature and slow: it cannot match the delicate efficiency of the human hand and brain. telework is about humanoids rather than robots. Mass Customization requires machines that can customize and individualize products in remote locations.

2.3.9 The Next Best Thing to Being There

What determines the tradeoffs of being there in person against "being there" in representation, in absentia or in spirit? Often it is simply cost and time. Increasingly it is also the range of choices. Very often it is the sense of opportunity cost: if you are physically engaged in one thing, how can you possibly be engaged in another? Telework does not recognize the alibis à la Perry Mason.

People hate making tradeoffs. They want to be there even if they can't. They want to have their cake and eat it too. They want to have the experience, but not forego other experiences. The time is becoming more precious as there are more choices available.

We do not want to go shopping for one thing, because it takes so much time that can be used to shop for other things. We do not want to thumb through all the catalogs – it takes too much time that can be used to explore so many other things. We do not want to browse through the internet and its assorted Amazon.coms because it ties us down. We want to have "virtual (software) agents" – or "virtual slaves"? – who would do everything for us. Is virtual slavery a sin?

Can virtual reality be "better" than "real" reality? When it is more interesting, offers more choices, saves time and imprints more intense and more indelible memories – it could be better.

In other words, sometimes we do not want to go to a soccer game even if we love soccer. We might prefer the teleexperience of TV, especially interactive telework when we can remotely control the cameras. We get a clearer picture of the game, have as many instant replays as we want, get spectacular close-ups, have a background announcer and still can sip our gin and tonic.

What do we miss? Traffic jams, anxiety, a bad view, hot smells and fellow spectators that we do not particularly care about. Pay-per-view TV has recognized this: for some sports events it is already charging more for TV viewing than for actually being there. TV monitors complement direct viewing from the most expensive subscriber suites, many spectators bring portable TVs into the bleachers (and actually follow them), larger public gatherings and conventions are habitually equipped with huge TV screens, and so on.

Some "remote" researchers are concerned that telework and telework reduce "socialization" opportunities, as if the traditional workplace was somehow designed for that purpose or even provided useful conditions for it. Without doubt, teleworkers are perceptibly more satisfied with their work.

A teleworker might feel lonely in the world of traditional commuters, but not in the world of interconnected communities of other teleworkers. The traditional workplace could be a truly lonely place for those who still have to go and remain there, when nobody else comes and all peers work at home.

Why should absenteeism and turnover be a problem in the traditional workplace? Can we even start to define absenteeism and turnover within the teleworking mode? telework naturally attracts and rewards self-motivation and task-orientation: in fact, it helps to enhance and develop such desirable traits.

Although traditional organizational loyalty and commitment of teleworkers is somewhat weakened, it grows even stronger in the direction of professionalization, process team and expert group affiliation, consumer community formation and other networking phenomena. Any company that rewards autonomy, professionality and task-performance will recover most of the old-fashioned loyalty and commitments from teleworkers.

The concept of the functional "department" is not useful in the teleworking mode and it should be abandoned. The notions of supervision and span of control are also being redefined. Supervisor-subordinate relationships are much less effective and necessary in teleworking, requiring a task-centered/goal-setting management. Face-to-face communication is less needed among self-motivated employees, as is true with any independent agents.

The "gender problem" is not clarified by teleworking. While teleworking men tend to be highly skilled professionals, teleworking women tend to be semi/unskilled data-entry clerical workers. Perceptions of work status are still differentiated: men view telework and home office as a high-status mode to be sought for and even envied if unattainable by others; women still tend to view their physical commuting to a remote workplace as a status symbol and telework-at-home as a lower-status mode. This is bound to change with the next generation.

Predictably, union objections to telework are strong and are increasingly motivated by the loss of influence over the remote worker. Autonomous, independent and self-motivated workers or citizens have never been good "material" for unionization.

Especially "knowledge workers" and "knowledge companies" are benefiting the most from teleworking in the knowledge era.

If we define knowledge as the ability to coordinate one's action towards purpose(s), then the knowledge production potential of telework is truly unsurpassed. With the exception of desk-top manufacturing (Selective Laser

Sintering), work at distance is by definition mostly information processing and remote coordination of action. This cuts the reliance on poor-information exchanges at the coffee machine and the war stories-based semi-tribal community is thus engendered. New forms of communication emerge, based on effectively organized exchanges of coordinative information, i.e., knowledge. Traditional "tribal" networks are effectively transformed into strategic alliances of highly autonomous agents. The expensive and wasteful processing of confused and haphazard "coffee-machine" information is replaced by virtually instantaneous and continuous transfers in a targeted and purposeful mode.

Unintended and inefficient socialization opportunities of the traditional workplace are being replaced by desired, necessary and meaningful socialization modes of people who have shared enough information already and decide to go ahead with face-to-face meetings, especially between employees and their customers and suppliers. Employee-to-employee socialization has to be to the benefit of the company and both parties involved.

Most difficulties with telework are found in the transitional or experimentation stages: the traditional corporation remains traditional in its organization, values and habits, but it already tinkers with all kind of high technologies which require qualitatively different support nets – not only doing things differently, but also doing different things. Mismatched technologies and their support nets are likely to confuse and mislead workers, managers and researchers too.

So, quite rapidly, e-mail is being transformed into e-business, telework into telebusiness, and telework into work cloning and remote action.

In the U.S.A., the e-mail medical consultation and treatment is taking hold. Insurance companies are starting to pay for e-mail online exchange between doctors and patients (about $25 for each exchange). The doctors can offer advice about post-surgical care, diet, changing a medication, etc., without the annoying office visits and frustrating telephone tagging. Physicians gain valuable time to spend with patients who actually need face-to-face interaction.

For patients too, e-mail medicine is a godsend. They can ask their questions in the evening, without missing work and catching viruses in a doctor's waiting room. E-mail exchanges are more relaxed, more conversational, people feel closer to their doctors. Comprehensive strategies of cure and prevention can be hammered out through this collaboration. Specialized individual websites can be set up, X-rays shared and analyzed, prescriptions renewed.

Disintermediation goes hand-in hand: private providers fill prescriptions by telephone or e-mail and send the medicine to their client patients directly, quickly and with precision, bypassing the mess of traditional pharmacy.

The world's first global online pharmacy is *RxNorth*, providing about $800 million worth of low-cost drugs a year to the elderly, uninsured or underinsured Americans. Run from a small village in Manitoba, it provides employment to more than 4000 Canadians.

Clearly, a comprehensive electronic health care information system can be evolved on such a basis, reducing medical errors and promoting better care. The productivity of physicians is improved, overhead costs reduced and access to doctors improved. Patients with diabetes, asthma and heart problems benefit most. Modern patients want to be able to communicate through e-mail and messaging. The customer is in control, in command of his life and well being.

Companies are supporting medical e-mailing as a way to maintain employees' productivity by eliminating unnecessary appointments and so driving down the cost of health care.

It is clear that telecommunications allow direct teleinteraction with customers, employees and suppliers through disintermediation. There is less need for dealers, intermediaries, operators, code-punchers and other bottlenecks, forcing customers "on hold." The Web market is growing explosively, predicted to reach over 550 million people within the next three years.

Corporate business systems are connected directly with their corporate constituencies, via the Web, intranets and extranets, by providing self-service web-sites for their customers. Self-service, telework, disintermediation, mass customization and outsourcing to the customer go hand in hand.

2.4 MBA Global Education

Education is the next internet frontier. After the wave of e-commerce, first business-to-consumer, then business-to-business and business-to-itself, the "e-ducation" wave will start propagating through the Net. Over 100 million adult Americans are already using the internet. The foundations for e-ducation are firmly in place.

First, business moved to the Net, then, the Net moved into business; now the Net is being absorbed into every aspect of business. Soon, education, especially business education, is going to "consume" the Net. E-business companies will demand it. Schools and countries that choose to ignore this will go the way of big department stores.

Universities, especially their business schools, have to reinvent themselves, reengineer their organization and curricula, and move to the e-engineering phase on the Net. Otherwise, their student will go to schools online, like Cisco, GE, IBM, AT&T, and other corporate online academies. Whichever schools, companies and countries establish the best internet educational capabilities, there is where the new era capital shall flow.

Traditional business schools have already started losing their best and brightest. Many prospective MBAs are increasingly choosing to go directly to e-business corporations and study and train at their own schools and academies. At the same time, E-commerce degrees, programs, certificates, majors, minors, specialties, concentrations, courses, fellowships and assorted "research centers" are proliferating on global campuses. Should e-business be taught as a separate academic subject or should it become an integral part of a general business curriculum? Money, prestige and the ability to attract the most desirable students hang in the right balance.

2.4.1 MBA and the Schools of Business

To attract new MBA students, one has to ask: What are they looking for and what do they need most? The answer surely is not: More of the same, only better.

MBAs do hope to enter the New Economy, master global communications and the internet, absorb networks and networking, become masters of e-business and e-commerce and become attractive to the insatiable corporations of the New Economy.

Doing the same thing better is not sufficient in the era of discontinuous, rather than continuous, improvement. That is how Lou Gerstner turned IBM, a spoiled child of a bygone era in American business, the famously self-absorbed company, into the open architecture ethic of e-business and the internet. Its shares now fetch nine times what they did when the new CEO walked in the door.

No MBA program can survive by teaching, no matter how excellently, the old-IBM world. Only the new teaching, of and beyond the new-IBM world, will do. The traditional MBA has to be reengineered into a "Global E-MBA," only more fully and more rapidly than IBM itself.

The internet, E-commerce, and telecommunications and network communities are the main components of the necessary retooling and reengineering of the MBA. All business schools are devoting vast resources to writing new case studies about the internet, overhauling existing courses and using online material to supplement traditional lectures. Corporate recruiters will snap up MBAs who seem to understand how the World Wide Web is changing the economy. And prospective students will shun any school they see as lagging behind the internet revolution.

General Electric has directed managers in every department to rethink their business with the internet in mind. At schools like Wharton, Northwestern, Massachusetts Institute of Technology and New York University, professors say they are able to allow students to study e-business intensively: they bought and brought the faculty together to fill out its course roster, eliminate overlaps and inaugurate a major in technology and e-commerce. MIT is one of several schools that have set up research centers along with the new majors. Its Center for eBusiness draws faculty from the business school and from the media and computer science laboratories.

Vanderbilt University's business school in 1995 became the first major school to offer such an e-business program. Recruiters are crowding e-business majors at Vanderbilt. It's easy to raise money for programs labeled "e-business," the dot-com millionaire alumni are more than willing to donate to them.

That the internet is crucial to the future of business schools is widely accepted and agreed upon. But how e-business should be taught – as a separate major or as being fully integrated into the entire curriculum – is still a subject of heated debates.

Similar debates raged in the 1970s and 1980s over the wisdom of separate international management concentrations. With globalization now an important theme in most courses, the international majors that still exist are rapidly dwindling in popularity – witnesses to serious strategic misreading of global trends at some schools. Now it is happening again.

Of course, in the long run it makes no sense to have a separate major about e-business. All business will be e-business as all business is international or global.

2.4.2 Need for Integration

There is of course a significant preponderance of flakiness, incompetence, overvaluation, naiveté and plain greed in the above-described E-wave. The

E-phenomenon itself is still poorly understood, not well researched and not yet academically respectable, well taught or theoretically-grounded. All this simply underlines the need for more serious, academically and professionally respectable integration of the MBA and e-business.

Will the current E-commerce wave become the right trend towards that end? We argue: No.

This trend tries, unfortunately and so far successfully, to isolate IT/S and all the related areas into separate specialties. Instead of integrating them seamlessly into the New Economy curriculum, it perpetuates the old model by simply adding yet another function, dimension or focus. One has to agree with Edward A. Snyder, the dean of the Darden School of Business:

"E-commerce degrees are silly in the same way that teaching international business in a global economy is silly." (NYT, Sept. 22, 1999, p. G12)

The subject of E-commerce should become an integral part of the business curriculum. In that sense it should disappear and be dissolved in the modern way of doing business. It should not remain artificially separated from it.

This understanding comes only from experience and common sense. Whenever a new field or function is simply added as a separate attachment, it turns into a fad, spends itself and fails. Only fully integrated areas persist and flourish.

Take quantitative analysis and operations research: their isolation and separation led to their downfall. Only after their full and seamless integration could they become true and equal parts of the system.

Take the "international" dimension. The global economy is international by definition. Its "internationality" cannot be singled out, separated and "taught." That's why "international business" made sense in the 60s and 70s. Now, all business is international, all business education is international, and thus all MBA degrees are international – by definition.

That is why international MBA programs require all their students to take serious study tours abroad for credit.

One cannot master this new internationality, i.e., globality, by emphasizing and concentrating mainly on things that are different. Only through deeper a understanding of what makes our businesses increasingly similar, common and comparable, one achieves "globality." The era of specialized, isolated and culturally embedded management systems is already over.

Take TQM. Quality and its management should be seamlessly integrated into the entire business curriculum because quality is an integral part of business. Any separation of degrees, concentrations and certificates must therefore qualify as being "silly" in Dean's Snyder's language, as quoted above.

Quantitative analysis, internationality, TQM and E-commerce are not functions and dimensions business, like production, marketing or finance. They should not be separated because concentrating in them is "silly," while concentrating in finance is not. A finance major is assured to be proficient in quantitative analysis, international issues, quality and the internet – if he is any good and useful. An E-commerce major, however, is not assured a similar knowledge and proficiency of finance (marketing, production, etc.).

2.4.3 What is the Global E-MBA?

As one should not teach "international" business in a global economy, one should also not teach E-commerce or E-business in the New Economy. (Recall Dean Snyder's comments.) When looking for a high-quality MBA, one should look at the level of integration of e-courses in all business and management courses (production, marketing, finance, strategy, etc.), and the level of similarly integrating the "international" dimension into its entire curriculum. Within a decade, all business will have significant global and electronic dimensions.

So, the Global E-MBA program must have both its "internationality" and "e-commerce" fully integrated in the curriculum. These two dimensions go hand in hand.

There is nothing more "international" in today's business than the internet, telecommunications and global hypercompetition. Companies are not so much interested in doing "international" things, as in doing things that are international. The difference is fundamental: International accounting can be conceived, but E-commerce is international.

The E-MBA program will have to bring this globality and E-commerce into all of its traditional areas and courses. Students should not study marketing and e-marketing, finance and e-finance or production and e-production separately or even in separate courses. Such divisions will disappear.

For example, taking a course in marketing would make a student proficient in e-marketing to the extent that no special, additional e-course would be needed. That would free the IT/S resources to do truly path breaking and innovative stuff. A similar diffusion happened with so called "quantitative methods," which are now mostly dissolved into all high-quality courses in any area.

Some new courses are of course needed too. Certainly Supply chain (or network) management cannot stand alone and must be part of the broader E-curriculum. The Network Economy, network corporation and network organization must be established on a sound scientific basis. Courses in Knowledge and Knowledge Management (KM) are of course unavoidable in an economy virtually running on knowledge and information fuels. Companies will have to learn to make knowledge assets durable, difficult to imitate, and difficult to substitute. Value-added management is a necessary part of virtually all courses.

Bargaining and negotiation, demand forecasting, technology choice/risk, relationship (alliance) management, design of adaptive organizations, managing through the creation of communities (communities of customers, communities of suppliers, etc.) are all being transformed in the new context. New authority structures will emerge and new stakeholder relationships will be formed. Theories of governance will have to be altered with the notions of "belonging" revised.

Is there a Global E-MBA in your future?

The answer becomes most obvious when you contemplate the opposite: how are your prospects going to be affected without the mastery of e-business, E-engineering, Mass Customization, added value management, knowledge management, IT/S, networks and networking, integrated supply nets, and global hypercompetition? What kinds of modern companies can even exist without such strategic building blocks of their competitive advantage?

So there is your answer: integrate e-commerce, global markets, and quality and knowledge management, all of them, into your curriculum. Not as specialties or concentrations, but naturally and seamlessly, as if you already were a manager of the 21st century.

2.4.4 Mass-Customized MBA

Of course, an MBA program, as all other university programs, must ultimately enter the internet era. Not to teach, but to practice e-education and e-MBA. Study programs must be individualized and mass customized in order to produce a variety and differentiation of thinkers and problem solvers, not just carbon copies of mass-produced "doers" who carry out order and add very little in terms of originality, innovation, strategic differentiation and competitive reframing.

Jean Piaget taught us that the principal goal of education is to produce individuals who are capable of doing new things, not simply repeating what other generations have done – that is, men who are creative, inventive and prone to discovery.

The second goal of education is to form minds that are capable of critical thinking, can verify assertions and do not accept everything they are offered at school. The greatest dangers that remain are mass sloganeering, collective opinions, and ready-to-wear trends of thought.

Each of us has to be able to resist individually, not just *en masse*, to criticize, and to distinguish between what is proven and what is not. So we need students who are active, who learn early the ability to learn and discover by themselves, partly by their own spontaneous activity and partly through the material we set forth for them. Such people can learn early to tell things apart, to identify what is verifiable and what is simply an opinion or the first idea that came their way.

Most of our MBA programs are far from such educational ideals.

The keywords are individualization, differentiation, distinction, originality and critical thinking – in short, the *Mass Customization of education*, of MBA programs in particular.

Every day it seems another business school announces the launch of an online MBA program. These programs are beginning to gain respectability. They partly deliver Mass Customization by enabling students to get their personalized education anytime and anywhere. However, they still lack many of the important features at the core of the Mass Customization model.

Schools will find it quite challenging to offer a service *tailored to one* when they are traditionally used to treating their consumers as xerox copies and in large groups.

Students, and especially MBA students, together with their current or future employers, should be *treated as customers*. The customer pays for the product and is therefore entitled to high quality at low cost, in a tradeoff-free fashion. As with customers, it is all about choice and creating individually tailored programs. Educated consumers are our best customers and they are entitled to and should demand at least:

- A flexible program that offers the freedom to study where, when, and how they want to.
- A rich menu of courses that can prepare them for new global careers.
- A faculty with demonstrated knowledge of subject matter (publications) and teaching expertise (critical thinking).

- Student body and faculty diversity that reflects the global nature of business.
- Quality education with high academic standards at an affordable cost.
- Education that incorporates new technology in the learning process.
- Applications should be accepted year round, online, with admissions decisions produced continuously, within a couple weeks.

2.4.4.1 Faculty

Schools usually decide in advance (forecasting) what courses will be offered and who will teach them in a given term. Students then select classes from that inventory.

One of the tenets of modern business and Mass Customization is to replace inventories with flexible capabilities that can be rapidly deployed. These principles should be not only be taught but also practiced. Faculty will simply post a choiceboard or menu, like Online Course Exchange (OCE), of subjects they are prepared to teach. A course will be activated when enough students sign up for it (i.e., JIT course delivery). Courses are then rolled out quickly and faculty needs to prepare them in advance. Over the long term, faculty will be expected to continually develop new capabilities that can be turned into courses.

There will always be a need for teaching core classes in order to satisfy accreditation requirements. The rich set of electives is necessary to meet the market test of supply and demand.

2.4.4.2 Online Course Exchange

A robust and interactive online system is fundamental to the success of a mass-customized MBA. Students have access to an OCE course catalog that can be searched by academic subject, faculty name, and other meaningful criteria. Students use the system to sign up for classes and view current class enrollment sizes. A class is offered once enough students sign up. A feature of the mass-customized MBA is that class tuition is based on enrollment size. As more students sign up for a class the cost can be spread out – students gain some control over the cost of their education.

The OCE allows students to form *communities of interest* that serve several purposes. Students are able to insure that the classes they need are available at a lower price by registering as *en bloc*. If a needed course is currently not being offered, students have the means to request a new course, in which case a current faculty member can address the gap. Groupware and videoconferencing tools are used to facilitate group activities.

2.4.4.3 Suppliers

Publishers of business textbooks, journals, videotaped courses, CD ROMs and other learning aids are integrated with the OCE. JIT courses will have pedagogical materials ready for student distribution on a short notice. Publishers can monitor enrollment activity to estimate whether a course is likely to be activated and what will be its enrollment size. Publishers and teachers also have an opportunity to collaborate on the development of new materials. In order to insure quality control over the process, publishers will be required to receive an Acceptance Certification before being granted access to OCE.

2.4.4.4 Students

The program has a lot of built-in flexibility for students. That allows students to better demonstrate their academic potential, performance and evaluation to academic and admission committees. Students attracted to this program are likely to be highly motivated individuals who do not need externally imposed discipline to work hard. The diverse nature of the faculty and the opportunities for online learning may attract diverse students who seek real world learning experiences.

2.4.4.5 Support Net

Behind the scenes are a number of resources and personnel that are important to the program's continuous renewal. The school has a collection of software applications, audio/video equipment, and recording rooms to assist faculty in creating online courses. An active team of recruiters has the important task of identifying and recruiting qualified auxiliary faculty members. Other personnel manage the relationships with suppliers. A customer support team will be available to assist all the program's stakeholders. The online system will need to be maintained and continuously improved.

There are also cultural changes required for the success of this program. Skeptical state boards of education will have to be convinced of the legitimacy of the program. Employers need to buy into this concept as well otherwise graduates will have a difficult time finding employment. This program will appeal to a much needed new breed of MBA students. The faculty will also be doing either new things or old things in new ways, enhancing distinction and differentiation.

Chapter 3

PRODUCING NETWORKS:
Management and Self-Production in Networks

3.1 New Economy of Networks

There is an increasing sense that the affairs of business, management and economics have been fundamentally transformed by the emergence of information and knowledge technology, global hypercompetition and customer sovereignty. Labels like the New Economy, Network Economy, or Digital Economy are proliferating and capturing the sense of a profound change. The new paradigm is still emerging, its contours hard to discern, and its rules still churning and evolving: it can only be captured in the process of becoming, not in the state of being.

One thing is clear: the boundaries, the barriers and the walls between products and services, industries, sectors, companies, functional departments, etc., are going to be significantly diluted, if not destroyed in the New Economy.

Management systems are accelerating their evolution. Only since the Second World War have we witnessed at least four significant evolutionary stages. Practicing management of the nineties is rapidly becoming obsolete. Practicing anything older than that amounts to assured loss of competitive advantage for a firm, region or entire nation. In order to understand the nature and the speed of management change, we have to understand its main evolutionary stages. In order to understand and practice its current paradigm, *extended-network orientation*, one has to understand the *why*, not only the *what* and *how* of management. Logically, at times of rapid change, the *what* and *how* of management become rather futile investments – only the *whys* can carry us from stage to stage.

The four evolutionary stages include: (1) *Final-Product Orientation*, where final-product improvement is the primary focus and the production process is

159

secondary; (2) *Process-Operations Orientation*, where process improvement comes into focus and Total Quality Management (TQM) emerges; (3) *Integrated-Process Orientation*, where the focus shifts from continuous improvement to discontinuous redesign and from operations to process architecture – business process reengineering (BPR) emerges; and finally, (4) *Extended-Network Orientation*, when the internal process becomes integrated in the extended network of external embedding. Only in the last stage, the currently reigning paradigm, both customers and suppliers become truly integrated as driving forces of the enterprise.

3.1.1 Evolution of Management Systems

After World War II, the traditional paradigm of product-oriented mass production (linear assembly lines, organizational hierarchies of command, product quality control, and mass consumption) had reached its peak in the fifties and sixties. In some lagging business cultures, the traditional paradigm is still being practiced today.

Soon afterwards, the Deming-Juran process quality teachings spearheaded a new quality orientation (later referred to as TQM) and propelled Japan directly to the post-war *process focus* (process quality control, just-in-time, continuous improvement), while the U.S. went through a painful and prolonged product-to-process transformation, ultimately leveling the playing field by the mid eighties.

At the end of the eighties, business *process* reengineering (BPR) concentrated on the radical redesign of the production process through the reintegration of task, labor and knowledge. As a result, lean, flexible and streamlined production processes were created, capable of fast-response, Internet-based integration for both business-to-business (B2B) and business-to-customer (B2C) interfaces, including mass customization.

In all three described stages, the competitive advantage was derived almost exclusively from the *internal resources* of the firm. At the end of the nineties, the most radical shift occurred as the competitive advantage became increasingly derived from the *external resources* of the firm – through the extended networks of suppliers and customers. In Figure 3.1 we display the main differences between product, process, and networks – the three dominant categories of management systems evolution.

In view of Figure 3.1, the managerial focus first shifted from product to the internal process. It has become clear that improving quality of the process leads to a better-quality product, but not vice versa. Improving the process was first carried out by continuous improvement, concentrating on improving the operations (circles). Then the emphasis shifted from operations to process relations (arrows), that is, to a *discontinuous* improvement by redesigning the process architecture, by reengineering the process. In all these efforts, the firm's focus was rooted in developing the internal sources of competitive advantage, knowledge, innovation and productivity.

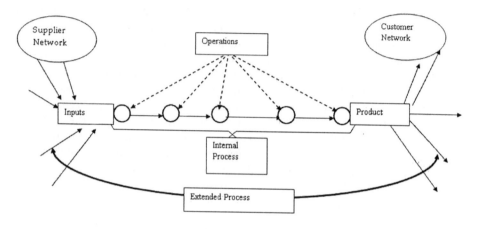

Figure 3.1 Product, process, and networks.

Only in the last paradigmatic shift was the internal process expanded into the extended process, including supplier networks and customer communities as main, this time external, sources of competitive advantage. Such a shift changes the very notion of competitive advantage, the sources of knowledge and the concept of the firm itself. It also brings forth and fosters a new set of relationships with customers and suppliers. The firm's internal sources and resources become insufficient in the New Economy: the firm can be only as good as is the network of which it is a part.

No firm can be an island. Being an island of hierarchical command in the sea of free markets, or an outpost of efficiency in the sea of mediocrity, or a bastion of secrecy in the ocean of global communication – all such traditional corporate images are harbingers of doom. *No firm is an island.*

The extended-process paradigm has ushered in the competitive advantage of cooperation, alliances, networks, knowledge, shared innovation and total communication.

3.1.1.1 Summary of the Four Stages

We summarize the individual stages in terms of their dominant characteristics:

1. *Final-product orientation.* The final product is primary, the production process secondary. Both operations and the processes are considered to be technologically fixed or "given." The process is broken into a large number of small elements, causing sequential product variability. Product quality is "inspected in," mostly at the end of the process. Statistical quality control, inventory control, cost minimization, mass production assembly lines, work specialization, hierarchies of command, mass consumption, reliance on statistical mass markets and their forecasting are among the defining characteristics of this stage. All basic methods of forecasting, consumer and market research, quality and inventory control, product and brand management, etc., were essentially developed during this stage and refined and adapted in later stages. In some business cultures, they still remain the cornerstones of current management.

2. *Process-Operations Orientation.* It is the high-quality process that assures high-quality products and not vice versa. This fundamental insight brought the process into primary focus. The process is still considered to be technologically "given" and within the domain of engineering and engineers. The main focus is on the improvement of process operations. Quality of the process was understood as the quality of its operations. Concepts of Total Quality Management, Continuous Improvement (Kaizen) and Just-In-Time systems have characterized this stage. Typically, the management hierarchy remains unquestioned and is preserved or even conserved, while the role of high and information technology is discounted, global markets are still ignored and alliances and cooperation are atypical. The process architecture is kept intact and remains "given."

3. *Integrated-Process Orientation.* The focus of attention shifts from operations (circles) to "linkages" (arrows) – towards the process architecture itself. The *reengineering* of the process, re-integrating individual components into larger, more autonomous and even self-manageable wholes, has characterized this stage. The production process was not assumed to be technologically "given" and predetermined by engineers. The production

process became a business process and thus subject to qualitative redesign and reengineering (BPR). Discontinuous improvement replaced continuous improvement. Traditional vertical hierarchies of command have flattened out into more horizontal, process-oriented networks. Mass customization, disintermediation, knowledge management and autonomous teams have emerged as a direct consequence of BPR.

4. *Extended-network orientation.* Finally, the entrepreneurial company of autonomous agents and teams, operating in an environment of intracompany markets within intercompany networks, emerges. Networks of suppliers and communities of customers have extended the internal network into a functional and competitive whole. Both internal and external sources of knowledge and competitiveness now form core competencies. Intranets and extranets have provided a communication medium for business-to-business and business-to-customer exchanges. Quality has become bundled together with cost, speed and reliability. Tradeoffs are now being reduced and eliminated.

Observe that the internal or extended process orientation of the last two stages led the focus on the action of *process coordination* to become the main source of corporate competency and competitive advantage. Purposeful coordination of action is knowledge, both human and corporate. So, it is not too surprising that the interest in knowledge management has accompanied the emergence of process focus in both internal and external networks.

3.1.1.2 Stakeholding in Networks

The major global players are rapidly developing supplier and customer networks. They are being interconnected by Internet-like corporate intranets and extranets. *Network extranets* allow online and immediate communication among all network participants and allow the same information to be shared by all at the same time.

Extranet communication enables companies to go beyond just-in-time systems and establish *immediate information sharing*. Extended process coordination becomes vastly enhanced along the entire value (supply) chain. Companies can concentrate more fully on innovation, optimization and alliance building.

Networks are the new frontier.

3.1.1.3 New Rules

Communication services used to be a sector of the economy. Now, communication *is* the economy. Whatever happens in the world of business (and increasingly in other areas too) is fundamentally shaped, influenced and molded by human communication and telecommunications technology. There have been *Infohighway*, *Infobahn*, and *Infostrada*, but the times of such turnpikes are numbered. With WiFi (wireless fidelity), the entire space becomes the medium when we are dealing with knowledge and wisdom, rather than just information.

Most Americans are increasingly communicating and working through the new space, as a virtual unit of one, interacting through the densely "wired" network space.

Self-service, work-at-home, do-it-yourself, telecommuting and telework are among the flourishing activities of the New Economy.

Among the many sets of new rules advanced for the New Economy, we choose very popular and simple ones, offering a number of metaphors for the uninitiated. Yet, the deeper contents behind such simple metaphors could be significant and demanding.

From "New Rules for the New Economy" (Kelly, 1998):

  1. Embrace the Swarm
  2. Increasing Returns
  3. Plentitude, Not Scarcity
  4. Follow the Free
  5. Feed the Web First
  6. Let Go at the Top
  7. From Places to Spaces
  8. No Harmony, All Flux
  9. Relationship Tech
  10. Opportunities before Efficiencies

This metaphorical "Newspeak" has to be translated and explained in order to appreciate the full impact of the New Economy. Below we provide some paraphrasing and reinterpretation for each of the "Kelly Rules":

1. *Embrace the Swarm.* This refers to the decentralization and distribution of efforts. Power flows away from the center – in business, politics or culture. Distributed, networked power (empowerment) is becoming stronger and more effective than its centralization. Network connectedness is the new

measure of complexity and performance. Biological connectedness is the foundation of emergent performance, knowledge and results. Autonomous networks of autonomous firms, teams and individuals are the foundation of the New Economy.

2. *Increasing Returns.* As the number of nodes increases arithmetically, the value of the network increases exponentially. After centuries of expounding the "Law of Diminishing Returns," networks are increasing their returns to scale: the larger the network (of computers, faxes, businesses, people, etc.), the larger the return to the individual user. The number of connections provides the power to sustain explosive compounded growth – creating a positive feedback of a self-feeding process.

3. *Plentitude, Not Scarcity.* Falling raw-material prices, productivity driven disinflation and even deflation, manufacturing techniques that are capable of perfecting copying, multiplying and propagating virtually everything: products, services, information and knowledge – abundance rather than scarcity increasingly drives economic value and business thinking. The average weight of products is dropping, including automobiles. We move towards a "weightless economy" as information replaces mass. The plentitude, not the scarcity, of networks is the basis of their ever-increasing value. Opportunity maximizing, rather than profit maximizing, for the individual *and* for the others, is the main characteristic of the New Economy.

4. *Follow the Free.* Gold is scarce and therefore less and less valuable; a network is valuable and priceless and the access is virtually free and open to all. Falling prices and disinflation characterize the abundance-based economy. The best is the cheapest; the very best is virtually free. Having the only one (scarce) fax machine in the world is of no value; having the access and use of millions of them is the real value. As price goes down, supply increases; so does the demand. The only scarce factor in economics is time, and therefore human attention. Let your customers complete and finish your products and services. Don't charge for use, charge for joining.

5. *Feed the Web First.* Rather than maximizing the firm's value, it is important to first maximize the network's value. The net must survive and become strong, otherwise the firm perishes. A strong company makes strong employees; a strong network makes strong companies: the network is the first allegiance of your firm's employees. All commerce migrates to the network economy, avoiding networks amounts to economic suicide, resisting them is a modern folly.

6. *Let Go at the Top*. Do not wait for failure, devolve proactively, and slough off the old at the height of their success. Make disassembly, reverse logistics, and material recycling a part of the production process: close the organization. Accelerating innovation process overlaps one success over another success, avoiding the eventual failure or obsolescence in between. Do not get stuck in a local optimum, search for the global optimum. Autopoietic "creative destruction" is an integral part of creation.

7. *From Places to Spaces*. Physical proximity, geographical distance and the sense of place are being replaced by the sense of space (anywhere, anything, anytime). The "Internet time" is the same everywhere in the world, as is the time space. From marketplace to market-space and from business place to business-space – these are the trends of free network participants, spelling the demise of intermediaries, agents, dealers and middlewomen (or middlemen). Move from value chains (and its intermediaries) to value networks; disintermediate as fast as you can. All nodes of the network are "intermediaries" to each other. About the only new "go-betweens" are intelligent agents, cybermediaries, or infomediaries (aggregators and syndicators of electronic contents).

8. *No Harmony, All Flux*. A sense of turbulence, chaos, instability, and a continuous churning of the environment can be counteracted only by the harmonizing and synchronizing effects of innovation. But equilibrium is dynamic and chaos could be a highly harmonious order, just slightly beyond the edge of traditional human perception and understanding. The harmony of chaos, the other word for complexity, has to be grown or produced, not simply installed.

9. *Relationship Tech*. Traditional productivity is a nearly meaningless byproduct in the network economy. Relationships amplification is the main economic event: the cause of productivity. Linkages and relationships enhancing technologies – wireless soft technologies are replacing the hard technologies of the hardwired world of the past. Self-service, not service, is the mode of the New Economy. *Pro*ducing and con*suming* has fused into a single economic process: "Prosuming." Relationship and connection enhancement is the new technological frontier. Interconnectivity generates trust; trust is the basis of the free-market economy.

10. *Opportunities before Efficiencies*. Being efficient in performing a known, well defined task cannot beat the inefficient discovery of new opportunities

for new tasks. Opportunity is the source of new wealth. It is better to be inefficient in powerful innovation than to be efficient in an out-of-date routine task. Only innovation creates space for more innovation. Producing new opportunities is better than optimizing existing ones; designing optimal systems is better than optimizing existing systems; and productivity is therefore the wrong goal to pursue in the New Economy of opportunities. To be productive in the wrong job is worse than to be less productive in the right job.

We can formulate another set of rules, leading us directly to the Global Management Paradigm (GMP) later.

1. *Networks and networking.* Information technology and systems (IT/S) allow new levels of connectivity between businesses, producers, customers and providers, as well as among employees. Market-type networks thus penetrate corporate boundaries and guide communications and economies within companies. Networks have become the base of new organizational theory and practice in a New Economy.

2. *The customer is the strategy.* No more empty exercises in strategic planning at the highest levels: the customer determines and drives the strategy of the whole enterprise. It cannot be any other way. The role of management is to "read" the customers' strategy correctly and implement it properly. Customers, not the "strategists" have the most knowledge and can best judge what they want and thus what the corporate strategy should be.

3. *Knowledge a capabilities is the main capital.* Modern corporations need knowledge; they buy other corporations to gain knowledge and strategic capabilities, not to derive short-term financial payoffs. New ideas, innovation, and vigorous managerial skills are the most expensive and the hardest form of capital to engage and maintain. Money, technology and labor gravitate towards knowledge and are driven and guided by it, not vice versa.

4. *Teams and teamwork.* In a New Economy, teams and teamwork are no more clichés and oxymoron's as they were in traditional command hierarchies. Teamwork and alliances with partners, associates (previously employees), suppliers, and customers, based on trust and team rewards, creates new organizational space capable of dealing with global hypercompetition. Partnership and trust are derived from a mutually assured advantage.

5. *Sharing of wealth.* Wages and salaries of individual employees are being complemented by co-ownership of corporate equity. Stock options are being extended to employees, not only to executives. Employee stocks and profit sharing are also on the rise. Each employee could become a capitalist, engaged and involved with his enterprise as an owner, not just a hireling.

6. *Personal, informal cooperation.* Informal environment, creative chaos and incessant innovation spawn self-organization and self-management. Managers become coaches, mentors, advisers and partners or associates.

3.1.1.4 Biological Imperative

Economies, markets and organizations are organisms, not mechanisms, so biology, rather than physics and engineering, is a proper metaphor and paradigm for their investigation and understanding. Biological systems are communicating networks, mechanisms are not. Among the earliest proponents of the biological imperative in economics were F. von Hayek and O. Morgenstern.

Oskar Morgenstern used to say that if you throw a monkey-wrench into a machine, it stops. If you do the same to an economy, it adjusts, like a biological organism.

Chaos, complexity and autopoiesis are invading the predominantly Newtonian and Descartian economic universe. Economies do not work as clocks or machines, but as eco-societies. Instead of energy, materials and land, information and knowledge are becoming sources of value. Instead of command, control and feedback, there is autonomy, self-organization and self-production. Hierarchies and division of labor are being replaced by self-organizing teams, synthesis of minds and unity of purpose. Creativity, innovation, adaptation and trust are becoming "hard" strategic realities of economics, business and management – neither of them very machine-like.

Instead of linear, mechanical models of input, output and feedback, we are appreciating the circularity, organizational closure and essential autonomy of economic systems. Wheels and cogs, accelerators, multipliers and other artifacts of mechanical engineering are being rapidly replaced by diffusion, propagation, self-production, self-sustainability, and evolutionary adaptation.

All modern businesses are in two kinds of "business": 1. To produce and consume something other than itself, i.e., output, product, service or information – through *heteropoiesis*; and 2. To produce and consume itself, i.e., its ability to coordinate action, in order to produce goods, services or information – through *autopoiesis*.

In order to produce something else, a corporation has to be able to first *produce itself*, i.e., recreate and renew its ability to produce, to coordinate its own action.

Like with any living organism, in order to produce the "else" – product, replica, copy – a corporation has to produce "self," the main prerequisite for producing "the other." The self-production of a corporation, its ability to coordinate its action, is autopoiesis.

At certain stages it is heteropoiesis that dominates business concerns: what, where, how much and when to produce. At other stages it is autopoiesis that dominates the focus: how and why to produce *anything, anywhere, anytime.*

Information is the input of heteropoiesis, knowledge is the flow of autopoiesis. The modern corporation (self-renewing network) produces knowledge first and product second. Traditional hierarchy produces product first and knowledge production is left to spontaneous forces, not explicitly managed and not viewed as a main competitive advantage.

The process of self-production is called *autopoiesis*, in contrast to heteropoiesis (production of the "other"). Self-produced systems or networks are referred to as *autopoietic systems*.

Autopoiesis or self-production can take place when there are distinct and autonomous individuals or agents interacting and communicating in a specific environment and according to specific behavioral *rules of conduct and interaction.*

An autopoietic organization (which we shall discuss in later sections) can be defined as a network of interactions and processes, involving at least:

1) *Production (poiesis)*: the rules and regulations governing the entry of new components, such as emergence, input, birth, membership and acceptance.
2) *Bonding (linkage)*: the rules governing associations, arrangements, manufactures, functions and positions of components during their tenure within the organization.
3) *Degradation (replenishment)*: the rules and processes associated with the termination of membership, like death, separation, consumption, output and expulsion.

Network organizations are autopoietic, based on the circular closure of the above three self-feeding and mutually adjusting production processes.

3.1.1.5 Evolutionary Approach

The biological imperative has to be considered very carefully. There is an entire school of "biological economics" or "bionomics" which applies traditional mechanistic economics to biological systems (profit maximization, economizing, feedback, entropy, utility maximizing, etc.) and then re-imports the results back as "biology" into economics or business management. That is what the New Economy needs least: further amplification and re-importation of neoclassical concepts of economics. Biological systems are autopoietic and self-organizing, exquisitely coupled with their environments – they are not economizing or profit-maximizing machines.

While it is less than desirable to export old mechanistic economics into biology, it is much needed to import some good systems-based evolutionary biology into the New Economics.

In spite of the evolutionary behavior of economic and management systems, economics itself is not an evolutionary science. It is still rooted in the mechanistic precepts of Newton and has not reflected on the evolutionary approaches initiated by Darwin. For economics, the social world is simply clockwork, where change is continuous within the mechanism, but its structure remains unchanged and unchangeable. The notions of the organization/structure dichotomy and autopoiesis are mostly unknown; an evolutionary view is impossible.

Another *caveat* is needed: adopting the so called Darwinian view is not necessarily a sign of accepting the biological imperative. Darwin's views were often simplified through a mechanistic analogy and thus became indistinguishable from Newtonian ideas. While God-designer was replaced with Nature and divine law with natural law, very little has changed. According to Becker: *"Having denatured God, they deified Nature."* So, in economics, the structure is natural and not man-made, and thus beyond the power of man to change.

Man is conceived as being a passive pawn of Nature and not the source of action and knowledge needed to change the system. A deified natural order discourages questioning of the essential assumptions of economics.

Yet, people are not passive at all: they build human institutions, manage human systems and engage in purposeful action. *An institution is collective action to control, liberate, and expand individual action.* Collective knowledge frames individual knowledge.

For any individual coordinated action to be successful in achieving its purpose, it must be respected and sanctioned by other individuals. Limiting one person's action frees the action of others; one person's liberty requires the respect of others. Every right must be rooted in requisite duties and responsibilities.

Individuals are constrained and affected by institutions, but their action is being protected if they follow the rules of conduct evolved by the institution. So, their power and freedom are actually enhanced by the institution, compared to the "power" of an isolated individual. Without institutions, human action would be severely curtailed, subject to clash and conflict with any other individual action.

The classical theory of economics does not recognize institutions, the individual is choosing from *given* alternatives. He cannot generate alternatives, change the rules, or act as a volitional person. He maximizes his utility, like a simple minded, tautological machine. The passivity of such an individual is secured.

Humans, human systems, and social institutions simply do not behave that way. They are acting, not just choosing. They always act within the context, culture, institution and individual circumstance. Causes of their actions are in the future (positive feedback of organisms), rather than in the past (negative feedback of machines). Future expectations and desires are the causes; its effects are in the present, in the action. No certainty applies; uncertainty rules.

To reduce the uncertainty of positive feedback, people act through social institutions and their systems of rules. Human systems, like biological systems, are self-producing, autopoietic.

3.1.1.6 Strategy Paradigm Reversal

Strategy, strategic planning and strategic reengineering are also undergoing fundamental redefinition. In 1994, H. Mintzberg wrote his magisterial *The Rise and Fall of Strategic Planning*, with the emphasis on the "fall" rather than on the "rise."

Most of the defenders of traditional strategic planning appear to be fighting to get some respect: keep their jobs, positions or theories. The declining role of traditional forecasting is well known and not too surprising in an unstable, less predictable, more chaotic business environment. In the New Economy, instead of forming goals based on predicting the future environment, and *then* mobilizing the ways and resources for reaching them, the process of strategy formation is being reversed by the practice of global hypercompetition.

First, one enhances current processes and resources into core competencies. *Then* one formulates the goals for the most effective utilization and further enhancement of these competencies for satisfying the customer. Instead of the [goals → ways → resources] dogma-sequence of the forecasting-based strategy, modern and flexible corporations are utilizing the [resources → ways → goals] sequences of foresight-based strategy formation, rooted more firmly in organizational abilities, competencies and knowledge, not in the blurred and expensive hopes of stability and predictability.

In the era of increased need for flexibility and responsiveness, global competitors can and do copy any market "position" or static competitive advantage rather quickly. The advantages derived from static positioning can therefore be only temporary. Is it wise to invest in and solidify with something that cannot last and is easy to emulate?

What can companies do in this environment of "quick copying"? Do they mutually annihilate each other? Do they engage in hypercompetition or "mutually destructive competition"? Of course not. They form cooperative networks of mutually assured advantage and they differentiate.

Such companies form long-term strategic alliances and collaborative organizational networks. In order to collaborate effectively, they have to become flexible so that they can effectively complement their partners. Their best bet in facing their partners, suppliers and customers is to move beyond operational effectiveness towards dynamic core competencies, flexibility and – *knowledge.*

Building up organizational knowledge – the corporate ability to coordinate action well – is the new strategy. Knowledge is inexhaustible, it can be continually renewed and expanded, and its copying is a form of flattery and provides competitive stimulation. Knowledge acquisition is not easy and is always special and individual.

Pursuing both operational efficiency and effectiveness could be at the core of creating competitive advantage, as can be the pursuit of strategic reengineering of processes and their operations. The goals must be an integral part of any strategy formation, whether they enter *a priori* or *ex post.*

The reality is a bit more complex. *Vis-à-vis* their competition, companies can perform *the same* processes and activities in order to attain *the same* goals, but do it more cheaply, quickly and more reliably – simply better. That is *operational efficiency.* Other companies could aim for the same goals, but perform their processes and operations in *different ways* in order to achieve their goals more effectively. That is *operational effectiveness.* This strategy is best exemplified by the reengineering of business processes and operations (BPR). Many companies are also engaging the same processes and operations (core competencies) towards the dynamic pursuits of different, frequently changing goals. They engage in *strategy formation*, moving beyond the efficiency or effectiveness of operational pursuits. Yet other companies have found it quite beneficial to perform different processes and operations in order to attain different goals. That is *strategic reengineering*.

Modern customers clearly prefer to "have it both ways": cheap and good, fast and cheap, good, fast and cheap, etc. – i.e. with little or no tradeoffs among the multiple dimensions of competitive performance.

In fact, customers view these multiple dimensions as *integrated packages*, with no tradeoffs allowed or desired. It is not perceived as high quality if it comes at a very high cost; it is not perceived as cheap if it takes forever; and it cannot be perceived as customer value if it is not cheap, fast and of high quality in relation to the competition. These integrated value packages cannot be disintegrated into tradeoffs.

The producers find it easier to deal with tradeoffs: they can easily deliver something very cheaply, very quickly or of very high quality, but not all of these at the same time. Producers prefer to work in a tradeoffs-based environment, while customers would prefer to live in a tradeoffs-free environment.

The producers, who come closest to satisfying the customers, by recreating a tradeoffs-free environment for them, create also the strongest long-term competitive advantage for themselves. How does one build a tradeoffs-free environment? By doing things differently and by doing different things – all in the direction and for the purpose of tradeoffs elimination.

Let us consider the traditional *productivity frontier*, comparing the delivered non-price buyer value and the relative cost position, as in Figure 3.2. The frontier describes the maximum value that a company can deliver at a given cost under the best currently available circumstances. Observe that only companies operating below the productivity frontier are in a tradeoffs-free environment and can improve by moving towards the frontier. Once on the frontier, such companies can only trade off value against cost, by moving laterally along the frontier, back and forth.

As the productivity frontier shifts outward (due to technological improvements), the companies scramble again for a temporarily tradeoffs-free environment, only to see their "advantage" quickly dissipated as competitors copy each other and are forced to face the customer-unfriendly tradeoffs again.

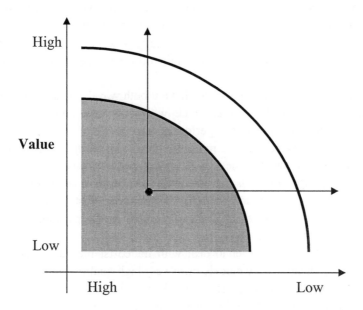

Figure 3.2 Tradeoffs-based improvement.

The situation in Figure 3.2 is loaded with old and traditional assumptions. The tradeoffs between value and cost are assumed to exist *a priori*, in the very way the frontier is drawn. No differentiation of means and goals is present; companies cannot design their own frontiers by engaging in different activities and different ways of carrying them out, etc. This is not how it works in the real world.

In Figure 3.3 we represent how companies redesign and reengineer their own processes and operations so that the frontier (tradeoffs) is eliminated and the tradeoffs-free environment can be continually expanded and improved upon. The shaded area (the universe of corporate activities) of Figure 3.3 represents a distinct advantage and improvement over the shaded area of Figure 3.2. The situation in Figure 3.3 is a true, long-term strategic advantage, while the situation in Figure 3.2 requires continuous operational improvements and tradeoff choices, without fully satisfying the customer.

Strategic reengineering is about creating competitive advantage through the choosing of different goals and different activities (or the different ways of carrying them out) so that a tradeoffs-free environment is created or at least approached as closely as possible, delivering a unique mix of value to the customer. The Japanese have shown the way in the 1980s by purposefully eliminating the tradeoffs between defects and costs. All other types of tradeoffs can be similarly eliminated by BPR-oriented companies, *capable of doing things differently and doing different things.*

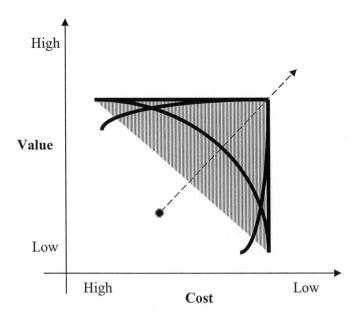

Figure 3.3 Tradeoffs-free improvement.

Modern strategy is not about making tradeoffs – i.e., choosing one inferior alternative over another – but about creating superior alternatives for the customer and thus for the company.

Conclusion

The New Economy has emerged. Its new rules are still in the flux, churning back and forth like the economy itself. No doubt that the U.S. economy is entering its uncharted waters with full force and determination. A high productivity growth rate, strong GDP growth, low unemployment, soaring markets, disinflation, self-service, home office, telecommuting, consumer community and the all-pervasive Internet characterize this entry.

Silicon Valley keeps thriving because it follows the principles of network interactions. Individuals switch from one company to another, but their companies form a range of informal alliances, sharing their core competencies, keeping the knowledge capital in the region. Productivity in the IT/S era is measured by *added value* (the revenue earned from products less all the costs of making the products).

IT/S is trying to keep pace with the network economy. Small entrepreneurial businesses are booming. The uncharted waters of the New Economy are becoming clearer and more manageable every day – an invitation for the still hesitant and still reluctant nations and regions.

3.1.2 The New Economy and the Cluetrain Manifesto

In the heydays of the New Economy there were attempts to formulate the beginnings of behavior and communications in networks. Some of the theses of the so called Cluetrain Manifesto still provide an interesting summary of the new consumer/employee perspective with a strong human systems management orientation.

Below we provide a short summary of selected ideas with a commentary and reinterpretation where appropriate and useful. These observations are rooted in the Internet and global communications networks: it is obvious that traditional concepts do acquire different meanings in the electronic space of networks. The notions of communication, conversation, coordination, individualization and so on, are crucial in networks. Networks are still *human systems* and the Internet has become a *human institution*.

Markets are conversations.

Markets are increasingly becoming free of place and location, moving into the realm of two-way communication for the purposes of causing or eliciting action. The nature of conversation is communication and the purpose of communication is action.

Markets consist of human beings, not just demographic sectors.

Markets (and its sectors, segments or niches) do not buy anything; individuals do. Each individual customer is a market. The shift from mass markets to individual or small-group markets within the global economy is increasingly powerful.

Conversations among human beings must sound human and be conducted in a human voice: typically open, natural, and uncontrived.

Humans do not like to communicate in slogans, sound bites and little ditties of the mass media. Mass media, like mass producers, have to individualize their product, mass customize their delivery, and move from a one-way broadcast to a two-way communication.

The Internet is enabling conversations among human beings that were simply not possible in the era of mass media.

The new conversation and communication space is the Internet.

Now customers can talk to producers (C2B) and among themselves (C2C). Also producers can talk among themselves (B2B) and also to customers (B2C). These rich communication links were simply not available before. Even "bloggers" (web log communicators) are influencing business, politics and entertainment in unprecedented ways.

The Internet is a powerful tool for dismantling the rigid hierarchies of command, ushering in the flat and flexible, horizontal organization of networked teams. The Internet allows knowledge transfer and sharing, dismantling excessive specialization and division of labor, producing an integrated, process-oriented enterprise.

Both consumers and employees, through their conversations, create communities and become members of these communities. Corporations do best in promoting and enhancing these communities. The corporation itself is becoming a community of members/employees. These new social forms are powerful producers of new organization, new knowledge and new strategy.

As a result, markets are getting smarter, more informed and better organized. Participation in a networked market changes people fundamentally.

People in networked markets have figured out that they get far better information and support from one another than from vendors.

Networks are smarter and more powerful than classical hierarchies. Interlinked communities of consumers, customers and employees are much harder to deceive or exploit. However, they could also be much more loyal, rewarding and wealth generating than the mass markets – if accepted and listened to.

There are few secrets. The networked market participants know more than companies do about their own products, services and strategies. They also tell everyone else.

The Internet makes corporate communications more transparent and secrets less rewarding. Open-book management among employees, among suppliers in the value chain, and among the community of consumers is more profitable than the traditional locking-up of great ideas in corporate safes. Hiding data, misinterpreting facts and continually apologizing through mass media is ineffective because it belongs to a different era.

The Internet allows employees and consumers/customers to communicate directly, without an intermediary of a special department, designated person or voice-mail interface. Corporate boundaries are getting blurred and often appear eliminated through the intensity of these conversations.

Corporations have to learn to speak in the same voice as these networked conversations. In just a few more years, the current "voice" of business – the sound of mission statements and promotion brochures – will seem contrived and artificial.

Companies that don't realize their markets are now person-to-person networks, getting smarter and joined in conversations, are missing their opportunities. Companies can communicate with their markets directly, not through "media."

Online markets are communities (networks of communicating agents) of autonomous individuals, not a passive mass of statistical categories, samples and averages. Companies should join these conversations and participate in them. Companies need to lighten up, take themselves less seriously and get a sense of humor.

Bombastic boasts, like "We are positioned to become the preeminent provider of XYZ" – do not constitute a position. So-called strategic positioning has passed. Companies cannot fix themselves into rigid and tradeoffs-based strategic "positions." Corporate strategy is derived from and made by communities of their customers and consumers. Strategy is not made at the top of the pyramid, the place quite remote and isolated from the realities of the market.

The Public Relations department does not relate to the public but creates a barrier, a language firewall. Companies should not be afraid of their markets.

The Public Relations department serves as a buffer and an intermediary; it should be disintermediated first. All contacts should be direct with those directly responsible.

Trust, as knowledge, has become a productive force and an economic category. Trust, as knowledge, has become a form of capital.

Smart markets will find suppliers who speak their language. The notion of loyalty is much stronger in networks precisely because the relationships can change and be renegotiated so fast. To be "loyal" in the mass market is short-lived, fickle and very expensive to sustain. In networks, natural loyalty is continually reproduced from within, based on quality, merit, and satisfaction.

To speak with a human voice, companies must first belong to a community of their suppliers and customers. Human voice means speaking natural human language. Living in human language is possible only through living in a human community.

Corporate culture is embedded in human or community culture and should not be separated from it through self-inflicted schizophrenia.

Companies that make a religion of security are protecting less against competitors than against their own market and workforce. Such obsessive secrecy is out. Companies keep secrets from their public, customers, suppliers, employees and media, very rarely from their competitors. That is very costly, counterproductive and self-damaging.

As with networked markets, people are also talking to each other directly inside the company – and not just about rules and regulations, boardroom directives and bottom lines. Such employee conversations are taking place on corporate intranets. The best intranets are built bottom-up by engaged individuals cooperating to construct a corporate conversation.

A healthy intranet organizes workers in many contexts and its effects are more significant than the agenda of any trade union.

Corporate intranets and supplier extranets are Internet-based networks of communication and knowledge sharing. They should not be imposed and "managed" from the top, although they can be so triggered. Their true value is in self-management and self-organization, producing autonomy and self-assumed responsibility – true jewels in corporate abilities and competencies.

Rigid organizational charts worked in an economy where plans could be fully understood from the top of management pyramid and detailed work orders could be handed down. Today, the organizational chart is horizontal, hyperlinked network, not hierarchical structure.

The self-organizing and self-producing networks, emphasizing ability and knowledge, have replaced organizational charts of vertical pyramids, emphasizing position and power. Modern organizations are neither military nor religious hierarchies of control and influence. They are engines of ideas; producers of knowledge.

Hierarchies invite intense competition in terms of politics, power, positioning and social climbing. They require very little competition in market results, profits and skills. Political competition rules over economic competition, and economic cooperation is often subdued by political cooperation. That cannot be self-sustaining in the age of Internet.

However subliminally, at this very moment millions of people online perceive companies as little more than quaint legal fictions that are actively preventing their conversations from intersecting. Smart companies join the conversation, transform themselves into the medium of discourse between employees and customers and become an integral part of the Internet-based New Economy.

Any writer of a Manifesto of 95 theses, if not Martin Luther, is bound to run out of steam and slip into repetition, clichés and unrealistic dreams of the working class and its powers. The power is not in the class but in the knowledge. Workers have not created the Internet and they are the slowest in adapting to it. Yet, the Internet is the right tool for transforming all workers into entrepreneurs and capitalists. Then they would have nobody to fight but themselves.

Communities of suppliers/partners, producer/providers, employees/associates and customers/consumers are spontaneously self-organizing into vast Internet-based networks, producing their own language of discourse, their own values and the new rules of conduct and behavior. The process of networking is as inevitable and unstoppable as globalization itself. The Cluetrain Manifesto is often naïve and visionary, but provides a very important contribution to the efforts of summarizing and systematizing newly emerging human contents of the Internet-based New Economy.

3.2 High Technology Management

The nature of technology has changed in the global era: it is becoming more integrative and more knowledge-oriented, it is available all around the globe and it includes logical schemes, procedures and software, not just tools and machinery. It tends to complement or extend the user, not to make him a simple appendage. The notion of technology has to be redefined: it should be viewed as a form of social relationship, with hardware and software enabling the brainware and technology support infrastructure.

Let us start by recalling the views of Stiglitz (1999) on technology transfer:

"History teaches us that transferring hardware is insufficient and ineffective. Codified technical information assumes a whole background of contextual knowledge and practices that might be very incomplete in a developing country. Implementing a new technology in a rather different environment is itself a

creative act, not just a copied behavior. Getting a complex technical system to function near its norms and repairing it when it malfunctions are activities drawing upon a slowly accumulated reservoir of tacit knowledge that cannot be easily transferred or 'downloaded' to a developing country."

Although Stiglitz still uses the labels of explicit and tacit knowledge, it is in order to emphasize the insufficiency of information, codified "knowledge" and the hardware-software mindset. *Information can always be "downloaded," knowledge cannot.* Knowledge has to be produced within the local circumstances and structural support.

Technology has been one of the main engines of economic development since the Industrial Revolution. Yet, its operational definition has been neglected and most people know it either from macroeconomics simply as "T" (in some arcane formula) or through a listing of hardware or "machinery" (like drill, computer, robot or crane). Such levels of treatment are clearly inadequate in the era of Information and Knowledge Technology or more generally *High Technology* – i.e. forms of technology that increasingly have to be managed by managers, not only designed by engineers. The managerial perspective on technology has been missing.

At its most fundamental, technology is a *tool* used in transforming inputs into products or, more generally, towards achieving purposes or goals. For example, the inputs can be material, information or services. The product can be goods, services or information. Such a tool can be both physical (machine, computer) and logical (methodology, technique). Technology as a tool does not have to be from steel, wood or silica, it could also be a recipe, process or algorithm.

Many IT/S technologies are *high technology*. But what is high technology? Why is it labeled "high"? We often know it by listing: optical fibers, reprogrammable robots, ceramic engines, satellite communication devices and systems, optical scanners, etc. – all are high technology. But why?

Technology is not just hardware, machine or equipment. It is much more than that. In order to utilize technology efficiently and effectively, we must grasp its broader definition and its broader embedding in the requisite enabling infrastructure. What would an automobile be without the network of highways? A computer without its software? A robot without a knowledgeable workforce?

How inadequate it would be to view IT/S as mere hardware, as computers without their networks, lasers and optical fibers without their telecommunication applications, a fax machine without at least one counterpart. Technology is a package of hardware, software, brainware and the support net. In many modern technologies, the hardware is becoming a commodity, the least decisive component, a mere physical casing for the real power of effective knowledge contents. The enabling infrastructure, or technology support network, is often becoming the most important component of technology: in the near future it will not be the number of computers per capita, but the density and capacity of their network interconnectedness which will determine their effective use.

It's not what you use or how you use it, but what you use it for and why. The shift from "what and how" to "what for and why" is virtually a defining factor of the *high* technology. It is the high technology that is characterized not by the change in hardware or software, but by the requisite change in the enabling infrastructure: it requires doing things differently and doing different things, not merely doing the same things better or more efficiently.

3.2.1 Components of Technology

Any technology can be divided into several clearly identifiable components:

1. *Hardware*. The physical structure or logical layout, plant or equipment of machine or contrivance. This is *the means* to carry out required tasks of transformation to achieve purpose or goals. Hardware therefore refers not only to particular physical structure of components, but also to their logical layout.

2. *Software*. The set of rules, guidelines, and algorithms necessary for using the hardware (program, covenants, standards, rules of usage) to carry out the tasks. This is the *know-how* – how to carry out tasks to achieve purpose or goals.

3. *Brainware*. The purpose (objectives and goals), reason and justification for using or deploying the hardware/software in a particular way. This is the *know-what* and the *know-why* of technology. That is, the determination of what to use or deploy, when, where and why.

These three components are interdependent and equally important. They form the *technology core*. Components of the technology core are co-determinant, their relations circular (non-linear and non-hierarchical) and mutually enhancing.

This concept of technology is clearly illustrated when we consider a car as technology:

An automobile consists of its own physical structure and logical layout, its own hardware. Its software consists of operating rules of the push, turn, press, etc., described in manuals or acquired through learning. The brainware is supplied by the driver and includes decisions where to go, when, how fast, which way and why to use a car at all.

One could similarly define computers, satellites or the Internet in terms of these three dimensions. Any information technology or system should be clearly identifiable through its hardware, software and brainware.

There is a fourth and the most important aspect of technology:

4. *Technology Support Net.* The requisite physical, organizational, administrative, and cultural structures: work rules, task rules, requisite skills, work content, standards and measures, styles, culture and organizational patterns.

3.2.2 Technology Support Net

Any technology core (hardware, software and brainware), in order to function as technology, must be embedded in a supportive network of physical, informational, and socioeconomic relationships which enable and support the proper use and functioning of a given technology. We refer to such a structure as the *technology support net* (TSN).

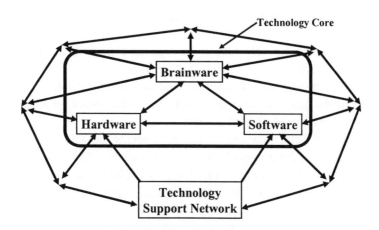

Figure 3.4 Structure of technology.

TSN is a network of flows: materials, information, energies, skills, laws, rules of conduct that circulate to, through and from the network in order to enable the proper functioning of the technology core and the achieving of given purpose or goals.

Ultimately, all the requisite network flows are initiated, maintained and consumed by people participating in the use and support of the use of a given technology. They might similarly and simultaneously participate in supporting many different technologies through many different TSNs.

The entire structure of the technology core and its support network of requisite flows are sketched in Figure 3.4. It should now be clear that the shape and form of the TSN is the main determinant of technology use.

Every unique technology core gives rise to a specific and requisite TSN and thus to a specific set of relationships among people. Ultimately, the TSN can be traced to and translated into the relationships among human participants: initiators, providers and maintainers of the requisite flows in cooperative social settings.

In this sense, every technology is a *form of a social relationship* brought forth from the background environment. Only in this sense, and only as such, can it be properly understood, discussed and managed. Let us look at an automobile as technology again. Its TSN consists of an infrastructure of roads, bridges, facilities and traffic signals, but also of maintenance and emergency services, rules and laws of conduct, institutions of their enforcement, style and culture of driving behavior, etc.

A large number of people have to be organized in a specific and requisite pattern in order to enable cars to function as technology.

All four dimensions are necessary in order to define technology: Technology is an interacting unity of hardware, software and brainware, embedded in its requisite support network of relationships.

It is clear that technology and its four components can only be defined from the vantage point of the user or observer, not in a context-free or absolute sense. In other words, roads, bridges and traffic signals can be technologies themselves, with their own hardware, software, brainware and support nets.

For example, traffic lights are a part of the TSN of an automobile, but their own hardware can be driven by their own software (a computer-controlled switching program or schedule) and brainware (purposes of safety, volume and flow control, and interaction with pedestrians). This technology core has its own support net of electricity, signal interpretations and car traffic. The traffic light is a technology of its own.

Similarly, a piece of software from some technology can itself become viewed as technology (for achieving specific business purposes or goals) with its own hardware, software, brainware and TSN. The success of Microsoft is rooted in this realization.

Such an observer-dependent definition of technology is also important for identifying important complementary, competing and collaborating technologies through the revealed intermeshing of individual TSNs into larger hyper networks. The relationship between the technology core and its requisite TSN is that of mutual enhancement and codetermination. A specific technology core requires a specific TSN, but the core itself is further shaped and defined by the intensity and depth of its embedding in its requisite TSN.

Although the technology core of the automobile gives rise to a new and proper TSN, the evolution and properties of the automobile TSN determine specific adaptations of the evolving technology core of the automobile. Through this co-evolution technologies mature and are characterized by a closer and more efficient fit between their core and TSN environment.

3.2.3 High Technology

The concept of the technology support net allows us to *separate* the technology core of hard-soft-brainware from its requisite embedding. Different cores can fit the same net, different nets can be tried for the same core, and so on. In this sense, any technology can be characterized as being "misplaced" or "unfit" as well as "right," "fitting" or "appropriate." In the cases of mismatch, both aspects of technology (core and TSN) have to be adapted in order to assure appropriate functioning.

Different changes in the core, both in hardware or software and brainware, will have differentiated effects on the requisite TSN. According to the nature and extent of such changes, we can offer the following definitions:

1. *High technology* is any technology core that affects the very architecture (structure and organization) of the components of the technology support net.

High technology therefore changes the qualitative nature of tasks of TSN and their relations, as well as their requisite physical, energy and information flows. It also affects the skills required, the roles played, the styles of management and coordination – the organizational culture itself. In short, it allows (and often requires) not only to *do things differently* but often to *do different things*.

Clearly, high technology has to be differentiated from [just regular] technology:

2. The *technology* core affects only the efficiency of flows over the TSN, i.e., it activates only quantitative changes over the qualitatively identical architecture of the TSN. It allows users to perform the same tasks in the same way, but faster, more reliably, in larger quantities, or more efficiently, while preserving the qualitative nature of flows and the structure of the support, skills, styles and culture. Technology allows us to do the same thing, in the same way, just more efficiently.

3. The *appropriate technology* core essentially preserves everything: the support net as well as the flows through it; its effects are neutral with respect to the TSN. It allows users to do the same thing in the same way at comparable levels of efficiency. Improving efficiency is not the purpose here, preserving and protecting the TSN is. Appropriate technology is very important in situations where the stability of the support net is primary for social, political, cultural or environmental reasons.

Introducing the electric typewriter core into the support net of the manual word processor core in the TSN of the electric (or manual) typewriter requires fundamental changes in net architecture: tasks, inputs, skills and culture. Even the support intermediaries (typists) are mostly eliminated. The word processor enters the classification of high technology.

To summarize our definitions: while technology improves the functioning of a given system with respect to at least one criterion of performance, high technology breaks the direct comparability by changing the system itself, therefore requiring new measures and new assessments of its productivity.

High technology cannot be compared and evaluated with the existing technology purely on the basis of cost, net present value or return on investment: it would be like comparing apples and oranges. Only within an unchanging and relatively stable TSN would such direct financial comparability be meaningful. In other words, you can directly compare a typewriter with a better (electric) typewriter, but not a typewriter with a word processor. Therein lays the management challenge of high technology.

Appropriate technology implies that rather than improving the measures of performance, it is the preservation of the TSN itself which is the driving purpose of technology implementation.

The notion of high technology is therefore relative to the vantage point of the technology being replaced. No technology remains fixed and – being a form of social relationship – it evolves. Technology starts, develops, persists, mutates, stagnates and declines – just like living organisms.

The high technology core emerges and challenges existing TSNs which are thus forced to co-evolve with it. New versions of the core are being designed and fitted into an increasingly suitable TSN, with smaller and smaller high-technology effects. High technology becomes just technology, with more efficient versions fitting the same support net. Finally, even the efficiency gains diminish, emphasis shifts to product tertiary attributes (appearance, style) and technology becomes TSN-preserving appropriate technology. This technological equilibrium state is at times interrupted by a technological mutation – new high technology appears and the cycle is repeated.

The automobile was high technology with respect to the horse carriage, it however evolved into technology and finally into appropriate technology with a stable, unchanging TSN. The only high-technology advance in the offing is the electric car – because of its need for wholesale restructuring and redistribution of the TSN.

Implementing high technology is often resisted. This resistance is well understood on the part of active participants in the requisite TSN. The electric car will be resisted by gas-station operators in the same way automated teller machines (ATMs) were resisted by bank tellers and automobiles by horsewhip makers. Technology that does not qualitatively restructure the TSN will not be resisted and never has been resisted.

The proverbial "Resistance to change" is not a universal human trait. In fact, humans like change, seek it out and thrive on it – as long as the change preserves the support network they are part of. The electric typewriter, electric tooth brush or the more powerful tractor were never resisted. Technologies and appropriate technologies are not resisted, high technologies are.

Middle management resists business process reengineering because BPR represents a direct assault on the support net (coordinative hierarchy) they thrive on. Teamwork and multi-functionality is resisted by those whose TSN provides the comfort of narrow specialization and command-driven work.

3.2.4 High-Technology Environment

We can compile a short comparative listing (Table 3.1) of the current impacts of the transition from Technology to High Technology.

Table 3.1 Technology vs. high technology impacts.

Technology	High Technology
Efficiency	Effectiveness & Explicability
Economies of scale	Economies of scope
Know-what	Know-how & Know-why
Data & Information	Knowledge & Wisdom
Specialization	Reintegration
Working harder	Working smarter
Centralization	Decentralization
Hierarchy	Network

Within the framework introduced here, one cannot fail to observe that modern information- and knowledge-based technologies (including techniques and methodologies) currently tend to be high technologies with high-technology effects. They integrate task, labor and knowledge, transcend classical separation of mental and manual work, enhance systems aspects, and promote self-reliance, self-service, innovation and creativity. The "low" technologies, no matter how new, complex or advanced, are those which still require the dividing and splintering of task, labor and knowledge, increase specialization, promote division and dependency, sustain intermediaries and diminish initiative.

Not all modern or advanced technologies are high technologies: they have to be *used* as high technologies, function as such, and be embedded in their requisite TSNs. They have to *empower* the individual because only through the individual can they empower knowledge. It would be hasty to claim that all "information" or "informating" technologies (IT/S) have integrative effects. Some information systems are still designed to "improve" the traditional hierarchy of command and thus preserve and entrench the existing TSN: the administrative model of management. They further aggravate division of task and labor, further specialize knowledge, separate management from workers and concentrate information and knowledge in centers.

As knowledge surpasses capital, labor and raw materials as the dominant economic resource, technologies are also starting to reflect this shift. Because knowledge is not a "thing," residing in a super-mind, super-book or super-database, but a complex relational pattern of networks brought forth to coordinate human action, technologies are rapidly shifting from centralized hierarchies to distributed networks.

The use of computers provides a good example. The original centralized concept (*one computer, many persons*) is a knowledge-defying idea of our computing prehistory and its inadequacies and failures have become clearly apparent. The era of personal computing brought powerful computers "on every desk" (*one person, one computer*). This short and transitional period was necessary for getting used to the new computing environment, but was inadequate from the knowledge-producing vantage point. Adequate knowledge creation and management come mainly from networking and distributed computing: *one person, many computers*. Each person's computer must form an access to the *entire* computing landscape or ecology: the Internet of *other* computers, databases, mainframes, as well as production, distribution and retailing facilities, etc.

Why has the very term "high technology" emerged only in recent decades, while "technology" was quite sufficient for centuries before that, even during and after the Industrial Revolution? Why is there this virtually global need to start differentiating technologies into "high" and the rest? There is no simple explanation: we have shown that high-technology impacts always existed and were built into the very foundations of the concept of technology.

One explanation could be related to the unprecedented breadth of the high-technology impacts today, due to the widespread intermeshing of technology support nets. High technologies do not appear one by one, more or less sequentially, but due to cross-synergies seem to advance on a broad front of virtually all economic sectors simultaneously.

For the first time our technology empowers individuals rather than hierarchies. It transfers influence and power where it optimally belongs: at the *loci* of the useful knowledge. Knowledge, innovation, spontaneity and self-reliance are becoming increasingly valued and promoted. Hierarchies and bureaucracies do not innovate, free and empowered individuals do.

3.2.5 An Example of High Technology

We have used the automobile as an example to demonstrate the importance of the technology support net (TSN) in defining technology and the interactions of its components, hardware, software and brainware. We have also insisted that only a qualitative *change* in the TNS can bring forth high technology impacts.

Certainly the automobile, an appropriate technology of today (albeit with some high technology components and subsystems) is promising to become high technology again, in the near future. The accelerating trends towards gas/electric and electric automobiles, accompanied by the development of hydrogen fuel cells and sun powered batteries, are the harbingers of the high technology transformation of the automobile.

But it is not just the fuel source but the very structure of the hardware, software and brainware that has to change.

A good example is the recent development that can be referred to as the *distributed engine* or more popularly as *e-Traction*. The idea is a century old and comes all the way from the Bohemian designer Dr. Ferdinand Porsche, who did not find the necessary support net for his inventions, either in the internal combustion engine dominated environment, or in his country of origin. In the early 1900s a 25 year old Porsche of Hofwagen-Fabrik Jakob Lohner & Co. developed electrically powered wheels and used them in roughly 300 different vehicles. In Amsterdam, for instance, both the fire brigade and "Amstel" brewery trucks briefly drove with this type of traction.

Porsche himself learnt from the Czech engineer Hans Ledwinka, the father of all-wheel brakes, air-cooled rear engines, articulated headlights and independent rear suspension. Ledwinka's designs of the Tatra 77 and T87 (the famous *Tatraplan*) were so admired by Hitler that he cajoled Ledwinka into making him detailed drawings – then passed them on to Porsche and the Volkswagen Beetle was "born," conceived by a Czech who died penniless in 1967.

Most gas/electric or electric vehicles today still work by connecting peripheral wheels to a central motor. A Dutch company "e-Traction" of

Apeldoorn has tested a bus in which the motor and wheel form a single unit. Such automobiles can have as many autonomous engines as there are wheels.

This is not a simple refinement, but a qualitative restructuring of the automobile, promising more miles per charge, better safety, easier maintenance and quiet and clean performance. It has a small combustion engine for charging the batteries, but the main propulsion comes from two electric motors with the tires attached that serve as the rear wheels. Many companies have since tried to popularize the distributed engine, and a few are currently producing them – including WaveCrest Laboratories in Virginia, powering bikes and bicycles. Another innovator is Solectria, a company in Woburn, Mass., that has produced simpler drive trains for more than 100 gas/electric buses.

The e-Traction is however the main player. It has already built a wheel motor for a forklift truck. In mass production, two wheel motors would cost no more than the large engine and other parts that the motors would replace on a regular diesel-powered bus.

The circular shape of e-Traction's motor is not unusual, but the basic parts are reversed. Usually an electric motor consists of a ring-shaped part that does not move, called a stator, through which a current runs, developing magnetic forces that turn the shaft that runs inside it, the rotor. Here, the shaft is fixed and the ring turns. If the shaft was to serve as an axle, and the ring was to have a tire attached, the result would be a motor that serves as a wheel. Such an arrangement would have only one moving part, and would eliminate the parts of the drive train, which transfers power from the engine to the wheels. So, it would eliminate the differential, or gears that allow a vehicle's wheels to turn at slightly different speeds.

Here, speeds are independently controlled. Electric wheels provide a simple way of making a vehicle four-wheel drive. And if one wheel started to slip in acceleration or braking, a central computer could determine that far faster than existing traction control or anti-lock braking systems and make adjustments.

Further, e-Traction squeezes into the wheel an electronic part called the inverter, which changes the direct current from the battery into an alternating current for the motor. Converting the current elsewhere in the bus would require running long AC cables to the motor, and such cables lose energy. Running DC cables from the battery to the wheel and converting the power there to AC increases efficiency. In addition, some electronic tricks can make the motor turn at speeds fast enough to run the bus without gears. The result is to drop the gearbox, a source of weight and friction. Unlike vehicles with internal combustion engines, most electric vehicles do not need variable transmissions, but they do need a gearbox of some kind. If something went wrong with the motor, with the inverter or with the chips that control the motor, a mechanic could replace them all in about 25 minutes by swapping out the wheel.

Clearly, a new support network of charging, service and maintenance is bound to emerge. The road and tires would have to be better because the electronics in the motor are in direct contact with the road, not protected like the rest of the bus is by shock absorbers. But the loss of the gearbox is a major benefit. Meanwhile e-Traction is also working on a Mercedes Jeep borrowed from the Royal Netherlands Army and a Range Rover. Both will have four motors, one on each wheel.

The future of the in-wheel electric engine seems brightening. At the recent Tokyo Motor Show, it was the distributed engine that was the choice in many of the hydrogen-powered concept cars. One hundred years after Porsche.

3.3 Autopoiesis

It is now useful and necessary to introduce the basic concepts and principles of autopoiesis or the self-production of networks. Although of biological origin, the theory of autopoiesis is eminently applicable to social, business and management systems – because they are mostly human systems. Human systems are mostly spontaneous, self-organizing and self-producing organisms, not mechanistic machines.

3.3.1 Machine/Organism Dichotomy

We owe Peter M. Senge (in de Geus, 1997) for applying the idea of the Machine/Organism dichotomy in the language of business. If the corporation is an autopoietic system – as we argue elsewhere – then the following insights reveal the assumptions (explicit or implicit) about corporate organization. Any observer of a corporate organism can adopt one or the other pole of the M/O spectrum. Machine (M) is heteropoietically constructed by an external designer who remains separate from it. Organism (O) is autopoietically influenced and directed by its own constitutive components.

Further distinctions between the **M** and **O** perspectives are also of interest:

1. **M**: Owned by someone, both whole and in parts, by external (absentee) owners. **O**: Owning higher organisms, especially human beings, fully or partially, is (in some cultures) considered fundamentally immoral.
2. **M**: Conceived and constructed by its builders to pre-specified purposes of the owners. Goals are externally imposed and "engineered." **O**: Self-produced, guided by their own, internal purposes, goals and objectives. External goals can be imposed (or enforced) but not "engineered" and internalized.
3. **M**: Its operations controlled by operators, controllers and "controlling" agents. **O**: Living beings and the processes of living are not mechanistically (directly) controllable, but can be *influenced*.
4. **M**: Created heteropoietically (produced by someone else, imposed externally), as a hierarchy of power and command. **O**: Created autopoietically (self-produced by itself, evolved internally) as a network of interrelationships and influences.
5. **M**: Fixed, static and predictable. Cannot change, grow, multiply, adapt – without somebody *making* it. **O**: Developing, evolving, dynamic and unpredictable. Can change, grow, multiply, adapt – through its own interactions and influences, on its own.
6. **M**: Identity, if any, imposed externally by its designers, builders and engineers. **O**: Identity, personality and character brought forth and manifested from within, from its internal organization of processes and functions.
7. **M**: No autonomy. All actions are reactions to external commands and programmed (engineered) rules. **O**: Autonomous or semi-autonomous. Self-generated goals lead to self-engendered actions.
8. **M**: Maintained, repaired, overhauled and rebuilt externally, through identical member parts. **O**: Capable of regeneration, self-renewal and reproduction, maintaining its identity beyond present members and constituents.
9. **M**: Member parts are (human) resources or reserves for externally controlled operations. **O**: Members are humans working in human communities.
10. **M**: No learning takes place: machine structure is fixed and cannot learn as an entity. **O**: All living organisms can learn, as an entity and through all of its components.

We have gotten used to viewing our companies as dead machines, contrivances and mechanisms. We use them as we would use machines and tools to achieve our goals. Humans do not wish to become machine-like, in order to fit the machine. They strive to make the machine fit, expand and enhance *their own* humanity – unless they are stopped dead in their tracks.

The original Czech word for business is *zivnost*, the making of living. The Swedes call it *näring liv*, the nourishment for life. The Chinese call it the *meaning of life*. To paraphrase Senge, business, i.e., *working together*, can be and can again become a deep source of life meaning. All the rest is just a job.

3.3.2 Autopoiesis (Self-Production) of Networks

With the advancement of the Internet, telework, telecommunications and remote knowledge sharing, we are witnesses to the emergence of distributed, self-produced and self-renewing networks or *eco-societies*, interdependent communities of businesses, individuals and groups. Many social networks emerge spontaneously, i.e., produce themselves through the rules-driven, recursive interaction of their own components. Not all social systems are machine-like or mechanistic contrivances produced by external agents, designed, controlled, planned, predicted, engineered and reengineered incessantly. Most new networks are self-produced and self-sustainable.

For example, consider the development of open-source software, like the Linux operating system. Once the software core was "seeded" on the Internet, it started functioning as a catalyst for further programming action of many persons, who contributed their own ideas, efforts and improvements, sharing their work freely with one another. With no centralized meta-designer, Linux has emerged as a spontaneous joint creation of thousands of people, spawning a worldwide community of Linux providers and users.

Self-producing networks amount to communication and action-based *eco-societies* (or eco-communities), self-sustainable in their environment, coordinating their own action, creating their own language, making sense of their surroundings, interpreting signals and producing survival-enhancing decisions.

The process of self-production is called *autopoiesis*, contrasting with heteropoiesis (production of the "other"). Self-producing systems or networks are referred to as *autopoietic systems*. Autopoiesis or self-production can take place when there are autonomous individuals or agents interacting and communicating in a specific environment according to specific organizational *rules of conduct and interaction*. On a lower level, biological (living) systems are also similarly autopoietic, based on coordination and communication of their components.

3.3.2.1 Organization and Structure

Business "organization" has become a misnomer because it does not allow us to distinguish between the main network concepts of *organization* and *structure*. It is with labels like *network "organization"* where the inability to separate organization from structure becomes a self-inflicted wound of organizational theory. We shall use labels like *business corporation* and *social system* in order to move the organizational research into its network stage, past the habitual labels. *Business corporation* can now have *both* organization and structure.

Any dynamic system must be based on the notion of dynamics-generating process (or processes), not on the notion of function. Function is a purpose, goal or objective externally assigned by the observer, not internally constitutive of the system. A business system is defined by its key processes, or core competencies of production, service, transportation, transformation, communication, and so on. These processes require *coordinated action*, which are coordinated sequences of real (not merely represented) activities, operations, exchanges and transfers.

Coordination is traditionally carried out by command or instruction (go there, do this) and in the new economy *by rules* (if this, then do that), covenants and habits – all embedded in the requisite *language* of coordination. Processes are therefore not only coordinated but also concatenated into interrelated sequences and chains, forming complex and cross-dependent linkages of parallel and sequential processes – producing *networks of coordinated processes*.

The network of interrelated processes is driven and recursively coordinated by the rules of behavior, including response, cooperation, competition and communication. Order-commands leads to non-recursive, externally driven one-time actions (go there, do that), while rules assure internal replication and recurrence (if this, then do that).

3.3.2.2 Concepts and Definitions

Identical processes (networks of processes) can be coordinated by different rules (systems or networks of rules). It is the system of the rules of coordination, rather than the processes themselves, which define the nature of recurrent execution of coordinated action. Recurrence is the necessary condition for learning and knowledge production.

The network of rules of coordination is that what distinguishes and defines the *organization* of a business corporation or system. *Organization refers to the network of rules of coordination.*

Every object, every corporation and every system is organized and characterized by its organization. Because any organization, being a network of rules, drives and replicates system action, it is at the foundation of system dynamics, executing and replicating its action.

Structure is fundamentally different from the network of rules of coordination (organization). It refers to the spatio-temporal distribution of outcomes or products of the rule-coordinated processes. Structure is a specific manifestation of the underlying organization within the specific context and conditions under which the rules were applied. The same organization (rules of coordination) can be manifested in a number of different structures. The same structure could only by chance or serendipity emerge from different organizations. Organization gives rise to structure, as action gives rise to outcome. *Structure is a static "snapshot," spatio-temporal arrangement of components and outcomes*, a manifestation of the underlying recursively dynamic organization of processes and their rules of coordination.

Example. Consider an object; a chair for example. Its organization is a set of rules that make it distinguishable and recognizable as a chair and not a table or dresser. How do we recognize a chair? By its organization, from the way it is put together: the legs (or base), the seat and the back are related according to certain rules. The back is more or less perpendicular to the seat, no table has a back, but all chairs do. "Chairs" without backs are seaters or benches, not chairs. Organization allows us to recognize any chair as a member of the family or *identity class* of chairs. Structure here refers to a particular and specific manifested *form* of the underlying organization: material (wood, plastic, metal), curvature (linear, bent, ornate), padding (soft, hard, molded), incline (straight, reclining), etc. Structure allows us to recognize this particular chair, my chair, your chair, "Morris chair." While organization refers to the identity class of chairs, structure refers to a specific, particular member of that class. The same is true for trees, dogs, persons, societies and, of course, institutions and corporations.

The common notion of *function* is fundamentally different from both organization and structure: function is *imputed externally* by an observer, more or less autonomously. An observer can stand on a chair, sit on a table, kneel on a bench or sleep on a billiard table – there are no limits to function. A corporation can serve as a Laundromat for dirty money. *Function defines neither organization nor structure, nor is it defined or implied by them.*

Corporations are identified by their organization (network of rules of coordination) and differentiated by their structure (specific spatio-temporal manifestations of applying the rules under specific conditions or contexts). Every corporation has its organization *and* its structure. The two are not the same. These two concepts should not be confused or their distinction blurred if the study of corporations and other social institutions is to proceed and progress.

Why is the blurring or ambiguity of the two concepts inadmissible or even dangerous? In order to understand and study the dynamics of a system (corporation), one has to first understand and study its organization, not its structure. One has to study the cause, not the outcome. If one wants to change a system (or corporation), one has to first change its organization (rules of behavior), not its structure (the arrangement of components and outcomes).

Changes in organization lead to changes in structure, *but not vice versa*. Changes in structure do not lead to changes in organization. *Organization drives the structure, structure follows organization. The observer imputes function.* Confounding the three concepts of corporate organization, structure and function amounts to a self-imposed limitation. Organization, as a network of rules, if executed, leads to the recurrence and self-replication of the coordinated processes. In order to achieve recursive behavior, organization cannot be linear and open-ended, unidirectionally traversing from input to output, but must be "closed upon itself," i.e., *circular* and thus *organizationally closed*.

Organizational closure is a prerequisite for self-renewal, self-replication and recursive regeneration of the system. The coordination of processes in organizational closure assures that the same network of processes and their coordination rules is produced again. Thus, not any set of rules, but only a circularly "closed" set of rules brings forth the self-perpetuation and self-sustainability of a system. An *organizationally closed* system produces itself: it recursively recreates its own network or processes and rules of coordination that produced it. *An organizationally open* system is linear and unidirectional: it does not produce itself; it does not recreate the network of rules and processes that produced it. It "spends" itself in one direction and has to be repeatedly and externally triggered and re-triggered by either command or feedback. Without renewing the external trigger-input it would exhaust its potential and cease its activity or production.

Organizationally closed systems are self-renewing; organizationally open systems are self-limiting. Self-organizing and self-managing systems, like spontaneously emerging and self-renewing cooperative networks, must be *organizationally closed.*

3.3.2.3 Organizational Embedding

The requirement of *organizational closure* should not be confused with the simpler and mostly artificial notion of so called "closed" and "open" systems in traditional systems theory or theoretical physics. There are no environmentally "closed" systems. An organizationally closed system is not "closed to its environment," nor is it somehow insensitive or irresponsive to environmental signals and perturbations. Organizationally closed systems thrive on active, highly evolved and often intense environmental interactions. Rules-driven systems, lacking external command and information feedback, persist only through their effective adaptation to external perturbations.

Environmental perturbations, signals and triggers affect the structure of the system. System's organization, being closed in the sense of self-consistency, is not that easily perturbed. An autopoietic system is not only open to its environment (like through a specific feedback channel), but it is closely and intimately *coupled with its environment.* We can conclude that such a system is *structurally embedded* in its environment, while remaining organizationally autonomous and closed. Only organizational autonomy and stability, combined with structural adaptability and environmental coupling, can assure a system's persistence in a chaotic and inchoate environment.

Rose is a rose is a rose… a chair remains a chair, even when its structure is continually remade to fit the circumstances. A wolf remains a wolf even though it sheds and "remakes" its coat with changing seasons. Harvard remains Harvard and IBM remains (hopefully) IBM even if their components and structures are continually adapting to changing circumstances. *Self-renewing corporations are organizationally closed and structurally open.* A rabbit survives in a harshly changed environment not by ceasing being a rabbit (dissolving its organizational closure), but by changing and adapting its structure (coat, food, reflexes and preferences). A corporation survives through maintaining its organization (closure) while adapting its structure by coupling it better with its sustaining environment.

One should see, after some reflection, that it is the *organizationally open* (linear) systems (like hierarchies, command systems, input-output and information-feedback mechanisms) that are less responsive to their environment, structurally more rigid and thus less adaptable. It is the *organizationally closed* systems (self-renewing networks, markets, and spontaneous social orders) that are actually more "open" to their environment; they are only structurally embedded within it.

3.3.2.4 The Role of Feedback

We should digress on the role of feedback. Feedback is often considered to be a crucial link with the environment, assuring the "openness" of the system via (symbolic) information linkages.

Any system that is separated from its environment by non-permeable boundaries or information filters, can "read and calculate" its environment only through symbolic, interpretational *information feedback*. Such feedback often provides the only link or channel of communication with the environment. Without such a "channel" the system would become a "foreign body" within its own environment.

This is why hierarchical command systems – organizationally open and structurally closed – must be equipped with the infrastructure of channels that are redolent of feedback. Data collection, data interpretation, information gathering, questionnaires and polls, special information channels, special information processors, consumer research, promotion, calculations and modeling, are the main connections penetrating otherwise impermeable boundaries.

A strong presence, large variety and technological effectiveness of information feedback are the best evidence of system's relative "closure" and its essential separateness or "decoupling" from the environment.

Organizationally closed and structurally open systems do not depend on specific channel processing of symbolic information. Structurally embedded systems respond to *action itself* (to in-formation), not to a symbolic description of action (information).

Responding to action is a sign of structural coupling, while responding to the description of action is a sign of information feedback.

Organizationally closed systems respond to coordinated action and do that by structurally coupling themselves with their environment. Organizationally open systems can only respond to information (description of action) feedback *because* they are not structurally coupled with their environment, but are essentially separate from it.

Example. We can gather information – through feedback – about consumer preferences: flavor, container size, consistency, level of expected demand and shelf life of, say, yogurt. Then we respond to this environmental "signal" by producing the requisite containers, flavors, quantities, etc. Our level of separation from the environment remains high and essential. Or we can couple the system with the environment of its consumers, allowing the consumers to become part of the production process and allowing them to express their preferences directly through the action of choice. That would mean choosing the flavor, container size, quantity and consistency (of yogurt) directly, through completing the production process and not far from the point of consumption.

While such *mass customization* is based on action and structural coupling, traditional mass production is based on the description of action and information feedback, creating a separation from the environment. Traditional hierarchies of command are dependent on mass consumption and production, consumer research, forecasting and anonymous "shelf transaction." Self-renewing corporations and networks thrive on mass customization, "prosumerism," online responsiveness and fully individualized (non-anonymous) market transactions.

The structural coupling of corporations with their environment is an important concept, going way beyond traditional feedback. A structurally coupled corporation responds to action, not to descriptions or predictions.

3.3.2.5 Summary of Autopoiesis

Biologists Varela, Maturana, and Uribe have initially introduced the concept of autopoietic systems in biological systems. An autopoietic system has been defined as a system that is generated through a closed organization of production processes such that the same organization of processes is regenerated through the interactions of its own products (components), and a boundary emerges as a result of the same constitutive processes. An autopoietic organization is conceived as an autonomous unity of a network of productions of components participating recursively in forming the same network that produced them. These components form such a unitary network in the space of their existence.

Such an organization of components and component-producing processes remains relatively invariant through the interaction and turnover of components. The invariance follows from the definition: if the organization (the relations between system processes) changes substantially, there would be a change in the system's categorization of its identity class. What is changing is the system's *structure* (its particular manifestation in the given environment). The nature of the components and their spatiotemporal relations are secondary to their organization and thus refer only to the structure of the system.

The system's boundary is a structural manifestation of the system's underlying organization. The boundary is a structural realization of the system in a particular environment of components. In physical environments this could take the form of a topological boundary. Both organization and structure are mutually interdependent.

The concepts of the autopoietic nature of a system were developed in terms of a living (biological) system as a model of self-production. Yet self-production has the potential to mean and be interpreted through many different ways by a variety of observers. "Autopoiesis" has been coined (not translated from Greek) as a label for a clearly-defined interpretation of "self-production." This phenomenon of self-production can be observed in living systems. A cell, a system that renews its macromolecular components thousands of times during its lifetime, maintains its identity, cohesiveness, relative autonomy, and distinctiveness, despite such turnover of matter. This persisting unity and its holism are called "autopoiesis."

All autopoietic systems must be social systems. In other words, all autopoietic, and therefore all biological (living) systems, are also social systems. Also, the topological boundary, that has been necessary to describe an autopoietic system within a favorable environment of physical components (such as those within and around a cell), may not necessarily take a physical form in other types of systems, e.g., in social systems.

In social systems, dynamic networks of productions are being continually renewed without changing their organization, while their components are being replaced; the birth or entry of new members replaces perishing or exiting individuals. Individual experiences are also renewed; ideas, concepts and their labels evolve, and these, in turn, serve as the most important organizing factor in human societies. The organizing core for the implementation of ideas must be the emergent society as an autopoietic entity.

Autopoietic systems can persist in their autopoiesis for many decades (humans, trees), for many days (cells) or for mere flashes of hours, minutes, seconds, or milliseconds (osmotic growths). The "lifespan" of autopoiesis in no way enters (or should enter) into its definition. Autopoiesis is bound to exhibit gradation: it does not "jump" into being in a magic instant – it becomes. It also gradually degrades itself as the processes of autopoiesis weaken and dim more or less rapidly.

3.3.2.6 Autopoiesis and Knowledge

Structurally closed corporations are producing knowledge; structurally open corporations are producing data and information. The difference is fundamental. System organization is a circularly closed network of process-coordinating rules. Because system knowledge (and its linguistic embedding) is defined as a *purposeful coordination of action*, system organization is the source of production, renewal and depository of system knowledge.

While information, a description of action, is just input into organizationally open, linear input-output systems, knowledge is the *action itself*, coordinated by organizational rules.

Modern corporations also have to draw a clear distinction between action and its description, i.e., between knowledge and information.

Information is input, knowledge is the process itself. Knowledge producing systems are fundamentally different from data and information producing systems. The former are rules driven, organizationally closed and structurally open, the latter are the opposite: command driven, organizationally open and structurally closed.

In this sense, any corporation serves a twofold purpose: 1. To produce and consume something other than itself, i.e., output, product, service or information – through its *heteropoiesis*; and 2. To produce and consume itself, i.e., its own ability to coordinate action, in order to produce goods, services or information – through its *autopoiesis*. In order to produce something, a corporation has to first be able to *produce itself*, i.e., recreate and renew its own ability to produce, to coordinate its own action. Producing a product presents a different focus and different challenges than producing the knowledge necessary for producing that product.

Like with any living organism, in order to produce the "else" – product, replica, and copy – a corporation has to produce the "self," its main prerequisite for producing "the other." The self-production of a corporation, its ability to coordinate its actions, is autopoiesis. At certain stages, it is heteropoiesis that dominates business concerns: what, where, how much and when to produce. At other stages, it is autopoiesis that dominates the focus: how and why to produce *anything, anywhere, anytime*. Information is the input of heteropoiesis; knowledge is the stuff of autopoiesis. Autopoiesis is the prerequisite of heteropoiesis, not vice versa. The modern corporation (self-renewing network) produces knowledge first and its product second. The traditional hierarchy produces the product first and the knowledge-production is left to spontaneous forces, not explicitly managed and not even viewed as a main competitive advantage.

At the beginning of the third millennium, the world has changed fundamentally. It has moved from information to knowledge, from organizational openness to organizational closure, from feedback to structural coupling, from hierarchy to network, from commands to rules, and from heteropoiesis to autopoiesis. Business and economic systems are no longer viewed as machines and contrivances (products of heteropoiesis) but as organisms and ecologies of organisms (products of autopoiesis).

3.3.3 The Model of Autopoiesis

Autopoietic organization is defined as a network of interactions and processes, involving at least the processes of:

1) *Production (poiesis)*: the rules and regulations governing the entry of new components, such as emergence, input, birth, membership, acceptance.
2) *Bonding (linkage)*: the rules governing associations, arrangements, manufactures, functions and positions of components during their tenure within the organization.
3) *Degradation (replenishment)*: the rules and processes associated with the exit or termination of membership like death, separation, consumption, output and expulsion.

In Figure 3.5, the three poietic processes are interconnected into a *cycle of self-production*. Observe that all such circularly concatenated processes represent productions of components necessary for the subsequent processes, not only the one labeled as "production." Although in reality hundreds of processes could be so interconnected, the above three-process model represents the minimum conditions necessary for autopoiesis to emerge.

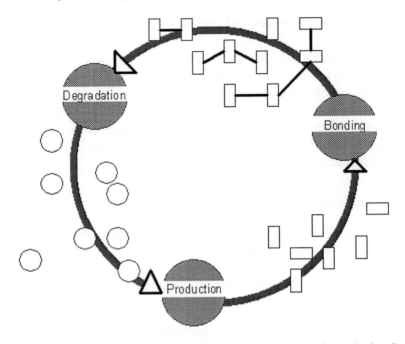

Figure 3.5 Circular organization of interdependent processes and their "productions."

An organization becomes autopoietic if *all three* types of constitutive processes are well *balanced* and function *in harmony*. If one of the three processes is missing, or if one or two types predominate (out-of-balance system), the organization can either be heteropoietic or allopoietic, i.e., capable of producing only "the other" rather than "itself." For example, production and bonding without requisite degradation would quickly deplete the environmental substrate and come to a developmental halt, like crystals and crystallization. Production and degradation without effective bonding would lead to ephemeral and oscillatory systems, and so on.

Any self-sustaining system will have the processes of production, bonding and degradation concatenated in a balanced and harmonious way, so that the production rate does not significantly exceed the replenishment rate, and vice versa. *Self-sustaining systems will be autopoietic in an environment of shared or common resources.*

3.3.3.1 Sustainability and Self-Sustainability

Any self-sustainable system must secure, enhance and preserve communication (and thus coordinated action) among its components or agents as well as their own coordination and self-coordination competencies. Systems with limited or curtailed communication can be sustained and coordinated only through external commands or feedback; they are not self-sustaining. *Hierarchies of command are sustainable but not self-sustaining.*

Consensual (unforced) and purposeful (goal-directed) coordination of action is knowledge. Self-sustaining systems must be organized so as to continually "produce themselves": their own capability of their own action coordination. Even though we often talk about sustainable systems, it is the *self-sustainability* of systems that is of real interest. The question is not how can *we* sustain a given system, but how can a system sustain *itself* in a given milieu?

Sustainability and self-sustainability are directly related to system organization and its self-production (autopoiesis). How systems are organized is much more important than how a system's individual agents think or what values they uphold. *Self-sustainable* systems are autopoietic and must therefore be organized for autopoiesis. Merely *sustainable* systems are heteropoietic because their sustainability does not come from within (from their own organization) but from the outside: from planned, system-sustaining activities of external agents. *Non-sustainable* systems are allopoietic, i.e., they are organized to produce things other than themselves. Allopoietic systems necessarily deplete their environment.

Heteropoietic systems can be sustainable as long as external agents sustain their system-sustaining efforts. Only autopoietic systems replenish their own environment and thus can become self-sustaining. Self-sustainable systems must maintain their ability to coordinate their own actions – producing *knowledge.* Self-sustaining systems must be knowledge producing, not only labor or capital consuming entities.

In summary, the presented view of sustainability can be characterized as follows: both sustainability and self-sustainability are time and context dependent system properties emerging from system organization. System organization must be continually produced or renewed via operating a common, shared resource system, optimally managed through the competition and collaboration of agents.

Continued functioning of the organization requires continued coordination of action, i.e., continued production of knowledge. Most systems can be sustained over long periods of time through an external supporting agent that disburses ideas, efforts, money or resources. Once this external agent withdraws its support, a system's sustainability can be directly challenged. *Externally sustainable systems do not have to be internally self-sustainable.* Any relationship External agent → Sustainable system can be transformed into a *self-sustainable metasystem* [External agent ↔ System]. While an external agent can in principle make any system sustainable, only an integrated agent-system can become self-sustainable: through making the external agent an internal part of the system.

3.3.4 Regional Enterprise Networks

Regional enterprise networks (REN) of small and medium businesses must be self-sustainable in their own environment. Increasingly, modern electronic networks enable small businesses to tap into the global reservoirs of information, expertise, and financing that used to be available only to large companies. Even individual agents become empowered through this process, and gain significant autonomy that enables them to participate in the autopoiesis of temporary corporations.

Free markets connect business agents into networks quite spontaneously, based on trade and other exchanges of mutual interest. In these tacit networks, firms remain interconnected on the basis of short-term collaboration in order to execute transactions, recurrently establishing, canceling and re-establishing their multidirectional relationships. Such networks are dynamic, reshaped and reformed according to changing contexts, interests and conditions.

The industrial districts (ID) of Italy are local hyper networks based on autopoiesis and innovation. A good example is the Prato region. In the 1970s, a failing textile mill was broken into eight separate companies and a major portion of the equity was sold to key employees. This was the seed, which had catalytic properties: by 1990, more than 15,000 small textile firms (averaging less than 5 employees) were active in the region. Textile production has tripled while the textile industry has declined in the rest of Europe.

What is at the core of ID success? The answer appears to lie in the mastering and controlling of the entire customer-supplier value chain, that is, the entire production process. The ID small businesses are not just separately scattered competing units, nor are they simple appendices to large companies or conglomerates. Instead, they respond to customer markets directly, through activating linkages most suitable for specific customization. They emerge, persist and disintegrate according to alternative manifestations of the customer-supplier value chain.

In Figure 3.6, the chain (or network) of small businesses covering the defining (initial) value chain is sketched. As the alternative chains develop (in response to new customers, technologies or products/services), like chains I and II in Figure 3.6, the original businesses lose the competency to "cover" all activities of such newly concatenated process sequences. A space for new businesses or business expansions has opened and is flexibly filled. Some original companies, unable to adapt, may go out of business, their knowledge agents reabsorbed into newly emerging units. As long as the ID responds and "covers" the ever-changing chains, the network remains self-organizing (autopoietic) and self-sustaining.

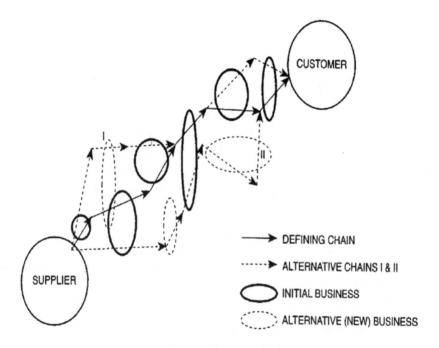

Figure 3.6 Industrial district formation along the value chain.

It is the chain, or process-induced productive synergy, which distinguishes ID from a simple collection of scattered, independent businesses.

There are many types of network organizations, driven by different goals and purposes. Some of them are simple tax/financial alliances, while others aim at sharing or controlling the market. There are networks that are "covering" the entire value chain and are flexible and adaptive enough to maintain and expand their "coverage" through the dynamic reshaping of their own linkages – such networks survive and prosper.

Autopoietic industrial districts have to adapt to the global environment and adopt the ways of strategic mass customization, knowledge production and development of intracompany markets. Mass customization will allow them to reach new and changing customers on a global scale, knowledge production assures innovation, sharing and propagation of knowledge along the chain or network, and intracompany markets make these businesses flexible, efficient and highly productive. Whatever socio-institutional arrangements can bring forth and strengthen these three basic requisite competencies will stay at the core of ID future success.

3.3.5 TCG Triangulation Networks

Australian TCG (Technical Computer Graphics) provides a good example of a self-producing network in a business-firm environment. There are no coordinating divisions, "leading firms," or management superstructures coordinating or "managing" TCG's twenty four companies; the coherence, growth and maintenance of the network is produced, according to J. Mathews, by a set of *network-producing rules*:

1. Mutual independence, binding firms through bilateral commercial contracts. This prevents the formation of an internal hierarchy.
2. Mutual preference among member firms in the tendering and letting of contracts.
3. Mutual non-competition among members, in order to establish requisite levels of self-denial and trust.
4. Mutual non-exploitation among members, based on "cost-plus" contracting, not on profit maximization.
5. Flexibility and business autonomy: no need for group approval of any transaction – if no rules are broken.
6. Network democracy without a holding company, "central committee," major owner, controller or formal governance structure.
7. Non-observance of rules leads to expulsion.
8. All members have equal access to the open market.

9. Entry: new members welcome, but financed by debt, not through drawing on existing group resources.
10. Exit: no impediments to departing firms.

The above ten rules constitute the corporate covenant and autopoietic organization of the TCG network. They insure that the network continually produces itself and maintains its coherence over time. There has never been a bankruptcy within the TCG network. In a changing environment, the TCG network grows outwards and adapts to a global market place through a "triangulation process" of collaborative alliances and through spinning-off new companies. A triangle is a strategic alliance of <TCG + external company + customer>. The bonding and concatenation of "triangles" expands the network.

3.3.6 Eco-Societies and Social Autopoiesis

"One could say that the expulsion of the biological and natural ecological determinants of human existence has been one of striking features of sociological studies since the 1930s."

Edward Shils, 1985
The Calling of Sociology

Global awareness is increasingly being translated into ecological awareness. Human systems are coexistent with their environment and the ecological awareness is naturally higher then that of the traditional hierarchies and their environmental exploitation.

By ecological awareness we mean responsibility to social, biological and physical environments of human systems. All three environments are interrelated and cannot be approached separately – disconnected from human knowledge and human systems.

So, we speak of *eco-societies*.

Economics, management, sociology and business itself cannot successfully transfer into the global era without making the environment their primary concern. Human systems are organisms and not machines.

Machines do not adapt to their environments, organisms do.

Again, rather than the physics and engineering of the past, we draw on biological knowledge and wisdom in constructing our conceptual understandings, necessary for effective action.

Society, according to Shils is the whole of interdependent parts, each of which is the "environment" for all the others. This *holistic view*, recognizing the whole as a unity of parts that affects the interactions of its parts. Holistic does not coincide with the popular "wholistic" and does not come from "holy." J. Ch. Smuts' holism, as the opposite or complement of reductionism or atomism, is based on the essential circularity of autopoietic systems: a whole is a unity of parts that affects the interactions of those parts. There can be no parts apart from the whole, and the whole cannot be contemplated apart from its parts: the whole is the parts.

We attempt to show that (1) many important social systems are self-producing (autopoietic), rather than purposefully "engineered" or constructed (heteropoietic), and (2) all self-producing (autopoietic) systems, including biologically living systems, must also be social systems.

3.3.6.1 Individuals in Networks

"Cells move, die, divide, release inductive signals or morphogens, link to form new sheets, and repeat variants of the process. Genes control the whole business indirectly by governing which morphoregulatory or homeotic product will be expressed."

Gerald E. Edelman,
Bright Air, Brilliant Fire

Since Huxley's *The Individual in the Animal Kingdom*, the idea of individuality has continued to present fundamental difficulties in biology. Is a colony of "white ants" an individual? Huxley proposed that: "Wherever a recurring cycle exists (and that is in every form of life) there must be a kind of individuality consisting of diverse but mutually helpful parts succeeding each other in time, as opposed to the kind of individuality whose parts are all co-existent."

It is the individuality of a cyclically recurring network of "ordinary" individuals, that is crucial for an enhanced understanding of self-sustaining social systems or networks.

Individuals are substantially defined by networks in which they are embedded. Also corporations can only be as good as the networks they are parts of. This is not true of only human systems. Every organism, even if spatially and temporarily isolated, can emerge, survive, and reproduce only as part of a larger *social network of organisms*. Similarly, each cell, organelle, or neuron can exist only as part of a group or society of cells, organelles, or neurons. Each component of an autopoietic system can emerge, persist, and reproduce only within the complex of relationships that constitute the network of interconnected components and component-producing processes.

Survival activities (economic and ecological) of separate organisms directly form and reform their local societies of interactive populations, which are further concatenated into regional networks and then into *full ecosystems*.

This type of "Gaia hypothesis" is not new in the history of science; A.A. Bogdanov formulated it quite clearly:

"The entire realm of life on earth can be considered as a single system of divergence, based on the rotation of carbon dioxide. This rotation forms a basis for complementary correlations between life as a whole – the 'biosphere' – and the gaseous cover of the Earth – the 'atmosphere.' The stability of atmospheric content is sustained in the biosphere, which draws from the atmosphere the material for assimilation."

Bogdanov, the father of Tectology (the precursor of modern autopoiesis), has thus conceptually coupled the biosphere, atmosphere, hydrosphere, and lithosphere into a single holistic system of mutually co-evolving coherences. We shall review historically more interesting precepts of Tectology in the later section.

3.3.6.2 Social Self-Organization

"If Nature possesses a universal psyche, it is one far above the common and most impelling feelings of the human psyche. She certainly has never wept in sympathy, nor stretched a hand protectively over even the most beautiful or innocent of her creatures."

Eugäne Marais,
The Soul of the White Ant

"Have you ever seen, in some wood, on a sunny quiet day, a cloud of flying midges – thousands of them – hovering, apparently motionless, in a sunbeam? ... Yes? ... Well, did you ever see the whole flight – each mite apparently preserving its distance from all others – suddenly move, say three feet, to one side or the other? Well, what made them do that? A breeze? I said a quiet day. But try to recall – did you ever see them move directly back in the same unison? Well, what

made them do that? Great human mass movements are slower of inception but much more effective."

Bernard M. Baruch,
Foreword to Mackay's Extraordinary Popular Delusions

It is time to define social systems and to elucidate the meaning of "social" for the purposes of eco-societies.

Social systems are renewable, self-producing networks characterized by internal (rather than external) coordination of individual action achieved through communication among temporary agents. The key words are coordination, communication, and limited lifespan of the agents.

It should be self-evident that the general notions of coordination, communication and individual lifespan acquire different meanings in different contextual embeddings.

Coordinated behavior includes both cooperation and competition (and all forms of conflict), in all their shades and degrees. Actions of predation, altruism, and self-interest are simple examples of different and interdependent modes of coordination. Communication could be physically, chemically, visually, linguistically, or symbolically induced deformation (or in-formation) of the environment and consequently of individual action taking place in that same environment.

I, as an individual, can coordinate my own actions in the environment only if I coordinate them with the actions of other participants in the network. So, I have to in-form (deform or change) the environment so that the actions of others are suitably modified: I have to communicate. As all other individuals are attempting to do the same, a social network of coordination emerges, and, if successful, it is being "selected" and persists. Such a network improves my ability to coordinate my own actions within the environment effectively. Cooperation, competition, altruism, and self-interest are therefore inseparable.

Social systems are not limited to human systems, especially when addressing the issues of ecological self-sustainability. Human systems simply in-form a special meaning in the universal acts of coordination, communication, and the birth-death processes in social systems.

For example, a group of fish thrown together by a tidal wave is a passive aggregation, *not* a social system. A swarm of moths lured to a porch light is an active aggregation, *not* a social system. A flag-pattern of athletes constructed through bullhorn-shouted commands from a coordination center is a purposeful heteropoietic aggregation, *not* a social system.

All of these can transform into social systems as soon as *internal* communication patterns become established; such patterns should temporarily persist (become autonomous), even after removing the external impetus.

The mere externally induced interaction of components does not suffice; billiard balls interact and so do wind-blown grains of sand – nobody would call them social systems.

Human waiting queues are often engineered and externally induced (enforced, not voluntary) interactions. To a large degree however, they do exhibit, at least temporarily, the voluntary self-organization characterized by its own specific behaviors, rules of conduct, choice of distance and modes of communication.

Similarly, schools of fish, swarms of bees, flocks of birds, packs of animals, and even the spontaneous wave-patterns of Olympic-games spectators are, however, no matter how ephemerally fleeting, social systems.

Any social system, in order to adapt and persist in its environment, must be capable of reshaping itself, controlling its growth, and checking the proliferation of individuals. In other words, the long-term persistence of a social system is critically dependent on precariously balanced birth and death processes. There can be no collective life without individual death.

A proliferation of individuals without balancing death processes and without death-inducing communication is "cancer" – a short-lived, environmentally destructive, unconstrained outburst of life-like processes. A dominant death process, without sufficient birth-process complements, takes any social system towards its decadence, demise and extinction.

Life of a social system, and thus life itself, is based on a dynamic and autopoietic equilibrium between birth and death processes. Life is therefore a social phenomenon: life of an individual cannot take place outside a social network, and the individual life itself must be socially embodied at the level of its components.

No communication and no death imply no life.

3.3.6.3 Detection of Autopoiesis

How can we detect autopoiesis in biological, chemical and social systems?

We refer the reader to Zeleny and Hufford's (1992) detailed analysis of 1. Biological (living) systems, 2. Chemical systems and 3. Spontaneous social systems. Here we present their conclusions:

1. The Eukaryotic Cell.

The generalized non-plant eukaryotic cell may be described as having a plasma membrane which surrounds the cytoplasm and cytoplasmic components of the cell. The cytoplasm contains the nucleus, mitochondria, Golgi apparatus, endoplasmic reticulum, various vesicles, lysosomes, vacuoles, cytoplasmic filaments and microtubules, centrioles, and other components of the cell. After applying the principles of autopoiesis to the generalized eukaryotic cell, it can be concluded that the cell forms an autopoietic unity in the space of its components.

Lynn Margulis is one of the few biologists who viewed eukaryotic cells as autopoietic populations of components. "We are walking communities," she insisted (Mann, 1991).

2. Osmotic Growth.

Stephane Leduc (1911) described an "osmotic growth," a membrane of precipitated inorganic salt, as having many processes, functions, and characteristic forms that appear to be analogous to those found in living systems.

Unlike typical experiments in simple precipitation, where two solutions are mixed and a cloudy solution of insoluble salt results, osmotic growths precipitate and grow over a period of minutes to days and go from a thin transparent membranous state to an opaque state. Actual photographic sequences can be found in Zeleny, Klir, and Hufford (1989).

After applying the principles of autopoiesis to the evaluation of osmotic growths (specifically the calcium chloride/tribasic sodium phosphate system), it can be concluded that an osmotic growth forms an autopoietic unity in the space of its components.

At the macroscopic level, the osmotic precipitation membrane exhibits fluidity, elasticity, and resealability identical to the properties of the plasma membrane. As the internal osmotic pressure increases, an expansion occurs (not a rupture) allowing components from the internal and external spaces to flow through the membrane and "couple" within the membrane. The osmotic growth phenomenon occurs because the operational integrity of the precipitation membrane is maintained.

Osmotic growths are, temporarily or even fleetingly, autopoietic. This implies that if we hold the current autopoietic theory to be correct and intact, then we must reassess our definition (redefine our criteria) of what it means to be "living." Life could be a specific form of organization of matter, rather than the specific matter so organized.

3. Kinship System.

As our third system, the kinship system is an example of a spontaneous social order that has a substantial impact and great significance in the life of social, economic, and political networks. A kinship system constitutes, prototypically, an autopoietic system that is produced and maintained through organizational rules (which are potentially codified) of a given society. No matter what the particular mix of its components (men, women, and children), the kinship system organizes its social domain and coordinates its social action in a spontaneous, self-perpetuating fashion. It must continually adapt to the external challenges and interferences of the society, social engineers and reformers.

Social networks, embodying kinship systems, are not static and unchanging structures, but highly dynamic ones. Cochran et. al. (1990), in their study of kinship systems, established that the distribution of different types and roles of network participants (kin, friends, neighbors, formal ties) remains relatively stable, even though the names and faces of network members keep changing. In the language of autopoiesis: It is their organization that remains stable, while their structures and components continually change.

Social networks can therefore change in their structure or in the nature of their component relationships (organization). One can therefore study shifts in the network's structure, turnover among its members, and changes in the character of continuing network ties. For example, in spite of frequent movements and changes of neighborhoods, American white children maintain the largest stable social networks (8 adults, 8 peers) while relatively immobile Swedish children maintained the smallest (4 adults, 4 peers).

Viewing families and kinship networks properly as autopoietic systems could lead to a new and important understanding of the effects of residential mobility, divorce rates, death and disease disruptions, loss of employment, or state intervention on the structure, organization and durability of social bonds in important social and support networks – primary, functional, peripheral and formal.

Through social autopoiesis, one also can learn more about which social environments produce desirable social supports in transaction with parents. What is the role of friends and relatives? What is the role of parental self-confidence, and how can it be enhanced? What is the role of a parent's level of formal education? How do intervention programs interact with the spontaneous self-organizational nature of social autopoiesis? The research agenda of self-producing social systems is remarkable in its challenge and significance.

It was the economist, F.A. Hayek (1975), who integrated the concepts of self-production directly into the domain of social systems:

"Although the overall order of actions arises in appropriate circumstances as the joint product of the actions of many individuals who are governed by certain rules, the production of the overall order is of course not the conscious aim of individual action since the individual will not have any knowledge of the overall order, so that it will not be an awareness of what is needed to preserve or restore the overall order in a particular moment, but an abstract rule which will guide the actions of the individual."

Consequently, the individuals in a society spontaneously assume the sort of conduct and evolve the rules that assure their continued existence within the whole. Of course, the conduct and rules must also be compatible with the preservation of the whole. Neither the society nor the individuals could exist if they did not behave in this manner. The overall order, preservation of the society, is not the "purpose" or the "plan" of the individuals. The individual actions are motivated by their own goals and purposes.

3.3.6.4 Boundaries of Social Systems

In kinship systems, boundaries are usually well defined. The distinction between family and non-family members is rarely ambiguous or subject to fuzzy interpretation. A definite family boundary can be established, although it is not necessarily topological. In the context of the family, the concept of boundary might be defined as the members included in a set. Family members are usually distinguished from their environment (from the "society") more sharply than any engineered or designed physical "membrane" can assure.

All social systems, and thus all living systems, create, maintain, and degrade their own boundaries. These boundaries do not separate but intimately connect the system with its environment. Even food moving through the mouth and the tube-like digestive tract is not necessarily "inside" the body, but remains "outside," in the "captured" or "enveloped" environment of the body torus. The same holds true for all other "boundary" organs; there is no inside or outside, and the boundary does not separate anything, except in the human observer's mind.

Boundaries do not have to be just physical or topological, but are primarily functional, behavioral, and communicational. They are not "perimeters," but functional constitutive components of a given system.

Boundaries do not exist just for a human observer to see or identify the system, but exist for the system and its components to interact and communicate with its environment. Take so called "giant organisms," like the Northern-Michigan creeping mega-fungus (30 acres, 100 tons) or the Utah Wasatch Mountains stand of some 47,000 quaking aspen trees (106 acres, 6,000 tons) "marching" harmoniously over the mountainscape. Humans can hardly see the "whole thing," identify its boundaries or "prove" its intactness.

Boundaries range from phospholipid bilayers, globular proteins, osmotic precipitates, and electric potentials, through cell layers, tissues, skins, metabolic barriers, and peripheral neural synapses, to laterally or upwardly dispersed boundaries of territorial markers, lines of scrimmage, social castes, secret initiation rites, and possessions of information, power, or money.

A company can have a number of geographically separate offices or be a virtual company, entirely "in the air" of electronic communication. The U.S.A. includes Alaska and Hawaii. A doctor does not leave the social system of a hospital while "on call" or connected with a beeper.

Although social systems are necessarily physical because their components realize their dynamic network of productions in the physical domain (their components are cells, termites, lions, adult humans, etc.), many computer simulations of autopoietic systems show that topological boundaries arise only if very minute rates of production processes are finely adjusted and balanced.

3.3.6.5 All Autopoietic Systems are Social Systems

Autopoiesis can take place only where there are separate and autonomously individual components interacting and communicating in a specific environment according to specific behavioral (including birth and death) rules of interaction.

Approaches which sacrifice this essential individuality of components, like the statistical systems of differential equations used in the traditional systems sciences, cannot model autopoiesis. They are definitionally incapable of treating autopoietic systems as social systems. Components and participants in autopoiesis must follow rules, interact, and communicate – they must form a community of components, a society: a social system.

F.A. Hayek pointed out that social engineers assume that since people have been able to generate some systems of rules coordinating their efforts, they must also be able to design an even better and "improved" system. The traditional norms or reasons guiding the imposition and subsequent restructuring of socialism embody a naive and uncritical theory of rationality, traced to Karl Marx's concept of social labor.

The removal of external pressures, support or props is one of the safest tests of the viability (i.e., autopoiesis) in *social* systems. If the coercive boundaries (physical or otherwise) are dissolved – and consequently the social system ceases to exist – then it was not autopoietic; if it reconstitutes its social boundary and spontaneously increases the level of cohesion, then it is autopoietic and self-sustaining.

It is only in the sense of such centrally-imposed "command" systems that we present our conjecture: *All autopoietic (biological) systems are social systems.*

We can restate autopoietic social organization as a network of interactions, reactions, and processes involving at least:

1) Production (poiesis): the rules and regulations guiding the entry of new living components (such as emergence, birth, membership, acceptance).
2) Bonding (linkage): the rules guiding associations, functions, and positions of individuals during their tenure within the organization.
3) Degradation (disintegration): the rules and processes associated with the termination of membership (death, separation, expulsion).

3.3.6.6 Biological Organisms are Social Systems

"The body of a mammal with its many vital organs can be looked upon as a community with specialized individuals grouped into organs, the whole community forming the composite animal."

Eugäne Marais,
The Soul of the White Ant

Although our purpose is not to analyze biotic systems in specialist's detail, let us explore the cellular organism and the human organism as social systems.

Biological organisms are not components-free black boxes but communicating, birth-death process balancing social systems. There is even the "competition" of cells and the selection and survival of the most "fit" during their embryonic development, dependent on the cell's rates of enzyme secretion, rates of cell proliferation, etc. There are communication, social neighborhoods, and birth-death processes taking place in cellular organisms.

3.3.6.7 Communication

Whenever a living cell is unable to communicate with other cells, it does not die, but rather grows uncontrollably, multiplying into other non-communicating cells, forming a malignant tumor which is unable to survive in its life-sustaining environment because it destroys it.

All organismic cells are interconnected through tiny channels in cell membranes or gap junctions. Through these channels, all molecular, chemical, metabolic, and electric communication among cells takes place. These communicative junctions are made of proteins (connexins) that align all cells into one continuous channel-network: a social system.

Malfunction in intercellular communication channels affects the intercellular social system and thus could "kill" the organism itself. If regulatory and inhibitory signals do not get through, the uncontrolled, deathless growth, and the voracious feeding on its own environment, would result.

To study cancer processes without studying cellular gap junctions could be ineffective. Clogged channels block social-regulatory signals and allow cells to go awry; clear channels allow the propagation of deadly signals. Gap junctions themselves are selective and self-regulatory; they tend to close and protect against chaotic signals and to open for and receive regulatory signals.

In order to treat cancers, one has to either re-establish communication channels and thus self-regulation, or block the growth of communication and support channels (like blood capillaries) in order to stop rampant proliferation. This is not a trivial mechanistic task; it can be mastered if we view biological systems as social systems.

3.3.6.8 Social Neighborhoods

Cellular neighborhoods, not only inheritable genetic "programs," are the main determinants of cells' functions.

Sociologically, autopoietic systems are better illustrated by the American plan of development, where one's status and fate are determined by one's neighborhood (location, location, location), rather than by the British plan, where one's status and fate are determined by one's ancestors.

The neural network especially, i.e., autonomous autopoietic system embedded in a larger complex of organismic networks, requires quick-response, flexibility and adaptability which cannot wait for a mutations buildup or rely on requisite but cumbersome "genetic alterations." Neural networks develop as autopoietic societies; individual cells wander around, get exposed to differential signaling of different cellular neighborhoods, and ultimately settle down (or get captured) within these neighborhoods, becoming functioning neurons of the visual, hearing, or smell regions of the cerebral cortex.

In cells, there is no master plan and there are no black-box feedback loops within feedback loops. There is only a society in autopoiesis, organizing matter of different structural attributes and properties (including viral DNA), thus arriving at different, sometimes important, structural manifestations. The mother cells do not impart specific information to their daughters about what to become.

3.3.6.9 Birth-Death Processes

In addition to communication and neighborhood influences, social systems are also characterized by a limited lifespan of individual agents-components, i.e., by death. If molecules would not break down, or cells, organisms, individuals and entire species would not die, there could be no social systems and thus no self-sustaining life on Earth.

Death dominates development. The vestigial webbing between human fetus fingers must be dissolved before birth. About eighty percent of the nerve cells of the baby's brain must perish within hours of their creation. A caterpillar's crawling muscles must be sloughed off in order to have a butterfly; female genitalia must be whittled away in order to have a male.

It is the uncontrolled and massive death of cells that is non-redeeming: Alzheimer's, Parkinson's, and Lou Gehrig's degenerative disorders result. Uncontrolled and massive birth is equally unredeeming: cancerous cell masses, killing their own environment (i.e., host organism) result. But individuals must die in order to help maintain their own social system.

Organic death is not a chaotic, haphazard, or disorganized part of social system autopoiesis; it is a harmonized, choreographed, and often suicidal dance of most exquisite complexity.

The emergence of autopoiesis is therefore inconceivable without the subsequent trimmings of apoptosis (meaning "falling from the trees"). The study of apoptosis is crucial in biology: in fact, no true biology can exist without it.

Death is not the absence of life, but a crucial building block of life. Life is never just an "individual" life, but a life of the social network that produced and sustained it. Life is a network of balanced, interrelated and communicating birth-death processes, extending beyond an individual's horizons and across generations.

This majestic view of an eternally self-renewing life has been best captured by Trygve Gulbranssen in his two novels – *Og bakom synger skogene* (*Beyond Sing the Woods*) and *Det blåser fra Dauingfjell* (*The Wind from the Mountains*).

Another good example is the immune system. Millions of T and B cells are continually generated, each capable of assaulting foreign proteins, but unfortunately also the body's own proteins. Up to 98 percent of them have to undergo immediate apoptosis in order to maintain the body's autopoiesis in a hostile environment.

Death is a productive process of the social system; it creates space, it generates production substrate, it brings in the innovation, and it allows trial-and-error adaptation to the environment. Individual cells are created in order to die, and thus their social system, i.e. living organism, can persist.

3.3.6.10 Evolution

"The idea that reason, itself created by the course of evolution, should now be in a position to determine its own future evolution is inherently contradictory, and can readily be refuted."

F.A. Hayek,
The Fatal Conceit

Social systems persist. They can persist or be conserved as societies of agents only if their individual agents are born, communicate, and die in equilibrium with themselves and their environment. Because of the turnover of their components, the social networks not only persist and are renewed, but they also evolve.

The unit of evolution (at any level) must therefore be *a network* capable of a variety of self-organizing configurations. It is the entire social network, including a neuronal group, that is being "selected," not its individual components. Such evolving networks are interwoven and co-evolving with their environment; they do not only adapt to the environment, but also adapt the environment to themselves – through mutually intimate structural coupling.

A bird must undoubtedly adapt to a mountain. However, a society (network) of birds can make the mountain adapt to them. For example, by over consuming a particular berry, the new brush growth is controlled, the mountain's erosion enhanced, and the production of both berries and birds constrained until a temporary balance is again restored. Colors of flowers have coevolved with the trichromatic vision of bees; shapes of flowers with the structural traits of insects and animals; modern breeders with the changing tastes and preferences of man.

The environment is not a structure imposed on living beings from the outside by "Nature," but is in fact a creation of those beings. The environment is not an autonomous process, but a reflection of the biology of the species. Just as there is no organism without an environment, there is no environment without an organism.

Such a co-creation view echoes Ortega y Gasset's powerful philosophy of "I am myself and my circumstance," or Varela's equally powerful "The world is not a landing pad into which organisms parachute; nature and nurture stand in relation to each other as product and process."

In this view of evolution of social networks there can be no intelligent distinction between inherited and acquired characteristics. What evolves is neither genetically encoded nor environmentally acquired, but is *ecologically embedded in a social network.*

There is no one fixed or pre-given world (a universe), nor is its dynamics simply observed or viewed differentially from a variety of vantage points (a multi-verse), but this world itself is continually re-shaped, and re-created by coevolving social networks of organisms.

3.3.6.11 Closure

"When I began my work I felt that I was nearly alone in working on the evolutionary formation of such highly complex self-maintaining orders. Meanwhile, researches on this kind of problem – under various names, such as autopoiesis, cybernetics, homeostasis, spontaneous order, self-organization, synergetics, systems theory, and so on – have become so numerous..."

F.A. Hayek,
The Fatal Conceit

One of the pioneering proponents of social self-production was F.A. Hayek. Only just before his death he came to realize that he was not nearly alone, that he was a part of transgenerational network, and that he sowed the seeds which are bound to lead – in the right season – to a rich harvest. This entire section was written in the memory of my honored teacher from Freiburg.

In terms of closure, let us reassert that all living systems, i.e., cells, organisms, groups, and species are social systems. Their interaction forms the entire terrestrial biosphere (or Gaia): a social system akin to the unified organism of a living cell, which itself is a social system of its constitutive organelles.

Connecting different species into a coherent, interactive, and self-organizing system cannot happen without death and dying – the fuel of environmental adaptation. The natural death of species does not signal the maladaptability of the species, but harmony, adaptability, and systemic perseverance of the social network of species. Death is a cosmological event – the most exquisite assurance of life yet to come. At one point, individuals of all species receive, by waves on the shore, sound of the wind, or with radio telescopes, that exquisite, life sustaining message. Like my friend Gordon Pask did when observing the Bay of Naples: "Now. Now it would be indecent not to die."

The connexins of cells, dances of bees, odors of fire ants, allochemicals of Douglas firs, and the language of humans are only the hints, only the shy peepholes into the veiled mysteries of life – and the promises of sciences yet to come.

3.3.7 Tectology and its Basic Concepts

A.A. Malinovskii (1873-1928), also known as Alexander Bogdanov, was the father of the *general theory of organizations* (Tectology: the universal organizational science). Tectology is the study of universal laws that govern the organization of all systems: a *general systems theory*.

The name tectology (after E. Haeckel) derives from the Greek *tekton* (builder): tekton + logos implies "the science of building," where "building" is interpreted broadly in the sense of organizing and organization.

In Bogdanov's view, a living organization was a special kind of "machine," which not only regulated and repaired itself (feedback cybernetics), but most importantly: it produced itself (autopoiesis). Bogdanov introduced the concept of *regulator* (modern feedback), as a device through which a process is maintained at a certain level (e.g., flywheel). He went significantly further with his concept of *biregulator:* two systems mutually regulating one another without an external regulator (or controller): they mutually regulate themselves. These two reciprocal aspects form a single *system of equilibria.*

It is essential to understand that a thermostat does not only regulate the temperature, but that temperature also regulates the thermostat – in a mutually affective, circular and non-hierarchical fashion. That is the premise Bogdanov had started from. Bogdanov's system (or complex) is not simply a collection of components and their relationships. His complex is a *process,* or a continuous flow of independent component-producing processes, concatenated in self-triggering circles of build-up and degradation.

3.3.7.1 Complexes: Formative Mechanisms

Three types of dynamic complexes were recognized: *organized, disorganized* and *neutral.*

Structural couplings between complexes and *their* (requisite) environments require formative and regulatory mechanisms to govern their production, build-up, maintenance, expansion, decline and degradation. Basic *formative* tectological mechanisms are: *conjunction* (or *conjugation), ingression, linkage, disingression, tectological boundary* and *conjunctive* and *disjunctive crises.*

Conjunction triggers the changes in organizational nets through forming linkages of common processes. These linkages are brought forth by mutual ingression (structural couplings) of elements. The nature of these linkages depends on the *plasticity* of conjugated complexes.

Negative ingression or *disingression* represents a breakdown in the linkage of a complex and a creation (or re-creation) of a new tectological boundary. Only through disingression can a complex remain structurally coupled with its environment; otherwise, it would become an isolated closed system (non-existent in nature).

The teclological boundary is not a crisp (or even fuzzy) distinction, but a dynamically shifting complex (or wave) of overlapping regions of neutral balances between the processes of ingression and disingression. Temporary breaks of the tectological boundary trigger conjunctive processes which lead both to new production or transformation of complexes and partial or full disintegration. Bogdanov refers to the break of the tectological boundary as a *conjunctive crisis,* and its subsequent reestablishment as a *disjunctive crisis.*

3.3.7.2 Complexes: Regulatory Mechanisms

Regulatory mechanisms are based on concepts of conservative selection, dynamic equilibrium and progressive selection.

Any complex must assimilate (select) and also dissimilate (dissipate) the requisite variety of the environment with which it is structurally coupled. Assimilative processes tend to establish, maintain and preserve the complex in a stable state of persisting autonomy. Each change towards preservation is balanced by the opposing changes of dissimilative processes. A *dynamic equilibrium* of change is thus established. This dynamic equilibrium (more precisely, *equilibration*) permits the human perception of the persistence of the complexes of nature.

In Bogdanov's view, simple units are coupled into linkages and chains. Linear chains are ingressively linked into non-linear and circular networks, continually building into higher-degree "chains." His links, chains and networks were the beginning of his proposed "mathematics of complexity."

As expected, Bogdanov was bound to find Darwin's mechanistic theory of natural selection to be "tectologically deficient." *Progressive selection* guides the emergence, growth and persistence of complexes: it could imply the preponderance of assimilation over dissimilation *(positive selection)*; or the reverse process, the preponderance of dissimilation *(negative selection)*. Positive selection produces greater heterogeneity of components and complexity of constitutive relationships. Negative selection leads to a greater homogeneity and structural simplicity of a given complex.

Bogdanov thereby stated the principles of modern autopoiesis (self-production) and the closed circular organization of processes. He understood that degradation and disintegration are also "productions" of components, results of progressive selection.

3.3.7.3 Tectological Implications

Why do organizational patterns appear stable? They must be stable if they are to be preserved or conserved. Their structural stability is brought about by progressive selection, both positive and negative. It depends on the smallest *relative resistances* of *all* its parts at any moment of time (the "weakest link" theory). The maximum relative stability is achieved through a uniform distribution of activities-resistances among the links of the whole.

Compare with the notion of self-management: concentrating all knowledge at the top (or in the center, brain or heart) of an enterprise has led to either systemic suicide or to authoritarian control. Only *distributed knowledge* is of value.

3.3.7.4 Transformation

Tectology becomes most useful in its search for solutions to organizational problems emerging from systemic divergence. Two solutions are possible: *systematic crisis* (destruction, catastrophe) or *systematic transformation* (contra-differentiation or integration). Man's prescriptive role is to produce new conjunctions among heterogeneous complexes. New conjunctions provide new impetus and material for subsequent regroupings and selections, i.e. for the structural transformation of the entire system.

Convergence of forms is different from their contra-differentiation. Convergence is the result of a similarly directed selection through the relationships in a similar environment. Contra-differentiation means that divergence is paralyzed by the direct conjunction of the diverging forms *themselves*. Bogdanov distinguished between tectologically "formal" convergence and the "real" convergence of systems of common "genetic" origin. He proposed that "real" convergence is essentially *indirect* contra-differentiation.

The so called centralist and skeletal forms are described as either egression (from "stepping out of line"), based on the authority-subordination principle, or degression (from "delegating to the lower level"), based on the decentralized, distributed principle. Only degression makes higher development of plastic forms possible, fixing their activities and protecting them in their environment.

Bogdanov also comments on the "irreversibility" of self-organizing processes. From the complementary asymmetry of *positive and* negative *selection* flows the basic, universal *irreversibility of processes in nature*. The negative selection occurs everywhere; what it "selects" is irrevocably carried away; destroyed forms leave the ecology of nature, nature itself becomes different and all that is new is created under the new conditions.

Being irreversible, the creation must be inexhaustible.

3.3.7.5 Crises

Bogdanov went well beyond the modern "catastrophe theory": His *crisis* is a change in organization, not just in structure. It is a transition from the current equilibrium to a new, limiting equilibrium (e.g., in mathematics, magnitudes are increasing and decreasing, while the real crises pertain to the origination and destruction of magnitudes).

There are two types of crises: crisis C (conjunctive) breaks up tectological boundaries and forms new conjunctions and linkages (e.g., merging of two drops of water); crisis D (disjunctive) breaks up the linkages and forms new tectological boundaries (e.g., dispersing a drop of water). All crises begin with phase C and end with phase D: one cannot break up something which has not been previously merged. Only when it is broken up, it becomes capable of merging.

3.3.7.6 Language

Bogdanov identified language as the "first tectological method" of humans. He understood that language, not linguistics, brought forth the organizational experience of society and thus he conceived of tectology itself as a kind of second-degree language: a coordination of tectological instruments (Mathematics would then be a special tectology of neutral complexes).

Every individual plays a part in systematizing and integrating collective organizational experiences of humanity. Such continued individual integration of know-ledge then guides human action. According to Bogdanov, *"Every person has his own small, imperfect and naturally constructed tectology."*

Language is a shared and consensual way of uniting, integrating and coordinating "individual tectologies," so that a coordinated action can take place. Knowledge can only exist in a social community of cognizing individuals: the knower must always be "a part of."

Language has made possible the exchange of ideas in human society. The exchange of ideas was a constant and vital necessity, for without it, it was impossible to coordinate the actions of people.

So, the key to knowledge lies in its *organization,* not in a mechanistic search for its "reality" or "essence."

In his own words: *"The truths of today will surely perish. But tectology gives us the guarantee that not even then could they be simply rejected, nor become, in the eyes of people of the future, pale and sterile errors."*

Chapter 4

PRODUCING DECISIONS:
Multiple Criteria, Tradeoffs and Conflicts

4. 1 Multiple Criteria Decision Making

In Human Systems Management we have to deal with multidimensionality. Humans are not machines and so they are not designed to a singular purpose or pursuit of a single objective. Humans and human systems live and exist in a complex world of multiple criteria.

Multiple-criteria decision making (MCDM) has become one of the fastest-growing fields of inquiry in the operational sciences since the early 1970s. The word "multiple" identifies the major concern and focus of this area: it is multiple criteria rather than a single criterion that characterize human choice, judgment and decision making.

It has become quite unsatisfactory to perceive the world in a one-dimensional way, and to use only a single criterion when evaluating or judging it. Humans always compare, trade-off, rank and order the objects of their experience with respect to many criteria of choice. Only in very simple, straightforward or routine situations can we assume that a single criterion of choice would be sufficient.

We may pick the largest apple from a basket (criterion of size), the cheapest brand of beer (price), the highest salary offer (monetary amount) or the shortest route home (distance). But often we worry whether the largest apple is the sweetest, the juiciest, the most aromatic and the freshest or whether we would enjoy eating it anyway. We may be concerned not only with our beer's price but also with its taste, caloric content, carbonation level and alcoholic content. We agonize about whether the highest salary offer is the one which also promises the highest rate of salary growth, whether it is accompanied by generous fringe benefits and whether the job provides comfortable working conditions or stimulates sufficient interest and provides a challenge. To arrive home at all we often have to consider the safest or the cheapest route, not only the shortest.

In a very definite sense we can talk about decision making only if at least two criteria are present. If only one criterion exists, there can be no tradeoffs and a mere measurement and search are sufficient for us to make a choice. For example, if you are asked to select the largest apple from a basket, are you engaged in decision making? Or is it sufficient to measure with respect to the criterion in question and search for the maximizing alternative? This does not imply that measurement and search are simple and easy tasks. However, if there is only a single criterion which can be measured, no decision making is involved. There can be no tradeoffs between profits and profits, costs and costs or utility and utility – so, no decisions can be made under a single criterion, only selecting more or less of the same thing. For that, one only has to measure and search.

Decision making occurs only when additional dimensions, such as an estimated reliability, a judge's credibility, or the cost of erroneous judgments are brought in. Clearly, no one-dimensional or single-criterion decision problem can ever exist. Other than choosing the tool of measurement, there remains very little to be decided.

Truly singular objectives or criteria occur only under very singular conditions of time pressure, emergency or crisis. Under such conditions, one often concentrates on a single criterion in order to simplify, speed up or control the decision process itself. As soon as the criterion has been determined, the decision has been implicitly made. It only has to be made explicit by the related tasks of measurement and search.

However, when facing multiple criteria, even if our measurement is perfect and the search along each of the dimensions is efficient, it still remains necessary to decide. Here, the choice is not implicit in the measurement.

The economist Milton Friedman summarized these distinctions as follows:

"An economic problem exists whenever scarce means are used to satisfy alternative ends. If the means are not scarce, there is no problem at all; there is Nirvana. If the means are scarce and there is only a single end, the problem of how to use the means is a technological problem. No value judgments enter into its solution; only knowledge of physical and technical relationships."

(Friedman 1962: 6)

Thus multiple-criteria decision making has emerged in response to the need for dealing with an economic problem, while traditional economics, decision analysis and utility theory have only dealt with the technological problem in Friedman's sense. Today, the very term "multiple-criteria decision making" has become synonymous with decision making.

4.1.1 Types of Criteria

We are concerned with multiple criteria. A number of different types of these guiding measures can be considered. We shall introduce only three basic criterion types: attributes, objectives, and goals.

4.1.2 Attributes

Attributes refer to descriptors of objective reality. A person might be described in terms of height, weight, color, age, wealth and so on. Other attributes might be more subjectively biased, for instance intellect, beauty or social status. One can choose any attributes as criteria of choice or decision making.

A theory dealing specifically with the aggregation of attributes into a single super-criterion of "utility function" is called multi-attribute utility theory (MAUT). The multi-attribute utility theory is based on traditional precepts of perfect rationality, utility or profit maximization, and predictability of aggregate phenomena. The theory is prescriptive, concerned with the choice among *a priori* specified, given, alternatives according to the principle of maximization of subjective expected utility.

The multi-attribute utility theory grew out of the one-dimensional utility theory and its central dogma of rational behavior. It goes as follows: if an appropriate utility is assigned to a possible outcome and the expected utility of each alternative is calculated, then the best course of action for any rational decision maker is the alternative with the highest expected utility. The theory thus reduces the complex problem of assessing a multi-attribute utility function into one of assessing a series of one-dimensional utility functions. These individually estimated component functions are then "glued" together, with the glue being the "value tradeoffs."

Determining the tradeoffs often requires subjective judgment from the decision maker, who must reflect deeply on the question: "How much achievement in terms of one objective am I willing to give up in terms of another objective?" The main purpose of the multi-attribute utility theory is to establish an aggregate super-objective and to maximize the overall utility as the ultimate single criterion. Certain processes are available to assist the decision maker in determining the tradeoffs that are necessary in order to arrive at a final utility aggregate. These tradeoffs subsequently disappear and are subsumed within the one-dimensional utility scale. If there are a large number of alternatives (but still relatively few criteria), it is preferable to attempt an explicit assessment of the overall utility function of the applicable multiple attributes. A proper assessment of an individual decision maker's utility and weight of importance given the various attributes is essential in determining a relatively accurate utility function. The determination of individual utilities and weights requires independence of attributes.

If independence among the attributes is lacking, it may be necessary to redefine the objectives (for example, combine purchase price and petrol mileage into the overall car cost for a period of five years). One of the most important tasks of the multi-attribute utility theory is to verify the independence of attributes (it is generally quite difficult for humans to say whether attributes are independent).

After independent attributes suitable for analysis have been established, all individual single-attribute utility functions must be constructed. Similarly, the weights of relative importance of the various attributes must be determined.

There is nothing in human experience to indicate that people actually employ such global or aggregate utility measures. They do appear to exhibit some consistency in their preferences, tastes and choices. Therefore, it is theoretically possible to construct models (aggregate utility functions) that predict decision-making behavior over certain classes of situations. Such models are not explanatory and do not reveal any causal mechanisms, but may display some potential predictive power.

Recent advances in neuroscience and the associated psychological data show convincingly that the conventional wisdom regarding rationality is incorrect. The human decision-making and problem-solving processes emerge from the way in which neural networks function: as a whole, as a spontaneously "wired" and self-organized "market" of endlessly propagated patterns that are non-aggregated and continually construct and reconstruct the observer's model of the world. Modern multiple-criteria decision making theory cannot ignore the most recent findings of neuroscience, or else human decision making and problem solving may never become sufficiently understood.

4.1.3 Objectives

Objectives represent directions of improvement or preference along individual attribute scales. There are only two such directions: more or less (maximize or minimize). For example, height in itself is an attribute, but finding the tallest among the alternatives, or maximizing height, is an objective. Thus an attribute becomes an objective when it is assigned a purpose, a direction of desirability or improvement (by a human). "To maximize horsepower" is an objective, directing the return for improved, specific achievement along the attribute horsepower. Such MCDM methodologies as multi-objective programming or compromise programming are designed to assist in resolving a conflict among a number of incommensurable objectives or objective functions.

Multi-objective programming

The main purpose of multi-objective programming is to find all non-dominated solutions of a given problem. The multi-criteria simplex method is the technique used. This method is designed to locate all non-dominated solutions. This methodology, which is rather complicated and technical, utilizes the simplex method of traditional linear programming as a computational base.

Interactive programming

The non-dominated set of solutions can be further reduced by considering different weights of importance via interactive programming or by iterative shrinking of the set of non-dominated solutions. Interactive MCDM procedures assume that the preferences of the decision maker form and evolve only in connection with a particular problem. In contrast to the multi-attribute utility theory, where we assume *a priori* articulation of preferences, interactive procedures assume no fixed or given preferences *per se*, but only situation-dependent, circumstance-shaped, evolving, changing preference patterns.

Compromise programming

Compromise programming combines the most useful features of multi-objective and goal programming. It is not limited to linear cases; it can be used for identifying non-dominated solutions under the most general conditions; it allows pre-specified goals; and, most importantly, it provides an excellent base for interactive programming.

In this context, we view compromise as an effort to approach or match the ideal solution as closely as possible. Compromise programming is based on the notion of distance or deviation from an ideal solution. The decision maker must identify an "ideal point" (the most preferred level of attributes associated with a set of conflicting objectives). This ideal point is most likely to lie beyond the set of non-dominated solutions. The objective of compromise programming is to identify those solutions closest to the ideal point.

De novo programming is then used to redesign the problem so that the ideal point itself becomes feasible (see appendix on De Novo Programming). In order to identify those solutions closest to the ideal point, we minimize the maximum weighted deviations between each attainable attribute value and the ideal value. Conversely, we can compromise from the "anti-ideal" (the worst possible outcome).

4.1.4 Goals

Goals are *a priori* determined specific values or levels defined in terms of either attributes or objectives. They can be precise desired levels of attainment or more fuzzily delineated, vague ideals. "Maximizing gas mileage" is a well-stated objective with respect to a car. "Achieving a gas mileage of twenty-six miles per gallon" is a clearly stated goal indicating a specific target or reference value for that objective. The most common methodology which is specifically designed to deal with the attainment of goals is referred to as "goal programming." While linear multi-objective programming deals with the minimization or maximization of various objective functions, goal programming is concerned with the conditions of achieving pre-specified targets or goals.

The setting of goals is a tactical device which often complements the pursuit of objectives. Setting a specific target, instead of posing a maximization or minimization objective, could present a clearer point of reference and provide a keener sense of direction. Once individual goals have been stated, the purpose of goal programming is to achieve the goal set as closely as possible; that is, to minimize the set of deviations or "distances" from the goals. All goals can be considered simultaneously or they can be taken individually.

There are three basic approaches to problems characterized by *a priori* set goals: pre-emptive goal programming, Archimedean goal programming and multi-goal programming. The three approaches differ only in their handling of objective function(s): they all rely on similar modeling of goals and constraints.

Pre-emptive goal programming involves a process of taking goals one by one in order of their pre-emptive priorities. Archimedean goal programming considers all goals simultaneously and uses a measure of the total "distance" from the pre-specified goal set. Multi-goal programming identifies all non-dominated solutions with respect to objective functions, as in multi-objective linear programming: there is no need to specify criterion weights (pre-emptive or Archimedean) and no aggregate preference or distance function.

The three approaches have been listed in the order of their weakening assumptions about the preferences of the decision maker: from a one-by-one artifact, through additive aggregate, to no-assumption framework; from their pre-emptive ordering of goal importance and their relative weighting, to no weighting required; also from a uniquely defined solution to a set of non-dominated solutions. If we replace *a priori* defined goals by the verifiably achievable ideal values, we enter the area of compromise programming.

It is clear from the preceding discussion of the various multiple-criteria decision making techniques that the basic solution concept applicable in each is the concept of non-dominance, derived from Pareto optimality. The Pareto optimality principle postulates that a state of world A is preferable to a state of world B if at least one person is better off in A and nobody is worse off. For multiple-criteria decision making purposes, we substitute criteria, attributes or objective functions for persons or commodities, and decision alternatives or solutions for states of the world. Solution B is dominated by solution A if in moving from A to B we improve at least one objective function and do not worsen any other.

It is useful to express non-dominance in terms of a simple vector comparison. Let x and y be two vectors of n components, $x_1, \ldots, x_n$ and $y_1, \ldots, y_n$ respectively.

Thus, let

$$x = (x_1, \ldots, x_n), \text{ and } y = (y_1, \ldots, y_n)$$

We say that x dominates y if

$$x_i \geq y_i \quad i = 1, \ldots, n$$

and $x_i > y_i$ for at least one i. Figure 4.1 provides a graphic explanation of these orderings.

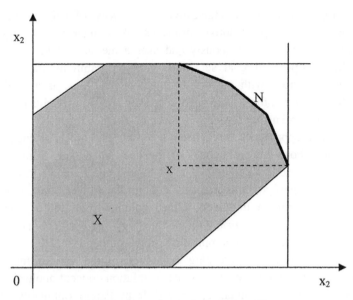

Figure 4.1 Set of non-dominated solutions N.

The set of all non-dominated solutions in X is designated N. The main property of N is that for every dominated solution (that is, every feasible solution not in N) a solution in N can be found at which no vector components are smaller and at least one is larger. Feasible set X, the shaded polygon area in the two-dimensional space of points $x = (x_1, x_2)$, consists of feasible combinations of x_1 and x_2. For example, x_1 and x_2 could represent production levels of Product 1 and Product 2 respectively. As objective functions, they would correspond to "Maximize quantity of Product 1" and "Maximize quantity of Product 2."

Observe that point x in X is dominated by all points in the shaded subregion of X, indicating that the levels of both components can be increased simultaneously. Only for points in N does this subregion of improvement extend beyond the boundaries of X into the infeasible region. Thus the points in N are the only points satisfying the definitions and they make up the heavily outlined portion of the boundary of X. All other points of X are dominated. (The set of non-dominated solutions is alternatively referred to as the efficient set, the admissible set or the Pareto-optimal set.)

4.1.5 Vector Optimization

John von Neumann and Oskar Morgenstern had the following to say about the vector optimization problem:

> *"This is certainly no maximum problem, but a peculiar and disconcerting mixture of several conflicting maximum problems... This kind of problem is nowhere dealt with in classical mathematics. We emphasize at the risk of being pedantic that this is no conditional maximum problem, no problem of the calculus of variation, of functional analysis, etc. It arises in full clarity, even in the most 'elementary' situations, e.g., when all variables can assume only a finite number of values."*
>
> (von Neumann and Morgenstern 1953: 10 – 11)

A vector optimization problem arises when two or more (K) scalar-valued objective functions (or criteria) are to be maximized over a set of feasible solutions:

$$\text{Opt } \{f(x) \mid x \in X \}$$

where $X = \mathcal{R}^N$ and $f(x) = [f_1(x), ... , f_K(x)]$.

A feasible solution x'' is non-dominated with respect to X and $f(x)$ if and only if $f(x') \neq f(x'')$ and there exists no $x' \in X$ such that $f(x') \geq f(x'')$. Solving a vector optimum problem means identifying all x'', that is the set $N(X)$, which are non-dominated with respect to X and $f(x)$.

Each component scalar-optimum problem,

$$\text{Opt}^+ \{f_k(x) \mid x \in X\}, k = 1, ... , K$$

has an optimal solution x^{k+} with $f_k^+ = f_k(x^{k+1})$. The vector $f^+ = (f_1^+, ... , f_K^+)$ represents an ideal value of $f(x)$ with respect to X. If $x^{k+} = x^+$, $k = 1, ... , K$, the vector optimum problem has a *perfect solution* $f^+ = f(x^+)$. This excepted, no feasible x yields a vector f^+. It is of course possible to redefine (or "reshape") X so that a perfect solution is brought forth and the vector optimization problem effectively resolved. This is effectively resolved by so called De Novo programming, discussed in other sections of this volume. At some sacrifice of realism, yet according to convention, we shall temporarily consider X to be fixed.

The perfect solution f^+ is complemented by the lowest, separately acceptable values achieved by anti-optimizing over the non-dominated set $N(X)$ of X. Each component scalar anti-optimum problem,

$$\text{Opt}^- \{f_k(x) \mid x \in N(X)\}, \quad k = 1, \dots K$$

has anti-optimal solution x^{k-} with $f_{k-} = f_k(x^{k-})$. The vector $f^- = (f_1^-, \dots, f_K^-)$ represents the anti-ideal value of $f(x)$ with respect to $N(X)$. If $x^{k-} = x^-$, $k = 1, \dots$, K, the vector optimum problem has an imperfect solution $f^- = f(x^-)$.

The imperfect solution is not acceptable as a whole (because it is necessarily dominated) although its individual component values are acceptable separately (as they could become part of $N(X)$).

Performance values of perfect and imperfect solutions identify the ranges of achievable values $[f_k^-, f_k^+]$, $k = 1, \dots, K$, defined over $N(X)$.

4.1.6 Scalar Maximization and Weights of Importance

Even though multiple-criteria decision making formally originated from vector optimization, the vector optimization problem has often been directly and without sufficient justification transformed into an aggregate (MAUT-type) scalar maximization problem. Most research then concentrated on determining the multiplier "weights of importance" for component criteria functions comprising the aggregate scalar function.

The vector optimization problem has thus been replaced by a scalar problem:

$$\max \{U [f(x)] \mid x \in X\},$$
or by
$$\max \{U [w, f(x)] = w_1 f_1(x) + \dots + w_K f_K(x) \mid x \in X\},$$

or by some other utility-function variation. The multiple-criteria problem has become a single-criterion problem.

$U [w, f(x)]$ is a unidimensional aggregation structure which subsumes and overrules individual decision criteria and renders their weights of importance, w_k, $k = 1, \dots, K$, as either meaningless or as simple normalizing multipliers. The larger the weight w_k, the more valued is the criterion performance contribution to the overall aggregate of $U [w, f(x)]$.

It is not self-evident why the notion of criterion importance should be closely related to or derived from the overall performance of aggregate superfunction $U[w, f(x)]$.

Maximization of the aggregate is in itself a criterion which can work against and overrule any *a priori* expressed notions of criteria importance. The only justification seems to come from accepting a sort of communal rule asserting that the collective is more important than the individual.

Consider a *simple example*. Let $w_k = 0.2$, $k = 1, ... , 5$ be equal weights of importance of five different decision criteria. In choosing among cars we may consider comfort, quality, price, reliability and mileage to be equally important criteria. Comparing two available cars, A and B, assume that the following criteria scores have been recorded:

A: (17; 1; 1; 1; 1)   U(A) = 4.2
B: (4; 4; 4; 4; 4)   U(B) = 4.0

The weighted aggregate $U[w, f(x)]$ thus attains values 4.2 and 4.0 for A and B respectively. An aggregate utility maximizer would choose Car A with $U = 4.2$, other things being equal. They would thus end up with an extravagantly comfortable car (score 17) of inferior quality, reliability and mileage at a very high price (scores 1). The whole point of specifying *a priori* equal importance of all five criteria has been missed. Unintentionally, one criterion (comfort) has become overwhelmingly important and all other criteria unimportant. There is no sense of balance, harmony or equilibrium: maximization of U overrides all such possible considerations.

Clearly, the individual decision maker does not seek to maximize any aggregate, superfunction or collective performance, but searches for a specific (here equally weighted) mix of actual criteria scores, ideal if possible, closest to the ideal if necessary. The search for a close-to-ideal equilibrium is of primary concern. The fact that some form of U could actually be maximized at such an equilibrium choice is the result of conventional tautology: that which maximizes U is preferred; that which is preferred maximizes U.

We may conclude that there are two types of basic decision-making assumptions:

Single criterion

Superfunction U is maximized, including the case of $w_k = 1$ for one $f_k(x)$. The weights of importance are simply normalization multipliers or discount factors that bring the achieved criteria scores differentially into the weighted total. Individual performances are less important than the overall performance; the collective dominates over the individual.

Multiple-criteria

The collective superfunction is not maximized; instead a balanced or equilibrium performance (close to the perfect solution) is sought in accordance with the expressed weights of criteria importance. Individual scores are more important than the aggregate; the collective is secondary, individual is primary.

Cultures and companies based on central planning, hierarchical command and collective decision making have a propensity to aggregate, reduce to a single formula, rely on the "overall" utility function and subsume separate criteria within one dominant single measure. Collectives and totalities disregard the individual and the individual's criteria for the sake of a higher, aggregate or collective purpose, like the utility function. Freely competing cultures and enterprises stress the individual and the individual's criteria as being autonomous, equal and separately or independently attainable.

4.1.7 Interactive Support

With the advances in decision support systems (DSS) and artificial intelligence (AI), the interest in human-machine interaction is also growing in the area of multiple-criteria decision making. Instead of the traditional prescriptive approach (external characterization of the best solution), the decision maker is aided in the very process of decision making and guided to allow internal conceptualization of what the best solution should be.

Interactive multiple-criteria decision making thus represents a fundamental departure from the traditional approaches of decision analysis. It reinstates the human at the center of the decision-making process and delegates external mathematical axioms of the prescriptive approach to the sphere of interesting scholastic speculations.

The best prescription of what is to be done comes from mastering that which is being done. The best outcome is bound to emerge from the best process. The opposite is not true: characterizing the best outcome does not guarantee anything about the process of reaching it.

It is now certain that humans do not follow any of the precepts of axiomatic rationality. Humans are fundamentally unconvincing *vis-à-vis* the axioms of rationality, yet their decisions continue to be superior to recommendations of expected utility maximization.

Human decision making cannot be and is not based on formulas. Formulas simplify, reduce and annihilate information. Humans do the opposite: they create or produce information and their decisions.

All important aspects of the decision-making process – criteria, alternatives, representations and evaluations – remain in a flux of mutual adjustment and co-determination throughout. Nothing is fixed *a priori*. The human decision-making process is a complex and circular search for internal consistency through layers of definitions and redefinitions of a problem.

All aspects of decision making are changing and mutually adjusting until a stable configuration or equilibrium among them is reached. The problem is thus dissolved, harmony achieved and there remains no other choice but the emerged stable pattern. Only then, retrospectively, may one look back and declare: "I have decided..."

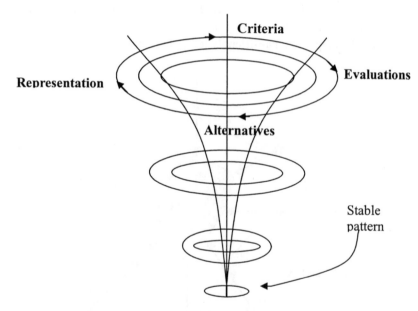

Figure 4.2 Circular and recursive search for a stable configuration (= decision).

In Figure 4.2 we sketch such a self-producing (autopoietic) process of decision making. Observe that all aspects (criteria, alternatives, representations and evaluations) are continually re-examined and readjusted throughout the process. Yet the process is not some pointless "muddling through" or chaotic whirlpool. It is a purposeful and often masterful search for harmony: a stable pattern which would (at least temporarily) dissolve the tension (or conflict) between what is and what remains desirable.

To interact with the decision maker for the purpose of forcing the use of *a priori* fixed formulas or patterns is fundamentally different from guiding the decision maker through the creative search process of Figure 4.2. Decision making is a process of successively redefining the problem.

What are the characteristics of the emergent conflict-free stable configuration? For example, an ideal solution (all criteria at their maxima with respect to a particular set of alternatives) can be brought forth and made feasible. Other such referential points, like anti-ideals (feasible minima of all criteria) or aspiration levels (set of desired goals) can also be used for the stable pattern characterization.

How are the multidimensional patterns to be represented? The number of requisite criteria typically exceeds three. Because we are not limited to numerical representation, spider-web diagrams (or "star" diagrams) provide the necessary graphics for developing human-friendly tools (Figure 4.3).

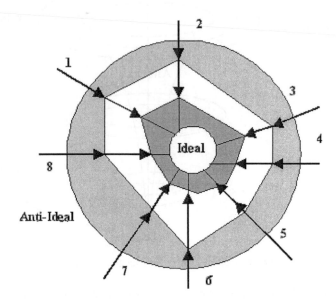

Figure 4.3 Spider-web diagram: eight criteria representation of progress from the anti-ideal to the ideal.

Observe that referential points can be displayed as circles (or any other pattern) in a spider-web diagram. Any feasible solution can be characterized by connecting its corresponding performances with respect to a large number of active criteria (8 in Figure 4.3). Such a representation is information complete: information is not reduced through a simplifying numerical formula. All alternative profiles are properly positioned with respect to active referential points and with respect to each other. Graphical and numerical comparisons of a large number of such profiles can be displayed. Shaded areas represent the extent of disparity (or conflict) with the referential patterns.

4.1.8 Multiple Decision Makers

All of the previous considerations have been related to a single decision-making agent. There is an ambitious and relatively unsuccessful streak in economics and multiple-criteria decision making literature, which deliberately proposes the problem of "multiple decision makers."

The problem of multiple decision makers appears to be somewhat artificially posed. Any multiple-criteria problem is usually unaddressed or unlabelled as to who "owns," is responsible for or champions the individual criteria involved. It could be a strategic entity of one, two, many or collective agents. Individual decision makers participate through their choice of criteria and through imposing or negotiating their weights of importance onto the overall decision-making process.

As long as we work with true (non-scalarized) vector optimization, nothing prevents us from allowing different criteria (and their subsets) to be championed (or differentially weighted) by different decision makers. Multiple-criteria problems are therefore also multiple decision makers' problems.

Each individual is (explicitly or implicitly) acting in the environment of multiple decision makers. Other agents' decisions (and performances of their criteria) affect the formulation and solution of any individual decision problem. Other agents' decisions become the constraints determining the "given" part of the individual decision-making context.

4.2 Concepts of Beauty, Quality and Harmony

Modeling challenges and modeling possibilities are increasingly involving qualitative rather than simple quantitative pursuits. The world and the world culture have changed: quality, not just quantity, matters.

Human concerns for preserving ecological, cultural, economic and social resources are undoubtedly going to rise dramatically in the future. Repeated examples of widespread destruction, collateral devastation and unwise or misinformed neglect of natural, built and economic environments should have driven the message home: we have brought most human societies to the edge of their cultural, economic and even biological sustainability. Yet, new conservation, preservation and enhancement efforts require modes of assessment, judgment and choice for which traditional economic analyses are clearly inadequate.

It would not be a problem to assess things that are single-dimensional, i.e., individually the cheapest, the most expensive, the simplest or the easiest to preserve. But we have to preserve things in terms of their entire complex social value: things that are beautiful, of the highest quality and of sustainable economic importance. Beauty and quality are not one-dimensional concepts like costs, profits or sales.

4.2.1 Beauty

We can all relate to some traditional definitions of beauty, like Aquinas's "That which pleases the eye (or nose, ear, mouth or touch)," or Adler's "That which pleases us upon being contemplated."

Such and similar concepts of beauty are highly subjective: whatever an individual experiences (through whatever senses or processes of contemplation) as beautiful is, at least for him, beautiful. Nothing particularly meaningful can be added here. *De gustabus non disputandum est.* Such beauty is all "in the eye of the beholder," a matter of individual perceptual and contemplative taste – extrarational, extrajudgmental and extrascientific.

However, every specific object (system, artifact, etc.) is identified as belonging to some generic class of objects, to its "family" of things. Each such object not only belongs to a class, but can also "occupy a position" within the class. For the purposes of comparison, assessment and judgment we rank, classify, group and order objects within their classes.

Each class of objects can therefore be characterized by real or conceived ideal levels of achievement along specific dimensions, criteria, qualities or attributes. From these, standards of excellence, quality or achievement can be derived, forming ideal objects, the most perfect representatives of a given class. These ideals can be either specific and real precedents or conceived or conceivable composites of specific and real dimensions (or experienced achievements).

Objects which in one way or another conform most perfectly to these ideals are more or less admirable, of high quality, or beautiful. Although individuals may differ in their tastes and judgments (or "measurements") of the conformance of a given object to standards of excellence, the classes, the standards and the ideals themselves can be obtained through knowledge, expertise and rational argument: they can be measured and discussed more or less objectively.

The most beautiful rose or flower is generally that which conforms most closely to a particular ideal of a rose within a given class of roses or flowers. This ideal can sometimes shift or be displaced, but the search for conformance or proximity endures: it serves as the mechanism of human construction (or "pullback" towards the point of attraction, the ideal) of beauty, quality or admiration.

Beauty is therefore related to conspicuous or prominent levels of achievement, like extreme, exaggerated, maximal/minimal, striking, etc. (but also the unusual, remote, rare and exotic), at least along some of the dimensions. At the same time, beauty is also related to pattern, symmetry, harmony, completeness, and balance.

Beauty's antonym, ugliness, does not imply "the other extreme or opposite," but rather mediocrity, plainness, blandness and indistinctiveness, combined with the want of symmetry, distortion, blemish, deformity or incompleteness.

Ugliness is a disordered and asymmetrical arrangement of bland and indistinct achievements. Beauty is a harmonious and balanced arrangement of noticeable and distinct achievements. Beauty is *negentropic*.

It is implied that different cultures will differ in their constructions of ideals, but the beautiful or the admirable is, across all cultures, that which most closely resembles or approximates those ideals. It is further proposed that awareness of differential ideals and the universal sense of harmony, symmetry and completeness allows for cross-cultural judgments of beauty, at least among the experts and connoisseurs. Many Chinese and Japanese can certainly appreciate the very best Western paintings or Western music, while Americans can exhibit similar appreciation of the very best Chinese screens or Japanese calligraphy.

4.2.2 Quality

It is to be expected that other notions based on proximity to ideal, prominence or perfection of achievement, like notions of quality, truth, goodness, liberty, equality and justice, will be strongly related to beauty.

Intuitively and experientially we find products and processes of high quality to be also beautiful, elegant and pleasing, i.e., harmonious, well balanced and complementary in appearance, function and use.

Many of the things we have said about beauty can be repeated for quality. Quality also pertains to objects within a given class and it is related to the class ideal or assemblage of representative standards and perfections. Quality is also by definition multidimensional and multifaceted. Perception of quality is derived from the proximity, approximativeness or resemblance of such ideals. The ranges of quality are related to the remoteness or distance from the ideal. The degrees of quality, as the degrees of beauty, can be assessed, evaluated and measured.

Traditionally however, for example according to J.M. Juran, quality is defined as "fitness for use" and "conformance to standards." Japanese define quality as the totality of characteristics used to determine if and how an intended application has been fulfilled. Another view sees quality as the minimum level of service to satisfy the target clientele. The closest and most useful concept of quality is implied by the Japanese term *shitsu*, implying a balance among measured values. None of these definitions is complete or suitable for our purposes.

What is the difference between quality and the concept of beauty discussed above? It seems that beauty can be perceived for its own sake, i.e., without any reference to its production, use or application. Quality is much more explicitly produced by man and fully intended for the purposeful uses of man. Beauty does not have to be confirmed by use or action, it can be simply contemplated. Quality can only be revealed through use or application towards goals.

A rose or sunset can be beautiful, but we do not necessarily speak of their quality. A specifically bred rose, produced for the purposes of competition or sale to customers, can be a quality rose. Many quality products and processes can be (and often are) beautiful: the two concepts, beauty and quality, emerge through very similar mechanisms. Even the products and processes of nature could be designated as being of quality – if they are applied towards the uses of man.

Beauty is assessed by judgment; quality can only be ascertained by use. Beauty can be assessed as a pure proximity to ideal, quality, because of the subsequent use, has to take the costs into account. Beauty emerges from the quest for perfection; quality emerges from the quest for usable (or affordable) perfection. Beauty is assessed by the observer (or contemplator); quality is brought forth by the user (actor, customer, and consumer).

Quality is related more to beauty than productivity. Both quality and beauty are directly related to human creativity and both are therefore readily acceptable. The notion of productivity is of later origin and is not readily or intuitively accepted by man.

Quality refers to a differentially weighted complex of multiple criteria or dimensions, approximating the ideal complex as closely as possible under the constraints of affordability of use and costs.

Both the ideal and the two constraints of affordability are being continually displaced by the very acts of production and use. The notions of quality, much more intensely so than the relatively stable notions of beauty, are therefore rapidly and continually shifting. Pursuits of both beauty and quality are never ending, but the pursuit of quality is aiming at continually changing ideals.

4.2.3 Harmony

There is a class of naturally or spontaneously produced systems which are not necessarily beautiful or of high quality, but their preservation is even more crucial: the physical, biological and social ecosystems.

Beauty relates to the harmony perceived in things and products. Quality relates to the harmony perceived in the affordable use of things and products. What about the perceived harmony among the processes "producing" these things and products? These are ecosystems: the primary "quality" of ecosystems is harmony.

Harmony, as opposed to chaos or conflict, is sustaining, productive and order-giving principle. All living systems are dependent and sustained by a "consuming order." All order is produced by the harmonious concatenation of the production processes – ecosystems. All living systems are dependent on harmony.

Harmony among the production processes leads to harmony in the use of products (quality, economy) and also to harmony within the products themselves (beauty, culture). Destroying the harmony of the processes, i.e., ecosystems, definitionally annihilates the harmony of the products, i.e., quality, economy and beauty.

Harmonious "social" organization is a network of interactions, reactions and processes involving:

1) production (poiesis): the rules and regulations guiding the entry of new living components (such as birth, membership, acceptance);
2) bonding (linkage): the rules guiding associations, functions and positions of individuals during their tenure within the organization;
3) degradation (disintegration): processes associated with the termination of membership (death, separation, expulsion).

All these circularly concatenated processes represent types of "productions" of components necessary for other processes. To emphasize this crucial point we speak of poiesis instead of production and autopoiesis instead of self-production. Although in reality hundreds of processes can be so interconnected, the above three-process model represents the minimum conditions necessary for autopoiesis to emerge, as has been discussed in Section 3.

The preservation, sustainment and enhancement of *harmony, quality* and *beauty* – if necessary in that order of importance – is the new challenge and charge of mankind.

The self-producing and self-organizing circle of ecology, economy and ethics must be restored and never broken again.

4.3 Tradeoffs-Free Decision Making

Traditional business and economic decision making is still plagued by the unwieldy and cumbersome concept of tradeoffs. One is still being "advised" – even within the prevailing MCDM methodology – to give up something in order to gain something else. So, one is forced to keep traversing and "racing through" assorted efficiency frontiers, productivity boundaries, efficient and non-dominated sets, tradeoff curves, etc., in search of good, acceptable tradeoffs.

In the era of information technology and systems (IT/S), mass customization (MC) and Network economy, the customer is king. No customer could ever possibly want any tradeoffs – if he had a choice. No customer wishes to sacrifice cost for quality, or speed for cost, or quality for speed. All customers and consumers want to have it all: superior quality, cost, speed and a whole host of other things. No wonder that the title of the recent business bestseller was titled *Free, Perfect, and Now*, that is, global customers want it at lowest cost, highest quality and as fast as possible. No truly economic agent would ever prefer to trade off one criterion for another, unless forced to.

The producer is in an entirely different position: he prefers tradeoffs because it is so much simpler to produce or focus on one thing or one criterion at a time: quality or cost or speed, etc., but not more or all of them simultaneously. Because some producers deliver quality, some other cost, and yet another speed – the customer is forced to choose and accept tradeoffs, one way or the other.

This traditional *tradeoff asymmetry* between producers and customers is rapidly disappearing. In the global economy, successful producers have to deliver the highest quality at the lowest price at the maximum speed, and without tradeoffs. This is the primary rule of the Internet-based network economy. The tradeoffs are being *eliminated* because they are not needed, not wanted and not necessary. Tradeoff curves, productivity boundaries and efficient sets are harking from the times long gone and are being discarded together with their tradeoffs. Such is the price (and the benefit) of progress.

4.3.1 On the Nature of Tradeoffs

Tradeoffs are often erroneously presented as being the real properties of specific criteria, objectives or dimensions. So, statements like "there are tradeoffs between cost and quality" are often accepted at their face value, as facts of reality. Similarly accepted have been the tradeoffs between unemployment and inflation (so called Phillips curve), often viewed as natural properties of the measures of unemployment and inflation, for many decades and by the majority of economists.

Criteria are and always have been just measures or measuring sticks for evaluating (measuring) objects of reality (things, alternatives, options, and strategies). There clearly is a fundamental difference between measures and the objects to be measured. Measuring "tapes" (size, weight, sweetness, etc.) are to be distinguished from apples, oranges and other sets of feasible alternatives themselves.

There can be no tradeoffs between measuring tapes. Tradeoffs are and always have been the properties of the measured objects. Measures of unemployment and inflation do not produce tradeoffs, the economy (the measured object) does. Measures of cost and quality do not produce tradeoffs, the set of alternative choices or options does.

Therefore, statements like "there are tradeoffs between multiple criteria" are fundamentally incorrect because criteria are measures. It is *only* the size, shape and structure of the feasible set (the measured "object" of alternatives, options and strategies) that is capable of producing or bringing forth any tradeoffs.

4.3.2 Examples of Tradeoffs

Phillips Curves

Whenever unemployment is low, inflation tends to be high and vice versa. This inverse relationship between the two economic measures is called the Phillips curve (since 1958).

Regardless of Phelps's and Friedman's insistence that there was no stable tradeoff between unemployment and inflation, and that the whole Phillips curve was based on fooling people, contradictory 1975 data were simply labeled "stagflation" and the false "tradeoff" notion was retained.

Information technology has not been taken into account. Computer software enhances brainpower, just as electricity, motors and chips added brawn to the old economy. Increasing returns to scale and falling prices (once you develop software, duplication is cheap) assure the growth of networks as their value multiplies.

Finally, in the U.S. at least, software has been recognized as a "business investment" and the tradeoff era has ended.

Hardware versus Software

A well-known tradeoff concerns the increasing hardware performance requiring considerable amount of electricity to operate and cool the increasingly complex chips. The producers adjusted to this "natural" tradeoff by producing desktop computers increasingly dependent on an electric power outlet.

In this way, improving computer performance would require more and more electricity and the sorely needed portables and handheld wireless devices would never come to being. The solution lies in eliminating the tradeoffs, not in accepting them or adapting to them.

Eliminating tradeoffs means abandoning improving silicon hardware and developing clever software. Drastically simplifying the hardware and shifting many of the most complex operations to software, so called Reduced Instruction Set Computing, is the answer.

Modern computing is very little hardware and a lot of software. Modern Code Morphing Technology puts the software in the center and cuts the power needs by one-tenth of Intel's best chips.

Always bet on brainpower, never on battery power – especially in MCDM.

Mass Customization

Tradeoffs between cost and quality are well known. Mass production offers cheaper products at lower quality and poorer fit; custom-made production offers better quality and tailored fit at higher price. For centuries consumers had to accept this tradeoff. The advance of mass customization eliminated the tradeoff: modern consumers can have high-quality, made-to-measure, individualized products at the same or lower price than mass-produced items.

Information technology, the Internet and smart software allow mass customization to penetrate into all product and service categories. Mass customization has eliminated tradeoffs. Again, if businessmen concentrated on choosing the "best" tradeoffs and decision makers kept surfing the non-dominated set, no mass customization would ever emerge.

Health Care Services

Health care delivery is traditionally loaded with tradeoffs. Yet, clearly, health care consumers desire high-quality products and care at a reasonable cost, delivered quickly and with positive outcomes. People do want tradeoff-free health care.

Information technology brings self-reliance, self-service and self-care, combined with preventive focus, into the picture. No amount of technically excellent care will produce optimal outcomes if health consumers are not actively engaged in managing disease and its prevention.

Health care providers are no longer supplying a service, but providing consumers with the tools that facilitate their self-care activities and efficiency. The web site SelfCare.com is the harbinger of tradeoffs-free health care. At-home medical testing kits now include HIV, colon/urinary, drugs, pregnancy, cholesterol, blood pressure, etc. Home usage of these kits, analyzers and monitors eliminates scores of assorted tradeoffs.

Inventory tradeoffs

Inventory management is a good example of tradeoff elimination. Traditionally, the cost of inventory was traded against the cost of reduced lead times, setup cost against holding cost, cost of inventory against cost of downtime and cost of shortfall, holding cost against cost of overtime, subcontracting or cost of shortage, holding cost against price fluctuations or shortages, etc.

All such tradeoff problems were spurious and incorrectly stated. They are not solvable by fiddling with order quantities, as JIT (Just-in-time) systems have showed. For example, safety stock is not just a matter of deciding how much inventory to carry: one can improve quality, reduce variability, reduce lead times or even improve forecasts in order to eliminate inventory tradeoffs entirely. Reducing the number of parts in product design, reducing the variety, switching to mass customization, etc., are other potent strategies for inventory reduction.

4.3.3 New Thoughts on Tradeoffs

A new, somewhat discomforting, possibly radical and certainly challenging idea has started making rounds in better business management literature: "Are tradeoffs really necessary?"

The answer is no: *tradeoffs are not necessary*. Pursuing and achieving lower cost, higher quality and thus improved flexibility, all at the same time, is not only possible but clearly desirable and – within a New Economy – also necessary.
Conventional wisdom recommends dealing with multicriteria conflicts via "tough choices" and a "careful analysis" of the tradeoffs. Lean manufacturing has apparently eliminated the tradeoffs among productivity, investment, and variety. "Quality and low cost" and "customization and low cost" were long assumed to be tradeoffs, but companies are forced to overcome the traditional tradeoffs.

Yet, according to Hayes and Pisano, many Japanese factories have achieved lower cost, higher quality, faster product introductions, and greater flexibility, all at the same time:

"Lean manufacturing has apparently eliminated the trade-offs among productivity, investment, and variety," they observe.

Similarly, B. Joseph Pine II, Bart Victor, and Andrew C. Boynton, in their article "Making Mass Customization Work," recall that [in the old paradigm]: *"Quality and low cost and customization and low cost were assumed to be trade-offs."* They also speculate that: *"...companies can overcome the traditional trade-offs."*

Turning to a more professional literature, John C. Anderson et al., reviewed "The Need to Make Trade-offs" in 1989 and concluded:

"Recently, trade-offs have been called into question as operations are being designed which have better quality, lower cost and faster delivery than the competitors. These operations have moved to a new level of performance rather than making trade-offs on an existing level. Because of these new insights, the exact nature of trade-offs is no longer clearly understood [emphasis M.Z.]."

The above conclusion presumes that the exact nature of trade-offs has somehow been understood before. However, their criticism is leveled at the wrong culprit and a rather infertile remedy is proposed:

"More research needs to be done to clarify the precise nature of trade-offs in operations. In addition, the existing literature on trade-offs has failed to make use of standard economic paradigms and theories. The economic literature is a rich source of micro theories concerning trade-offs in decision making. This literature could be extended to operations strategy, but has not been to date."

Needless to say, the "standard economics paradigms," the economic literature or multiattribute utility theory have virtually nothing to say about the "exact nature of trade-offs." They simply demonstrate that trade-off evaluations and decisions are frequently painful and almost always tedious.

Can one decrease cost and increase quality at the same time – and continue doing so? The answer is yes: tradeoffs are properties of badly designed systems and thus can be eliminated by designing better, optimal systems.

4.4 Conflict and its Dissolution

Human decision making and judgment are often studied with the help of the above described model-morphism. Another important phenomenon subjected to such approach, even on a commercial scale, is the notion of conflict.

Conflict, in psychology at least, is the situation in which two or more motives are partially blocking each other. The prime source of conflict is thus assumed to lie in cognitive differences concerning the perceptions and interpretations of components comprising a given decision situation. Conflict thus becomes a cognitive conflict, generated by poor communication, misunderstanding, ideological inflexibility, etc., and the means toward its resolution are naturally directed toward affecting a cognitive change: discussion, argumentation, persuasion, negotiation, "shuttle diplomacy," threat, punishment, and other means of temporary conflict suppression or concealment.

Are perceived cognitive differences the causes or the symptoms of the underlying conflict?

If they are the causes, then removing cognitive differences will be presented as a path to conflict resolution. However, removing cognitive differences is clearly impossible – unless we resort to a substantive *Gleichschaltung*.

If cognitive differences are mere symptoms, i.e., outward manifestations of the underlying conflict, then the path is clear: we have to search for the real causes.

It would amount to a gross simplification to assume that conflict arises simply because of inadequate communication, misinformation, or misunderstanding. That would imply that there is no "real" conflict at the bottom of human existence; all is due to stubbornness, ignorance, and ill-conceived goals. Conflict resolution then would be simply a matter of skillful negotiation, bargaining, persuasion, propaganda, strategic threats, "brainwashing," and other means of eliciting desired "cognitive change." No disease can be cured by removing its symptoms. It can only be temporarily concealed and obscured to our senses.

Communication also does not seem to be too essential for conflict resolution. In fact, one could submit that the amount and intensity of conflict in modern society simply increase with the advances in the means and intensity of communication. The most stable and effective agreements are frequently results of tacit and implicit "understandings," often with no explicit communication present. We may observe commonly shared values among non-communicating entities, as well as values increasingly diverging in step with intensified communication.

4.4.1 Definition of Conflict

Conflict occurs when two or more distinct alternatives, selected as the means for achieving stated objectives, are mutually exclusive.

With respect to the above definition of conflict, we can identify the following necessary conditions of a potential conflict:

(1) One or more decision agents, i.e., organisms or machines capable of making

a choice: human decision makers or judges, Buridan's donkeys, rats or decision-forming contrivances. We shall denote them M, F, H, etc.

(2) Two or more available alternatives of choice, denoted by $0, 1, 2, 3$, etc., where 0 indicates a "no choice" alternative, or "no preference" vote.

(3) One or more objectives or criteria of choice, say a, b, c, etc., including rules, programs, drives, instincts, motives, etc., and other concepts which are used to evaluate the decision agents' choices.

One familiar source of conflict is a married couple. Let us clarify the essential aspects of conflict by drawing upon this rich source of exemplary cases.

We shall denote the conflict-free state between M and F, with respect to a given criterion, a, by their uninterrupted linkage, i.e., no action is being considered with respect to a:

$$M \, ^{a} F$$

Next, we shall attempt to introduce a conflict between M and F. Suppose that both M and F share an identical objective a, say, for example, to spend their vacation together in the most satisfying way. There are only two alternatives available, 1 and 2. (For example, 1 might represent Las Vegas and 2 denote Miami.) If then M selects alternative 1 and F chooses alternative 2 as their respectively preferred means of maximizing or achieving a, we can observe a classical case of conflict emerging:

$$M \, ^{a} 2 \ 1 \, ^{a} F \qquad (1)$$

Thus, the conflict-free linkage has been interrupted, and the presence of conflict is indicated by the break (space).

How would we code a conflict-free situation? Assuming no changes or relaxations in a, but providing a *new* option 3, then, for example,

$$M \, ^{a} 3 \, ^{a} F \qquad (2)$$

i.e., both M and F decide to go to Prague. Observe that (2) represents initial choices, unaffected by any communication, persuasion, or marital counseling. Such efforts are only relevant in (1); (2) is not their necessary outcome. More likely,

$$M^{a} 2 - F \qquad \text{or} \qquad M - 1 \, ^{a} F$$

would result. Observe that in both cases we could not leave the objective a unaffected. The conflict has not been actually removed but only concealed.

Further, the alternatives selected in (1) must be mutually exclusive, If we remove their mutual exclusivity, for example, by changing a to represent spending the vacations in the most pleasurable way *and alone*, we might get:

$$M \overset{a}{-} 2 - 1 \overset{a}{-} F \tag{3}$$

i.e., M goes to Las Vegas and F to Miami, and everybody is happy. No conflict exists.

Among the available alternatives we have listed 0 as a distinct possibility. It should be emphasized that not making a choice, i.e., selecting 0, is different from not initiating a search among potential alternatives. That is, 0 could be an outcome of applying some a if there is no 1, 2, 3, etc., which would lead to achieving a given objective. Observe that we can distinguish the following different conflict-free situations involving a "no-choice":

$$M \overset{a}{-} F \quad \text{or} \quad M \overset{a}{-} 0 \overset{a}{-} F \tag{4}$$

although they might appear as identical on the surface. That is, if a means to share a two-week vacation in the Caribbean for under \$100, then there is no conflict emerging between M and F.

If the selected alternatives are mutually exclusive, conflict might appear even in the presence of 0, as

$$M \overset{a}{-} 1 \ 0 \overset{a}{-} F \tag{5}$$

For example, if a means to have a good time together by going out tonight, and 1 happens to be a corner bar as the only alternative available (e.g., because of budgetary constraints), the conflict might still occur.

It is important to emphasize the following. Suppose that a means to have a good time together, 1 would be the corner bar, while staying home would be 2. Then, again,

$$M \overset{a}{-} 1 \ 2 \overset{a}{-} F \tag{6}$$

In both cases (5) and (6), the F might stay home, but the nature of the conflict is different. The rationale for introducing 0 is to allow a conflict of the decision agent with its environment or circumstances. That would happen when no alternative to achieve a exists, or its existence is not discovered or perceived.

The following question arises: does $M \overset{a}{-} 0 \overset{a}{-} F$ represent a conflict situation or not? According to our definition, there is no conflict between M and F; but both are in conflict with their environment as two separate individuals. The nature of such conflict emerges when the special case of a single decision agent is being explored. It is in this framework that the presence of 0 *always* indicates individual conflict. The following situations then should not be confused:

$$M \overset{a}{-} F$$

$$M \overset{a}{-} 1 \overset{a}{-} F \tag{7}$$

$$\text{and } M \overset{a}{-} 0 \overset{a}{-} F,$$

because they are quite different.

Before exploring the case of a single decision agent, let us further explain the second necessary condition: *two-alternative stipulation*. The definition implies that, if there is only one alternative, there cannot be any conflict, because the mutually exclusive choice cannot appear. In a sense, there is no choice available, because even the no-choice alternative 0 might not be available. The selection would always be 0 or 1 or 2 or... etc.: a conflict cannot appear.

There can be a two-alternative situation even when one option so completely dominates another that the situation is actually *perceived* as being a single-alternative one (for example, the choice between life and death). Such situations are capable of generating conflict.

Let us return to condition (3). Until now we have assumed a single, shared (or common) objective a. Each decision agent can make a choice by employing different or multiple objectives. However, the similarity, identity, or differentiation of objectives might not have anything to do with the conflict. Compare carefully the following:

$$M \overset{a}{-} 1 \ 2 \overset{a}{-} F \tag{8}$$

$$\text{and } M \overset{a}{-} 1 \overset{b}{-} F \tag{9}$$

In (9), for example, if *a* means to go out for a drink and *b* means to be in the close proximity of one's spouse, then *1* (a corner bar) might be the selection for both *M* and *F* and no conflict appears. A conflict could emerge if

$$M^a \; 1 \; 2^b \; F$$
$$M^a \; 1 \; 0^b \; F \tag{10}$$

Let us explore the case of a single decision agent, say *M*. Since there is no other decision agent, the only possible conflict can be either his inner conflict or a conflict with the environment. We assume that whenever a *single* choice from *1, 2*... can be made (i.e., *0* is excluded), there is no environmental conflict and, because the mutual exclusivity does not apply, there is also no other conflict.

Let us introduce symbol ε to indicate the "environment" – a passive decision agent of sorts. Then ε always matches a single choice but it does not match *0* or a multiple choice. For example,

$$M^a \; 1 - \varepsilon \tag{11}$$
$$\text{and } M^b \; 2 - \varepsilon \tag{12}$$

do not indicate conflicts. But the following modifications do represent conflicts:

$$M^a \; 0 - \varepsilon \tag{13}$$
$$\text{and } M^a \; 1 \; 2^a \; M \tag{14}$$

where (13) is a conflict with the environment and (14) is a conflict internal to M, even though generated by environmental conditions.

We are ready to explore multiple objectives in the case of a single decision agent. First, let us introduce some simple conflict-free situations:

$$M^a \; 1^b \; M \tag{15}$$
$$\text{or } M^a \; 1 \; 2^b \; M \tag{16}$$

where *1* and *2* are not mutually exclusive. More typical would be the following situations of conflict:

$$M^a \; 1 \; 2^b \; M \tag{17}$$

$$M \stackrel{a}{=} 1 \ 0 \stackrel{b}{=} M \tag{18}$$

Although further development and refinement of the *conflict algebra* introduced in previous paragraphs is both possible and desirable, it has not been the primary purpose of this exposition. Our task is to understand conflict itself.

Next we show that conflict can be characterized as being induced by the mutual exclusivity of distinct alternatives selected by decision agents. We shall introduce a concise and general definition of conflict: *Conflict is the absence of a prominent alternative.*

4.4.2 Conflict Dissolution

Since we limit graphical analysis to two-dimensional geometry, only the following cases are included among the discussed examples: (a) one decision agent with two objectives, and (b) two decision agents with single objectives. The number of decision alternatives can be as large as desired.

Let us graphically represent the conflict of (1), i.e., two decision agents with a joint single objective *a*, in Figure 4.4:

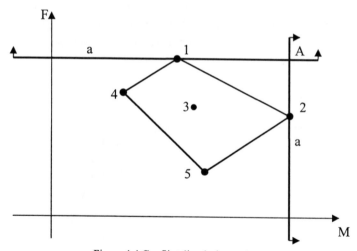

Figure 4.4 Conflict dissolution at A.

Observe that *M* and *F* maximize criterion *a* at *2* and *1* respectively. Even though they have a common objective and there are no cognitive differences, no mistakes or insufficient communication, there is a conflict. The prominent alternative *A* is either non-existent or it has not been considered by either *M* or *F*. It is *the absence of A* which causes the conflict to emerge. Note: should *A* become feasible, the conflict would be *fully dissolved*.

In Figure 4.4 we provide a more general representation of conflict. Let $X = \{1, 2, 3...\}$ denote the set of feasible alternatives and *M* and *F* two decision agents, each employing a single objective function.

The heavily traced boundary of *X* represents a *region of compromise,* a bargaining set. Observe that no compromise solution, including both extremes *1* and *2*, removes or resolves the underlying conflict. Conflict resolution via compromise is only a temporary disguise of the absence of *A*. At any compromise located on the heavy boundary of *X* there is at least one decision agent (or at least one objective) which stays unsatisfied in relation to what is actually achievable.

Even if *M* "persuades" *F* to go along and accept alternative *2*, and even if *F* is genuinely convinced that such negotiated outcome is the best for both *M* and *F*, *the conflict has not been resolved.* Sooner or later the suppressed perceptions and value judgments will claim their toll, a conflict will re-emerge, hasty agreements will not be honored, and deceit and treason will appear.

The methodology of so called "conflict *resolution*" clearly does not remove conflict; it might not even reduce conflict. It is a temporary disguise of a lack of innovation and creativity needed for inventing, discovering or considering prominent alternative *A*.

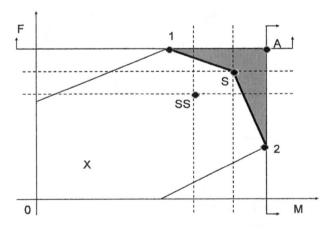

Figure 4.5 Intensity of conflict: size of the shaded area.

The shaded region between X and A approximately indicates the intensity or extent of present conflict. *The only way to dissolve conflict is to consider, find or create A.* The only way to reduce the intensity of conflict is to generate alternatives in the shaded area of Figure 4.5, i.e., those which are "closer" to A.

Negotiators, persuaders, diplomats, and bargaining experts are still devoting most of their efforts to inducing a "cognitive change" in the adversary party, to make *them* see it from *our* point of view. The powerful ones, the skillful ones, and the slick ones succeed and reap the short-term benefits (including Nobel prizes) of a temporary "conflict resolution." But the sources of conflict are left untouched. At the first opportunity, as the threats and power domination abate, the conflict will burst out with renewed vigor. Only the great statesmen in history knew the secret of finding a prominent alternative and were able to dissolve conflicts for generations to come.

Human objectives, values, perceptions, cognitive differences, etc., are the result of very complex evolutionary processes. Interactions of hereditary, cultural, environmental, and educational experiences, as well as a unique and non-reproducible history of evolution of an individual, group, nation or society – all such deeply ingrained characteristics are surely not reversible in a matter of days or weeks. Is the art of compromise simply a skill of persuasion? Of course not. The art of true compromise is the art of finding or creating a prominent, conflict-free alternative. Only a few practitioners are still applying this ancient art.

The preferences of two (or more) opposing decision agents are not necessarily in contradiction. They are implied by their respective value systems and assumption sets. Their cultural, social, and psychological histories are the clues to a discovery of these underlying value systems. The initial conflict between preferences can be traced and restated as opposing systems of assumptions. At least some of the assumptions must be common to both systems; otherwise there would be no basis for the conflict at all. (A New Yorker can rarely be in conflict with a Bushman, even if they meet.)

Partial commonality of assumptions suggests that there must exist a supra-system that implies *both* opposing systems of assumptions. The discovery of such a supra-system is similar to the discovery of a prominent alternative A. The new preference statements derived from a supra-system will be consistent and conflict-free and will render the original conflicting preferences irrelevant.

4.4.3 Significance of Conflict

Conflict provides the decision-motivating tension, the sense of frustration and dissatisfaction with the status quo. Since the underlying source of the pre-decision conflict is the non-availability of a prominent alternative, one must first attempt to create or make one available.

We can know the attribute measurements of alternative A. Is there any possibility for its empirical realization? Or, at least, something closer to it? Observe that the shaded area in Figure 4.5 provides a good normative guidance with respect to what kinds of alternatives should be generated.

One forms a "model" of a desirable alternative while it is still in the early stages of its development and before excessive sunk costs have been incurred toward its actual construction and physical development. Measures of distances between the most preferred levels of attributes (prominent point A) and the potential new alternatives are then used to produce an evaluation of their merits.

The notion of distance is a natural concept in conflict modeling. If a rat is taught to approach food at the end of a long corridor and then is shocked while retrieving it, thereafter, upon repeating the procedure, the rat will stop at a certain distance from the goal. If released nearer to the food, the rat will retreat to the same distance as before. The conflict is then modeled by the pull increasing with nearness and the tendency to retreat which also increases as the goal is approached.

The distance embodying is true also for human decision agents. Consider the situation in expression (18): M and the two objectives a and b. As M approaches closer to 1, he is also being painfully reminded ("shocked") of the discomfort of being too far from 2. After a while, M settles at a certain distance from both competing tendencies – a compromise solution. If there is no other real alternative, except 1 and 2, M might attempt to avoid or delay the choice by staying stuck at the *compromise distance* between 1 and 2. It is therefore possible that Buridan's ass will actually starve in front of the two identical stacks of hay, simply because they are mutually exclusive.

Since genuine conflict resolution is impossible and conflict dissolution might be a lengthy process of invention, innovation, and discovery, one can attempt *conflict reduction,* i.e., reducing the distance between A and a compromise solution. Such partial reduction of conflict intensity can be termed *conflict management.* We emphasize again that no traditional compromise resolution actually removes the conflict. The only way to dissolve a conflict is through the establishment of A.

Managers should learn how to remove the *essential conflict* through the identification of prominent alternatives, not how to remove the *apparent conflict* through the processes of persuasion or advocacy. Most available models start with: "Given a set of feasible alternatives X..." Because making a decision, as a means of conflict reduction or resolution, is tantamount to generating a prominent alternative; one would expect that the normative generation of new alternatives should become a primary concern of management.

4.4.4 Prominent Alternative

The concept of a prominent alternative is not entirely new. What is new is the recognition that its absence constitutes the source of most of conflicts.

Observe that alternative A represents a point at which multiple objectives are maximized: an overall optimum, an unattainable ideal. That does not mean that it does not serve as a norm or a rationale of human decision making. If we cannot achieve A, we should at least attempt to move *as close as possible* to it. The unattainability of an ideal should not serve as an excuse for trying to achieve the attainable only. Ignoring the ideal and settling down to what is "good enough" does not remove the conflict and it is incompatible with good management.

For example, so called "satisficing" means "resolving" the conflict by simply ignoring it. Point S in Figure 4.5 represents such a "good enough" solution, satisfying *a priori* determined goals and arbitrarily lowered aspiration levels. Even worse, a satisficer might set his goals even lower, choose point SS, and live smugly ever after.

It is hard to understand that some theorists could have taken satisficing seriously. They should not ignore the sarcasm of Simon's own definition: "Satisficing is the behavior of human beings who satisfice because they do not have the wits to maximize."

It was Schelling who observed that the most stable agreements and conflict resolutions are not conspicuously fair, or conspicuously in balance with estimated bargaining powers, but just plain "conspicuous." His focal points and conspicuous features are very similar to the prominence of A. Schelling demonstrated that people match each other's choices if there exists a prominent choice which can serve as an anchor for tacit agreement. The prominence principle can be viewed as a strategic principle, as a means of implementing tacit agreements among decision agents with at least partially coinciding motives in situations where explicit conflict-free compromise is impossible.

The task of looking for a prominent alternative does not reduce the need for bargaining and negotiating skills. It simply displaces the *locus* of their effectiveness from persuasion and from inducing cognitive changes to the domain of problem definition, formulation, and expansion. Identification of new and prominent alternatives along with their subsequent incorporation in a decision-making situation – that is even more than a skill; it is an art.

4.5 Theory of the Displaced Ideal

With the proliferation of variety of choice and mass customization of products and services, human preferences have become much less stable, much less predictable and much more context dependent: they are continually changing, flexibly responding to changing situations.

It is therefore necessary to develop decision-making models for adaptive human beings, rather then for traditional "rationality machines." The displaced ideal theory provides an alternative view of human decision making.

4.5.1 Means and Ends

In modeling human decision making there should be no separation of means and ends or alternatives and objectives. Both sides of the process, i.e. analysis of what is available and of what is desirable, are closely interdependent and interactive. There is also no clear primacy between means and ends; quite often an alternative is selected simply because it is there, available. One can recall the "let me see what they have and I will tell you what I want" attitude of a young shopper.

Neither means nor objectives are determined independently of each other. Objectives are evolved on the basis of available alternatives which are, in turn, adjusted and generated in accord with the existing objectives. Modeling of decision processes and economic behavior must take into account the fact that the means-ends dichotomy does not constitute the way in which people typically approach decisions.

There is no fundamental conflict between multiple human needs, objectives or goals. They are not conflicting in human minds, in their preferential sets. On the contrary, their complementarity and symbiosis is one of the striking aspects of human choice.

However, multiple objectives, *as a whole,* are in conflict with the means of their pursuit. Inadequate means are the source of perceived conflict among the ends. Objectives are in conflict with the natural, economic, technological and social limits that do not allow their full and simultaneous attainment.

Thus, a traditionally sharp separation of ends and means precludes any meaningful "conflict resolution" because it relegates conflict into the realm of values, rather than the realm of possibilities and options. Even today some authors still talk about conflicting objectives, conflicting values or conflicting needs. But there is no conflict between goals of increasing energy consumption and decreasing environmental pollution, *provided* that solar energy can be effectively harnessed.

Conflict between multiple objectives of a single individual thus reflects the underlying conflict between disparate and mutually exclusive alternatives. Similarly, conflict between multiple decision makers is a manifestation of the underlying conflict between mutually exclusive alternatives they prefer as individuals. Thus the sources of conflict can be traced to common conditions in both situations. We shall therefore not distinguish between individual and group decision making – it is always the individuals who make decisions.

4.5.2 Utility Maximization

We shall briefly summarize some of the underlying precepts of the utility-theory approach. It appears to be possible to deduce all of the theorems (that were originally derived from cardinal utility measures), from a simple *indifference curve* analysis, i.e., from the ordinal utility model. Consequently, intensities of human preferences, both intrapersonal and interpersonal, are not explicitly considered by modern utilitarians. Yet, expressions of degrees of preference, strength or intensity of choice, are imminent in most of human experience.

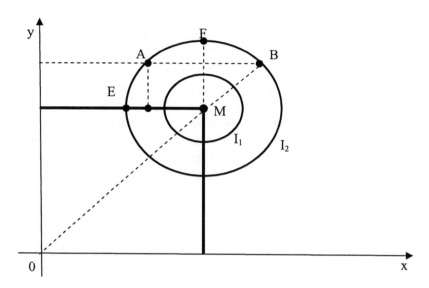

Figure 4.6 Preference space with "point of bliss" m.

Consider the preference space in Figure 4.6. Both axes, x and y, may represent a number of things: amounts of goods available, attribute scores or criteria, preferences of two different individuals and so on.

Maximum utility is achieved at M, the "point of bliss." Obviously, M is preferred to all points on lower indifference curves, i.e. $M > I_2 > ... > I_a > I_1$, while towards the points on the same curve, like A and B, we are assumed to be indifferent. In the absence of any availability constraints (or production possibility boundary) M would always be the choice.

However, if x and y are respective amounts of goods in one's possession, then the concept of indifference breaks down as follows: we can move from B to M directly by disposing of (freely or at costs) excess amounts of x and y. We cannot do the same from A. It is therefore difficult to maintain indifference between A and B, when clearly $B > A$. Similarly, $F > A$, $A > E$, etc. It turns out that indifference curves can be valid only in the southwest sub-region of M in Figure 4.6.

Most utility theory assumes that all alternatives are comparable in the sense that given any two alternatives, one or the other is strictly preferred or else the two are seen as being preferentially equivalent, i.e. choice indifferent. If one is presumed not to be able to express the intensity of one's preference then the notion of indifference, which is the most refined and most precise expression of preference intensity (i.e., one of zero intensity), becomes an artifact. One can express almost any intensity of preference – except indifference. *Indifference, as the extreme and the most precise expression of preference, is correspondingly the most difficult to assess explicitly.*

In Figure 4.7, observe how point A (and similarly any other point of the (x, y)-plane separates all points (given $x > 0$, $y > 0$) into four distinct domains. With respect to A, all points in domain II *dominate* (in this case, strictly dominate) all points in domain I. Points of III are not necessarily comparable with all points of I or II; the same is true for IV and I or II. Finally, no point of III is comparable with any point in IV and vice versa, evidently with the exception of A itself.

The relation of dominance is transitive. That is, if A dominates B, and B dominates C, then A dominates C. The utility maximization paradigm will not work except with a *transitive preference* field.

However, intransitivities of preferences frequently occur, especially if we are forced to choose between inherently incomparable alternatives. Although human choices may yield to a transitive ordering along individual *attributes in isolation*, their multidimensional consideration may not result in a transitive ordering of choices.

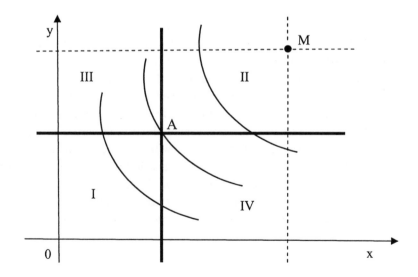

Figure 4.7 Intransitive preferences field.

No matter how intransitivities arise, we must recognize that they exist, and we can take only little comfort in the thought that they are an anathema to most of what constitutes theory in behavioral sciences today. We could say that they are only concerned with behavior which is transitive, adding hopefully that this need not always be a vacuous study. The truth is that transitive relations are far more mathematically tractable than intransitive ones.

Economics, however, should be positive rather than normative science. The traditional decision model is thus seriously flawed if it ignores the interaction that occurs between means and ends during the decision process.

4.5.3 Ideal Point

Economic theory usually acknowledges that there are no rigid limits to human wants but says nothing about the conditions under which wants are or are not satiated or exhausted. Under what circumstances does the gratification of wants give rise to saturation and under what circumstances to displacement: the arousal of new wants?

Realistic decision-making situations are of course *constrained*, the means are rarely unlimited.

Therefore, in constrained situations, as in Figure 4.8, reaching M becomes an unrealistic goal. The set of available alternatives is much too limited by the production possibility frontier or boundary P. Conflict between what is preferable and what is possible is thus established and a decision-making process will take place. Because of the fuzziness of M, the conflict is only perceived as a *sense of conflict* rather than being clearly defined and operational.

In order to define the extent of this conflict between means and ends, a decision maker explores the limits achievable along each particular attribute of importance. The highest achievable scores with respect to all such assessed attributes form a composite, an ideal alternative, I. In Figure 4.8 both M and I are graphically represented. Where M could be too difficult to identify, I is always simple to define and serves as a preferential approximation of M in decision making. The difference between these two reference points should be clear.

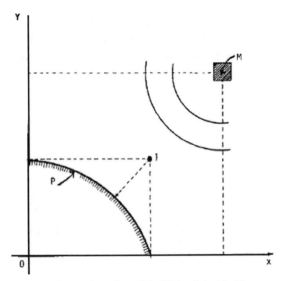

Figure 4.8 "Point of bliss" M and the ideal I.

General infeasibility or nonavailability of *I* creates a pre-decision conflict and generates the necessary impulse to move "as closely as possible" towards it. Because of the experienced conflict, the decision maker starts searching for new alternatives, preferably those which are closest to ideal *I*.

We should note that if such an ideal alternative is found, that is, the ideal becomes feasible, there is no need for further a decision-making process. Conflict has been removed and *I* is automatically selected since it is the best of all available choices.

Observe that in contrast to the relative stability of *M*, point *I can be displaced* rather frequently in dependency on changes of the available set. Ideal *I* becomes a moving target, a point of reference which provides a new model for human adaptivity, intransitivity and contextual adjustment of preferences.

Decision making is then a dynamic process of seeking *M* via *I*.

4.5.4 Displacement of Preferences

The processes of partial decision making may consist of discarding some inferior alternatives, reconsidering previously rejected alternatives, adding or deleting criteria, generating new alternatives, etc. As all alternatives are compared with the ideal, those which are the farthest from it are removed from further consideration. There are many important impacts of partial decisions. First, whenever an alternative is discarded there could be a shift in the maximum available score to the next lower feasible level. Thus, the ideal alternative is being displaced closer to the feasible set.

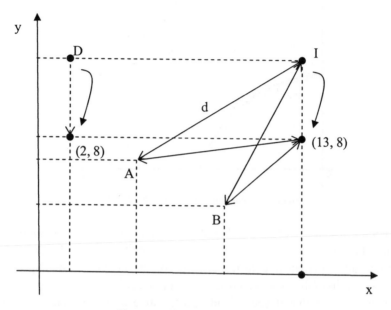

Figure 4.9 The displacement of ideal I.

Similarly, addition of a new alternative may displace the ideal farther away. Such displacements induce changes in evaluations, attribute importance and ultimately in the preference ordering of remaining alternatives. All alternatives are then compared with respect to the new, *displaced ideal.*

In Figure 4.9 and Table 4.1 we explore a simple case of displacements of the ideal point and their impact on the adaptive displacements of preferences.

Assume that the decision maker attempts to choose an alternative which would be *as close as possible* to the ideal. We shall employ the Euclidean measure of distance to provide distance ranking, i.e.,

$$d = ((x^* - x)^2 + (y^* - y)^2)^{1/2}$$

In the first case, the ideal point is $(x^*, y^*) = (13, 13)$ and the order of preferences thus induced is $A > B > D > C$. Let us now assume that point D has been shifted from (2, 13) to (2, 8). This can be due to an error in measurement, replacement of one alternative by another, addition or deletion of an alternative, a change in perception, etc. Consequently, there is a new ideal $(x^*, y^*) = (13, 8)$ (see Table 4.1) and the same Euclidean distance implies the following ranking: $B > A > C > D$.

Observe in Figure 4.9 that the preferences between A and B have been reversed because of the change in D. Also, consider the second case separately and note that B is optimal, followed by A, etc. Let us extend this second set of four available alternatives by adding a fifth one, say $E = (2, 13)$ as in Table 4.2. Although E is not optimal, the optimality ranking of previously considered alternatives has been reversed: A is now optimal, followed by B, E, D, and C. A nonoptimal alternative A has been made optimal by adding E to the feasible set.

Table 4.1 The displacement of the ideal.

Alternatives	1st Case			2nd Case		
	Attribute Values		Euclidean distance from the ideal	Attribute values		Euclidean distance from the ideal
	x	y		x	y	
A	6	7	9.2195	6	7	7.0710
B	10	4	9.4868	10	4	5.0000
C	13	0	13.0000	13	0	8.0000
D	2	13	11.0000	2	8	11.0000
Ideal	13	13	0.0000	13	8	0.0000

Note: The ideal is chosen as the best x and y values from the competing alternatives.

Table 4.2 The effect of the new alternative.

Alternatives	Attribute Values		Euclidean distance from the ideal
	x	y	
A	6	7	9.2195
B	10	4	9.4868
C	13	0	13.0000
D	2	8	12.0845
E	2	13	11.0000
Ideal	13	13	0

What is implied here is that in comparing A with B humans use I as a point of reference. Points A and B are rarely compared directly with each other. Rather, A is compared with I and B is compared with I separately and a comparison of A and B becomes an indirect consequence of this process.

The sequential nature of such comparisons leads to obvious changes in the number and nature of alternatives comprising the available set. Thus, a different ideal might be invoked in the different stages of the process. Intransitivity of choices can then emerge as a natural outcome of a consistent and rational decision-making process.

Consider the first case of Table 4.1 once again. We shall explore a particular triad of choices, say (A, B, D) in Figure 4.10. We shall assume that the decision-making process unfolds in stages and that inferior alternatives can be removed from consideration. For example, if $A > B$ and B and D have been already compared, then B can be removed from the set.

First, by comparing B and D one we conclude that $D > B$. Next, we observe that $A > D$ and D can be removed. To complete our triple comparison we compare A and B, yielding $B > A$, because the removal of D affected the displacement of I to I^*. Thus, in three stages, the decision maker stated that $A > D$, $D > B$ and $B > A$.

There is nothing inconsistent with the above intransitivity of preferences. The decision maker always minimizes the distance from the ideal but partial decisions about individual pairs of choices lead to its partial displacements. Observe that not all triads would be characterized by such intransitivity and that the sequential order of comparisons does matter. For example, starting with $A > D$ we then conclude that $A > B$ and finally $D > B$. Similarly, the sequence $A > B$, $D > B$, and $D > A$ preserves yet another transitive ordering. In this case the removal of B shifts I to (6, 13) and $D > A$.

We can conclude that in situations involving partial displacements of the ideal there is room for an appearance of intransitivity, especially if sequential and pairwise comparisons are carried out. If asked to compare all four alternatives as a whole, the decision maker would confirm that $A > B > D > C$, as derived earlier. As the number of alternatives to be compared increases, there is a tendency toward partial decision making and a reduction of the number of alternatives on the part of the decision maker. That leads to more frequent displacements of the ideal and intransitivity of choices could appear more frequently too. For example, extend (A, B, D) into (A, B, C, D) and perform the following sequence of comparisons: $A > C$, $B > C$, $D > C$.

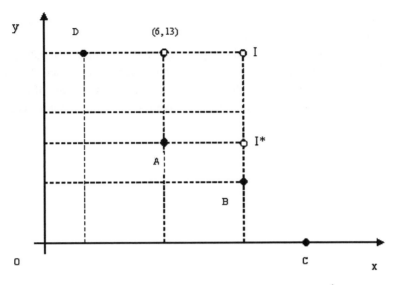

Figure 4.10 Example: adding D displaces ideal from I to I*.

Observe that C can be removed at this point. Then $D > B$, $A > D$ and so D can be removed. Finally, $B > A$. There is a large variety of ways in which to perform the decision-making sequence. A number of preference orders can be generated. Any number of alternatives becomes more difficult to assess as a whole if the number of attributes considered is large. Thus a link between intransitivity and dimensionality can be established.

Because the choice between A and B is influenced by the position of I (and therefore by some of the remaining alternatives) observe that the independence of irrelevant alternatives axiom has no place in describing human decision making. So-called "irrelevant" alternatives are actually very relevant and human preferences are a function of the available alternatives and change as these alternatives vary.

4.5.5 Conclusion

The decision-making process has been evolved by man through painful and unforgiving tests of human and individual history. Its dynamics, adaptability and flexibility have persisted and demonstrated a high degree of survival value. Approximate reasoning, fuzziness and dynamic readjustment complement this process. In dealing with complex reality, man, as a decision maker is irreplaceable. His capabilities have not been even approached by the most dizzying structures of mathematical analysis.

The man-evolved decision-making paradigm must be amplified rather than replaced, understood rather than ignored, respected rather than degraded. Normative models cannot be constructed without deep understanding of the most advanced decision-making methodology evolved so far: the human decision-making process.

Chapter 5

ATTAINING WISDOM:
Wisdom of Management Systems

There is such a thing as management wisdom.

Knowledge itself is of course necessary, but increasingly not sufficient. We do not have to know only what and how to do things, but increasingly, to attain wisdom, we have to ask why? A global managerial wisdom is emerging from confronting wisdom of the West with the wisdom of the East.

Modern managers have become too accustomed to the media and training gurus, propagating the fallacy that – for example – the so called Japanese-style of management is culturally different, Eastern in its outlook and collectivist in nature, and is therefore somehow "un-American" and somewhat difficult to transfer or adopt. While cultures remain different, their management styles are converging. Global markets and global customers are "forcing" the convergence through their increasingly global preferences.

Good management is good management – anywhere in the world. Bad management can increasingly be recognized by different cultures and experiences the world over.

Similarly, so called historical or cross-generational differences are becoming much less pronounced when we get to the level of wisdom. There could be new technological and organizational frameworks and requirements, but in the end, good management is remarkably recognizable in the practices of today as in the practices of hundred years ago. Only the bad management practices show a strong differentiation. Like in the Leo Tolstoy's famous opening line in *Anna Karenina*: *"Happy families are all alike; every unhappy family is unhappy in its own way,"* good management practices are remarkably alike; bad practices are quite different the world over.

Data is effervescent, ephemeral and context-free; information is rapidly exhausting itself and losing its competitive edge; knowledge is periodically being renewed and produced by learning; but a fundamental wisdom always applies...

it persists through the longest periods of human experience. It would not qualify as wisdom otherwise.

There is a deep-seated lack of historical awareness and alarmingly limited knowledge of Western management traditions and their interconnectedness with the broader traditions of the world. The role of teachings of Sarasohn, Deming and Juran in shaping Japanese-style management is well known. Less well known are the "pre-Japanese" American, European and Australian management practices, extending from the early twenties until now. Many of them not only constituted the foundations of Japanese-style management, but surpassed it in breadth, potential and proven practice.

In short, in the context of the Global Management Paradigm and at the level of wisdom, there is no fundamentally Japanese-style or American, German, Chinese or whatever management: there is *only good or bad management*, more or less suitable or fitting to a particular stage or area of global business evolution and its contextual ecology.

Rather than analyzing and describing some of the successful management *systems*, we have compiled their key maxims, excerpts and typical quotations that are strikingly and undoubtedly Western, American, capitalistic and individualistic in all respects. Yet, they have become global in their wisdom and timeless in their effectiveness, ethics and relevancy.

5.1 Management Wisdom of the West

In the following subsections we present a selection of ideas of remarkable business practitioners who are not only formidable doers, but who also can think and *write*. We select their key books and identify quotations of their management systems-forming understandings and explanations – *their wisdom*. They are arranged in small "no-comment-packets" for reader's easier consumption and reflection.

5.1.1 Henry Ford. Mostly from his book *Today and Tomorrow*, Doubleday, Page & Company, Garden City, NY, 1926; reprinted by Productivity Press, Cambridge, MA, 1988.

If you shoveled a building full of dollars, you would not have the same capacity for production and use, as you would have if you filled the same building with machinery and organization of human skill.

Money put into business as a lien on its assets is dead money. When industry operates wholly by the permission of "dead" money, its main purpose becomes the production of payments for the owners of that money. If quality of goods jeopardizes these payments, then the quality is cut down. If full service cuts into the payments, then service is cut down. This kind of money does not serve business. It seeks to make business serve it.

Live money in a business is usually accompanied by the active labor of the man or men who put it there. Dead money is a sucker-plant.

Another rock on which business breaks is debt. Debt is nowadays an industry. Luring people into debt is an industry. Possibly it is true that many people, if not most, would bestir themselves very little were it not for the pressure of debt obligations. If so, they are not free men and will not work from free motives. The debt motive is, basically, a slave motive.

Business that exists to feed profits to people, who are not engaged in it, stands on a false basis. This is being so well understood that it has become a part of the creed of commerce: that the service of business is wholly to the public and that the profits of business are due, first to the business itself as a serviceable instrument of humanity, and then to the people whose labor and contributions of effort make the business going concern.

To hold up prices is to tax the people more heavily than even a government could. Good management pays dividends in good wages, lower prices, and more business; it is very bad management that can see in a revival of national ambition only an opportunity to lay heavier burdens on the spirit of enterprise.

Labor is not a commodity. One's own workers ought to be one's own best customers.

In real business there is no gambling. Real business creates its own customer.

All of our new operations are always directed by men who have had no previous knowledge of the subject and therefore have not had a chance to get on really familiar terms with the impossible. Our invariable reply to "it can't be done" is, "Go do it."

Dies are set in the anvils and hammer-faces. As in the case of upsetting machines, each hammer is set with dies that enable it to perform a complete phase of the work of manufacture. There is no division of labor between hammers.

We will use material more carefully if we think of it as labor; we will not so lightly waste material simply because we can reclaim it – for salvage involves labor. The ideal is to have nothing to salvage.

Having on hand twice as much material as is needed – which is only another way of saying that twice as much stored human labor is needed – is precisely the same as hiring two men to do the job that one man ought to do. Hiring two men to do the job of one is a crime against society.

Our finished inventory is all in transit. So is most of our raw material inventory.

One cannot hope to live on a community – one must live in a community.

The function of the machine is to liberate man from brute burdens, and release his energies to the building of his intellectual and spiritual powers for conquests in the field of thought and higher action. One has only to go to other lands to see that the only slave left on Earth is man minus machine.

The stock market as such has nothing to do with business. It has nothing to do with the quality of the article, which is manufactured, nothing to do with the output, nothing to do with the marketing; it does not even increase or decrease the amount of capital used in the business. It is just a little show on the side.

If not a single share of stock were to change hands, it would make no difference to American business. And if every share of stock changed hands tomorrow, industry would not have a cent more or cent less of capital to work with. The whole stock activity, therefore, is on par with organized baseball...

The absentee stockholder is one of the principal, though concealed, items in the unnecessary and preventable costs of living.

Industry is not money – it is made up of ideas, labor and management, and the natural expression of these is not dividends, but utility, quality, and availability, Money is not the source of any of these qualities, though these qualities are the most frequent sources of money.

One of the great steps, which the United States might take, would be to wipe out all tariffs on imports. That would be a real contribution to the world, and also it would be a real contribution to American industry.

5.1.2 Ross Perot. Mostly from his February 15, 1988 article in *Fortune: "How I Would Turn Around GM."*

Financial people will be responsible for maintaining accounting information. People who know how to build cars and serve customers will make the product decisions. Accountants will not sap the productivity of car builders with guerrilla warfare.

Starting today, GMers are going to work together, using brains, wits, creative abilities and initiative as substitutes for money. GM will use money like a scalpel not a bulldozer. The serious problems facing GM have little to do with capital expenditures and everything to do with tapping the full potential of the GM team. If spending money were the answer, GM would already be the first and best at everything it does.

Listen, listen, listen to the customers and the people who are actually doing the work.

Customer problems will not be looked upon as legal problems but as service problems that must be solved immediately. From now on, the customer is king!

Eliminate all waste, starting at the top. Huge staffs, now in place, act as buffers shielding the people running the company from reality. These staffs will be abolished, opening up lines of communication.

Starting today, words like "management," "labor," "bonus-eligible," "salaried" and "hourly" will no longer be used. From this day forward, everyone is a GMer. Everyone will be a full member of a closely-knit, unified GM team.

As of today, all people who manage in an authoritarian way will be fired. First feed the troops, then the officers.

The primary financial incentive offered will be GM stock. There is only one way to make the stock go up: Be the best.

We've got to nuke the GM system. We've got to throw away Sloan's book [*My Years with General Motors*, former chairman Alfred P. Sloan Jr.'s description of GM's management system]. It's like the Old Testament – frozen thousands of years ago.

I come from an environment where, if you see a snake, you kill it. At GM, if you see a snake, the first thing you do is go hire a consultant on snakes. Then you get a committee on snakes, and then you discuss it for a couple of years. The most likely course of action is – nothing. We need to build an environment where the first guy who sees the snake kills it.

I'd get rid of the symbolic things that separate people. I took the position that anybody who needed a chauffeur to drive him to work was probably too old to be on the payroll.

5.1.3 George F. Johnson. Mostly from William Inglis's book *George F. Johnson and His Industrial Democracy*.

The trouble with most employers is that they don't see far enough ahead. If they did, if they had real vision, they'd see that they would be better off paying good wages and helping their workers to lead normal, happy lives, owning their homes and being a real part of the community. But the shortsighted employers want to make quick money, and think they can get it by paying as little as possible, exploiting their workers and the people who buy their product.

We could build up a great enterprise by making our workers comfortable, free of worry, whether in the factory or in their homes; by thinking of them and treating them as human beings, not machines to be run till they broke down and had to be scrapped; to make them as contended as we could within reason. Men everywhere respond to this kind of treatment. It is decent; it is common sense – and it pays too; pays everybody in the enterprise and the whole community.

Those who control labor must live with labor. The children of the workers should grow up with the children of the employers. Executives should be familiar with the lives of their workers – not in a prying sense, but in a social sense. They should be concerned with the happiness and the prosperity of the men and their families. It isn't so all-important that the owners shall prosper, but that people dependent on the industry shall prosper.

Aristocracy – aristocracy of labor, of wealth – I hate it. Just because others are shortsighted is no reason why should I be so. This industry is built on the ideal of democracy, of humanity – and therein lies its strength.

We have a rule that any worker or group of workers with a grievance may come at any time of the day directly to me – even in director's meeting. We keep the human touch.

But the strongest thing in our organization is the good faith based on solid friendship and mutual regard between the head of the concern and the workers – not policy but real friendship. That is our real foundation.

All our executive positions are filled by men who began at the bottom and worked all the way up.

If you want to be "one hundred percent American," be considerate and tolerant, broad and liberal – God-loving and man-loving. Then you will be "one hundred percent American," even though you happened to be born in Africa. Without this, you won't be "one hundred percent American," even though you and your parents, grandparents, and great grandparents were born on Bacon Hill.

There is more profit in selling millions of shoes to the multitude than in selling mere thousands to the lovers of luxury.

Every improvement we make, every improvement and every saving we put into effect is divided into three parts: the workers', the consumers' and the company's. That is one of the best ways to make a business successful and keep it so. People who sell our shoes and people who wear them know from experience that we provide them, at a lower price, the best leather and the most skillful workmanship. So long as we play fair with all three parties in the business, we can be reasonably hopeful of prosperity.

5.1.4 James F. Lincoln. Mostly from his book *A New Approach to Industrial Economics.* The Devin Adair Company, New York, 1961.

The usual absentee stockholder contributes nothing to the efficiency of the operation. He buys a stock today and sells it tomorrow. He often does not even know what the company makes. Why should he be rewarded with large dividends?

There are no layoffs at the Lincoln Electric Company when business slumps. Employment is continuous. There is only retirement at advanced age and the occasional drop-off, when the man does not fit.

There is no doubt that following habit relieves us of much mental effort. Following habit, however, prevents progress. Progress is made only by doing the new and habitually unusual. Progress can be made in no other way.

The worker today is an expert who has abilities that are far beyond the boss's. His contribution is completely necessary if industry is to succeed and progress.

Since the wish to make the product better in design and lower in cost is the desire of all involved, there will be continuous development of the latent abilities of all those who are responsible for this progress in the company. They will as a consequence be progressively more able, more productive and more efficient. They will constantly increase in individual stature.

The worker will be continuously employed. This will eliminate his fear of the future, which now makes him resist progress in efficiency.

The interests of labor, management and the customer are identical in the final analysis. They are the same people ultimately.

Only management is responsible for the loss of the worker's job. Only management can follow and develop a program that will bring in orders. The worker can't. Management, which is responsible, keeps its job. The man who had no responsibility is thrown out. Management failed in its job and had no punishment. No man will go along with such injustice, nor should he.

There are two groups who must be rewarded for increased profits. They are, first, the workers, from top to bottom, who increased the profit by their skill and cooperation. Second, of equal importance, is the customer, He paid for all the costs of production and all profit. He is the reason that industry exists.

The last group to be considered is the stockholders who own stock because they think it will be more profitable than investing money in any other way.

The stockholder, as listed here, is not the man who is the owner or who founded the business or supplied the original capital. Such founding owners usually are actual producers and should be so considered. But the absentee stockholder is not of any value to the customer or the worker, since he has neither knowledge of nor interest in the company; his only interest is in greater dividends and an advance in the price of his stock.

Cooperation between labor and management must be accomplished if we are to retain our present position in the family of nations. We are rapidly losing our place now in competition with manufacturers in Europe and Asia. If this continues as it is now going, we soon will be outdistanced.

Our present program of collective bargaining, management and labor together determine how much the customer will pay for the worker's remuneration and for his inefficiencies. The customer, who pays all costs, is not even consulted. It is not strange that the results from such irresponsible bargaining should be disappointing and often foolish, as we now see.

The proper responsibility of the industry is to build a better and better product at a lower and lower price.

There is no known limit to the cost reductions that can be made in the manufacture of any product if cost reduction is the actual goal of both management and men. But that goal is largely changed to increasing profits and dividends when the hired manager is under the direction of the stockholder.

As the rare geniuses that are in the industry disappear, the economy will be greatly changed by their absence. The individual owner and operator of an industry has an entirely different outlook and goal for his company than the hired managers who operate the large and complex organizations, which are the results of the present combinations of smaller companies that have been absorbed.

The industry's goal, if it is to succeed as it can, must be completely different from simply increasing dividends. The industry controls our standard of living. We cannot allow it to be converted to a source of profit only for a limited number of non-producing people.

Salesmen will change from peddlers to consultants. Their number will greatly decrease. Advertising will be changed from deception to instruction and it will also decrease in volume. The reputation of a product will be determined not by the quantity of money spent in advertising it, but by its actual use to the customer.

The goal of a properly led company is better quality at a lower price. If it does not or cannot do that, it should disappear and eventually it will. Competition will destroy it in a free market. That is what competition is for.

Efficiency cannot eliminate jobs because increased efficiency lowers costs, lower costs cause lower prices, lower prices expand the market, and an expanding market increases employment.

It is not part of the management's responsibility to be merely kind to workers. Managers are responsible for efficiency in their industry. Efficiency depends on human cooperation within the industry. If genuine cooperation is to be regained, it is absolutely essential that wage earner's present fear of losing his income be eliminated. Only removing the danger can eliminate that fear. Only guaranteeing continuous employment can do this.

It is strange that people suppose that men are more careful of other men's property than of their own. In fact, government operation always has been far more wasteful than private enterprise.

5.1.5 *Sir Fletcher Jones*. Mostly from his book *Not by myself*, Kingfisher Books Pty Ltd., Cheltenham, Vic., 1976.

Customer benefits come first, second and third.
Quality without compromise.

Management by Consultation.
Family & Staff Co-operative Ownership.

The retail salesman acted both as the buying agent for his customer and as the last element in the production line, which began with the cloth developers and ended "two feet from the customer."

Employee shares carry equal rights and all shares remain within the FJ Family. Any shareholder that left the employ before retiring age was expected to sell his or her shares. Shares held by present and past employees, and the widows of deceased employees now exceed 70 percent. Our shares should not be looked on as means of speculation. Each year in addition to our normal cash dividend, a dividend of 5 percent to 7 percent has been satisfied by the allotment of shares.

The only justification for the ownership of the means of production and distribution lies in a determination to "give more and more for less and less."

Fletcher Jones will remain interested in your garment as long as you are.

If you need to buy sixty dozen items it is better to buy them from two selected suppliers than from ten. A buying order is like a small piece of butter. A small piece of butter spread over many pieces of bread just cannot be tasted.

The retailer is the customer's buying agent. In Group Buying one details the customer's needs and plans to have the right garment in the right place at the right time and at the right price.

Any fool can buy successfully as long as he continually asks himself two important questions. They are: "where is the need?" and "whom shall we serve?"

From Company slogans:

It All Depends on Me.
Let the People Sing.
Use your head when buying a hat.
Look at your hat – Everyone else does.
No Man is Hard to Fit.
No Credit for Anyone.

We've had shops with no offices and desks in odd places. We've insisted on a cash-only policy for all customers. We've been obsessed with making sure our garments fit. We've stuck to a monetary mark-up system of pricing. We've hoped in all our ways to give more and more for less and less.

No man should leave the world as bad as he found it.

What a man says whispers – what he does thunders.

Correct fitting is three-dimensional. You have to fit a man's mind as well as his body. Then, when you think you've managed this, you find you have to fit his wife's mind as well.

If you are an industrialist who is interested in people you are more likely to be interested in decentralization than you would be if you were interested in profits or in personal convenience.

If it is good for one man to concentrate on a current problem, why not get a lot of men concentrating on the same well-defined problem and doing so in one spot altogether? We have found the stand-up meeting to be a good way of doing this.

KISS – Keep It Simple, Stupid.

A man needs more satisfaction from his work. The pay envelope is important. Of course it is. But job satisfaction is more vital. One of the tragedies of the so-called economics of scale in this modern world of ours is the way in which the importance of the individual seems to have become of decreasing significance.

"Lord, if Though dost allow me to have a shop some day, I promise Thee that I will run it from the customer's point of view."

We are going to build a new kind of factory. We will pull all these rules down from the walls: Thou shalt not this, thou shalt not that, thou shall this and that.

We will put up the only rule that matters, Do unto others as ye would be done by them.

No war, no strike, and no depression can so completely destroy an established business, or its usefulness, as can new and better methods, equipment and materials in the hands of an enlightened competitor.

The never-ending quest for better quality can surely be a good substitute for the individual's pride in craftsmanship, as in the days gone by. A continuing interest in the customer's property can be a substitute for the personal relationships, which might have existed between the craftsman and his customer.

5.1.6 Tomas Bata. Mostly from his book *Uvahy a proje*vy (Reflections and Speeches), TISK, Zlin, 1932. Reprinted by SUTB, New York, 1986. Also from A. Cekota's *Entrepreneur Extraordinary,* Edizioni Internazionali Sociali, Rome, 1968.

The only thing we can never consider being our private property is our life – we contributed nothing to its origin. It was loaned to us with the duty to pass it on to our descendants improved and enriched.

To make capitalists from all of our employees is one of the primary objectives of my business.

Buildings – they are just piles of brick and concrete. Machines – they are a lot of iron and steel. Only people can give life to it all.

I have no wealth – I have only shoes for customers and leather for workers. It is the same kind of wealth as a telescope is for an astronomer or a violin for a musician. Without it, I could not give work to my associates and shoes to my customers. I would be of the same value to the world as a violinist without a violin.

The profit sharing of employees is obviously not a new idea. At the present time, American entrepreneurs use it the most. However, I was looking for a way of employee profit sharing that would help to establish autonomy of the workshop.

The workshop autonomy is not only cheaper but also better. Nobody knows the job impediments better than I do, actually performing the work. The better the selection of the workshop participants and the smaller their turnover, the more successful the autonomy will be.

A competent executive is busy running around, searching for and educating people who could replace him and eventually take over his job altogether.

You will see Mr. President [*then T.G. Masaryk*], that every one of us, each employee, has an electrical robot at his disposal. I consider it one of my greatest achievements that these robots now perform the work, which used to leave bloody blisters on the hands of our fathers. Robots release the greatest powers of man – the powers of the human mind.

Americanism is an empty word. No "-ism" has ever helped anybody or resolved anything. And it never will.

High wages are achievable only through human intelligence.

We shall achieve real success only when we educate the people to manage and direct their own work. It is more difficult to teach people to think for themselves than to obey.

We know what our sales department would look like, with its many branches and stores, if we had not discovered the way to turn our store managers into entrepreneurs. These branches and stores enjoy complete autonomy.

Our enterprise is already directing itself to these principles. We have the financial ability to pay out at any time the claims of the employees. We do not utilize bank loans and credit. We pay our suppliers cash, immediately upon receipt of the goods. The money we owe to our employees is deposited in safe bonds, readily transferable into cash. We do not use the employees' savings for the operation of the business.

5.1.7 Homer M. Sarasohn. Mostly from his and Charles Protzman's 1948 book, *CCS: Industrial Management* and the February 6, 1989 article in *Forbes*, pp. 70-78.

Managers should look at every aspect of a manufacturing operation as a piece of an integrated system, and should think through the consequences for the entire system of fiddling with any of its parts.

Every company needs a concise, complete statement of the purpose of the company's existence, one that provides a well-defined target for the idealistic efforts of the employees.

Companies must put quality ahead of profit, pursuing it rigorously with techniques such as statistical quality control.

Every employee deserves the same kind of respect fellow managers receive, and good management is "democratic management." Lower-level employees need to be listened to by their bosses.

"We shall build good ships here: at a profit if we can, at a loss if we must, but always good ships." *Motto of Newport News Shipbuilding*

Every business enterprise should have as its very basic policy to aim the entire resources and efforts of the company toward a well-defined target, a target that would benefit society.

This present-day fad of aping the Japanese style of management is absolutely destructive of our own future. We've got to recapture the enthusiasm, the pioneering spirit that made America a world leader.

Human systems management wisdom is a truly beautiful thing to behold. It has been accumulated over the centuries and put to good use in the service of mankind. There is an inner beauty in doing things really well: there is quality, harmony and coordination, *there is a system.*

One of the truly remarkable global enterprises has been Bata Corp. and its even more remarkable system of management.

5.2 Bata System of Management

One of the entrepreneurs analyzed in the previous section is Tomas Bata. His management system was undoubtedly the most complete and most modern and successful. For Bata, a company was not just a money-making machine.

Bata enterprise was organized and behaving as a living organism – learning, adapting and self-organizing. It was also viewed as such by Bata and his *associates* – a label for employees copied today by Wall-Mart. Employees felt to be parts and components of a living organism, not of well-oiled, well-crafted machinery.

One of the associates, Max John, wrote: "During my employment with Bata, where I could rotate through all departments of the firm, I had an opportunity to comprehend the overall organization of production and interpersonal relations within the company. The organization and functioning of the company reminded me of the living organism, with all life processes being maximally efficient, often suggesting optimal behavior of a successful and healthy animal.

The brain of this organism was the board of directors and the heart of the circulatory functions was the central warehouse, working according to the principles of profit maximization…"

Bata recognized – long before current corporate personalities – that not money, not technology, not labor and not real estate, but *knowledge* is the most important form of capital and the sole source of a sustainable competitive advantage.

5.2.1 The System of "Eight Principles"

Bata Co. practiced the system of Eight Principles, or key conceptual dimensions and their practical realizations, which formed the Bata Management System (BMS):

Dimension	Realization
world class	global benchmarking
cooperation	work partnership
self-government	private corporation
participation	profit sharing
co-ownership	employee capitalization
self-management	shop autonomy
co-entrepreneurship	market/customer focus
competition	internal benchmarking

The *8P* system also integrated three additional dimensions, like independence, knowledge sharing and synergy, but these were derived or implied rather than being explicitly constitutive of the Bata System.

In short, Bata Co. was an integrated system characterized by co-ownership, profit sharing and the managerial autonomy of departments, shops and processes. The company was a privately held corporation, not a publicly owned one: there were no public stock and no public trading with company ownership. The company thus enjoyed a good measure of independence, self-government, flexibility and long-term strategic orientation. It created a harmonious, ecological co-existence and active co-evolution with its immediate environs (Zlín) and the Moravian region as a whole. Employees were partners and associates (*spolupracovníci*), capable of effective cooperation, sharing and considerable sacrifice. They all were held to the highest standards of excellence through internal competitive benchmarking and intracompany markets, as well as through vigorous global aspirations and world-class competitiveness.

All ranks of employees, from the "Chief" all the way down to apprentices, were able to realize not only their work lives, but their full professional careers and personal growth, as well as social development, through this self-renewing and self-enhancing corporate organism.

5.2.2 Evolution of Bata Co.

The Bata Enterprises, the first truly global corporation, was founded by Tomas Bata (1876–1932) who came from humble beginnings, as the son of a shoemaker in a small town in Moravia, to be one of the foremost entrepreneurs of the new state of Czechoslovakia in 1918. Strongly influenced by American industrial practices and the early thinking and experiences of Henry Ford, Bata combined them with the cultural distinctiveness of his native Moravia and created what is still known as the "Bata Management System." This participative, human-oriented system was many years in advance of its time, including concepts such as empowerment, worker participation and quality improvement.

Fortunately, Bata's system did survive his premature death in 1932 and the company found its largest success and expansion under the steersmanship of his step-brother Jan Bata. After the occupation of Czechoslovakia by Nazi Germany seven years later, the company headquarters relocated to the U.S. and Canada and it still operates globally today, domiciled in Toronto, Canada, under the leadership of Thomas J. Bata.

The Bata system of management found its roots in Henry Ford's ideas – those before 1926 – as summarized in his seminal book *Today and Tomorrow*. Ford's early view of management was based on worker autonomy, knowledge, just-in-time, waste minimization, quality and customer's involvement (customization). It was all but abandoned by Ford in his turnaround embrace of mass production, taylorism and hierarchical management in the 1930s.

But in Moravia, Tomas Bata remained true to Ford's original ideas and brought them to practical fruition in the late 1920s and early 1930s. Young Tomas, who repeatedly visited, trained and worked in the U.S.A., brought home the lessons of self-reliance, quality management, strategic flexibility, high technology, worker participation and use of knowledge as capital.

The first international conference on the Bata System of Management took place in Zlin, at the Tomas Bata University, on May 16-18, 2001. The second one has taken place in May 19-20, 2005.

Bata System of Management

The Bata system is a management system of extraordinary productivity and effectiveness. Its main characteristics include: integration instead of division of labor, whole-system orientation, continuous innovation and quality improvement, team and workshop self-management, profit-sharing and autonomy, workers' participation and co-determination, clearly-defined responsibilities, organizational flexibility, vigorous automation and most importantly an uncompromisingly human-orientated capitalistic enterprise. Every employee was a partner, co-worker or associate and all workers were to become owners and capitalists.

There are clearly identifiable principles which Tomas Bata evolved, adhered to and ultimately made to work. He proclaimed his first slogan "Thinking to the people, labor to the machines!" at the factory gate. He eliminated the intermediaries: a large network of Bata-run stores and outlets complemented and extended his production operations by integrating customers into the production process.

Bata also made the consumer and the public not only the purpose, but the very foundation of his enterprise. "Our customer – our master" and "Service to the public" were not just slogans, but sound principles of business. Production and profits were not the ends, but the means towards improving the individual lives of all Bata employees. Employment was stable and long term: a part of each worker's earnings was reinvested in the company (the initial endowment put up by the company) – each worker became a capitalist and partial co-owner.

Bata claimed that the quality of employee life was a primary concern of the employer (not of the state). He offered economic incentives to employees to stop drinking and smoking, or to lose weight. He provided family housing (with gardens) and a minimum social infrastructure: hospitals, museums, churches, swimming pools, recreational facilities, sport stadiums, and roads – all part of the self-imposed responsibilities of Bata Enterprises.

He also established and ran his own school of management: an institution considered too important to be left to the external and traditional providers of business education. He was seeking enhanced self-reliance, independence and vertical integration: railroads, waterways, airports, land, forests, even local government – all became connected to his enterprise. He strove to operate with no debt and with no credit: all state taxes were paid according to obsessive principles of integrity.

Thanks to these and similar principles, Bata's business grew and flourished even during the worldwide depression of 1929–1932. He was fully aware of the qualities of his system: he knew it was a whole which could not be copied in parts – there were no "company secrets." Often he assured his associates that no fair competition could ever pose a threat to their performance.

However, the Bata system was gravely damaged by the "unfair competition" of politics and Nazi ideology in 1939, and then it was vilified and later proscribed by Marxists and communists of the post-1948 era. Bata's own family, managers and workers were forced into exile.

Operational practices

Bata's strong symbiosis of workers' autonomy and empowerment through technology was unique and even by today's standards still remains somewhat "futuristic." Let us consider a short sample of Bata practices:

1. the process of continuous innovation and improvement; the total system of preventive maintenance: machine shop working as "clockwork;"
2. in-house adaptation and rebuilding of all purchased machinery; 10 percent of the engineering employees involved directly in the R&D function;
3. the assurance of continuously high-quality output with processes streamlined to eliminate breakdowns and stoppages and individual workers given quality responsibility;

4. total manufacturing flexibility was achieved by:
   (i) breaking the traditional large factory plant into smaller, semi-autonomous and specialized workshops; and
   (ii) making all machines self-contained, independently powered and motorized by electric motors (referred to as "electric robots" by Bata);
5. changes in product styles and types were achieved quickly (in a few hours) by rearranging machine sequences and layouts, by pulling out machines temporarily ("decoupling the line") and by designing all adjustments and customization into the final stages of the production process;
6. a close personal "ownership" relationship between workers and "their" machine: not only was there no suspicion of the machinery but there was also no neglect, only pride of ownership, emotional involvement and total care;
7. all operators were able to stop production line conveyors at will; all waste in production was minimized (everything had to be just in time for the next step); all machines were designed to serve "the process," not just perform individual operations;
8. dedication to automation: one of the Bata machines "did everything but talk and sing" (the note-scribbling overseas visitors were never able to copy it; a machine called the "Union press" produced a pair of shoes in a single movement);
9. a perfect, semi-automated, rotational system of preventive maintenance of all machinery (including full overhauls and updates), carried out without ever stopping the production.

Human capital at Bata Enterprises

Another set of Bata's concepts is related directly to people. The need for the total involvement of top management was never questioned. In order to be promoted to a top managerial position, one had to personally make a pair of shoes. All executives remained close to their product and actually had to learn how to make it themselves.

Quality circles also emerged spontaneously, because they had to. More interesting is that top executives (and T. Bata himself) were part of the continuous quality improvement process: their suggestions ranged from a company-store door design to teaching all workers statistics and profit calculations.

Many decades before the collapse of management hierarchies, Bata and his entire directorship took their lunch in the company cafeteria (to assure proper quality of food and operations). It was insisted that each executive must be replaceable and that competent leaders must be continually trained and educated:

the company-run school and the Tomas Bata School of Work and Management were the answer. Bata was no fool: "High wages can only be attained through human intelligence," he insisted.

Bata was also an optimist ("A day has 86,400 seconds"): he simply knew it was possible to succeed. What about the Management by walking around? Jan Bata put his office in an elevator – in order to be close to his operations and associates. They rejected the notion that any acquired wealth must be taken from somebody else (the "zero-sum" fallacy). His workers were paid eight times more than the prevailing average. He projected that each worker should be able to retire at 50 and live from their accumulated capital. The best savings strategy, he taught, was the repayment of debts. He warned that producers asking for state customs and quota protections ultimately harm the public and minimize employees' gains. To beg for subsidies or bailouts was not only unworthy of a professional manager, but to Bata, any such managed competition was unacceptable.

He also dreamt, almost longingly, about the "new machines" which would ease human mental work, computations and accounting. He had big plans for such computing machines. Bata's response to the ravages of the Depression was masterful and yet not tried anywhere else: he achieved workers' approval to reduce wages by 40 percent; at the same time he took steps to reduce their cost of living expenditures by 50 percent; finally, he reduced the prices of all Bata products by 50 percent. It worked: Bata Enterprises and employees flourished even during the Depression.

Bata was fond of saying: "And how do they do things in England?" He liked to answer, rather proudly: "Just the other way around. In England there is no understanding between managers and workers. They do not trust each other. They even have powerful adversary organizations, separately for employers and employees. Employers are not allowed to raise wages without approval... workers cannot accept work on their own terms..."

Tomas Bata was never short of courage: "We are the pioneers. The cowards did not even start on the journey; the weak were lost on the way. Forward!"

Agenda for Change

The stages of progression towards the Bata System of Management (and organization) are not based on assorted techniques, methods, systems and technologies, but on nothing less than creating a corporate organism, bringing forth the living organization.

This *agenda for change* clearly requires a strong focus on what has to be preserved, not on what has to be changed. Once we know the core areas to be preserved, then we can manage the change effectively. One cannot know what to change unless one knows what *not* to change:

1. Decide which core areas (competencies and values) of the company are vital to its existence and should be preserved. Then make a commitment to changing all the rest.
2. Establish clear lines of authority, responsibility, decision-making powers, and guidelines for behavior in the core areas.
3. Develop (and derive from experience) well-defined rules and regulations for enforcing proper conduct in the core areas.
4. Create systems to monitor and evaluate performance and to assure discipline in the core areas as much as needed or necessary. This is your corporate core.
5. Educate new recruits and present employees to fully understand and appreciate the importance of preserving the core and conforming to its standards. Now you can change.
6. Communicate and continually reinforce the importance of the core standards in evolving new organizational forms, systems and structures of management, communication and experience. Your corporation is ready to learn.
7. Introduce incentives and rewards for outstanding implementation and performance by individuals or groups, with respect to preserving core values and projecting them into new structures. Reinforce corporate learning.
8. Recognize and award exceptional persons, for outstanding service and leadership, socially, publicly or privately, in order to rebuild a self-sustaining organizational culture.
9. Relax the external forms of enforcement, extend greater freedom, and gradually allow self-discipline, peer pressure and sense of corporate identity to take the place of external authority.
10. Identify and support each individual in terms of his or her own personal growth and a self-rewarding experience within the company. The person's adherence to the company becomes an expression of identity of personal and corporate growth.

5.2.3 The Aim of an Enterprise

Myron Tribus has presented Bata's perspectives on business aims at the First Bata Conference in 2001. He referred to David Maley and his analysis of various factors essential to business success. There are three significant factors which could be arranged in three different ways, depending upon what the management thought was the aim of the enterprise. Bata represents the fourth way…

The first arrangement corresponds to the dominant mode in most countries:

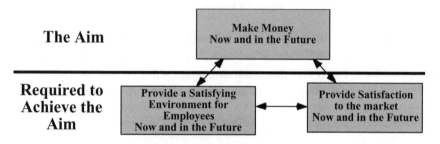

Figure 5.1 Shareholder dominance.

In this view the most important objective for the company is to make money. It is the main reason for the company to exist. "Increase shareholder value" is the watchword.

The second arrangement corresponds to the recommendations of people in the quality movement. "Put Quality First" is their slogan.

Figure 5.2 "The customer comes first."

The third possible arrangement, according to David Maley, is to make the welfare of the employees the first consideration, as shown in Figure 5.3.

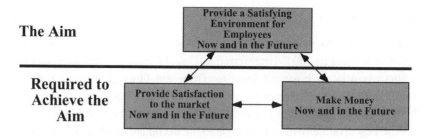

Figure 5.3 Employees first.

There are not too many companies following this third choice of aim. Pacific Southwest Airways in California advertises itself as looking after employees first, on the basis that if they do so, the employees will look after customers.

Bata followed a different aim, as suggested in the following diagram:

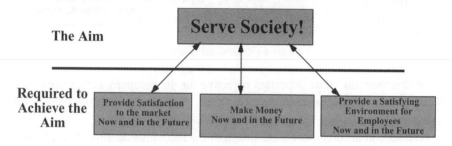

Figure 5.4 Bata's aim.

From both word and deed we learn clearly that Bata thought of his business enterprise as an instrument for social good. From very early on, in the early 1900s, he thought of his company as being the means to lift the standard of living of people not only in Zlin but everywhere in the world.

5.3 Bata Management Wisdom

Each country and region exhibits a wide range of cultural wealth: not only the visible things such as buildings, cathedrals and works of art, but also literature, music, paintings, theatre and film. These usually dominate thanks to their visibility and longevity. However, there exists a less visible wealth, embedded in the knowledge, abilities, methods and experiences of people, forming the root source (*urquell*) of all those visible "things" of cultural wealth. Knowledge is the unique foundation of the culture of any nation. Management knowledge and wisdom is the foundation of that. The Bata Management System can be considered such a foundation.

Because an authentic quotation is often more convincing than a theoretical explanation, we use Bata's own words, thoughts and concepts (presented in *italics*) as our leads to subsequent comments and explanations.

Reading a body of knowledge should be an input into the life of reflection, a road to wisdom. One can get lost in data, overloaded by information, there is never too much knowledge – but wisdom is the rarest of possessions.

Our life is the only thing in this world that we cannot consider to be our private property, as we have not contributed anything to its generation. It was only conferred to us with the obligation and expectation to pass it on to our posterity, multiplied and improved. Creation and enhancement of our own life is our duty and privilege: we are presenting the accounts of our conferred gifts of life to our contemporaries as well as to the next generations. Our accounting should not end in a deficit, a loss, or impoverishment of our contemporaries and successors. We start with the "debit" and we end with the "credit" and only we are responsible for the final balance. Life is a capital and therefore it must, in the same way as a fertile seed, create something more, something to be left for the "spring sowing"…

Because of such a thoroughly western credo, Tomas Bata left behind a body of practical work, a tangible small model of a working and managing society, as he created in Zlin. He was an *entrepreneur*.

An "entrepreneur" (not "businessman," "merchant," "dealer" or "shopkeeper") is a person who brings new products, new services and new values to the market. An entrepreneur opens new markets. A person that just keeps a tobacco shop or an inn cannot be considered an entrepreneur – he is but a tradesman (or an innkeeper). An entrepreneur does not just maintain his livelihood, but through his undertakings creates value for others. An entrepreneur does not steal, because stealing is not a creation.

During his trips in the U.S.A., Bata tried to find a job in order to learn how to work. He took machine operation tests, but he never got any job: *I underwent maybe twenty of such tests a day, six times that within a week. My mind became depressed and dispirited. I did not care about the dollars imported from America. I wanted American dollars. I wanted to measure myself directly with an American.*

We all have to measure ourselves with our peers. However, we all have the basic freedom to choose our own peers. How we choose our benchmarks, how we choose the measures of our success and happiness, determines more then anything else what we become.

Once being on such a journey, I said to myself that I would not eat until I get a job. And I got one. From a vagabond, a useless person, all of a sudden I became a nobleman. My hands were torn and bruised, but my head was sitting firmly in its place. That was the beginning for Tomas Bata. He realized early that a dollar is not a dollar. A dollar earned is different from an imported dollar, and that is different from a dollar gained or stolen. A dollar earned by his own work and directly in America, in a competition with his chosen peers, is the "real" American dollar – and that is the one Bata cared for. It makes no sense to compare or "benchmark" yourself to those who are similar or even worse than you are. You have to compare yourself only with your superiors – and only through such choice become better yourself.

In America I liked the better and more equal relationship between worker and employer: I am the master, you are the master, I am a businessman, and you are a businessman. I wished that such a way of life would also exist here in Zlin. I wished that we would all become equal, somehow. It is here where we can trace the first beginnings of Bata's workshop self-management. But workers in those days still preferred to remain hired laborers; they did not want to "become equal." Trade unions supported them in their passivity and irresponsibility. Who has ever heard "each worker a capitalist!" It needed a new frame of thought, an entrepreneurial thought.

Should you ever want to build a big enterprise, build up yourselves first. Only a great person is capable of creating a great enterprise. Each (real) entrepreneur produces three things: him or herself, the enterprise, and the product – in that sequence of importance. First come values, convictions, a vision, character, persistency, knowledge and capabilities. The next is the enterprise: its ability to produce and provide service, the knowledge of how to do things right, and also how to do the right things. And then, in the end, there is the product and the service that should satisfy the customer better and provide more value than any other does.

While working I did not think of building a company, but of building up the people. I have empowered man so that he could be more efficient and serve people better. Then he would build a good company. The principal duty of an organizer is to create psychological and moral foundations – as in any institution of learning. Corporation as an institution of learning? The moral, ethical and psychological basis of an enterprise is emerging. A successful enterprise is based on (proper) relationships and attitudes toward work, co-workers and customers. No hired laborer of any enterprise can create anything himself. He must become a collaborator, a participant, a co-owner and co-entrepreneur.

Only the field plowed by the farmer himself would yield rich crops. Only the shepherd, the owner of his sheep, is ready to face the wolves and protect his herd. A hired laborer, who is not a sheep owner, would run away. To work "with his plow" is a duty of each entrepreneur. Only workers co-owning the enterprise will work for it and stand for it even in bad times. Hired laborers (and managers) will fill their little (or larger) rucksacks and run away at the first howling of the wolves.

Bata liked to dwell on the obvious: *A day has 86,400 seconds.* What does it mean?

Clearly, a day has 86,400 moments. You arrive within a moment, and leave as well. You are able to decide in a moment. Even a brainwave of a new idea hits within a moment. Our own life, our work and entrepreneurship consist of moments. Each moment is valid. Most of us probably know people working days and nights, sometimes even during weekends, they do work constantly: in a car, in a bathtub, during a walk, while doing other work. However, moments are running through their fingers and they never have any time. Having no time does not mean working – and working continually does not mean working well. Why do people who have no time usually achieve so little? Because they do not understand their moments. They do not know that it is not important to dig a big hole through the night; what matters is whether it is really necessary to dig it. Asking questions first, asking why? It takes all night to dig a hole, and it takes a moment to make a decision that it is not needed. Therefore: do only what is essential, but do it fast and effectively. Then also your day will consist of 86,400 valuable moments.

What were the kinds of slogans such people would put on their factory walls?

Let's be creditors, not debtors!
A clever man starts where a blockhead ends
Cleanliness + order = quality
Everybody should be an entrepreneur at his workplace
Pay in cash, do not borrow
Help yourself

Do not continue with already bad work
The customer's wish is our law
Strong individuals love life
Learn languages
Strength means speed
Experience – mother of knowledge

Of course, money was also very important to Bata, but not as a direct goal, but as means toward greater, more important goals.

Those who are only chasing after money will never catch up with it. Do work well and honestly; try to do it better than your neighbor. Money will come running after you. Money is like a shy doe or a beautiful woman – you have to approach them slowly, indirectly, from a distance, with patience. Money itself is not the target – what matters is the process of earning money. For sure you do not want to do business here, to grab some money there, and jump from one job to another, from one business to another. You want a steady, increasing and lasting flow of money, the process itself. You do not want a job, you want a career. You want those shy does and beautiful women – as well as money – to come to you, to search you out.

Let me advise you, because I am a good manager; I have learned how to earn pennies as well as millions. The accent is on the word "earn." Not just make, get, steal, borrow, win or swindle – but *earn!* He, who wants to work least for the highest income, will remain poor forever.

As there does not exist any textbook or tried and tested method, I decided to build my own system, which – as I hope – would help mankind. The name of this system is: "An example." Learning and teaching through examples is undoubtedly the most powerful form of leadership. Only a great person is able to use this method successfully. People without vision and moral values, people without character, or without deep knowledge and skills – should not stand up as role models or examples. Let us not be afraid of great persons as they will not hurt you. They will always serve as a creative example and motivation. One should be afraid of weaker people, whatever high place they occupy: these people, being driven into the corner or dissatisfied with themselves, can damage or destroy you and their surroundings.

The prerequisite for the prosperity of our enterprise is that you should not imagine the enterprise as yours, or existing only for you. Our enterprise has not been built up merely to provide its founders with a livelihood. In our enterprise we are bringing new, until now unknown, wealth and education to our people.

The aim of the entrepreneurship is the service to the public, the service to the people and the service to the world – always and only the service. In entrepreneurship, the leading and managing by service is necessary for achieving success. Enterprises, not the state, are the bodies bringing quality of life and possibilities of education to the nation. A country without good enterprises, a country of consumers rather than producers, is not a very good country.

Enterprises are part of the nation's culture. We do not recognize a cultural nation by cathedrals, museums, schools, music and paintings, but mostly by its culture of work and attitudes toward work, by its working environment and the respect toward education. Foundations of national culture are rooted in the culture of the enterprise and entrepreneurship.

In order to build a strategic environment for motivation, innovation and entrepreneurship, one has to engage all employees: *We are granting you a share in the profits not because we feel a need to give some money to people, out of the goodness of our hearts. No, in taking this step we have other goals. By doing this, we want to achieve a further decrease of production costs. We want to reach the situation in which shoes are cheaper and workers earn more.*

We are therefore offering you a share in the profits your workshop makes. The independently working workshops or departments are small and consequently everybody should help to increase profits of his workshop. The accounting is so simple that everyone can understand it and the account of losses and profits will be posted every week in the particular department. Should your department, in certain weeks, show a loss, it would not be to your detriment, as you are not going to share in the losses.

Here we find the participation in profit sharing combined with workshop self-management. The functions of co-ownership and co-entrepreneurship are integrated. Why is the participation in the department's loss excluded? The profit is created in the workshop, but the loss is the "co-responsibility" of the management that did not create good enough conditions for profit realization.

Having no shares in profits already penalizes the workshop. Moreover, if losses continue to occur for a longer period, a workshop's existence in the enterprise would be endangered: no enterprise can tolerate permanent losses. Individuals, teams and departments who do not add value should not take part in the enterprise.

By profit sharing we intend to boost the moral and material well-being of our workers. A worker should understand our business, should grow with it. We wish that all our workers became financial partners in our enterprise. We ask that you use your higher income to improve the living standards of your families and enhance your education. Only then we can hope that the enterprise will recover the invested funds. Your increased capabilities can be applied to work for the enterprise or to public service of our country. Each worker should become a capitalist, a capital participant of the enterprise – co-entrepreneur. Education, schooling and training were not considered as costs, an item being cut first when the money is short. Education is an investment: a strategic instrument to improve output and competitiveness – in a properly organized enterprise.

Workshop Self-Management. Participation in profits did not mean traditional profit sharing through yearly redistribution of bonuses and extra salaries. This is not co-entrepreneurship, but a "collective consumption." Participation in profits is an integral part of workshop self-management. In order to let people participate in profits, they have to have optimal conditions for profit creation:

1. The profits should be calculated at very short intervals: once a week (in today's Kyocera Co. daily).
2. Everyone participating in the scheme should be able to calculate the size of his own share.
3. The profit-sharing scheme should be based on the distribution of workers into smaller teams, so that every participant in the scheme would partake in the self-management of the workshop.

Knowledge is not missing from the above rules. In order for people to take part, *they have to know* what to do and when and why to do it. They have to know how to improve production processes and management of workshops in order to produce necessary profits. Creation of profits precedes its distribution. It is much more difficult to teach people to think and act on their own, than it is to teach them to obey and follow orders.

The workshop autonomy is not only cheaper, it is also better. When actually doing the work, I know better than others where the problems are. Execution of the work is the best source of knowledge about the work. The person performing the work is at the same time the bearer of this knowledge. It is implicit in the quality of performance if the worker possesses the necessary array of specific skills and knowledge. The problem is how to co-ordinate these different, complementary "complexes of specific skills." It is possible to do that either by command – like in the traditional system – or through self-management and a system of intracompany prices. A reliable price system is the best coordinator of human economic activity, and no system of rules and orders can be so efficient.

Using an intracompany pricing system, each department in the production chain had to purchase the necessary "goods" from the preceding department. After completing its work, a workshop's "goods" are sold to the next workshop in the value chain.

Bata industrial transportation was based on establishing a special relationship with the truck driver. This relation was stipulated by a contract. After a certain mileage – as a rule within two years – the driver became *the owner* of the truck. He had a mileage tariff guaranteed by the contract. It consisted of a calculated price for fuel, truck servicing, and amortization of the truck's purchase price and profits for the driver; by this contract he became an individual *entrepreneur*. It is self-evident that these drivers took proper care of their trucks even before they became their owners. This system was virtually faultless.

Through my work, I usually realize my own ideas. Most people's work consists of following the commands of others. Even when working sixteen hours a day, I do not feel that I work more than others, because I find pleasure in my work and I learn from it. The work could mean "suffering" for a hired worker as he cannot wait to see his salvation in the words "Thank God, the workday is over." He starts his life after the working hours. The worker who is also the co-worker and the co-owner realizes his own thoughts and ideas; his well paid work brings inspiration, education and satisfaction in life.

Management of an enterprise cannot be done without trust. If I did not trust people and had to check everything by myself, it would cost more than the damage that might have eventually arisen from breaking my trust. An enterprise of long-term significance cannot be managed without the trust. The wealthiest companies are noted by their high degree of trust in employees, the poorest by a high degree of mistrust. The trust, as knowledge, is a productive force, being the most valuable capital for an enterprise society.

We should make the greatest effort to know the truth about the world and ourselves. We should neither deceive nor flatter ourselves, but we must not allow others to deceive or flatter us either. Recognition of the truth includes self-recognition – understanding the truth about oneself and about the company. The worst attributes of an entrepreneur are self-appraising, self-bragging and self-assessment. Only the others, the customers and the market, can evaluate our qualities and added value.

To help the foreman acquire property by giving him presents makes no sense whatsoever. It would be too easy. All it would require would be distributing initially certain amounts of money; just as the farmer's wife puts false eggs into a basket in order to lure the hen to lay real eggs. By dispensing gifts of money to people, we achieve exactly the opposite results – because people have a better memory than chickens. People become dependent on handouts and ignore their abilities of self-reliance. It is the question of morale, education and building up necessary self-discipline and self-confidence.

The desire to become irreplaceable is the motive of progress, but the wish to remain irreplaceable slows down the progress. The desire to excel and to measure up with the best in the world constitutes a wealth of the nation. If a man becomes indispensable, it is both an award and obligation at the same time. The need to be useful to others, not only to oneself, represents a higher-level need than the need for liberty. However, if a man wants to remain indispensable, he becomes a drag on the progress of society. Great people are always surrounded by better and more capable people – in order not to be or remain indispensable. Lesser people always surround themselves by worse and even less capable people – so that they could remain indispensable. Capable people never consider themselves indispensable. Incapable people on the contrary, jealously guard, defend and by any means disseminate their myths of indispensability.

An incapable director looks jealously around himself and wishes to get rid of anybody who could outdo him and possibly replace him. A capable director, on the other hand, continuously searches for people able to be trained to replace him as soon as possible. He realizes that having successfully done his job, he is needed higher up and that somebody else has to succeed him at the lower level. One manager is chasing away applicants with a stick; the other searches with in vain for human "eagles," who are so rare. One executive surrounds himself with eagles; the other "leads" numerous gaggles of geese and squadrons of ducks. Eagles do not fly in formations.

We should engage only in the activities that serve the public. This does not mean that we shall not work for our families and ourselves, but that we should not harm the public and public affairs while doing so. Enriching ourselves on the account of others – by stealing, lying, misinforming, censoring or doing bad work – could harm the public. What in the beginning promises gain to us at the expense of the public, harms both sides in the end.

Calculations should not be hidden in the boss's safe, but entrusted to all employees, and indeed to every cutter. Consequently, all our business secrets became suddenly and easily available to our competitors – who observe all our moves and could imitate every step we make. It turned out that people couldn't successfully work if they were not fully acquainted with everything pertaining to their department. Self-management of teams requires work and management with "open books." Modern Open Book Management means transparency and working "in full light." Self-management cannot function correctly in an atmosphere of suspicion, non-transparency and fear. Fear and suspicion do not have any place in modern enterprise and entrepreneurship. Fear must be driven out from the enterprise, as Professor Deming taught. Not only the fear of employees, but also the fear their bosses have of the employees and the public.

Any thought or idea is silly and useless as long as it remains imprisoned in the human mind. It resembles a rough diamond before it is cut and polished. Thought also needs cutting and polishing and only the human brain can accomplish this. Physicist Michael Faraday used to follow the maxim: "Work-Finish-Publish." It is the leading spiral of intellectual and creative work. All three phases of the spiral must be equally balanced. Publication of the finished work is the "polishing" of diamonds. It is the confrontation with other human brains; it is the service to the public. Fearful people are afraid to give publicity to their ideas and to publish their work. They are afraid of other weaklings who are again afraid to hear or read whatever is new and original. In such a culture of fear and mistrust, only a few real "precious stones" of spirit get cut and polished.

In our sales rooms, bargaining does not exist. Our first word is also our last, at home as well as abroad; we endeavor to fulfill even the unexpressed wishes to the best of our ability. Bargaining means that your price is not the lowest one, or that you do not even know it; in any case, it means that you are not competitive. Pay a visit to a Turkish bazaar and you will meet a thousand years of tradition of bargaining and haggling over prices to a quite unbelievable extent. Then you will understand the correct meaning of the expression "Turkish economy" and why Turkish businessmen remain poor, as does Turkey itself.

The price is a dictator. The price is an integral part of the product. With other characteristics of the product it creates an organic unity. Price and product are separated only in medieval bazaars of negotiation and bargaining with naive customers.

Buildings – they are only heaps of bricks and concrete. Machines – they are only pieces of iron and steel. Only the humans give life to it all. If you have buildings and machines, you only have dead assets, without life and function. You do not know what to do, how to do it and why to do it. You lack the most important assets: human knowledge and wisdom. Only people and their brains can put all that concrete and bricks, and iron and steel into motion. Many enterprises of today are still "brick and mortar," buildings full of machines – and full of people. They are full of people, but are missing their brains. Economic theory does not yet work with the concept of knowledge. It knows only buildings, machines, labor and land – which really is very little.

Bata Co. Environment. We can attempt to describe the external and cultural environment of the company, although only in a short outline. For Bata, the order and cleanliness was a strategic principle, not a simple cultural self-expression. Machines and floors were painted white, so that the smallest drop of oil or dirt signaled an eventual future defect or potential failure. Tools were kept in red painted choice-boards with black moldings, so that even from a distance a missing tool noticeably signaled its absence.

Bata machines were not bolted to the floor, but independently mobile on special platforms equipped with independent electric engines. It was an enforced rule that a transported machine or material ought to *remain in motion.* Material must not be in the way, must not delay work and must not, in any case, be abandoned: idle items were confiscated by the "yard squad," which took the goods into the storage area and released them back only after storage fees, transportation costs and penalties were paid – up to the full purchase value of the items.

Green plants, flowers and water fountains decorated all, outside and inside – all was carefully kept like a garden. Smoking was forbidden throughout the entire factory area. The company's own fire brigade took care of the safety of the enterprise. By the end of the year, firemen got their financial bonuses based on *the smallest* (not the largest) number of fire interventions.

Following the same spirit, in Prague-Jarov there is now a car repair shop where cars are washed and polished *before* the process of repair. The repair of high quality goods cannot be done in dirt, oil and mud. How many times have you met a repairman, bricklayer, carpenter or other "professional" that leaves behind havoc and dirt, quite unprofessionally? Add the first principle of professionalism – Put Into Original State (PIOS) – to the principles of keeping and improving the original state.

Whenever I find badly trimmed edges or a crooked heel on finished shoes, I do not pay attention to that crooked work. What does interest me is how and why the character of the people working in that workshop could get so crooked. It is absolutely clear to me that people with a crooked character cannot accomplish a square piece of work. Quality of the product is not so important as the quality of the process leading to it. Quality of the process enhances quality of the product, but not vice versa. People who are working in the process control the quality of the process. The quality of people is a guarantee of a quality of the product, not the other way around. The crooked job is a simple consequence of a crooked mind. To repair crooked work is an ineffective loss of time. It is necessary to straighten the process and improve the character of people.

Do your work in such a way that the next worker in the chain wants it. Do not continue with bad work. Control and self-control of quality became a strategic necessity. Controllers assumed the role of ombudsmen for customers. The quality of the process and the quality of the person are more important than the quality of the product.

The customer is not interested in paying for useless movements of employees, wandering around workshops and warehouses, waiting for supplies, bringing material here and there, stoppages, lack of job assurance, etc. The customer is not interested if something has not arrived yet, they did not supply it, they did not pay, he did not come, something broke, etc. He is not even interested that markets collapsed, clients were lost, there is not enough cash, etc. Moreover, he is not interested in things like: we turned the bottom, within a week, next time and it will be better later. The customer is not an entrepreneur. *The customer is only interested in the low price, high quality and "yesterday's" delivery of goods or services.* Otherwise he would not be a good customer, but only an "accomplice" in the shoddy practices of business.

Quality originates in the process, not in the department of quality control. Nothing else but costs arises in the quality control department. It is the duty of the management to create the right conditions for every worker to do high quality and faultless job – not statistically, not on the second try, not on average, but *immediately and for the first time.* The "Our customer – our master" principle is also valid inside the company.

It is not as easy in our country. I intend, however, to realize my plans even if I should search with a candle in my hand for suitable people among the 14 million inhabitants of our republic. And I shall not rest until I find as many capable people as is necessary for manufacturing the tools and the machines best suited for our production. A truly good entrepreneur takes upon himself the functions of the human resources department. He must be ready to change his management team and monitor, challenge and question people, even several times, before their work brings advantages and added value to all.

One man can, within one day, do the mental work worth millions. But you cannot expect the same from a machine. This mental work can be found all around us, and a plenty still waiting to be done. All this unemployment and misery is caused by the fact that there is a lack of capable people willing to do mental work. Bata knew about physical labor very well; he liked to do it and appreciated it very much. As an entrepreneur, however, he recognized that the actual wealth is brought to the enterprise, region and nation mainly by mental work, not by the manual drudgery.

A profit brought to each participating party by a particular transaction should be considered as honest business. Business or industrial management should not increase the wealth of only one person, but also of all the others participating in business. A basic rule of a free market: all participants in the business transaction have to improve their starting positions. The rule of a free market becomes infringed when one participant bases his profit on the loss of the other. If I steal from others then I cannot be a capitalist, even if I parade around as a defender of the free market or entrepreneurship. A market, where Peter is robbing Paul, is no free market at all; it is its negation and denial. The necessary role of an entrepreneur as a creator of new values is now evident: both parts can only gain from the added value.

In countries with high business morale there is a high standard of living. Business and production – I mean industrial and agricultural production as well as crafts – create values. It is obvious that where the creators of values are mutually cheating and robbing instead of helping and supporting each other, poverty is the inevitable and necessary result. Low levels of mutual trust, high extent of stealing and glorification of cheating are rampant in poor countries. Poverty at the same time cannot pay debts, does not buy goods and requires a notary to verify every signature. A handshake, a given word or one's own signature have little value. It is very simple: a hundred earned by honest work, paid for a good product or service, is a new hundred reflecting a newly created value. These hundreds leave behind "a trace" of added value in the economy. A stolen hundred simply moves money from one pocket to another – without "a trace," without any value and economic effect. Therefore countries that are stealing remain poor in the long run. They do not have enough "traces" of added value. A hundred is not always the same hundred, especially not in a free market.

Our Customer – Our Master: The famous Bata motto, evidently the most important and probably even the most modern one. The customer is the only purpose and justification of production, like it or not. The customer is the reason for the construction, design, production, sale and strategy of an enterprise. The customer is always right, *even if he is not.*

Is then an entrepreneur only a passive servant of the customer, a simple reflection of his requirements, preferences and expectations? Not at all. A customer can be "made" satisfied even *beyond* his expectations; it is possible to fulfill the requirements not yet known to him and to meet preferences still yet to appear – a customer never sets limits on an entrepreneur's originality, creativity and anticipation.

What is the difference between a capitalist and an industrialist? Production processes and assets influence each other; one cannot exist without the other. A production produces capital; capital enables further production that produces further capital and so on ... $P \rightarrow C \rightarrow P \rightarrow C \rightarrow P \rightarrow C$ ... in a continuously repetitive chain. This chain represents a basis for all entrepreneurs. This chain enables two understandings or interpretations: 1) ... $C \rightarrow P \rightarrow C'$... or 2) ... $P \rightarrow C \rightarrow P'$... Both views work with the same "material." At first sight they function equally or similarly, but in spite of this there is a difference between them – in the purpose, accent, priority and strategy. The first one is the view of the capitalist, the latter of the industrialist. For capitalist, the purpose of production is capital, for the industrialist, the purpose of capital is production.

State what you decided to be: an industrialist, not a capitalist. Your success depends only and uniquely on the customer and therefore you should always defend his interests, as passionately as your own. Our public starts to understand that your vital task is not the accumulation of assets, but the service to the customer.

The basic principle of my entrepreneurial work is to turn my employees into capitalists. By this simple idea Bata immobilized the Marxists and other defenders of the struggle between capitalists and workers, entrepreneurs and employees. Bata enterprise consisted of small companies and entrepreneurs that took part in the profit of their department and participated in the enterprise with their own asset.

I would like to prove, not by words, but by deeds, that an enterprise managed according to our principles is invincible in the competitive struggle. I am not asking anybody to support my efforts, least of all the state. All I need is a chance and opportunity to continue my work. The state is not the right partner in an entrepreneurship as it functions on completely different principles and listens to drums that nobody else hears. But it must do no harm. As with a physician, the first principle of a statesman should be: Do no harm! And if you must, then harm at the minimum. State-managed enterprises do not increase the rate of affluence of the population because they avoid and stifle competition. Yet only competition forces an enterprise – no matter who manages it – to transfer the achievements of progress immediately to the worker and to the customer. A state should not be in or do business. A state should create optimal conditions for the economic competition and protection of the customer – thus for the enterprising behavior of private individuals.

State or private monopolies, curtailing the free way of life, or any kind of state protection of small or large enterprises from domestic or foreign competition, inevitably leads to a lower production morale and interferes with the progress in production... This was delivered at the Congress for Scientific Work Management in 1921. The best protection of entrepreneurship and entrepreneurs are not state subsidies and grants, but cooperation. Enterprises and entrepreneurs who do not associate into the networks of cooperation are the candidates for subordination to the state and its "protection."

Capitalism is not an ideology. Capitalism is not an ideological antithesis of socialism. Capitalism was not invented by anybody. Capitalism is a natural and spontaneous system that comes to life always when the pressure and ideological limitations cease. The ideology and politics of capitalism create obstacles to human development, changing its natural characteristics and changing it into a materialistic pretender that it has never been. Therefore, capitalism is an unfulfilled experiment and a moving target. It is constantly developing and adjusting, unshackled in propositions, dogmas and slogans. It does not fit and will never fit into textbooks. Its domain is action, work, effort and struggle to achieve. It does not tolerate a bureaucracy, it flourishes on trust, cooperation and high goals.

The prosperity of citizens as well as manufacturers is being created by the cooperation between inventive designers and courageous entrepreneurs who are ready for sacrifice. Handicraft brings misery to those who practice it and to the consumers as well. Technology is the source of productivity growth, and the growth of productivity is the source of wealth. If a machine can deliver the same quality at lower costs, it is surreal to continue tying up hands and brains.

For us only the world's best is good enough. In a global economy there is no other criterion of success that is as reliable, accurate and irreplaceable, as the *world class.* The aim is not necessarily to become the best in the world; the aim is to compare ourselves with the best in the world.

If you measure yourself with the best in the world it does not mean you are the best in the world. Not being a genius is no sin. But not recognizing a genius is a sin, failure and basic privation of an individual – a punishment that affects not only him, but all.

It does not matter what you are producing – be it machines or potatoes – try to do it on a worldwide scale. We should move from the idea that the world was created to serve us to the idea that we were born to serve the world. Even the smallest, unimportant item should be made perfectly. Take any product, even a mousetrap, if it is the most perfect one in the world, the world would beat the path to your doors, as Emerson said. It is all about ideas, innovations, creativity and the service to the public.

I do not posses a fortune – I have only shoes for my customers and leather for my workers. It is a property similar to the telescope for an astronomer or a violin for a musician. If I did not have it, I could not give jobs to workers and shoes to customers. I would be worth just as much as a musician without a musical instrument. For the real entrepreneur money is an instrument, not a purpose. An entrepreneur without money is like a musician without a violin. Therefore, it is useless to envy entrepreneurs their money, as without it they would become shopkeepers. A shopkeeper works for his own consumption and needs little money. An entrepreneur works to develop the enterprise, therefore he must have money and his consumption is inevitably the least important goal.

It is very difficult to force a man to create something new in his "mental workshop," to concentrate exclusively on his task and stop thinking of external things. Nobody has yet invented something or performed a demanding mental effort without concentrating fully from the beginning to the end. Discipline, order and concentration in one's mental workshop were what Bata struggled for.

Every human activity must eventually manifest itself in numbers. Don't be afraid of numbers and learn to work with them. If you *really* mean to improve something (a process, product, work, life), you have to measure and describe the original state and compare it to the actual state – and you need numbers for this measuring and comparing.

Nothing is difficult, if we have the will; not only some, but a profound, persistent and unyielding will. All that breaks down around us, dies because of the worst illness of our era: the lack of the most difficult of arts – the art of will. A will to succeed, be outstanding, differ by the force of your thoughts and by the persistence of your actions, not by the color of your hair, your tie or the whiteness of your smile – that is the art of will.

In the Middle Ages, people's lives were uneventful and static. The medieval man invested his money in immovable properties. Invest your money also into movable properties: in education, knowledge, and abilities. Learn to move; do not be afraid to change. Is a man forced to learn only from "his faults"? No. *Learn always and only from the faults of others.* It is always too late to learn from one's own mistakes.

Charity does not help people. They must be taught to help themselves through regaining faith in themselves. We may give a hungry man a fish, then another one, and tomorrow yet another. But he will remain hungry, dependent and poor. If we teach him how to catch fish, we shall lead him to independency and a good life. It is too easy to distribute alms, gifts and tender mercies. But it is difficult to really help people, to teach them and thus make them free. To teach someone how to catch fish – is surely a different kettle.

Public service. The purpose of entrepreneurship is service to the public, improving the quality of life, looking for better solutions, products and processes for a better life for all, not only for enterprise owners. Why? Only under such conditions can an enterprise continue in its prosperity and thus bring higher profits and earnings to all its members.

Become the first servant of your customers and collaborators. Organize your job in such a way that even your partners can do their job in high quality and without drudgery. Trust your machines, and techniques, and make sure that your machines do the hard work for people. Only the boss-servant gains the authority of his collaborators. His authority then does not arise from his position or function, but from his personal qualities and courage to serve others.

Many people are afraid that in the future technological inventions will enslave humanity. Such people have not found the way to make machines their servants. A fear and anxiety of technology and progress seem to be a lasting characteristic of many cultures and subcultures. In the past, people were afraid of automobiles, afterwards of telephones and planes, then robots and computers, now they are afraid of the Internet, telecommunications, electronic books and RFIDs. Some people are even using the most advanced technologies in order to block and retard technological progress. They do not see technology as a service tool, they do not look at themselves as masters of technology – they become its subordinates, servants and slaves.

New inventions bring new, better working methods. In our days, it is impossible to force people with impunity to continue using outdated and useless working methods during their entire lives. The whole society suffers if a man is prevented from changing his craft. A fight against unemployment is not based on the protection, "revitalization" and preservation of the old ways of work, processes and crafts. It requires in an active support and creation of entirely new jobs, processes and crafts. To do useless, unnecessary and ineffective work is not in the interest of a good enterprise.

The market is more important than production. The market, or the ability to realize produced goods or services on the market, is more important than the production itself. To produce for stock, to produce unmarketable goods, regardless of the effort or quality of work, is a useless and ungrateful action. To do business by peddling "unmarketable production" is amoral and humiliating. To produce well means producing in a marketable way. Unmarketable goods are not good goods, even if they were "the best." If there were no sales, then there would be no production. Production is necessary, but not sufficient. Sales are necessary and sufficient. The ideal is to produce only those things that have already been sold.

A wage is a crop and is based only on what "resulted" from the efforts of the enterprise's employees. You cannot pay wages from anything else than the added value of an enterprise, department, team or individual. Added value is the only source of wages. Only a good enterprise can pay good wages. Even a ministry or bank can pay good salaries – from the money of taxpayers and other people.

Who pays our wages? The company? Not at all! It is the public who pays. One of the wage laws is that everybody pays to be served well. In any enterprise it is the public, the customers, who pay the wages. An absent shareholder does not finance any of the necessary operational costs. His money is "dead." The customer is to be therefore rewarded the first and the most reliably. The customer has to become an integral part of the enterprise and entrepreneurship.

What is the *raison d'être* of the employment in any enterprise? Each employee must be paid for his work more than he would get if he undertook it "on his own." In the negative case he would leave and go into business for himself. In a good enterprise the problem is concentrated on the best utilization of the potential of each individual. Why should the customer be satisfied? In order to purchase products and services of comparable quality, reliability and delivery time at the lowest possible prices. Maximum wages for employees, minimum prices for customers: the strategy of a well-organized enterprise, the road to success.

On the division of labor: *I bought my own material, I cut it and I clipped it, I distributed it among the workers, I myself inspected and accepted each and every pair, I paid my workers and I did all the booking and accounting, all with the greatest speed and with considerable saving of time, material and money. My skill reached such proficiency that during a single Saturday I was able to take care of 100 workers for the whole week: analyze their product sales, the quality of their work, count their production pair by pair, issue new work for each worker separately, enter it into their own work-books, calculate and pay their wages and account and record all the customer-supplier affairs normally related to production or sales. As a result, I was able to devote the entire week, except Saturdays, to work.*

Bata was a small entrepreneur before he became a large-scale industrialist: he succeeded to manage 100 employees on Saturdays and he devoted the remaining time to adding value – to a productive work. A good entrepreneur and manager cannot grow up from the weeds of specialization and division of work, but from the craftsmanship, professionalism and expertness in a given area.

A human being should be able to change diapers, plan an invasion, butcher a hog, seize a ship, design a building, write a sonnet, settle bills, build a wall, tear down a wall, straighten a broken bone, comfort a dying man, follow an order, give an order, cooperate, act alone, solve an equation, analyze a new problem, pitch manure, program a computer, prepare a tasty meal, fight courageously and die gallantly. Specialization is for insects.

There are three kinds of values, all of which are wanted by everybody and needed by anybody for any work in the world. They are: capital, knowledge and freedom. In spite of this, people are slaves of debts, passions and non-discipline; young people without their own money, knowledge and freedom are flying around the flashing lights of empty promises of hope until they end up totally exhausted and with their wings already burned. There is no help for these people, be it school, money or freedom. The purpose of preparation of the next entrepreneurs-to-be is to become masters of capital, knowledge and freedom – not their servants.

You can apply to any leader the biblical maxim: "Whoever would want to be the greatest amongst you, let him be your servant." Check the bible for the principle of "servant leadership." Management by service, service to customers and service to the public are principles of any leader-servant and management by service. "Our customer – our master" remains the expression of a leading principle, the principle of a management by service. Those who do not see any humiliation in the service to others, but only a higher calling and a gift of leadership, would never become servile lackeys. Those who show contempt for the service to others are flunkeys, not leaders.

Point Number 4. You, as well as anybody from your family, will not accept any bribe, in whatsoever form and under whatsoever circumstances, from any of our suppliers, customers, assistants and whoever else. Otherwise you will be immediately fired without any compensation and your entire deposit with us will be used in favor of the Company Support Fund, not forgetting your obligation to pay a compensation for the damage caused by your inappropriate actions. Kindly, sign here. Introduce the Point Number 4 also in your enterprise, in your parliament, in your government and in your constitution... unconditionally and without any recall. Point Number 4 is the prerequisite of successful entrepreneurship.

An enterprise is a living organism – an organization of people and machines united to serve the existence of other people and to ensure, by such service, also their own existence. An enterprise is a living body, not a machine. It is the cooperation of employees in ensuring their own ability to serve. The responsibility for the life of an enterprise rests with the entrepreneur, employer, or chief officer.

Bata's view of state entrepreneurship, expressed so eloquently in modern "putinism," is that it: *1. Deprives citizens of economic activities and lowers them to the level of serfs to bureaucracy. They become dependent on the state, specifically on its bureaucracy; not only politically, but also economically. 2. Weakens the criteria of performance and usefulness by removing the competition. 3. Forces too many people to draw their incomes from faceless and nameless state property. 4. Transfers its business losses and management deficiencies to its employees and customers, through political and economic interventions.* A state entrepreneurship is not entrepreneurship but a manipulation of money belonging to other people, using non-economic instruments. Political parties surely should not be in business and maintain the control in economic management of an enterprise, community or region. The consequence of such non-economic, political "management" could be nothing but a decline, stagnation, corruption and loss of competitiveness.

5.4 Wisdom and Culture

Wisdom of enterprise is necessarily related to culture. Wise business leaders must see themselves as being embedded in culture, not as being separate from it. In order to become a part of national or increasingly global culture, modern business must not only be efficient, effective and ethical, but also become a cultural institution. Only then can its culture be preserved and propagated – like the one of the Bata Management System – through many generations and over large geographical spaces.

It has become part of conventional wisdom, especially in the currently integrating Europe, to draw sharp demarcation lines between economics and culture. Cultural elitists and intellectual snobs cannot stand the thought of lowly and "vulgar" business, management or economics, while economists, politicians and businessmen have come to view culture as some sort of externality, a charitable afterthought, an "extra" indulgence, or business-like investment.

Buying, displaying and consuming products of culture, does not imply living in culture or even living culturally. Also, living comfortably, efficiently and fully in a well organized family unit, without the intrusion of post-modern art, does not necessarily indicate cultural impoverishment. Producing a good automobile in a good and employee-friendly factory environment is as much a reflection of culture as "producing" new waves of pop music or "celebrity" paintings.

There exist entire nations, governments and states which self-characterize themselves as being "cultural" or "of culture," while still supporting the production of conspicuous marble lobbies of modern monetary "cathedrals," in spite of the progress towards education, the Internet and telecommunications.

Others point proudly to the exquisite achievements of their predecessors, the ancient builders, architects and engineers, while being themselves manifestly incapable of securing civilized conditions and security for their own employees and citizens.

There are economic and business theories and practices that are purposefully and radically non-cultural, unable to expand (or even express) human values, professional pride, sense of achievement, quest for quality and joy of satisfaction. There are still societies totally (and even programmatically) avoiding modern learning and therefore degrading their own culture.

Economics, organization and quality of production, service and employment, should not be separated from culture. In many ways they constitute culture's most reliable and most expressive manifestations.

How can unsatisfactory working conditions, shoddy production practices, governmental arrogance and disregard for its tax-subjects, inefficient and inconvenient services, unimaginative management and a disordered, dirty environment be manifestations of culture or a cultural society? Is not a satisfying, well organized, high-quality and high-productivity enterprise an important and challenging embodiment of human culture? Is not an affordable, useful, safe and high-quality product an equally important measure of nation's culture as are "primitive" straw hats, "hand-painted" kitsch, street bazaars, folk "art" and other products of post-modern culture?

A century or two ago, it was the builders, the producers, the artisans, engineers, inventors, architects and mathematicians, often integrated within a single person, who were widely recognized as creators and contributors to culture, along with musicians, painters, educators and writers. *Management, business, organization and entrepreneurship cannot be value-free or culture-free; they are not separated from culture and thus should not be devoid of culture.*

What is culture?

Culture usually refers to the learned or created (heteropoietic) environment, providing the milieu for human communication, interaction and adaptation within broader ecological surroundings.

Culture is essentially non-biological and non-genetic: it cannot be inherited, it has to be learned. It can be preserved and enhanced only through education, training, learning and experience. Culture has its social (interpersonal relationships, rules of behavior, and patterns of organization), material (arts, crafts, products) and spiritual (values, ideas, goals) dimensions, often inseparable and always complementary.

Even most higher-organisms seem to exist in some sort of "culture," based on simple mimicking, aping, repeating, conditioning, observing, etc.

Culture is mostly autonomous and self-organizing, sufficiently independent of the underlying bio-genetic evolution. However, some genetic influences (basic human "substrate") undoubtedly contribute to cultural differences. Similarly, business and management cultures of different nations will differ because of their differential location, history, focus and educational efforts.

But culture is dynamic and not static. It evolves, changes, and continually renews itself on the basis of its own inner rules of conduct and behavior, yet it is reacting to external signals, pressures and deformations. Culture, as a network of relationships, is recursively self-renewing (autopoietic), but not once-and-for-all produced (allopoietic). Culture is and always must be the product of culture as life itself is the product of life. Culture cannot be designed externally by social engineers.

Autopoietic culture persists in spite (and even because) of the continuous flux (birth and death) of its individual components (specific human beings): it maintains its autonomy, adaptability and inner order over time. *Allopoietic culture* (an artificial "machine" produced by propaganda and social engineering) collapses with the demise or exit of its key individuals: it is not self-renewing. "Culture" which emerges and declines with the life cycle of a specific cohort of individuals is not culture: it has not been transferred through learning.

Human culture, the whole human society, is an autopoietic complex of its individual (also autopoietic) component cultures of nations, races, tribes, families, enterprises, groups and regions, defined and existing in specific time, space and language.

Such all-human culture evolves and manifests itself only locally. The old slogan "Think globally-act locally" is not just a cliché, but an expression of wisdom, a prerequisite for successful human cultural existence.

Language provides the necessary environment for human cultural self-production and evolution. It facilitates consensual coordination of human action. Linguistic differentiation, the "Tower of Babel," is therefore a necessary reflection of historical specificity of the time and space of ancient protocultures.

Products of previous cultures (architecture, art, music) are not necessarily reflections and certainly not products of contemporary cultures. Yet, current cultures do use, exploit, destroy and even appropriate the cultural products of the past.

A well run, well organized and competitively productive enterprise, providing work fulfillment and secure family lives for thousands of human beings, often represents a more potent and more expressive cultural achievement than a hand-made mug, self-absorbed painting or forgettable piece of pop music.

Culture is very selective: it continually screens and filters its candidate manifestations. Although culture produces, quite naturally and neutrally, both good and bad, art and kitsch, efficiency and sloth, it is only what is judged and perceived as good, beautiful and of quality that is allowed to enter and become part of the persisting selection of culture. It falls only on the contemporaries to do the producing, but mostly on their posterities to do the selecting.

A Nation's culture cannot be measured only by its past achievements (i.e. achievements of a preceding culture), but mainly by its current behavior, rules of conduct and production relationships.

Economy and business should be recognized as an integral part of human culture. The art of organizing production, consumption and the society at large is truly the greatest of arts, to be practiced only by the most competent and qualified artists, not by the intellectually residual elite of technocrats.

So far, we do not require much education, standards, experience or knowledge from politicians, businessmen and executives. Still, one cannot even be a veterinarian or experiment with guinea pigs without acquiring minimal education and demonstrating the required skills and capabilities. Yet, we do allow and often condone social experimenting with millions of human beings on a large scale, conducted by individuals with superficial knowledge, minimal or limited experience and an inadequate or obsolete education.

APPENDIX (Selected Formal Models)

In the following appendices we gather some systems techniques that could also be considered appropriate for human systems management studies. Human systems management, relying on concepts like autopoiesis, tradeoffs elimination, multiple criteria, mass customization and optimization, must be capable of supporting at least some of these concepts through formal modeling. Because these models are mainly of interest to researchers and experts, we have gathered them here, outside the main text which is addressed to a more general, non-specialized audience of managers, executives and students.

Appendix 1

Simulation Model of Autopoiesis

In 1974, three Chilean scientists, F.C. Varela, H.R. Maturana and R.B. Uribe, published their seminal article, entitled "Autopoiesis: The Organization of Living Systems, Its Characterization and A Model," providing a new direction for understanding and modeling living systems.

Autopoietic organization is realized as an autonomous and self-maintaining unity through an independent network of component-producing processes, such that the components, through their interaction, generate recursively *the same* network of processes which produced them.

The product of an autopoietic organization is not different from the organization itself. A cell produces cell-forming molecules, an organism keeps renewing its defining organs, a social group "produces" group-maintaining individuals, etc.

In contrast, the product of an *allopoietic organization* is different from the organization itself; it does not produce the components and processes that would realize it as a distinct unity. Thus, allopoietic systems are not perceived as "living" and are usually referred to as mechanistic or contrived systems. For example, spatially determined structures, like crystals or macromolecular chains, machines, formal hierarchies, etc., are allopoietic.

It is important to distinguish between the *organization* and *structure* of an organic system in this context. We shall paraphrase the original thoughts advanced by Maturana and Varela. A network of interactions between the components, renewing the system as a distinct unity, constitutes the *organization* of the system. The actual spatial arrangement of components and their relations, integrating the system temporarily in a given physical milieu, constitutes its *structure*. The unity and holism of systemic organization *and* structure represents what is commonly referred to as a *system*.

Therefore, two distinct systems may have the same organization but different structures. Structural changes do not reflect changes in the system as a unity as long as its organization remains invariant. A system and its organization cannot be explained by simply reproducing its structure. The structure of a system determines the way its components interact between themselves, with their environment and with the observer.

AUTOPOIETIC MODEL OF A CELL

One of the simplest autopoietic systems exhibiting the minimum organization of components necessary for autopoiesis is the model of a biological cell. There is a catalytic nucleus capable of interaction with the medium of environmental "substrate" so that the membrane-forming components can be continually produced. The resulting structure displays a membranous boundary that defines the system as a separate and autonomous unity in the space of its components.

In accordance with this basic organization of a cell, the simplest model of its autopoiesis must consist of a medium of substrate, a catalyst capable of producing more complex component-links, which are in turn capable of bonding, ultimately concatenating into a membrane surrounding the catalyst.

We shall designate the basic components of the model by the following symbols:

hole (H)	(space)
substrate (S)	$\bigcirc$
free link (L)	$\square$
singly bonded link (B)	$\boxdot\ -$
fully bonded link (B)	$-\boxplus-$
catalyst (C)	$\bigstar$

The original Varela-Maturana-Uribe model was based on the following organization of components:

1. Production

$$2\bigcirc + \bigstar \rightarrow \square + \bigstar + (\text{space})$$

A catalyst and two units of substrate produce a free link and a space, while the catalyst is assumed to be essentially unaffected by this operation. Production can take place when a pair of substrate is in the predetermined neighborhood of the catalyst.

2. Disintegration

$$\square \quad + (\text{space}) \rightarrow 2\bigcirc$$

$$- \boxed{\prime} \quad + (\text{space}) \rightarrow 2\bigcirc$$

$$- \boxminus - + (\text{space}) \rightarrow 2\bigcirc$$

Any link, free or bonded, can disintegrate into two units of substrate. An additional unit of substrate will occupy an available space, which must be in the neighborhood of a disintegrating component.

3. Bonding

$$\boxed{\prime} - \boxminus - \ldots - \boxed{\prime} + \square \rightarrow \boxed{\prime} - \boxminus - \ldots - \boxminus - \boxed{\prime}$$

A free link can bond with a chain of bonded links; two chains of bonded links can be bonded into one, or re-bonded after their connecting link has disintegrated; two free links can be bonded together to start a chain formation.

Observe that disintegration and bonding are operations that do not require a catalyst; they are "self-catalytic." That does not mean that the catalyst has no influence over those operations. For example, bonding can take place only beyond a predetermined catalytic neighborhood while disintegration can appear anywhere in the space.

More detailed rules, guiding the movement of all components and specifying the necessary conditions for the three interactive rules above, are disclosed in the next section.

Each component (and its corresponding neighborhood) is allowed to move over the space according to predetermined rules. A set of dominance relations must be established in order to prevent different components claiming the same space during the same unit time-interval. Any component can claim a space, a link can displace a substrate, and a catalyst can displace both substrates and links.

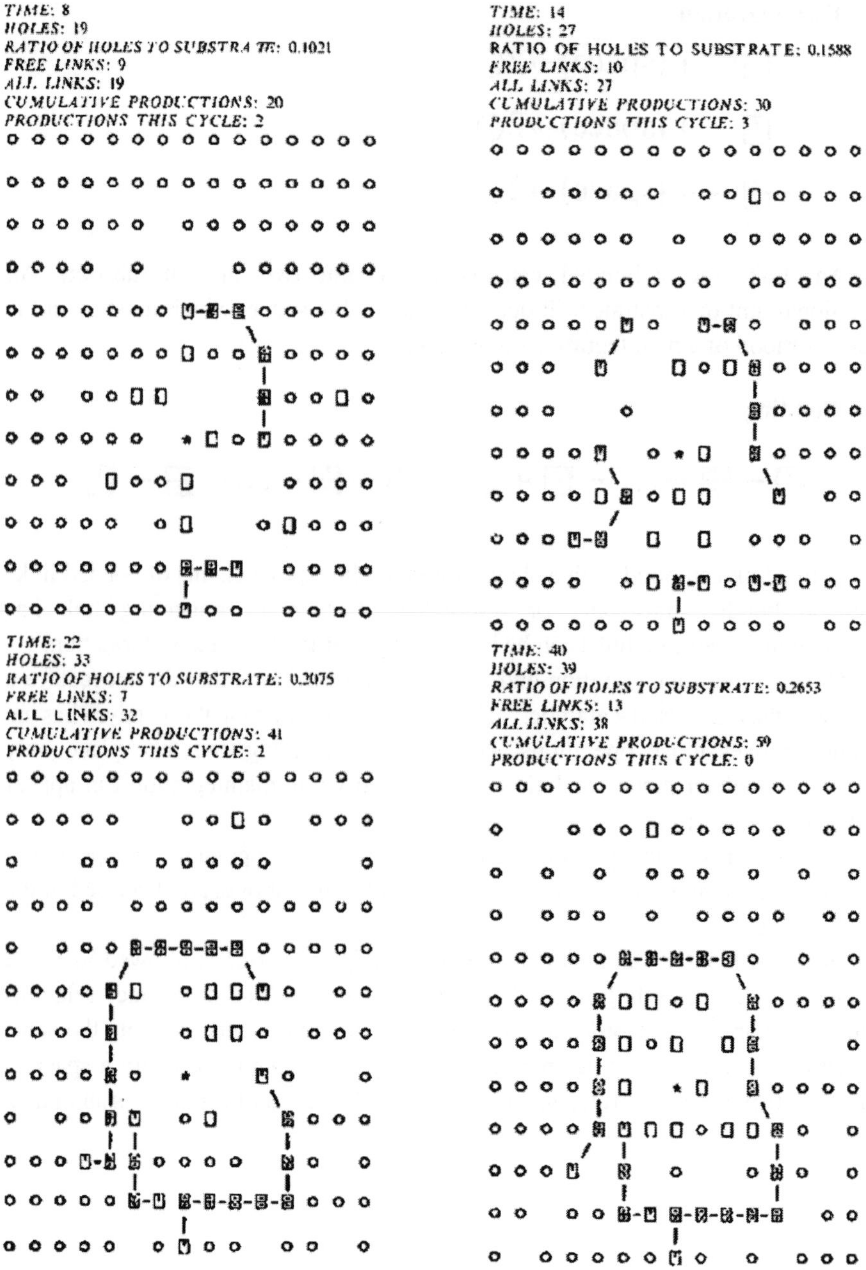

TIME: 8
HOLES: 19
RATIO OF HOLES TO SUBSTRATE: 0.1021
FREE LINKS: 9
ALL LINKS: 19
CUMULATIVE PRODUCTIONS: 20
PRODUCTIONS THIS CYCLE: 2

TIME: 14
HOLES: 27
RATIO OF HOLES TO SUBSTRATE: 0.1588
FREE LINKS: 10
ALL LINKS: 27
CUMULATIVE PRODUCTIONS: 30
PRODUCTIONS THIS CYCLE: 3

TIME: 22
HOLES: 33
RATIO OF HOLES TO SUBSTRATE: 0.2075
FREE LINKS: 7
ALL LINKS: 32
CUMULATIVE PRODUCTIONS: 41
PRODUCTIONS THIS CYCLE: 2

TIME: 40
HOLES: 39
RATIO OF HOLES TO SUBSTRATE: 0.2653
FREE LINKS: 13
ALL LINKS: 38
CUMULATIVE PRODUCTIONS: 59
PRODUCTIONS THIS CYCLE: 0

Figure 1 The emergence of an autopoietic unity: computer printouts.

The relation of precedence $*$ > $\Box$ > O > (space) establishes this partial dominance. We do not allow any movement of bonded links.

Each link can have at most two bonds: it can be either free, single bonded, or fully bonded. Additional bonds are of course possible, but they induce frequent branching of chains, creating other, catalyst-free enclosures. Multiple bonds are indispensable for modeling in a three dimensional space.

Non-branching chains of bonded links will ultimately form a membrane around the catalyst, creating the enclosure impenetrable for catalyst $*$ and free links $\Box$. These two components are effectively "trapped" and forced to function for the benefit of the autopoietic unity. Substrate units O can pass freely through the membrane and thus keep the catalyst supplied for the production of additional $\Box$. Any disintegrated links, causing ruptures in the membrane can be readily and effectively repaired by the ongoing production. The unity of the system is recursively maintained through a series of minor structural adaptations.

In Figure 1, we present a sample of some APL printouts, providing typical "snapshots" from the "history" of an autopoietic unity.

A FORMAL MODEL OF AUTOPOIESIS

We shall outline at least the settings of a grid on which autopoiesis experiments can be carried out. Let us define a two-dimensional (Cartesian) *tessellation grid*: a space of an autopoietic automaton. The *grid* G consists of a countably infinite set of *positions*, each position is referred to by a unique pair of integers *(i, j)*, positive or negative. For practical purposes we shall consider that the underlying network of positions forms an n-dimensional Cartesian grid, i.e., it has the nature of an *Abelian group*.

An Abelian-group cellular automaton Γ is an ordered quintuple:

$$\Gamma = (Q, M^\circ, +, f, H)$$

where

(i) Q is a set of states.
(ii) $M^\circ = \{M_1, ..., M_m\}$ is a generator set of a finite-generated Abelian group having group operation "+", i.e., vector addition.
(iii) f is the local transition function, a *set of rules*, a mapping from $Q(t)$ to $Q(t+1)$.
(iv) H is the quiescent state, such that $f(H_1, ..., H_m) = H$.

The *neighborhood* of any position k in G is defined as the set

$$N(k) = \{k, k + M_1, k + M_2,..., k + M_m\}.$$

The meaning of f is that an assignment of states to $N(k)$ helps to determine the next state of k.

A *form F* is an assignment of states to all positions of an automaton. A *finite* form is one in which all but a finite number of positions are assigned to the quiescent state H. The operation of F is assumed to proceed in unit time intervals, $t_0, t_1 = t_0 \pm 1$, ... while the local transition function is being applied *simultaneously* to all positions of G during each time-interval, thus generating a sequence of forms $F_0, F_1, F_2, \ldots$

Example. Conway's "Life" cellular automaton can be described as follows:

$Q = (0, 1)$, $H = 0$, *and* G is the Abelian group generated by

$$M^\circ = \{(1, 0), (0, 1), (1, 1), (-1, 0), (0, - 1), (- 1, - 1), (1, -1), (-1, 1)\}$$

under the operation of vector addition. Each position has exactly eight neighboring positions, the *Moore neighborhood N (k)* for a given k, determined by M°. Let f be defined as follows:

1) If at time t the state of k is 0 and there are *exactly* three positions in state 1 in $N(k)$, then at time $t + 1$ the state of k will become 1.
2) If at time t the state of k is 1 and there are exactly two *or* three positions in state 1 in $N (k)$, then at time $t +1$ the state of k will remain 1.
3) If at time t position k and its $N(k)$ do not satisfy either condition 1 or 2, then at time $t \pm 1$ position k will be in state 0.

These three conditions adequately define f and enable us, given any configuration at time t, to effectively determine the configuration at time $t + 1$.

Modeling of Autopoiesis

We shall allow the neighborhood of a position to "wander" throughout a constant Abelian space. That is, a state is distinct from a position of the space and is identified with a shifting set of "interdependent positions" in the space.

Each position is identifiable as (i, j), $i, j = 1, \ldots, n$. We define a complete general neighborhood of $k = (i, j)$, $N(k)$, as follows:

$$N(k) = \{k + \lambda_r M_r \mid r = 1, \ldots, 8\}$$

where M_r indicates one of the eight possible directions over a Cartesian grid and λ_r represents the number of steps taken. Thus, the *Moore neighborhood* is characterized by all $\lambda_r = 1$, the *von Neumann neighborhood* has $\lambda_r = 0$ for all "diagonal" directions and $\lambda_r = 1$ for the rectangular ones, etc. By varying the λ_rs from 0 to n we can generate a large variety of neighborhoods, depending on a given context.

We shall turn our attention to a very simple and specific neighborhood, depicted in Figure 2, We assume that any movement can proceed in a rectangular fashion only and the complete neighborhood consists of all positions reachable through either one or two moves, i.e., $\lambda_r = 1$ or 2 for all rectangular movements. Thus,

$$M^\circ = \{M_r \mid M_1 = (-1, 0), M_2 = (0, 1), M_3 = (1, 0), M_4 = (0, -1)\}$$

In Figure 2 observe that M_1 through M_4 correspond to four basic directions: North, East, South and West. A complete neighborhood of any position (i, j) is reachable by one or two rectangular moves. The *Moore neighborhood* is indicated by the eight marked elements. To establish a circular relation between operators M_r, we shall define
$M_{4 + 1} = M_1$.

We can demonstrate the usage of basic movement operators as follows:

$$(i, j) + M_1 = (i - 1, j)$$
$$(i - 1, j) + M_3 = (i, j)$$
$$(i, j) + 2M_1 = (i - 2, j)$$
$$(i, j) + M_2 + M_3 = (i + 1, j + 1), \text{ etc.}$$

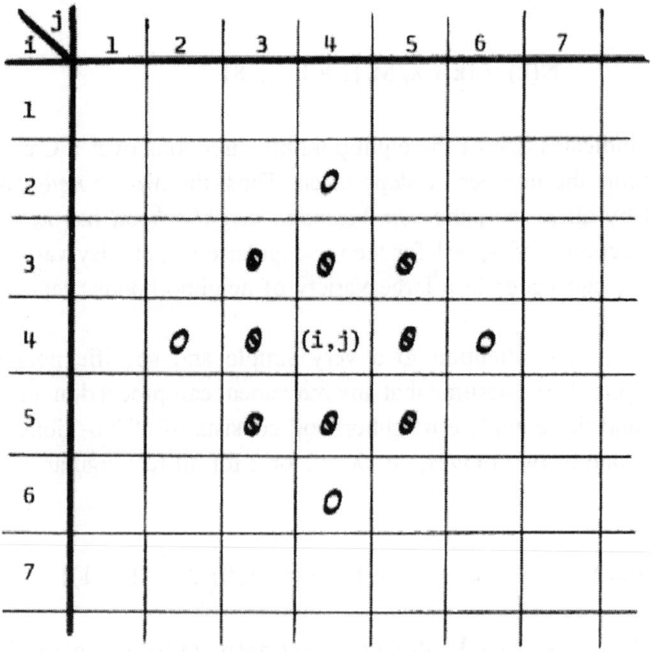

Figure 2 Moore neighborhood.

The set of all possible states, Q, is defined as follows: $Q = \{H, S, L, B, C\}$, where

$$H(i, j) = H(k): \text{space (a quiescent state)}$$
$$S(i, j) = S(k): \text{substrate}$$
$$L(i, j) = L(k): \text{(free) link}$$
$$B(i, j) = B(k): \text{bonded link}$$
$$C(i, j) = C(k): \text{catalyst}$$

In general, $k \equiv (i, j)$ and $E(k) \equiv E(i, 2)$, denotes a position k being in state E, i.e., any element of Q. In Figure 2, observe that for $n \le 3$, i, $j \le 2$, $i, j \ge n - 1$ only *incomplete* neighborhoods can be defined. We shall state simple *boundary conditions:*

$$E(i, 2) + M_1 = E(i, 2)$$
$$E(2,j) + M_2 = E(2,j)$$
$$E(i, n - 1) + M_3 = E(i, n - 1)$$
$$E(n - 1, j) + M_4 = E(n - 1, j).$$

Since all movements over $N(k)$ are carried with respect to k, we can further simplify our notation by not repeating k every time. Thus, we use E instead of $E(k)$, $E(M_r)$ instead of $E(k + M_r)$, etc.

For example, for $k \equiv (i, j)$ and $M_r \equiv M_1$, instead of $E(k + M_1 + M_1)$ we use $E(2M_1)$ to designate that position $(i - 2, j)$ is in state E.

There are two essential ways of moving over $N(k)$:

i)   select a direction M_r and a number of steps λ_r, and then identify the state of $(k + \lambda_r M_r)$.

ii) select a state E and then identify all positions of $N(k)$ being in that state as well as the directions to reach them from k.

With respect to (ii), for example, M_E indicates that $(k + M_E)$ position,

$$M_E \in M°, \text{ is in state } E. \text{ In other words}$$

$$E(M_H) \equiv H(k + M_H) \equiv H(M_H).$$

We shall omit the detailed modeling and formal coding of the necessary Movement, Production, Bonding, Disintegration and Re-bonding functions which have to be carried out in order to complete the model. An interested reader can find the entire functional model of autopoiesis in the work of Zeleny on "Self-Organization of Living Systems: A Formal Model of Autopoiesis," *International Journal of General Systems*, 4(1977) 1, pp. 13-28.

Because we are dealing with an evolutionary system, we have to also use a "blind generation procedure" of random numbers in order to determine movement, production, bonding, disintegration and re-bonding of individual components. This is necessary to preserve sufficient randomness because a real-world environment has no known, complete, finite description or prediction.

EXPERIMENTS IN SELF-ORGANIZATION

The formalization of parallel processes is very flexible. Catalytic neighborhoods can change their sizes and shapes, as well as the neighborhoods of other components. The rates of production and disintegration can vary over time or in dependency on their previous values. Multiple catalysts can be introduced, stationary or in flux with respect to each other. The influence of chance can be further amplified or totally removed (by extending the set of movement rules). The amount of matter in the system can be kept either constant or external inflows or outflows of the substrate introduced. The system can be induced to disintegrate totally or to "freeze" into a stable allopoietic structure.

Systems with turbulent behavior or only partially delineated membranes can be observed as well as the systems whose membranes are ever-expanding. Systems with broad or narrow membranes, substrate-seeking "amoebas" floating through space, and hundreds of other varieties can be evolved by adjusting and harmonizing a few parameters or rules.

We can even provide a connection between a particular structural adaptation and the change in the organization itself. The interacting rules, which are otherwise invariant, can thus be allowed to change according to appropriate meta-rules. Such self-affecting systems are then capable of self-reproduction and therefore evolution.

We shall next describe a few simple experiments performed with the APL-AUTOPOIESIS model (M. Zeleny and N.A. Pierre, "Simulation Models of Autopoietic Systems." In: *Proceedings of the 1975 Summer Computer Simulation Conference*, Simulations Council, La Jolla, California, 1975, 831-842.)

Function and Form

We have already discussed the distinctions between systemic organization and structure. The same autopoietic organization is realizable through different structural forms although its basic unity of function and its identity as a unique system stay unchanged. Structural adaptations are triggered by specific perturbing changes in its environment. We can talk about structural coupling: the effective spatio-temporal correspondence of changes of state of the organism with the recurrent changes of state of the medium while the organism remains autopoietic.

This structural rapport of the system and its environment allows us to simulate complex structural histories, in a controlled and predictable way, without changing system organization.

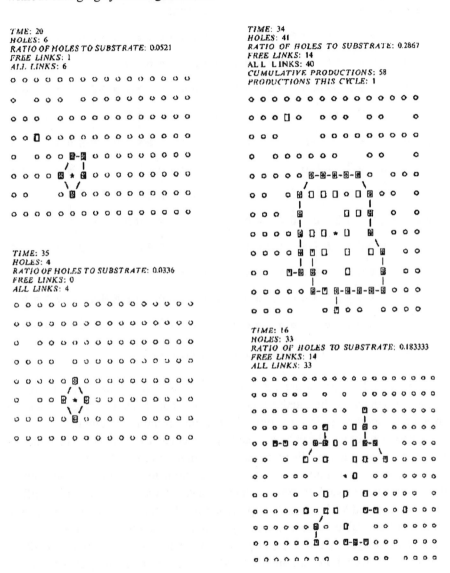

Figure 3 Emergence of pre-designed structural forms.

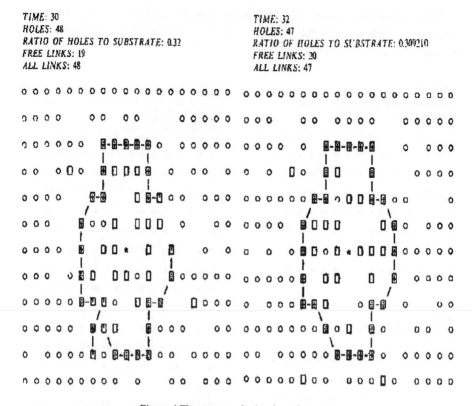

Figure 4 The structure in the sign of a cross.

For example, such structural variables as size and shape can be simply studied. Changes in the catalytic neighborhood could elicit a large variety of structural responses, as in some typical "snapshot" printouts in Figure 3.

Autopoiesis of a cell can be affected by particular structural adaptation and its functions of production, disintegration and bonding affected to their extremes. An allopoietic structure, a crystal, might ultimately form. It can neither disintegrate nor expand or move. Either a weak catalytic reach or a high inflow of substrate could lead to such "allopoietization." On the other hand, an increased outflow of available substrate, creating disproportionately many spaces, would cause the catalyst to move rapidly over the space and the turbulence of its neighborhood would prevent orderly bonding – no membrane may ever form.

One can also simulate a growth in system size quite simply, by establishing a state-dependent change regime in the size of the catalytic neighborhood. Also, very complex shapes and patterns can be simulated as arising from structural adaptations of the autopoietic system. In Figure 4 we have an example of an autopoietic cell acquiring the shape of a cross. Theoretically, any complex shape can be brought forth through induced structural adaptations.

Biological Clock

All living systems exhibit a variety of biorhythms and cyclical adaptations. The most prominent is the aging phenomenon, a clearly observable "life cycle" of growth, plateau and decline. Organizational stability and permanence of an autopoietic system is the permanence and stability of its structural history, not of its existence. All known autopoietic organizations have "built-in death." They either crystallize into allopoietic debris or disintegrate back into their components.

No autopoietic cell can escape death. Observe that it is unreasonable to assume that the catalyst is unaffected by its participation in the production of links. Each single act of production diminishes its catalytic power. Initially, when there is a lot of free substrate, the number of produced links is naturally very high. At the same time, the number of spaces necessary for disintegration is still very low. As a result there is a large initial build-up in the amount of organized matter (free or bonded links).

As the amount of free substrate decreases and the number of spaces increases, the two rates, production and disintegration, achieve a balance which is characteristic for a relatively stable period of self-repairing membranous enclosure. The production still continues, although at a much lower rate; the more production events are performed per unit of time, the weaker the catalyst becomes. Thus, we observe the fastest "aging" of the catalyst in the initial stages of the most vigorous production activity.

Although this "aging rate" becomes progressively slower, the production rate is ultimately exceeded by the disintegration rate and the total amount of organized matter starts to decline. Because the spaces become fewer again and there is more substrate available, the aging and loss of catalytic power speeds up at this later stage in a burst of activity before total catalytic exhaustion. The disintegration rate is already low before the death itself and becomes only a slow decay afterwards.

There is a large variety of other emergent rhythms that can be detected in the behavior of this autopoietic cell. For example, there is a natural cycle observed in the ratio of spaces to substrate even when the rates of production and disintegration are kept stable. More substrate leads to more links and higher incidence of bonding. Consequently, the actual amount of substrate is less while the number of spaces is up. That allows more links to disintegrate, creating more substrate and fewer spaces again.

Multiple Catalysts

Obviously there can by any number of catalysts functioning in a given space. When they are distant enough they can enclose themselves quite independently and function without mutual interference. A group of autopoietic cells can be observed, each and all in a dynamic equilibrium with their environment.

The most interesting case arises if we assume that at a certain stage the catalyst is allowed to divide itself into two identical replicas. For example, the first total closure of a membrane provides the trigger which causes such catalytic replication. The new catalyst then occupies any immediately adjacent space. Their respective neighborhoods overlap to a large extent. Note that a large portion of the original membrane will disintegrate because no re-bonding is possible in the area of the overlap.

Because a catalyst cannot pass through bonded segments, it will ultimately float out of this new opening. The two catalysts of equal power will float apart and gradually enclose themselves by two separate membranes. The larger is the overlap of their respective neighborhoods, the stronger is this initial "pulling apart." Gradually they disconnect themselves, almost gently (See Figure 5).

Apparently a self-reproduction has been simulated. There are two identical and independent autopoietic cells as a result of a simple mechanical division of a cell. A fairly close replica of the initial cell is obtained without the benefit of copying, coding or information processing programs.

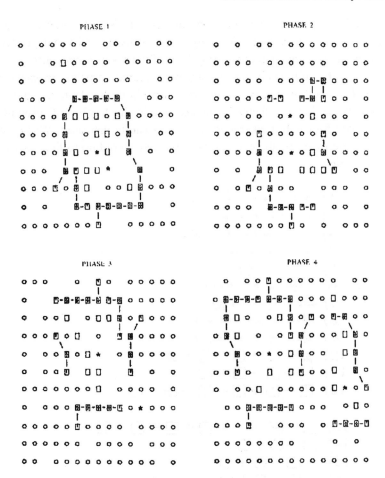

Figure 5 Computer simulation of cellular division.

Autogenesis of Life: A Simple Scenario

We shall consider a uniformly distributed environment of basic particles of matter (marked by •), devoid of any information and structure. Such a universe is initially in a thermodynamic equilibrium. Let us assume that there is a separate locality where the local values of the mean density and temperature can differ from the equilibrium conditions. Only the particles • can penetrate the boundaries of such locality, both ways. All other structurally higher combinations of the basic particles are trapped inside the boundaries.

The following set of 19 rules (one of many possible) would induce a self-organization of an autopoietic unity (like a living cell) independently of particular chemical and structural properties of the basic components.

Observe that ultimately the density of substrate particles increases as it is required for a cell to emerge. At the same time both the stable and the unstable compounds are being effectively trapped within the locality of disequilibrium. The chance of a catalyst emergence is being steadily increased. When a catalyst emerges, one or more, the cell can be produced according to the rules we have already studied.

1) $\bullet + \bullet \rightarrow \bullet - \bullet$

2) $\bullet - \bullet + \bullet \rightarrow \perp$

3) $\bullet - \bullet + \bullet - \bullet \rightarrow +$

4) $\bullet - \bullet + \perp \rightarrow \odot$

5) $\odot + \bullet \rightarrow O$

6) $+ + \bullet - \bullet \rightarrow O$

7) $\perp + + \rightarrow \bigstar$

8) $\perp + \bullet \rightarrow \bullet - \bullet + \bullet - \bullet$

9) $+ + \bullet \rightarrow \perp + \bullet - \bullet$

10) $\bigstar + O + O \rightarrow \square + \bigstar$

11) $\square + \square \rightarrow \square - \square$

12) $\square - \square + \square \rightarrow \square - \boxplus - \square$

13) $\square - \boxplus - \cdots - \square + \square \rightarrow \square - \boxplus - \cdot$

14) $\square \rightarrow O + O$

15) $- \square \rightarrow O + O$

16) $- \boxplus \rightarrow O + O$

17) $O + \bigstar \rightarrow \pentagon$

18) $\pentagon + \bullet \rightarrow \bigstar + \bigstar$

19) $\pentagon \rightarrow \bigstar + O$

We can imagine that there are dormant and potentially active layers of rules that are being brought forth to their action through the emergence of the necessary particles, molecules or compounds. Finally, the last three rules allow for "self-regeneration" of the catalyst and its replication. That triggers the autopoietic division of the cell and induces self-reproduction.

Appendix 2

Eight Concepts of Optimality

Traditionally, "optimality" refers to the maximization of a *given* function with respect to *given* resource constraints. This is not how the business world operates – neither should it. "Optimizing a given with respect to a given" would drive any business quickly to a competitive halt.

Optimization must reflect the reality of human decision making, not the reality of axioms-derived mathematical constructs. In order to optimize human systems, one has to create and produce new, situation-responsive constraints in full correspondence with new, situation and constraints-responsive objectives or criteria. Optimization is about finding the best, constructing and designing it, not about doing the best with the already given, fixed and properly sclerotized.

This "flexible path" of optimal system production within broader human systems management has to be taken, because the notion of optimality and the process of optimization are pivotal to the areas of economics, engineering, as well as management and business.

What does it mean to state that something is "optimal"? If optimal means "the best," then asking "What is the best?" remains a legitimate and, in mathematical programming, still mostly unanswered question.

Any maxima or minima could be declared optimal under specific circumstances, but optima are not necessarily maxima or minima. The two concepts are different: maximizing (or minimizing) is not optimizing.

Although dictionaries commonly use optimization as a synonym for maximization, we shall develop the concept of optimality in the *sense of balance* among dynamic multiple criteria or objectives, while remaining in balance with the evolving constraints.

When there is only a single dimension or attribute chosen to describe reality, maximization or minimization with respect to constraints can be acceptable, if not sufficient. When there are multiple criteria (measures or yardsticks), as is true in most situations, then optimality and optimization (in the sense of balancing) need to be developed.

341

Optimization applies to an *economic problem*: when scarce means (resource constraints) are used to satisfy alternative ends (multiple objectives). If the means are scarce, but there is only a single end, then the problem of how to use the means is a *technical problem*: no value judgments enter into the solution, no balancing is needed, and no optimization can take place. Only the knowledge of given physical and technical relationships is needed.

In other words, if all our constraints are "given" (fixed) and if our objective function is single, then the solution is fully defined and predetermined by mathematical problem formulation. This *a priori* solution just needs to be revealed, explicated or computed by a fixed, given algorithm. No optimization is possible because everything is given and predetermined.

The technical problem is not what we wish to address when dealing with optimality and optimization in human systems management.

Optimality is Not "Satisficing"

Balancing of multiple criteria is about optimization, not about "satisficing." It is about finding the best, not about finding just the good enough or satisfactory. That is not good enough. H. Simon acknowledged this quite simply by saying: *"No one in his right mind will satisfice if he can just as well optimize."*

Surprisingly, multiple criteria or multiple objective functions – the necessary prerequisites for optimization – were not recognized and acknowledged by the optimization sciences until the early 1970s. Optimization in the sense of balancing multi-dimensionality is not compatible with the traditional concepts of "optimality" characterized by scalar or scalarized schemes, based on unique solutions under complete information. These are rather limited mathematical constructs, ineffective in capturing the richness and complexity of human problem solving, decision making and optimization.

We must learn to understand decision making not merely as a computation of the given, already-constructed world, but as a way of constructing our local world, ordering individual and collective experiences. It is necessary to acknowledge multiple concepts of optimality.

Multiple Concepts of Optimality

There are some basic prerequisites that must be at the root of any effective optimization scheme.

For example, what is determined or given *a priori* cannot be subject to subsequent optimization and thus, clearly, does not need to be optimized: it is given.

What is not given must be selected, chosen or identified and is therefore, by definition, subject to optimization.

Consequently, different optimality concepts can be derived from different distinctions between what is given and what is yet to be determined in problem-solving or decision-making formulations.

It is similar to the theory of effective change: In order to know what to change, one must know what must be conserved. If all is given then no space for change has been opened. Without change there can be no optimization.

For example, if we determine the value of the objective function *a priori*, set it at a predetermined value (like in Simon's *satisficing*), then we cannot optimize it (nor maximize or minimize it). If we set a value of the constraint *a priori*, then we cannot adjust and optimize that constraint. Constraints have to become goals or objectives in order to be optimized. Even if we do not determine the value of the objective *a priori*, but the constraints are fixed, we still cannot optimize it – it is strictly implied (given) by the constraints.

Traditionally, by optimal solution or optimization we implicitly understand maximizing (or minimizing) a single, pre-specified objective function (or criterion) with respect to a given, fixed set of decision alternatives (or resource constraints). Both criterion and decision alternatives are given, only the known (optimal) solution remains to be revealed, extracted through calculation. That is not optimization by any stretch of imagination.

There are at least *eight distinct optimality concepts*, all mutually irreducible, all characterized by different applications, interpretations and mathematical formalisms.

1. Single-Objective Optimality

This is not really optimization but refers to the conventional maximization (or "optimization") problem. It is included here for the sake of completeness, out of respect for tradition and as a potential special case of *bona fide* optimization.

To maximize a single criterion, it is fully sufficient to perform technical measurement and algorithmic search processes. Once the set of constraints X and an objective function f are formulated or specified, the "optimum" (that is, the maximum) is found by computation, not by decision processes or balancing. The search for optimality is reduced to "scalarization": assigning each alternative a single number (a scalar) and then identifying the largest-numbered alternative.

Numerical example. Consider the following linear-programming problem with two variables x and y, and a single objective function f is maximized and subject to five resource constraints:

$$\text{Max } f = 400x + 300y$$
$$\text{Subject to} \quad 4x \leq 20$$
$$2x + 6y \leq 24$$
$$12x + 4y \leq 60$$
$$3y \leq 10.5$$
$$4x + 4y \leq 26$$

The maximal solution to the above problem is $x^* = 4.25$, $y^* = 2.25$, and the optimal value $f^* = 2375$. Observe that all is given here and therefore any consideration of *market prices* of resources is not needed. In human systems, *no resources can be optimized without considering their market prices.*

However, if $p_1 = 30$, $p_2 = 40$, $p_3 = 9.5$, $p_4 = 20$, and $p_5 = 10$ were respective market prices (\$/unit) of the five respective resources, then the total cost of the current resource portfolio, i.e. purchased quantities of individual resources (20, 24, 60, 10.5, 26), would be $B = \$2600$.

2. Multi-Objective Optimality

More generally, if optimality is to be distinct from a simple-minded maximization, it should involve balancing and harmonizing *multiple criteria*. In the real world, people continually resolve conflicts among multiple criteria, which are competing for their attention and assignments of importance. This corresponds to the vector optimization problem.

Such maximization of individual objective functions should be non-scalarized, separate and independent, that is, not subject to a superfunctional aggregation which would effectively reduce multi-objective optimality back to single-objective maximization. There would be no other reason for considering multiple criteria other than for constructing the aggregate. All initially rich information would be lost in the aggregate. Multiple criteria, if they are to be meaningful and functional, should be optimized (or balanced) in the non-scalarized vector sense, in mutual competition with each other.

Numerical example.

$$\text{Max } f_1 = 400x + 300y$$
$$\text{and } f_2 = 300x + 400y$$
$$\text{Subject to} \quad 4x \leq 20$$
$$2x + 6y \leq 24$$
$$12x + 4y \leq 60$$
$$3y \leq 10.5$$
$$4x + 4y \leq 26$$

The maximal solution with respect to f_1 is $x^* = 4.25$ and $y^* = 2.25$, f_1 (4.25, 2.25) = 2375. The maximal solution with respect to f_2 is $x^* = 3.75$ and $y^* = 2.75$, f_2 (3.75, 2.75) = 2225. The set of optimal (non-dominated) solutions X^* includes the two maximal solutions (extreme points) and their connecting (feasible) line along the line $4x + 4y = 26$. For example, 0.5(4.25, 2.25) + 0.5(3.75, 2.75) = (4.0, 2.5) is another non-dominated point in the middle of the line. Holding the same market prices, total cost of the resource portfolio remains $B = \$2600$.

3. Optimal System Design: Single Criterion

Instead of optimizing a given system with respect to a selected criteria, humans often seek to form or construct an optimal system of decision alternatives (optimal feasible set), designed with respect to such criteria. Single-criterion design is the simplest of such concepts: it is analogous to single-criterion "optimization," producing the best (optimal) set of alternatives X at which a given, single objective function f is maximized and subject to the cost of design (affordability).

Numerical example.

$$\text{Max } f = 400x + 300y$$
$$\text{Subject to} \quad 4x \leq 29.4$$
$$2x + 6y \leq 14.7$$
$$12x + 4y \leq 88.0$$
$$3y \leq 0$$
$$4x + 4y \leq 29.4$$

where the right-hand sides (resource portfolio) have been optimally designed.

Solving the above optimally designed system will yield $x^* = 7.3446$, $y^* = 0$ and $f(x^*) = 2937.84$. If market prices of the five resources ($p_1 = 30$, $p_2 = 40$, $p_3 = 9.5$, $p_4 = 20$, and $p_5 = 10$) remain unchanged, then the total cost of the optimal resource portfolio (29.4, 14.7, 88, 0, 29.4) is again $B = \$2600$.

4. Optimal System Design: Multiple Criteria

As before, multiple criteria cannot be scalarized into a superfunction. Rather, all criteria compete independently or there would be no need for their separate treatment.

Numerical example.

$$\text{Max } f_1 = 400x + 300y$$
$$\text{and} \quad f_2 = 300x + 400y$$
$$\text{Subject to} \quad 4x \leq 16.12$$
$$2x + 6y \leq 23.3$$
$$12x + 4y \leq 58.52$$
$$3y \leq 7.62$$
$$4x + 4y \leq 26.28$$

The above represents an optimally designed portfolio of resources: the maximal solution with respect to both f_1 and f_2 is $x^* = 4.03$ and $y^* = 2.54$, f_1 (4.03, 2.54) = 2375 and f_2 (4.03, 2.54) = 2225.

This can be compared (for reference only) with the f_1 and f_2 performances in the earlier case of given right-hand sides. Assuming the same prices of resources, the total cost of this resource portfolio is B = $2386.74 $\leq$ $2600. One could therefore design even better performing portfolios by spending the entire comparative budget of $2600 (or the additional $213.26).

5. Optimal Valuation: Single Criterion

All previously considered optimization forms assume that decision criteria are given *a priori*. However, in human decision making, different criteria are continually being tried and applied, some are discarded, new ones added, until an optimal (properly balanced) mix of both quantitative and qualitative criteria is identified and constructed. There is nothing more suboptimal than engaging a perfectly good set of alternatives X towards unworthy, ineffective or arbitrarily determined criteria (goals or objectives).

If the set of alternatives X is given and fixed *a priori,* we face a problem of optimal *valuation:* According to what measures should the alternatives be evaluated or ordered? According to criterion f_1, f_2 or f_3? Which of the criteria best captures our values and purposes? What specific criterion engages the available means (X) in the most effective way?

In order to evaluate X, should we maximize f_1 or f_2? How do we select a criterion if only one is allowed (possible) or feasible?

Numerical example.

$$\text{Max } f_1 = 400x + 300y$$
$$\text{or} \quad f_2 = 300x + 400y$$
$$\text{Subject to} \quad 4x \leq 20$$
$$2x + 6y \leq 24$$
$$12x + 4y \leq 60$$
$$3y \leq 10.5$$
$$4x + 4y \leq 26$$

The maximal solution with respect to f_1 is $x^* = 4.25$, $y^* = 2.25$, f_1 (4.25, 225) $= 2375$. The maximal solution with respect to f_2 is $x^* = 3.75$, $y^* = 2.75$, f_2 (3.75, 2.75) $= 2225$. Is 2375 of f_1 better than 2225 of f_2? Only one of these valuation schemes can be selected.

6. Optimal Valuation: Multiple Criteria

If the set of alternatives X is given and fixed *a priori*, but a set of multiple criteria is still to be selected for the evaluation and ordering of X, we have a problem of multiple-criteria valuation: Which set of criteria best captures decision maker's value complex? Is it (f_1 and f_2)? Or (f_2 and f_3)? Or perhaps (f_1, f_2 and f_3)? Or some other combination of multiple criteria?

Numerical example.

How do we select a set of criteria f_1 or f_2, or (f_1 and f_2) that would best express a given *value complex*? Value complex refers to the set of values and purposes guiding our criteria-selection criteria.

$$\text{Max } f_1 = 400x + 300y$$
$$\text{and/or Max } f_2 = 300x + 400y$$
$$\text{Subject to} \qquad 4x \leq 20$$
$$2x + 6y \leq 24$$
$$12x + 4y \leq 60$$
$$3y \leq 10.5$$
$$4x + 4y \leq 26$$

The maximal solution with respect to f_1 is $x^* = 4.25$, $y^* = 2.25$, f_1 (4.25, 2.25) $= 2375$. The maximal solution with respect to f_2 is $x^* = 3.75$, $y^* = 2.75$, f_2 (3.75, 2.75) $= 2225$. Should we use f_1 or f_2, or should we use both (f_1 and f_2) to achieve the best valuation of X according to our value complex? Only one of the possible (single and multiple criteria) valuation schemes is to be selected.

7. Optimal Pattern Matching: Single Criterion

All previously considered optimization concepts assume that relevant decision criteria are given and determined *a priori*. Yet, that is not how human decision-making processes are carried out: different criteria are being tried and applied, some are discarded, new ones added, until a proper balanced mix (or portfolio) of both quantitative and qualitative criteria is arrived at.

Like any other decision-problem factors, criteria should be determined and designed in an optimal fashion. There is nothing more wasteful than engaging perfectly good means and processes towards unworthy, ineffective or arbitrarily determined criteria.

There is a problem formulation representing an "optimal pattern" of interaction between alternatives and criteria. It is this optimal, ideal or balanced problem formulation or pattern that is to be approximated or matched by decision makers. The single-objective matching of such *cognitive equilibrium* (Zeleny 1989, 1991) is once more the simplest special case.

Numerical example.

Should we maximize f_1 or f_2? How do we select a single criterion if only one is allowed, possible or feasible?

$$\text{Max } f_1 = 400x + 300y$$
$$\text{or Max } f_2 = 300x + 400y$$

$$\text{Subject to} \qquad 4x \leq 29.4 \text{ or } 0$$
$$2x + 6y \leq 14.7 \text{ or } 41.27$$
$$12x + 4y \leq 88 \text{ or } 27.52$$
$$3y \leq 0 \text{ or } 20.63$$
$$4x + 4y \leq 29.4 \text{ or } 27.52$$

The above presents two optimally designed portfolios of resources with respect to f_1 and f_2, respectively. Among the possible patterns are ($x^* = 7.3446$, $y^* = 0, f_1(x^*) = 2937.84, B = \$2600$) and ($x^* = 0, y^* = 6.8783, f_2(y^*) = 2751.32, B = \$2600$).

Suppose that the value complex requires that the chosen criterion should minimize the opportunity cost of the unchosen criteria, other things being equal. Choosing f_1 would make f_2 drop only to 80.08 percent of the opportunity performance, whereas choosing f_2 would make f_1 drop to 70.24 percent. So, f_1 has a preferable opportunity impact, and the first pattern and its resource portfolio would be selected.

A value complex indicating that deployed resource quantities should be as small as possible would require choosing f_2 and thus the second pattern.

8. Optimal Pattern Matching: Multiple Criteria

Pattern matching with multiple criteria is more involved and the most complex optimality concept examined so far. In all "matching" optimality concepts there is a need to evaluate the closeness (resemblance or match) of a proposed problem formulation (single or multi-criterion) to the optimal problem formulation.

Numerical example.

How do we select a set of criteria f_1, f_2 or (f_1, f_2) that would best express our current value complex?

$$\text{Max } f_1 = 400x + 300y$$
$$\text{and/or Max } f_2 = 300x + 400y$$

$$\text{Subject to} \quad 4x \leq 29.4 \text{ or } 0 \text{ or } 19.98$$
$$2x + 6y \leq 14.7 \text{ or } 41.27 \text{ or } 28.78$$
$$12x + 4y \leq 88 \text{ or } 27.52 \text{ or } 72.48$$
$$3y \leq 0 \text{ or } 20.63 \text{ or } 9.39$$
$$4x + 4y \leq 29.4 \text{ or } 27.52 \text{ or } 32.50$$

The above describes three optimally designed portfolios of resources with respect to f_1, f_2 and (f_1, f_2), respectively. So, among the possible patterns are $(x^* = 7.3446, y^* = 0, f_1(x^*) = 2937.84, B = \$2600)$, $(x^* = 0, y^* = 6.8783, f_2(x^*) = 2751.32, B = \$2600)$ and $(x^* = 4.996, y^* = 3.131, f_1(x^*) = 2937.84, f_2(x^*) = 2751.32, B = \$2951.96)$.

If the value complex requires that B = \$2600 is not to be exceeded, we could "match" the third optimal pattern to that level by scaling it down by the optimum-path ratio r = 2600/2951 = 0.88. The new pattern is then (x^* = 4.396, y^* = 2.755, $f_1(x^*)$ = 2585.30, $f_2(x^*)$ = 2421.16, B = \$2600). If producing both products is of value, then the choice could be maximization of both f_1 and f_2.

Summary of the Eight Concepts

In the next Table we summarize the eight major optimality concepts according to a dual classification: single versus multiple criteria and the extent of the "given," ranging from "all-but" to "none except." The traditional concept of optimality, characterized by too many "givens" and a single criterion, now appears to be the most remote from any sort of optimal conditions or circumstances for problem solving as represented by the multiple criteria cognitive equilibrium (optimum).

Table 1 Eight concepts of optimality.

Number of Criteria / Given	Single	Multiple
Criteria & Alternative	"Traditional" Optimality	MCDM
Criteria Only	Optimal Design (De Novo Programming)	Optimal Design (De Novo Programming)
Alternatives Only	Optimal Valuation (Limited Equilibrium)	Optimal Valuation (Limited Equilibrium)
"Value Complex" Only	Cognitive Equilibrium (Matching)	Cognitive Equilibrium (Matching)

The third row of Table 1 can be solved by De Novo programming in linear cases. In the next section we summarize the basic formalism of De Novo programming, as it applies to linear systems. It is only with multiple objectives that optimal system design becomes fully useful, even though a single-objective formulation can also lead to some performance improvements.

Appendix 3

De Novo Programming

In this section we summarize the problem of resource portfolio optimal design and provide its formal computational procedure for linear-programming cases. This method is referred to as De Novo Programming, meaning that the levels of resources are not known and given *a priori*, but are purchased *de novo*, as a new, optimal portfolio at prevailing market prices.

De Novo Programming relates to the second row of the previous table of the eight concepts of optimality.

Consider a simple production problem involving two different products, say suits and dresses, in quantities x and y, each of them consuming five different resources (nylon through golden thread) according to technologically determined requirements (technological coefficients). Unit market prices of the resources are known, as are the levels (number of units) of resources currently available (given portfolio of resources). The data are summarized in Table 1.

Table 1 Original data for production example.

Unit Price $	Resource (Raw Material)	Technological Coefficients (Resource Requirements)		Number of Units (Resource Portfolio)
		$x = 1$	$y = 1$	
30	Nylon	4	0	20
40	Velvet	2	6	24
9.5	Silver Thread	12	4	60
20	Silk	0	3	10.5
10	Golden Thread	4	4	26

In Table 1, observe that producing one unit of each product x and y ($x = 1$ and $y = 1$) requires 4 units of nylon [$(4 \times 1) + (0 \times 1)$), 8 units of velvet (($2 \times 1$) + (6 $\times$ 1)], etc. The total number of available units of each material (in the resource portfolio) is given in the last column of the table.

The current market prices of the resources (first column) allow us to calculate the costs of the initial resource portfolio (last column):

$$(30 \times 20) + (40 \times 24) + (9.5 \times 60) + (20 \times 10.5) + (10 \times 26) = \$2600$$

The same prices can be used to compute the unit costs of producing one unit of each of the two products:

$$x = 1: (30 \times 4) + (40 \times 2) + (9.5 \times 12) + (20 \times 0) + (10 \times 4) = \$354$$
$$y = 1: (30 \times 0) + (40 \times 6) + (9.5 \times 4) + (20 \times 3) + (10 \times 4) = \$378$$

In other words, it costs $354 to produce one suit and $378 to produce one dress. Suppose that we can sell all we produce at the current market prices of $754/unit of x and $678/unit of y.

Expected profit margins (price – cost) are:

$$x: 754 - 354 = \$400/\text{unit}$$

$$y: 678 - 378 = \$300/\text{unit}$$

Being traditional profit maximizers, we are interested in maximizing the total value of the profit function $f_1 = 400x + 300y$. For a second criterion, let us consider some quality index: say 6 points per x and 8 points per y (scale from 0 to 10), so that we can maximize the total quality index, or function $f_2 = 6x + 8y$.

We are in a position to analyze the outlined production system with respect to *both* profits and quality. Maximizing levels of x and y (best product mix) can be easily calculated by simple techniques of linear programming (here we need only the results).

1. Function f_1 is maximized at $x = 4.25$ and $y = 2.25$, achieving a maximum of $(400 \times 4.25) + (300 \times 2.25) = \$2375$ in profits.
2. Function f_2 is maximized at $x = 3.75$ and $y = 2.75$, achieving a maximum of $(6 \times 3.75) + (8 \times 2.75) = 44.5$ points in the total quality index.

One can trade off quality for profits by moving from $x = 3.75$, $y = 2.75$ to $x = 4.25$, $y = 2.25$ and back. Because we can produce only one product mix at a time, we can choose to maximize profits (at $x = 4.25$, $y = 2.25$) *or* quality (at $x = 3.75$,

$y = 2.75$), but *not both*. The choice is difficult because of the induced undesirable tradeoffs between profits and quality.

Let us now purchase a portfolio of resources different from that in Table 1. This new production system is comparable and compatible in all respects, except for the last column of Table 2.

Table 2 New data for production example

Unit Price $	Resource (Raw Material)	Technological Coefficients (Resource Requirements)		Number of Units (Resource Portfolio)
		$x = 1$	$y = 1$	
30	Nylon	4	0	16.12
40	Velvet	2	6	23.3
9.5	Silver thread	12	4	58.52
20	Silk	0	3	7.62
10	Golden thread	4	4	26.28

We are now in a position to analyze the newly proposed production system (Table 1) under the same conditions.

1. Function f_1 is maximized at $x = 4.03$ and $y = 2.54$, achieving a maximum of $(400 \times 4.03) + (300 \times 2.54) = \$2375$ in profits.
2. Function f_2 is maximized at $x = 4.03$ and $y = 2.54$, achieving a maximum of $(6 \times 4.03) + (8 \times 2.54) = 44.5$ points in the total quality index.

Observe that both previously attained separate maximum values of f_1 and f_2 have been matched. *Both* maximum profits (\$2375) and maximum quality index (44.5) are achieved through a single product mix: $x = 4.03$ and $y = 2.54$. This particular product mix was infeasible in the previous system. By making it feasible, we have eliminated all and any tradeoffs between the criteria of profits and quality.

The initial system (Table 1) was operated at the cost of \$2600. The newly designed system (Table 2) is realizable at the following cost:

$(30 \times 16.12) + (40 \times 23.3) + (9.5 \times 58.52) + (20 \times 7.62) + (10 \times 26.28) =$ \$2386.74

The superior performance of the newly designed system comes at \$213.26 less than the inferior "optimal" performance of the initial system.

Optimal Portfolio of Resources

The above example demonstrates that the chosen portfolio of resources is crucial for assessing maximum achievable levels of profits, costs, quality, flexibility, etc., at which the corresponding production system can be operated.

A simple rearrangement of resource levels (comparing Table 1 with Table 2) "reshapes" the management system (the set of feasible alternatives) and leads to superior performance at lower costs. Why?

No productive resources should be deployed individually and separately: they do not contribute one by one according to their marginal productivities. Productive resources *perform as a whole* system: they should be determined and deployed *jointly as a portfolio.*

We have identified the portfolio of resources as being critical to a system's performance and maximum productivity. Other factors, like technology, education, skills, work intensity, innovation, flexibility, quality, etc., could only realize their full potential if applied to optimally-designed and tradeoffs-free systems.

Herbert E. Scarf, in his ORSA/TIMS Plenary Lecture on May 9, 1989, characterized linear programming (LP) as "an exercise in applied mathematics which has nothing to do with market prices." Mathematical programming and most of operations research are therefore apparently unrelated to the main institutions of economic theory and do not deal with the optimal allocation of resources.

Factors of production are not separable and individually productive and thus cannot be independently "given." Traditional marginal productivity theory presumes the independent productivity of individual inputs. To change one resource while holding all the others fixed tells us nothing and never occurs in reality. To hold the number of trucks fixed while changing the number of drivers tells us nothing about the optimal number of trucks and drivers. Such marginal thinking ignores the fundamental complementarity between inputs. Machines and other capital equipment are designed with specific engineering characteristics appropriate to given fuels or to specific types of materials. Production is not and cannot be about "varying factors one at a time" or extracting meaningless "shadow" prices when real market prices are missing.

Only through the operation of undistorted, reliable and "unregulated" market forces does it become possible to utilize resources efficiently over time in any given allocation, i.e. to avoid their overutilization or underutilization. In optimally designed portfolios of resources, all "shadow" prices must be positive and equal to each other: no further trade-offs or re-allocations should be possible in optimal systems; no "post-optimality" analysis applies.

Profit Maximization

Free market systems are rooted in the assumption of profit maximization by individuals and corporations. Yet, rational economic agents can maximize profits in *at least two* fundamentally different and mutually exclusive modes:

1. Manage (operate) a *given* system – so that a profit function is maximized.
2. *Design* an optimal system – so that its management (operation) leads to maximum profits.

These two forms of profit maximization are clearly not identical. In the first case, one is doing one's best and squeezing the maximum possible profits from a *given* system. This is known as profit maximization. In the second case, one designs (re-engineers) a profit-maximizing system: doing one's best leads to maximum profits. This is also profit maximization.

Because the second case is, *ceteris paribus*, always superior to the first one, we are facing two strategically different concepts of profit maximization. It *does* matter – in business, economics or management – which particular mode of profit maximization the individuals, corporations or economic cultures prefer: free markets are bound to reward those who consistently adhere to *the second mode* of profit maximization – the optimal design of profit-maximizing systems.

Formal Summary of De Novo Programming

Formulate a linear programming problem:

$$\text{Max } Z \ Cx \ \text{s.t.} \ Ax - b \le 0, pb \le B, x \ge 0, \tag{1}$$

where $C \in \Re$ qxn and $A \in \Re$ mxn are matrices of dimensions qxn and mxn, respectively, $b \in \Re^m$ is the m-dimensional *unknown* resource vector, $x \in \Re^n$ is n-dimensional vector of decision variables, $p \in \Re^m$ is the vector of the unit prices of m resources, and B is the given total available budget.

Solving problem (1) means finding the optimal allocation of B so that the corresponding resource portfolio b maximizes simultaneously the values $Z = Cx$ of the product mix x.

Obviously, we can transform problem (1) into:

$$\text{Max } Z = Cx \quad \text{s. t. } \quad Vx \leq B, \quad x \geq 0, \tag{2}$$

where $Z = (z_1, ..., z_q) \in \Re^q$ and $V = (V_1, ..., V_n) = pA \in \Re^n$.

Let $z_{k*} = \max z_k$, $k = 1, ..., q$, be the optimal value for kth objective of Problem (2) subject to $Vx \leq B$, $x \geq 0$. Let $Z^* = (z_{1*}, ..., z_{q*})$ be the q-objective value for the ideal system with respect to B. Then, a *metaoptimum problem* can be constructed as follows:

$$\text{Min } Vx \quad \text{s. t. } Cx \geq Z^*, \quad x \geq 0. \tag{3}$$

Solving Problem (3) yields x^*, $B^* (= Vx^*)$ and $b^* (= Ax^*)$. The value B^* identifies the minimum budget to achieve Z^* through x^* and b^*.

Since $B^* \geq B$, the optimum-path ratio for achieving the ideal performance Z^* for a given budget level B is defined as:

$$r^* = B/B^* \tag{4}$$

and establish the optimal system design as (x, b, Z), where $x = r^*x^*$, $b = r^*b^*$ and $Z = r^*Z^*$. The optimum-path ratio r^* provides an effective and fast tool for the efficient optimal redesign of large-scale linear systems.

There are two additional types of budgets (other than B and B^*). One is B_j^k, the budget level for producing the optimal x_j^k with respect to the kth objective, referring back to the single-objective De Novo programming problem.

The other, B^{**}, refers to the case $q \leq n$ (the number of objectives is less than the number of variables). If x^{**} is the degenerate optimal solution, then $B^{**} = Vx^{**}$ (See Shi, 1995). It can be shown that $B^{**} \geq B^* \geq B \geq B_j^k$, for $k = 1, ..., q$.

Shi then defines six types of optimum-path ratios:

$$r_1 = B^*/B^{**}; \; r_2 = B/B^{**}; \; r_3 = \Sigma \, \lambda_k B_j^k/B^{**};$$
$$r_4 = r^* = B/B^*; \; r_5 = \Sigma \, \lambda_k B_j^k/B^*; \; r_6 = \Sigma \, \lambda_k \, B_j^k/B,$$

leading to *six different optimal system designs.* Comparative economic interpretations of all optimum-path ratios are dependent on the decision maker's value complex.

The following numerical example is adapted from Zeleny (1984, 1986):

$$\text{Max} \quad z_1 = 50\, x_1 + 100\, x_2 + 17.5\, x_3$$
$$z_2 = 92\, x_1 + 75\, x_2 + 50\, x_3$$
$$z_3 = 25\, x_1 + 100\, x_2 + 75\, x_3$$

Subject to

$$12\, x_1 + 17\, x_2 \leq b_1$$
$$3\, x_1 + 9\, x_2 + 8\, x_3 \leq b_2$$
$$10\, x_1 + 13\, x_2 + 15\, x_3 \leq b_3 \qquad\qquad (5)$$
$$6\, x_1 + 16\, x_3 \leq b_4$$
$$12\, x_2 + 7\, x_3 \leq b_5$$
$$9.5\, x_1 + 9.5\, x_2 + 4\, x_3 \leq b_6$$

We assume, for simplicity, that the objective functions z_1, z_2, and z_3 are equally important. We are to identify the optimal resource levels of b_1 through b_6 when the current unit prices of resources are $p_1 = 0.75$, $p_2 = 0.60$, $p_3 = 0.35$, $p_4 = 0.50$, $p_5 = 1.15$ and $p_6 = 0.65$. The initial budget $B = \$4658.75$.

We calculate $Z^* = (10916.813;\ 18257.933;\ 12174.433)$ with respect to the given B (\$4658.75). The feasibility of Z^* can only be assured by the metaoptimum solution $x^* = (131.341,\ 29.683,\ 78.976)$ at the cost of $B^* = \$6616.5631$.

Because the optimal-path ratio $r^* = 4658.75/6616.5631 = 70.41$, the resulting $\mathbf{x} = (92.48,\ 20.90,\ 55.61)$ and $\mathbf{Z} = (7686.87;\ 12855.89;\ 8572.40)$. It follows that the optimal portfolio $\mathbf{b}$, with respect to $B = \$4658.75$, can be calculated by substituting $\mathbf{x}$ into the constraints (5). We obtain:

$$b_1 = 1465.06$$
$$b_2 = 910.42$$
$$b_3 = 2030.65$$
$$b_4 = 1444.64 \qquad\qquad (6)$$
$$b_5 = 640.07$$
$$b_6 = 1299.55$$

If we spend precisely $B = \$4658.8825$ (approx. $\$4658.75$) the optimum portfolio of resources to be purchased at current market prices is displayed in (6), allowing us to produce x and realize Z in criteria performance.

Extended De Novo Formulation

There are many interesting extensions of De Novo programming in the literature. But the main extension always concerns the objective function. The multiobjective form of Max $(cx - pb)$ appears to be the right function to be maximized in a globally competitive economy. This is compatible with achieving long-term maximum sustainable yields from the deployed resources. Another realistic feature would be multiple pricing and quantity discounts in both resources and products markets.

Searching for a better portfolio of resources (redefining the $b_i s$ of right-hand sides) is tantamount to the continuous reconfiguration and "reshaping" of systems boundaries. Such practical considerations lead to a more general programming formulation, starting to approximate the real concerns of free-market producers.

For example, the following optimal-design formulation of the production problem, although still not fully representing the reality, takes full advantage of De Novo programming computational efficiency while delivering the necessary decision inputs:

$$\text{Max } z = \Sigma_j \, c_j(x_j)x_j - k\,[\Sigma_{i \in I1} \, p_i b_i]\pi_1 - \ldots - [\,\Sigma_{i \in Ir} \, p_i b_i]\pi_r$$

Subject to $\qquad \Sigma_j \, a_{ij}x_j - b_i \leq 0 \quad i \in I$

$$[\Sigma_{i \in I} \, p_i b_i]\beta \, \leq \, B,$$

where $I = I_1 \cup ... \cup I_r, I_s \cap I_{s+1} = 0, 0 < \pi_s < 1, s = 1, ..., r, \beta \geq 1$
and

$$c_j(x_j) = \begin{cases} c_{j1} & x_j \leq x_{j1} \\ c_{j2} & x_{j1} < x_j \leq x_{j2} \\ . \\ . \\ . \\ c_{jkj} & x_{jkj-1} < x_j, \end{cases}$$

where $c_{jh} \geq c_{h+1}, h = 1, ..., k_j$.

The formulation above is more practical than traditional LP-systems, but perhaps still far away from the really useful formulation of the real world-class management systems.

Appendix 4

The External Reconstruction Approach (ERA)

In De Novo Programming we have shown how to determine optimal quantities of resources for a company to create its own optimal portfolio. However, resource constraints are not only about the quantities (the right-hand sides of inequalities), but also about the constraints themselves.

Resources do not exist *per se*, but are identified and defined by human and corporate purposes and objectives. What is a resource for one company could be a product, scrap or free good for another.

Whenever an available resource is fully utilized, the corresponding constraint is called *active*. Whenever there is a surplus or overstock of a resource, the corresponding constraint is called *inactive*. Clearly, the purpose of any optimization is to make *all constraints active*, not to waste resources, not to carry unnecessary inventories "just-in case," but to make the systems operations lean and waste-free, "just-in-time."

Optimization techniques, like linear programming (LP) have nothing to contribute to the optimality of corporate resources because they accept and condone any number of *inactive constraints* and thus institutionalize waste and redundancy of resources. Even computationally, LP is grossly inefficient because *only the active constraints* determine the optimal solution of any linear system; once the set of active constraints is determined, no other constraints have to be examined, not matter how many.

The proposed External Reconstruction Approach (ERA) is based on a simple philosophy: because only the "active" constraints determine the optimal LP solution, there is no need to work initially with all the constraints. Our approach starts with a single constraint; additional constraints are subsequently appended *per partes* and only as many as are needed are used for characterizing the final solution. We may say that the set of feasible solutions (corporate portfolio of resources) is being externally reconstructed, *uno alla volta* (one at a time).

This *Uno Alla Volta* philosophy allows us to handle the *entire range* of LP problems: *from* all "soft" constraints to be "designed" optimally, *to* all "hard" constraints to be taken "as given." ERA can *design* an optimal system, fully or partially, or optimize within a fully *given system* (traditional LP formulation), which is a special case of the broader *de novo programming* formulation of the previous section.

Formulation

Consider first a standard linear programming formulation:

$$\text{Max } z = \sum_j c_j x_j$$

Subject to

$$\sum_j a_{ij} x_j \leq b_i \quad i = 1, \ldots, m, \tag{1}$$

$$x_j \geq 0, \quad j = 1, \ldots, n.$$

Let $x_j^*, j = 1, \ldots, n,$ denote the optimal solution to problem (1).

If we allow b_i to become *variables* b_i, i.e. soft (changeable) instead of hard (unchangeable) constraints, then the following *De Novo* formulation is of interest:

$$\max z = \sum_j c_j x_j$$

Subject to

$$\sum_j a_{ij} x_j - b_i \leq 0, \quad i = 1, \ldots, m,$$

$$\sum_i p_i b_i \leq B, \tag{2}$$

$$x_j \geq 0, \quad j = 1, \ldots, n,$$

$$b_i \in R, \quad i = 1, \ldots, m.$$

If $p_i \geq 0$ for all i, provided that we exclude the constraints i for which $p_i = 0$, then

$$B \geq \sum_j \left(\sum_{i \in I} p_i a_{ij} \right) x_j,$$

where $I = \{ i \mid p_i > 0 \}$. Defining

$$A_j = \sum_{i \in I} p_i a_{ij},$$

problem (2) becomes equivalent to

$$\max z = \sum_{i \in I} p_i$$

Subject to

$$\sum_j A_j x_j \leq B, \tag{3}$$

$$x_j \geq 0.$$

If all $A_j > 0$ and $B \geq 0$ (problem is bounded) then problem (3) has the following solution:

$$x_j^* = \begin{cases} B / A_j & \text{for } j = k \\ 0 & \text{otherwise,} \end{cases} \tag{4}$$

where k satisfies

$$c_k / A_k = \max_j \left\{ c_j / A_j \right\}.$$

Observe that solution (4) also fully solves problem (2) under the specified conditions.

Algorithm *Uno Alla Volta*

Assume, for simplicity, that $p_i = 1$, for all $i = 1, \ldots, m$. Then define:

$$B^0 = \sum_i b_i$$

$$A_j^0 = \sum_i a_{ij}. \tag{5}$$

Denote the solution to problem (3), with B^0 and A^0_j, as x^{*0}_j. Then we can formulate a family of r-constrained continuous "knapsack" problems:

$$\max z = \sum_j c_j x_j$$

Subject to

$$\sum_j a_{sj} x_j \le b_s, \quad s = 0,1,\ldots,r, \qquad (6)$$

$$\sum_j A^r_j x_j \le B^r,$$

$$x_j \ge 0, \qquad j = 1,\ldots,n,$$

where

$$A^r_j = A^{r-1}_j - a_{rj} \qquad (7)$$

$$B^r = B^{r-1} - b_r$$

Observe that problem (6) is reduced to problem (3) using definitions (5), for $r = 0$, since $a_{0j} = b_0 = 0$.

Let the solution to equation (6) be x^{*r}_j. Substituting x^{*r}_j in the constraints of equation (1), the following condition can be tested:
Is the following true?

$$\sum_j a_{ij} x^{*r}_j = b^{*r}_i \le b_i \qquad (8)$$

If condition (8) is violated, transform the r-constrained problem (6) into the $(r+1)$-constrained problem by appending an additional constraint identified as follows:

Let $r = r + 1$. Then

$$b_r = \max_i \{b_i\} \text{ for all } i \text{ such that } b^{*r}_i > b_i \qquad (9)$$

and the corresponding constraint is

$$\sum_j a_{rj} x_j \le b_r.$$

Recalculate A'_j and B^r according to definition (7) and solve the extended problem (6) to obtain new x_j^{*r}.

Remark. The recalculation of A'_j and B^r is also useful for accounting purposes and possible analysis of shadow prices. It continually tightens the "aggregate" constraint (3) and thus improves the efficiency of the algorithm. It is also advantageous to use x_j^{*r-1} as the initial solution for obtaining x_j^{*r} in problem (6).

There is some $r \le m$ such that x_j^{*r} satisfies condition (8) *for the first time –* provided that problem (1) has at least one feasible solution. Observe that such x_j^{*r} also solves problem (1), $x_j^r = x_j^{*r}$.

The implications of the able described algorithm appear to be of both theoretical and practical interest.

Numerical Example

Find x for the following problem:

$$\max 400x_1 + 300x_2$$

Subject to

$$4x_1 \le 20$$

$$2x_1 + 6x_2 \le 24$$

$$12x_1 + 4x_2 \le 60$$

$$3x_2 \le 10.5$$

$$4x_1 + 4x_2 \le 26$$

Step 1. Formulate problem (3) with definitions (5) and solve:

$$\max 400x_1 + 300x_2$$

Subject to

$$22x_1 + 17x_2 \le 140.5$$

Gives solution:

$$x_1^{*0} = 6.386\,3636, \quad x_2^{*0} = 0.$$

By substituting the above solution in the original constraints, we obtain x_j^{*0} and test condition (8):

$25.545454 \leq 20$	**No**
$12.772727 \leq 24$	
$76.636363 \leq 60$	**No**
$0.0 \leq 10.5$	
$25.545454 \leq 26$	

where **No** indicates a condition violation.

Step 2. Select the largest right-hand side value among all violated constraints (designated by **No**) and identify the corresponding constraint in the original set. Form and solve equation (6) for $r = 1$, using x_j^{*0} as the initial solution:

$$\max 400x_1 + 300x_2$$

Subject to

$$12x_1 + 4x_2 \leq 60$$

and

$$10x_1 + 13x_2 \leq 80.5$$

With the solution:

$$x_1^{*1} = 3.948\,2758, \quad x_2^{*1} = 3.155\,173.$$

Test condition (8):

$$15.793103 \le 20 \qquad \textbf{No}$$
$$26.827585 \le 24$$
$$60 \le 60$$
$$9.4655172 \le 10.5$$
$$28.413192 \le 26 \qquad \textbf{No}$$

Step 3. Select the largest **No** value, identify the corresponding constraint, and solve problem (6) for $r = 2$, using x_j^{*2} as the initial solution to:

$$\max 400x_1 + 300x_2$$

Subject to

$$12x_1 + 4x_2 \le 60$$
$$4x_1 + 4x_2 \le 26$$
$$6x_1 + 9x_2 \le 54.5$$

With the solution:

$$x_1^{*2} = 4.25, \quad x_2^{*2} = 2.25$$

Test condition (8):

$$17 \le 20$$
$$22 \le 24$$
$$60 \le 60$$
$$6.75 \le 10.5$$
$$26 \le 26$$

Condition (8) is satisfied *for the first time* (no violated constraints) and $x_1^{*2} = x_1^* = 4.25$ *and* $x_2^{*2} = x_2^{*2} = x_2^* = 2.25$ solves the original problem (1).

The ERA has a number of uses and potential applications:

(1) *Design of optimal* systems. If a system is to be designed *de novo*, i.e. optimal levels of b_i are to be determined for given prices p_i and the available budget B, then (3) and (4) are relevant and computationally sufficient.

(2) *Working with* mixed *constraints*. If some of the constraints *are given* and fixed, then one can use ERA to reconstruct only these fixed and potentially active blocks of the feasible set, while "designing" the remaining ones.

(3) *Solving traditional LP*. If *all* constraints are "given," we have a special case corresponding to the traditional LP. The ERA then proceeds all the way towards reconstructing the potentially active constraints of the feasible region. Its performance must be comparable to (at least, not worse than) the simplex method.

(4) *Multiple objective functions*. ERA is fully applicable to linear programming with multiple objective functions. Because of its "design" capabilities, it allows us to solve a multiobjective conflict through the redesigning of the system, rather than through the classical "trading off" within the limits of a given system.

Appendix 5

Human Judgment and Regression Analysis

The problem of weights in linear models is plaguing traditional regression analysis, especially models (linear in parameters) applied to the *study of human judgment* and capturing judgmental patterns. Here we discuss the "linearity trap."

A so-called *linear model,* based on the notion that the judge's predictions are a linear combination of available cues, either presented to or chosen by the judge, is employed in the task of making more explicit the corresponding weighting structure used in the judge's weighting policy.

The paradigm in question is very similar to the compensatory models discussed above and could be summarized as follows: the variables $x_1, x_2, \ldots, x_k$ are cues or information sources upon which the judgment is based and which are to be combined and weighted in order to arrive at the subject's final response or prediction. The basic model is:

$$R = \sum_{i=1}^{k} w_i x_i, \tag{1}$$

where R is the level of response and w_i are the weights assigned to available cues x_i. In the *lens model,* for example, R is predicted from linear combinations of cues while w_i are represented by the regression coefficients b_i and by the utilization coefficients r_i obtained through a series of experiments.

The *Integration Theory* approach is based on model (1) also, but the x_i are subjective scale values rather than physical or objective values, and the weights represent their respective salience or importance. The *ANOVA model* adds terms like $w_{ij} x_i x_j$ to Equation (1). For example if $k = 2$, we would write (1) as:

$$R = w_1 x_1 + w_2 x_2 + w_{12} x_1 x_2, \tag{2}$$

which, by introducing a simple change in notation, say, $w_3 = w_{12}$ and $x_3 = x_1x_2$, would become:

$$R = \sum_{i=1}^{3} w_i x_i,$$

(3)

where x_3 represents a new, "interactive" cue weighed by w_3. Although the term is a multiplicative function of x_1 and x_2 and thus the linearity is destroyed in two dimensions (i.e. x_1, x_2), the model remains linear in three dimensions (i.e. x_1, x_2 and $x_3 = x_1x_2$). Similarly introducing exponential terms, like x_i^2, x_i^3, ... , x_i^α, does not affect the underlying linearity of (1). We can write $x_i' = F(x_i) = x_i^\alpha$ and consider F as representing some particular subjective valuation or scaling function. Then (1) becomes:

$$R = \sum_{i=1}^{k} w_i x_i'$$

(4)

It is quite clear that the linear model is the unchanging core underlying most of the approaches in question. So called curvilinearity or configurality refers to a simple nonlinear rescaling of cues and thus only affects the ways in which cues enter the basic model (1). Additive and linear properties of (1) are not removed. To conclude, most approaches differ only in the ways by which inputs into (1), w_i's and x_i's, are obtained or measured. But they are identical with respect to the algebraic equation (1), which is the equation of a straight line for $k = 2$, and of a hyperplane in general.

This represents a good example of a *model-morphic approach* to research and experimental science. A mathematical model, like linear regression, weighted average, linear combination, etc., is selected first. The studied phenomenon, process or behavior is then restated and redefined – adjusted and transformed – in terms of variables and parameters of the selected model.

Such purposeful adjustment of reality in order to fit pre-existing modeling devices is referred to as model-morphism. Because it is clearly impossible to change mathematical archetypes (or archemodels), unless one develops a new modeling paradigm, the only degrees of freedom remaining are in adjusting the phenomena to be studied.

Purposeful Judgment

The difference between decision making and judgment is significant. While decision making implies subsequent action and thus a responsibility for one's decision, judgment refers to evaluation of alternatives and their choice *without commitment to action* and assumption of responsibility. Judges (and expert judges) do no have to bear the consequences of their valuation and choice; decision makers do. Different criteria, standards and attitudes toward risk will be displayed by decision makers and judges.

The purpose of decision making is action. The purpose of judgment is description of action.

Decision making can be characterized as purposeful judgment, the choice committed toward achieving a particular goal or goals. Whether the purpose of such a choice is an action or an expression of preference will influence the way in which the judgment is formed. This is to say that judgment is a form of information processing, while decision making is an expression of knowledge.

The very fact that a choice is being made implies that some kind of a *preference function* (or trade-off function, utility function, etc.), is ordering the available alternatives, and can be applied to *model the judge*.

Let us denote the preference function as U defined on the set of available cues (criteria), say:

$$U = f(x_1, x_2, \ldots, x_k). \tag{5}$$

Such a complex, nonlinear, explicitly unknown (and possibly indeterminable) preference structure U can be used to induce the necessary ordering of the available alternative choices. This is not meant to imply that people actually make their choices on the basis of complex, nonlinear preference structures but simply that their choices can be so described or modeled. In both the judgment research and the decision theory research an attempt is being made to approximate or capture the basic properties of U. Equation (1) represents the simplest and most widely used approximation.

Basically, the so called *policy capturing methodology* is an effort to estimate the weights in (1) in such a way that the predictions (or choices) based on (1) would at least statistically coincide with the predictions of a judge (based on U). In the next paragraph we show that the regression paradigm can never achieve such objectives.

The Linearity Trap

We shall develop our argument through the use of several graphs rather than obscure its impact by mathematical symbolism. Let us assume that only two cues, x_1 and x_2, are salient, so that a simple two-dimensional geometry can be

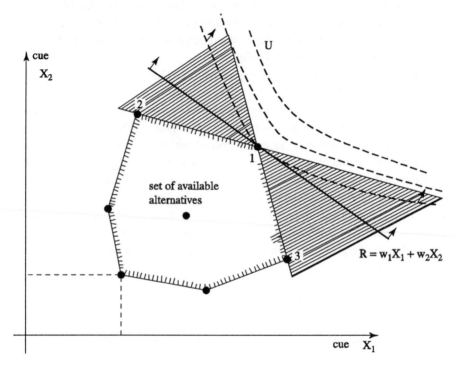

Figure 1 Relationship between the U-function and its linear approximation.

In Figure 1, a set of points in the (x_1, x_2)-space represents currently available alternatives for which the corresponding cue levels (or values) are read on the respective axes.

The desirability of x_i' increases in the direction of the arrows. Function U represents contours in the utility space, increasing in the direction of the arrows and achieving its maximum at alternative 1. Alternative 1 is the choice (or prediction) made by the judge revealing implicitly this particular form of U. It is important to see that (1) is an equation of a family of straight lines with R increasing in the same direction over the cue-space, or (x_1, x_2)-space, namely, $R = w_1x_1 = w_2x_2$. Particular values of w_1 and w_2 determine the slope of these linear contours, or their relative position with respect to the origin. In Figure 1 the weights are determined in such a way that R also reaches its maximum at alternative 1. In this sense it would lead to the same prediction and so would "capture" the judge's policy through a uniquely estimated set of weights.

However, in Figure 1 we observe that an infinite number of different straight lines (indicated by the shaded area), varying over a large number of weighing structures, would achieve exactly the same prediction, which is to reach their maximum at point 1, and therefore *also* "capture" the judge's policy.

Which set of weights then represents the "true" policy of the judge?

This is the *first failure* of the linear weighing model: it could be indeterminate in the sense that quite often an arbitrary (or random) choice of weights could predict equally well as the weights which were painfully extracted through the regression analysis – simply because they happen to fall in the same shaded area as in Figure 1.

The prominence of alternative 1 assures that almost any set of weights, including random and arbitrary selections, would make the linear model perform well on most statistical tests. But what if alternative 1 is removed or displaced? Is the captured policy still applicable?

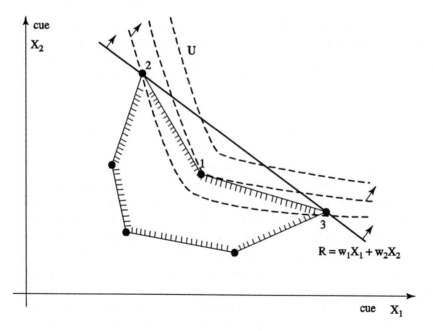

Figure 2 Linear function cannot enter the "gap".

Depending on a given situation, the positioning of individual alternatives could change. In Figure 2, let us assume that alternative 1 has been displaced closer to the origin (say because of a change in cue-level measurements).

Let us also assume that the same judge and therefore the same underlying U facilitate the choice. U is again maximized at alternative 1, which represents the highest utility to the judge. If we try to achieve the same point via the linear approximation - we fail. Observe that there is no set of weights in existence which would lead to the prediction of 1. For all possible combinations of weights we always end up at 2, or 3, or both.

This is the *second failure* of the linear model. There are cases, like the one in Figure 2, where the model will always differ from the *correct* prediction based on U. While 1 is the most preferred point, the linear approximation is always wrong in predicting 2 or 3.

The implication of this failure is potentially very harmful.

Let us assume that in Figure 1 the policy corresponding to the heavy straight line has been captured through a series of experiments and correlation analyses. If the judge applies U consistently, his choice would consistently be point 1 and the model would match his prediction most of the time. The policy has been captured.

Now let us assume that the same situation is presented to the same judge with a minor change: namely, point 1 shifts closer to the origin, behind points 2 and 3, due to a simple rescaling of the cue levels for point 1, as in Figure 2. The judge is still consistent. He applies the same U and correctly identifies 1 as the most preferred alternative.

But the experimenter is confused. Applying the previously "captured" policy leads him persuasively to points 2 or 3. He might start changing the previously "captured" weights or try to "recapture" them, but nothing would happen – either 2 or 3 would always be predicted by the model.

Is the judge inconsistent? Should he be aided in removing his inconsistency?

We might try to show him that if he would use the weights previously captured, he could "correctly" arrive at either 2 or 3. If we were skillful enough in our persuasive abilities, possibly backed by computer displays and graphics, we could actually train the judge to do what is not good for him. He could give in to our coaching and ultimately end up at 2 or 3, deriving an obviously lower level of utility than at 1.

There is also a *third failure* of the linear model. In Figures 1 and 2 we have considered only a minor change in the set of available alternatives. That is, in

Figure 1 the judge would probably agree and give us the set of weights similar to those we have captured. Also, in Figure 2, since there is no set of weights leading to point 1, he has no reason to disagree with the captured weights and probably would "reveal" that he is using the same set. But what if the same judge (and the same underlying U) faces two more tangibly different sets of alternatives?

Let us look at Figure 3 and note that the same set of cues is still used.

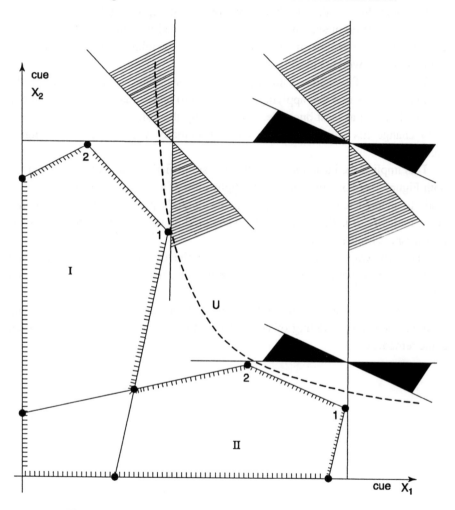

Figure 3 Different feasible sets have different effects on weights.

There are two separate sets of alternatives, I and II. The same judge applies his implicit U in both situations and predicts point 1 in I and point 2 in II as his most desirable alternatives. The same solutions might be achieved by choosing particular sets of weights, similar to those in Figure 1. The respectively shaded regions in Figure 3 indicate all possible weight combinations which would also achieve points 1 and 2.

Our point here is that the judge, by consistently applying U, would indicate that entirely different sets of weights have been used in achieving the respective predictions. As a matter of fact, the two sets of weights do not have a single combination of weights in common!

Which set of weights "captures" the judge's policy – the first one or the second one? Observe that applying only one set to both situations would lead to a wrong choice in at least one case. The only way the judge can remain consistent is to change his weights entirely and substantially with respect to changing contexts.

This implies the basic *fallacy* of the oversimplified concept of *consistency*. In both Figure 2 and 3, any "consistent" application of a "captured" weighing policy leads to inconsistency (with respect to the judge's preferential U) in a rather consistent way. It is the experimenter who could be inconsistent here, forcing his hopelessness on the judge.

The only way to achieve consistency in the dynamic, ever-changing and flexible environment is to be "inconsistent," i.e., dynamic, ever-changing and flexible.

We shall use some of our findings about the linearity trap in the following section, exploring modeling of consumer attitudes in marketing and proposing some remedies.

Appendix 6

Consumer Attitudes Modeling (ADAM)

In the previous section we have discussed the so called "linearity trap" and pointed out the inadequacy of linear models when it comes to the use of regression analysis in the human systems redolent of decision making, judgment and choice.

In consumer research, there have been countless attempts to measure consumer attitudes towards product brands with respect to multiple attributes of the product. There is a voluminous literature dealing with the simplest, so called compensatory multi-attribute attitude model:

$$A_j = \sum_{i=1}^{m} \lambda_i d_{ij}, \qquad j = 1, \ldots, n, \tag{1}$$

where an individual's attitude toward brand j is a weighted combination of the individual's evaluations of brand j with respect to m salient attributes. In model (1) we consider n brands, m attributes, m weights of attribute importance λ_is, and m respective perceptions or *scores* d_{ij} (also called beliefs), forming evoked set D.

To avoid the definitional ambiguities, we shall talk about alternatives of choice rather than brands, attribute attention levels rather than weights, and scores or degrees instead of beliefs. We shall retain the attitude score to designate the overall relative intensity of the preference for an alternative j.

Although intuitively appealing (and mathematically trivial), model (1) has shown considerable resistance towards turning explanatory and predictive. It has failed because of the *three failures* of linear models discussed in section 5 of this Appendix.

Because model (1) is simply an equation defining a family of hyper-planes in m-dimensional space, all conclusions of section 5 apply here.

We can only add that the weights of attribute importance λ_is cannot be correctly specified by the following type marketing research procedure: "In general, in deciding whether or not to buy a brand, how important to you is each of the attributes listed below?" Such an approach does not achieve much.

The attributes "listed below" do not establish a decision context: the respondent simply does not know and cannot know. Asking questions in the *default context* (no context at all) is the curse of any such research, not only in marketing.

The weights of importance must change and vary from one context to another. If she assigns a large weight to an attribute and she considers a set of products which all measure equally on scores d_{ij}, then the decision cannot be made because of the large weight. In such cases, the real decision maker ignores such an attribute.

All interviews elicit a description of intent or action in a context-free fashion. It cannot be otherwise. All decisions refer to action itself and all take place in a specific, given context. It cannot be otherwise. Context-free questions and answers can never match context-rich decisions and actions.

Let us summarize some other objections against the *direct assessment* of weights through context-free interviews or questionnaires:

(i) Most psychological studies indicate that an explicit importance-weighting process is unstable, suboptimal, and often arbitrary. The human ability to arrive at an overall evaluation by weighting and combining diverse attributes is not very impressive, because they are forced to think out of context in determining the weights.

(ii) The task of multi-attribute weighting is further complicated by a fuzzy logic employed by a decision maker when facing a not fully comprehensive problem. It is ambitious, for example, to expect decision makers to state that: "my $\lambda_i = 0.42$," or even "$0.45 < \lambda_i < 0.5$." More likely they express themselves in such terms as: "λ_i should be substantially larger than 0.5," or, "λ_i should be in the vicinity of 0.4, but rather larger," or some similar fuzzy statement.

(iii) The total number of all possible (and identifiable) attributes is usually very large, even in the thousands. Obviously we do not expect any person to assign priority weights to the hundreds of attributes reliably. Yet, the small set of salient attributes is evoked (usually 5-15 attributes) and may therefore be elicited by applying *some* weighting structure to the complete identifiable set of attributes, and then by disregarding those which have received their weight below some predetermined threshold level.

(iv) Observed changes in weights reflect their dependency on a particular set of feasible alternatives considered at a given time (choice situation). Thus, the changes in the evoked set of d_{ij}, D, would imply different λ_i.

Even the most prominent theories of choice behavior appear to be incomplete because they treat the underlying choice tendencies as static and independent of the particular set of alternatives being considered at any one time.

The dependency of weights on the set of feasible alternatives further indicates the importance of eliciting each buyer's "evoked set" of alternatives rather than having all respondents evaluate an arbitrary list of "all" or the "major" available attributes.

If weights do change, the kind and the number of attributes considered must also change, as well as their saliency. It is probably clear now why the parameters λ_i should be called attention levels rather than weights of importance. The attribute dynamics suggested here must be a part of any model having even a remote chance for a success. Let us assume that we can model the dynamism of attention levels in dependency on a given set of feasible alternatives. Then model (1) should work because λ_is would correctly reflect the underlying utility function U at all times, right? Wrong.

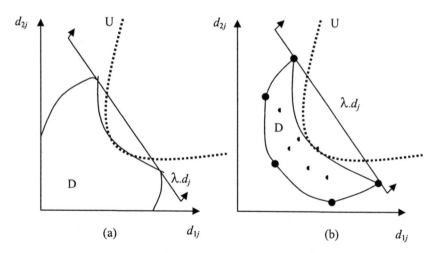

Figure 1 Failures of a linear model $\lambda.d_j$ to reach non-convex "gaps" in
(a) continuous and (b) discrete cases of D.

There is the condition of the convexity of evoked set D of d_{ij}. If D is not a convex set, i.e. it contains a gap or a dent, as for example in Figure 1, then there could be no set of weights which would help even the "correct" model (1) to achieve the solution compatible with the underlying U.

In general, the set D cannot be considered to be convex. In the marketing context especially, it will more likely resemble the set in Figure 1(b), i.e. a *point set* of discrete alternatives – a non-convex set.

That is, attributes are not generally available on a continuous scale but only through a given set of choice alternatives. An automobile with 1.37 doors, a 37.2 oz. Bottle of Coke, or a coat priced at $16.59 might not be feasible alternatives at a given time. Convex approximation of a non-convex set is not feasible. This corresponds to the third failure of linearity discussed in section 5.

It is important to realize that the three conceptual "failures" discussed earlier pertain to the linear compensatory model (1) and not to the particular ways of determining its weights. Whether the weights are obtained by direct questioning, regression analysis or individual multidimensional scaling, as long as the results are substituted into model (1), all three failures apply.

The so called computational approaches (weights are computed rather than elicited) alleviate some of the difficulties, namely the non-convexity problem. Their main weakness is that they "bootstrap" themselves into the attribute weights. That is, the differential weights are not related to any intrinsic properties in a given decision situation, but rather they are internally computed to satisfy the minimization of the Euclidean metric. Decision makers are presumed to use the weights so as to minimize a particular distance function. Consequently, any other distance metric used would imply a different set of weights under otherwise equal conditions.

The assumption that an individual prefers that alternative which is "closer" to his ideal point is very useful and it has been adopted in decision making. The issue of weights however, comes down to the following question: Do we minimize the weighted distance function or do we weight the attributes so that the distance function is minimized?

In the first case, the weights come from the outside; they are external and independent of a particular functional form of the distance measure. In the second case, as in computational models, the weights come from within and are serving only as a means of parametric minimization.

ADAM (Attribute-Dynamic Attitude Model)

We shall outline only the most essential features of the *Attribute-Dynamic Attitude Model*.

As stated earlier, any feasible alternative can be purposefully evaluated in terms of a vector of attribute scores, say $d_j = (d_{ij},..., d_{mj})$, where d_{ij} evaluates j^{th} alternative with respect to the ith attribute. The set of all such vectors d_j is denoted D.

Consider the ith attribute in separation. The set D now generates n numbers, $d_i = (d_{i1},..., d_{in})$, representing feasible levels of the ith attribute. Among these attainable scores, for any i^{th} attribute, there is at least one extreme value that is preferred to all remaining ones. Such a score shall be called an anchor value of the ith attribute. The set of all such anchor values for all attributes shall be called the anchor point or the anchor.

If $d_i^* = \mathrm{Max}_{j \in D} d_{ij}$ then the *anchor point* associated with the given set D is denoted as

$$d^* = (d_1^*,..., d_m^*). \tag{2}$$

Such an anchor d^* plays a prominent role in decision making. If there is some $j' \in D$ such that $d_{j'} \equiv d^*$, i.e. the anchor is attainable by the choice of j', then there is no decision-making problem because any utility function defined over D-space would reach its maximum at d^*.

The anchor is however, infeasible in general. That is, there is no alternative j' in D which would attain maximum scores with respect to all attributes simultaneously.

We now restate an earlier axiom (see Section 4.4) on which the whole theory presented here is based:

Axiom of Choice. Alternatives that are closer to the anchor are preferred to those that are farther away. To be as close as possible to the perceived anchor point is the rationale of human choice.

Considering the ith attribute in isolation we face a trivial decision problem: we simply choose the anchor value (feasible by definition).

Because we are always facing a multi-attribute problem, we have to reflect the cardinal preference of the decision maker, even with respect to the single attribute. Using the Axiom of Choice, observe that in the case of a single attribute, the anchor point is identical with the anchor value. The alternatives that are closer to d_i^* will be preferred to those being farther away. But what do we mean by "closer," "farther," or "as close as possible"?

Example. Three different alternatives are evaluated with respect to some easily measurable attribute, say "$ saved." We might obtain the following three-dimensional vector: (5, 10, 500). Obviously the first two values 5 and 10 are quite far from 500, with 10 being a little closer. Let us assume that the lucrative third alternative has proven to be infeasible and has been replaced by a new alternative, generating the so-modified vector (5, 10, 11). This change in the anchor value has also caused 10 to become much closer to the anchor than 5. The difference between 5 and 10 has changed from negligible to substantial. This is the "context dependency" in action.

The fuzzy language employed in the previous paragraph like "as close as possible," "closer," "farther," "substantial," "negligible," etc., reflects the reality of the fuzziness of human thinking, perception and preferences.

Referring to the Axiom of Choice, we would like to measure the distance of any alternative j from the anchor point, in order to identify the one which is the closest.

For this purpose we define

$$\overline{d}_{ij} = d_i^* - d_{ij},\tag{3}$$

and then minimize a distance function, $L_p(\lambda, j)$, defined as follows:

$$L_p(\lambda, j) = \left[\sum_{i=1}^{m} \lambda_i^p \overline{d}_{ij}^p\right]^{1/p}, \qquad 1 \le p \le \infty.\tag{4}$$

Observe that equation (4) represents the family of L_p-metrics, providing a wide range of geometric measures of closeness with respect to changing parameter p. Through varying p and λ_i', any monotonic, continuous and non-decreasing utility function can be expressed. Our point is that no utility function is explicated or assumed and the entire family of L_p-metrics can be considered.

If
$$\underset{j \in D}{\text{Min}}\, L_p(\lambda, j) = L_p(\lambda, j_p),$$
(5)

then, $j_p \in D$ is called the *compromise alternative* with respect to p. Actually, the power $1/p$ can be disregarded in equation (4), for $1 \le p < \infty$, since the compromises j_p would not be affected. To understand the role of the distance parameter p, we shall substitute $v_j = \overline{d}_{ij}$, omit $1/p$, and rewrite equation (4) as:

$$L_p(\lambda, j) = \sum_{i=1}^{m} \lambda_i^p v_i^{p-1} \overline{d}_{ij},$$
(6)

In equation (6), as p increases, more and more weight is given to the largest distance. Ultimately the largest distance completely dominates and for $p = \infty$, equation (6) becomes $L_\infty(j) = \text{Max}_i \{\overline{d}_{ij}\}$. We assume a given set of attribute attention levels λ_i, i.e. $\lambda = (\lambda_1, \lambda_2, \ldots, \lambda_m)$.

In Figure 2, assuming that the d_{ij} have been correctly assessed, we see that "as close as possible" can be interpreted as minimizing the distance between any j and the anchor in the geometrical sense. In Figure 2, the j ($\equiv j_2$) is the closest in terms of the Euclidean measure, i.e. $p = 2$. This is a special case from the family of L_p-measures, any or all of which can be used as well.

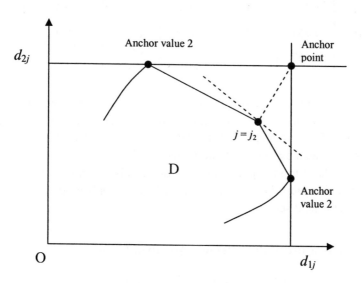

Figure 2 Measuring the distance from an anchor point.

By minimizing (6) for a given λ and *all* p, $1 < p < \infty$, we would generate the set of all j_ps, called the *compromise set*, denoted by C. Obviously C is the locus of points (alternatives) which are all "as close as possible" to the anchor point with regard to all reasonable geometrical interpretations. As a first approximation of C it will suffice to identify solutions j_1, j_2 and j_∞ as it is portrayed in Table 1.

Numerical example. Let the degrees of closeness – transformed into distances by equation (3) – be assigned to a problem with six alternatives and three attributes as denoted by the table below.

Table 1 Identifying alternatives {1, 2} as set C (in bold).

j	1	2	3	4	5	6
$\overline{d}_{1j}$	0.667	0	0.667	1	0.889	0.889
$\overline{d}_{2j}$	0.25	0	1	0	0.334	0.334
$\overline{d}_{3j}$	0.5	1	0	0	0.334	0.334
$L_1(j)$	1.417	1	1.667	1.75	1.557	1.557
$L_2(j)$	**0.757**	1	1.445	1.563	1.013	1.013
$L_\infty(j)$	**0.667**	1	1	1	0.889	0.889

The values of three L_p-metrics in Table 1 are obtained from equation (6) by using $\lambda_i = 1$ for all i (i.e. assuming equal weights) and $p = 1$, 2, and ∞ respectively. Observe that $j_1 = 2$ (bold) and $j_2 = j_\infty = 1$. Thus the compromise set C is approximated by the set of alternatives {1, 2}.

Clearly, we have to incorporate the attention levels λ_i explicitly in the model, and they should exhibit their dependency on D as it has been discussed earlier. We do this in the next section.

Entropy as a Measure of the Attribute Attention Level

We now define an *attention level* λ_i for the ith attribute:

An attention level λ_i , assigned to the ith attribute as a measure of its relative importance for a given decision context, is directly related to the average intrinsic information generated by the given set of feasible alternatives through the ith attribute, and simultaneously to the subjective assessment of its importance, reflective of the decision maker's cultural, psychological, and environmental history.

So, there are two components entering the formation of λ_i:

(1) A relatively stable concept of the attribute importance w_i, reflecting an individual's cultural, genetic, psychological, societal, and environmental background.

(2) Relatively unstable, changing concept of the "situational importance," say $\tilde{\lambda}_i$, i.e. an attention level based on a particular context as it is reflected in the composition of the evoked set of feasible alternatives D. These weights, $\tilde{\lambda}_i$, could change radically with changes in D and thus also with changes in the average intrinsic information generated by D.

Example. Let us assume that it has been assessed that "fluoride content" has the highest weight of importance in the hierarchy of toothpaste attributes considered by a given individual, say $w_i = 1$. The analysis of D then reveals that all alternatives are equal in terms of scores for this particular attribute i. Thus the attribute receiving the highest level of importance does not allow the individual to make a decision because it transmits no information to the decision maker. That is $\tilde{\lambda}_i = 0$.

Because decisions are being made, such an attribute must be dynamically re-assessed and the weight of importance shifts from "fluoride content" to say, "taste," and in spite of what might have been claimed *a priori*, that would now become the most important attribute. The definition of attention level presented earlier would assign 0 to "fluoride content" automatically and would thus exclude the attribute from the model. The definition becomes operational only if the "average intrinsic information" transmitted to the decision maker through the ith attribute can be measured.

One way to achieve such measurement efficiently is to base $\tilde{\lambda}_i$ on the traditional measure of the average intrinsic information, the *entropy measure*. The more distinct the individual attribute scores are, the larger is the corresponding $\tilde{\lambda}_i$. For this purpose we interpret $\tilde{\lambda}_i$ as a measure of the contrast intensity of the ith attribute.

Recall that vector $d_i = (d_{i1}, \ldots, d_{in})$ describes set D in terms of the ith attribute, $i = 1, \ldots, m$. Individual d_{ij} are assumed to represent the transformed degrees of closeness, ranging for example from 0 to 1.

To each d_i we assign a measure of i's *contrast intensity* or entropy, denoted by $e(d_i)$.

Let us also define

$$D_i = \sum_{j=1}^{n} d_{ij}, \qquad i = 1, \ldots, m. \tag{7}$$

If D is a finite set (as it can be reasonably assumed), then the traditional entropy measure can be adjusted to our purpose as follows:

$$e(d_i) = -K \sum_{j=1}^{n} (d_{ij} / D_i) \ln(d_{ij} / D_i) \tag{8}$$

where $K > 0$ and $e(d_i) \geq 0$ and ln is the natural logarithm. If all d_{ij} are equal to each other for a given i, then $d_{ij}/Di = 1/n$, and $e(d_i)$ takes on its maximum value, say e_{max}. Obviously $e_{max} = \ln(n)$. So, by setting $K = 1/e_{max}$, we get $0 \leq e(d_i) \leq 1$, for all d_i. Such normalization of the entropy measure is useful for comparative purposes.

Next we introduce the *total entropy* of D, defined as

$$E = \sum_{i=1}^{m} e(d_i). \tag{9}$$

Then the *measure of contrast intensity* of the ith attribute can be transformed into a weight of importance as a function of equation (8) in the following way:

$$\tilde{\lambda}_i = (1 - e(d_i))/(m - E). \tag{10}$$

Observe that a change in D could lead to the displacement of the anchor point. This, in turn, induces changes in d_{ij} and thus triggers further changes in relative contrast intensities of individual attributes. Ultimately, the change in D is reflected in a new set of $\tilde{\lambda}_i$.

For example, removing a particular brand (reduction of D) could increase the contrast intensity and thus generate additional decision-relevant information. Similarly, the influence of adding or deleting an attribute (changing the dimensionality of the D-space) can be studied. We can determine a combination of attributes providing the highest overall contrast intensity and thus potentially the most "valuable" attribute mix to a decision maker. Similarly the most "valuable" combination of alternatives can be determined.

Remark. Let us denote the *subjective* assessment of importance of the ith attribute as w_i, i.e. the component dependent on the stable factors defined earlier. The interaction between $\tilde{\lambda}_i$ and w_i could then be described as, for example,

$$\lambda_i = \tilde{\lambda}_i . w_i , \tag{11}$$

or, as in ADAM,

$$\lambda_i = \frac{\tilde{\lambda}_i \cdot w_i}{\sum_{i=1}^{m} \tilde{\lambda}_i w_i}, \qquad i = 1, \ldots, m. \tag{12}$$

Observe that both equations (11) and (12) are still rather arbitrary assumptions about the true nature of the weight interaction.

Numerical Example

Consider three attributes which were assigned subjective weights w_i (like using the traditional "in-depth" interview methodology associated with model (1)). Relevant numerical values for four feasible alternatives are summarized in Table 2:

Table 2 Measured scores of example data.

	i	j			
w_i	$f_i(j)$	1	2	3	4
0.8	$f_1(j)$	7	8	8.5	9
0.1	$f_2(j)$	100	60	20	80
0.1	$f_3(j)$	4	4	6	2

In Table 2, $f_i(j)$ indicates the "raw data" score directly measured for the jth alternative with respect to the ith attribute. The numbers in Table 2 could be dollars, grades, degrees, points, etc. Bold designation indicates the anchor values for the three attributes. The anchor point is then given as $f^* = (9, 100, 6)$. The degrees of closeness can be generated by any suitable seminal function, for example, $d_{ij} = f_i(j) / f_i^*$. We arrive at Table 3:

Table 3 The degrees of closeness d_{ij}.

j / i	1	2	3	4	Σ
1	0.778	0.889	0.944	1	3.611
2	1	0.6	0.2	0.8	2.6
3	0.667	0.667	1	0.334	2.668

Next we calculate $e(d_i)$ according to equation (8) where $K = 1/e_{max}$ and $e_{max} = \ln(4) = 1.3863$. The results are given in Table 4:

Table 4 Attribute i^{th} contrast intensities $e(d_i)$.

	d_{ij}/D_i			$d_{ij}/D_i(\ln d_{ij}/D_{ij})$		
	1	2	3	1	2	3
1	0.216	0.385	0.25	-0.331	-0.367	-0.347
2	0.246	0.231	0.25	-0.345	-0.338	-0.347
3	0.261	0.007	0.375	-0350	-0.197	-0.368
4	0.277	0.307	0.125	-0.356	-0.363	-0.260
Σ	1	1	1	-1.382	-1.265	-1.332

From Table 4 we obtain: $e(d_i) = 0.997$, $e(d_2) = 0.913$, $e(d_3) = 0.954$ and $E = 2.864$. Then $\tilde{\lambda}_i = 0.022$, $\tilde{\lambda}_i = 0.64$, and $\tilde{\lambda}_i = 0.338$ indicate the contrast intensities in equation (10) measuring the intrinsic average information transmitted by each attribute (compare with w_i in (12)). According to (12), we could calculate attention levels as: $\lambda_1 = 0.153$, $\lambda_2 = 0.555$, $\lambda_3 = 0.292$, to be entered in the formula of the distance function (Equation (4)). For the sake of simplicity, let us use a simple additive model of type (1) instead of the L_p-metric.

We shall compare its performance using w_i, λ_i and $\tilde{\lambda}_i$, as it is summarized in Table 5:

Table 5 Different weighing structures effect.

	1	2	3	4
$\sum_{i=1}^{m} w_i d_{ij}$	0.789	0.838	0.875	**0.913**
$\sum_{i=1}^{m} \lambda_i d_{ij}$	**0.869**	0.664	0.547	0.695
$\sum_{i=1}^{m} \tilde{\lambda}_i d_{ij}$	**0.882**	0.628	0.486	0.647

Bold designation indicates the maximum values. Thus, the traditional approach, using fixed and D-independent weights, would recommend alternative 4. The method of ADAM, proposed here, predicts alternative 1.

Anchor Point Displacement

Using the entropy measure, we can temporarily discard those attributes which exhibit low contrast intensity. The choice of salient attributes is thus made on a more objective basis and does not have to be left to an "expert judgment."

Such a decrease in the number of attributes could lead to a smaller D as some alternatives become dominated by others with respect to remaining salient attributes. This is of course is beneficial because consumers try to avoid choosing from a large number of attributes, minimizing tradeoffs and the post-decision regret.

The net result is the *displacement of* the anchor point. Consequently, all degrees of closeness d_{ij}, all attention levels λ_i and all compromise alternatives are to be recalculated and revaluated after each displacement. Consumers are sensitive to the changes in context. Attributes previously not considered could become salient and *vice versa*.

The displacement of the anchor does not have to be accomplished by its actual shift, but by *being perceived* at different locations (say via the influence of advertising, complexity and numerousness of attributes, proliferation of variety, different brands, etc.). In such cases, ADAM can fulfill an important normative role. It can cut through hundreds of alternatives and attributes much faster than any decision maker facing the jungle of brands, attributes and advertisement pressures.

One critical comment on model (1) was based on the convexity assumption in Figure 1. The methodology of ADAM works for both convex *and* non-convex situations equally well. In Figure 3, observe that j, chosen by implicit U, is inside the gap and cannot be reached by any linear function (which would always offer a wrong prediction, no matter how accurately and patiently we calculate the attention levels).

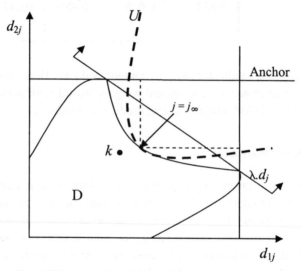

Figure 3 Nonconvex "gap" is reached by distance measures, not by $\lambda.d_j$.

ADAM, being based on the proximity of alternatives to the anchor point, can always enter the gap. In Figure 3, the alternative j is also the closest one according to the L_p-metric, i.e., $j \equiv j = \infty$ for $p = \infty$ in equation (4).

Appendix 7

Risk Measures and Portfolio Analysis

Most decisions in human systems are made under at least some conditions of risk and uncertainty. Traditionally, the amount of risk inherent in a given project, endeavor or portfolio is quantified by measuring the dispersion of potential outcomes around the mean (expected value) of a given probability distribution of uncertain returns. The measure of dispersion most favored by statisticians is the variance (or its square root, the standard deviation). A small variance implies that the distribution is closely massed around the mean value, and consequently one can predict the final outcome with a fair degree of accuracy. A large variance implies a high degree of uncertainty as to what the actual outcome is likely to be. In other words, risk is identified with the degree of dispersion of potential outcomes.

This is another example of model-morphism: the assumption that a studied phenomenon should conform its behavior to the readily-available, simple model. Simply put: because variance is such a simple statistical measure of dispersion, let variance measure risk.

One problem with equating risk and dispersion is that high variance implies not only high risk but also high potential for realizing returns well above the mean. Low variance implies high predictability of actual return but with little chance for exceptional outcomes. That is, investing in a low-variance project protects against extremely low returns, but one is also running a "risk" of *not* realizing potentially high returns.

Measures of Risk

"Some financial writers, unfortunately, have come to look upon the standard deviation of the distribution of returns as a measure not only of the variability (which it is) but of the risk inherent in a project (which it is not). In everyday usage, risk means the probability of a loss or the probability that a return will be lower than some target level."

E. Lerner[1]

What is risk? How can riskiness be measured? How do decision makers perceive and deal with risk? Can the degree of riskiness be described by a single-dimensional index, or is the risk inherently *multidimensional*?

Each risky alternative is characterized by a probability distribution defined over its possible (or conceivable) outcomes. According to the nature of the outcomes, such distributions can be continuous or discrete, bounded or unbounded, fully or partially known, subjectively estimated or objectively measured. It is obvious that the riskiness of a given situation is directly related to the position and shape of the probability distribution associated with the outcomes. If only one outcome can occur with a probability of 1 – that is, if the "distribution" of probabilities is degenerate, with a single "mass point" – then no riskiness is perceived or measured.

The major task is as follows: How do we ascertain that one distribution describes a situation which is perceived as being more (or less) risky than a situation described by another distribution? That is, how can we derive a measure of risk on the basis of the attributes of a given distribution?

We shall briefly summarize three typical approaches to the above question: The expected-utility approach, the mean-variance approach, and stochastic dominance.

1. Expected-Utility Approach The expected-utility approach does not attempt to measure the riskiness of a given situation as perceived by the decision maker, but rather tries to describe the decision maker's *attitude* toward risk *per se* out of context, without reference to a particular situation. This is done through structured and subjective interrogation of the decision maker about a battery of hypothetical (and artificial) situations.

---

[1] E. Lerner, *Managerial Finance,* Harcourt Brace Jovanovich, New York. 1971, p. 328.

Suppose there are n consequences $X_1, X_2 \ldots X_n$ associated with a given alternative or prospect x. Let the worst consequence be X_1 and the best consequence X_n, and let the corresponding distribution of probabilities of occurrence be $p_1, p_2 \ldots p_n$. The decision maker is being asked: Consider (1) an option X_i which you could obtain for sure, and (2) a risky option (a lottery, a gamble) characterized by X_n with probability π_i and X_1 with probability $1 - \pi_i$. At what value of π_i would you be indifferent between receiving X_i for sure and engaging in the risky gamble?

The question is repeated for all possible X_i, $i = 1, 2 \ldots n$. A set of probabilities $\pi_1, \pi_2 \ldots \pi_n$ is derived. The procedure is further simplified by assigning $\pi_1 = 0$ and $\pi_n = 1$.

The fundamental result of the utility theory is that each X_i can be replaced by the corresponding risky option characterized by X_1, X_n, and π_i. Observe that each consequence X_i occurs with probability P_i. The decision maker said that he or she was indifferent between X_i and a π_i chance for X_n and a $(1 - \pi_i)$ chance for X_1. Consequently, π_i and their positive linear transformations can be taken as representing the utilities of individual consequences X_i, that is, u_i (ranging from 0 to 1). The expected utility index is

$$\sum_i p_i u_i = \sum_i p_i (a + b\pi_i) = a + b \sum_i p_i \pi_i$$

The assessment of $u_i = a + b\pi_i$ results in assigning utility indexes u_i to consequences X_i. That is, a utility function u has been constructed so that it assigns a utility $u(X)$ to any possible consequence X over a continuous or discrete range of values.

Depending on the shape of u, the function can be said to reflect a decision maker's risk aversion (u is concave), risk preference (u is convex), or risk neutrality (u is linear).

This type of risk measure does say something about the decision maker's attitude toward the risky gambles as formulated by the analyst. It does not say much about the actual risk content perceived by the decision maker in a specific situation. All human action takes place within a given context.

2. Mean-Variance Approach This approach is based on the assumption that a larger mean (or expected value) of a given distribution is preferred to a smaller one, and a smaller variance (dispersion) is preferred to a larger one. The most common risk measure is the variance σ^2 or its square root, standard deviation σ, of a distribution characterized by mean $\bar{x}_i$. A rational decision maker is expected to maximize $\bar{x}_i$ and to minimize σ^2.

It has become obvious that variance *per se* does not measure risk. Many researchers have turned to as an alternative. While variance measures the total dispersion of possible outcomes around the mean, semivariance measures the dispersion of outcomes below some predetermined target value. Business executives' emphasis on "downside risk" indicates that semivariance may be a better approximation of their perception of risk than variance.

However, most executives perceive risk as a *probability* of not achieving a minimum target return. So, neither variance nor semivariance appears to be an adequate measure of risk. The same holds true for all proposed combinations of mean and variance, for example, $K\sigma - \bar{x}_i$ with $K > 0$, or a $\sigma^2 - (1 - a)\,\bar{x}_i$ with $0 < a < 1$. These are all one-dimensional aggregates or indexes, often one-sided and very difficult to justify.

Neither approach addresses the fundamental question of risk assessment: Can the risk associated with a given alternative be characterized and measured by a single number? Or is the concept of risk and its perception essentially multidimensional, comprised of a number of incommensurable and therefore irreducible components?

3. Stochastic Dominance Approach Because of the problems associated with the expected-utility theory, and because of the inadequacy of single-dimensional indexes in the mean-variance (or semivariance) approaches, we have to turn to *stochastic dominance*.

This approach is based on the assumption that only limited information is available about a decision maker's utility function u. It is assumed that all we can say about u is that it belongs to a broad family of real valued functions U. We shall discuss stochastic dominance in the next section.

What is a Portfolio?

The most common application of risk concepts appears in problems of portfolio selection and management.

We can use the term "portfolio" synonymously with the expression "collection of assets" or, even more generally, "collection of prospects." A portfolio could consist of both financial and real assets: savings deposits, bonds, treasury bills, debentures, equity shares, etc., as well as real estate, antique

Persian rugs, jewelry, paintings, antique coins, wines, or other collectibles. Portfolios also may include such prospects as investment ventures – both projected and on-going concerns.

Portfolio management, then, is the process of defining, evaluating, selecting, maintaining, adjusting, and dismantling an investment portfolio.

We are concerned only with portfolios which are held for the purposes of realizing a return on investment, either monetary or in kind. But there are other portfolios, especially individually held ones, which are solely for the purpose of consumption (that is, some wine cellars) or for purely aesthetic satisfaction. We have also introduced the concept of *portfolio of resources* or resource portfolio when dealing with De Novo Programming.

There is no investment without risk. Risk is one of the major criteria used in assessing a portfolio. It is therefore essential that we know how the risk involved should be measured.

Current Concepts of Risk

We say that a prospect return x_i is risky if it is characterized by a probability distribution $F_i(x)$. Let $\bar{x}_i$ and σ^2_i respectively denote the mean and variance of $F_i(x)$. The most common risk measures discussed in the literature are all *single-dimensional*. Some authors simply use σ^2_i or σ_i directly, with little regard for the actual investors' risk perceptions and behavior. According to them, the risk associated with x_i – say, R_i – can simply be measured by

$$R_i = \sigma_i^2 = \int_{-\infty}^{\infty} (\bar{x_i} - x_i)^2 \, dF_i(x)$$

in the continuous, and

$$R_i = \sigma_i^2 = \sum_{j=-\infty}^{\infty} (\bar{x_i} - x_{ij})^2 \, p(x_{ij})$$

in the discrete case; $p(x_{ij})$ designates probability of the jth level of return to the ith prospect, or X_{ij}. Standard deviation $\sigma_i = \sqrt{\sigma_i^2}$ is frequently used in both cases. This measure is often further modified as follows:

$$R_i = \alpha \sigma_i^2 - (1-\alpha)\bar{x}_i \qquad\qquad 0 < \sigma < 1$$

or

$$R_i = k\sigma_i - \bar{x}_i$$

or

$$R_i = \frac{\sigma_i^2}{x_i}.$$

Then there is a whole family of risk measures based on *semivariance*.

$$R_i = \int_{-\infty}^{t_j}(t_i - x_i)^\alpha\, dF_i(x) \qquad \alpha = 0 \qquad \left(R_i = \sum_{j=-\infty}^{t_i}(t_j - x_{ij})^\alpha\, p(x_{ij}) \right)$$

One can substitute various parameters for t_i: a desired target level return, the break-even point, or even $\bar{x}_i$. Most writers also prefer to set $\alpha = 2$.

A different type of measure was can be based on *entropy* and it reaches its maximum value for uniform distributions:

$$R_i = -\int_{-\infty}^{\infty}\ln[f_i(x)]dF_i(x) \qquad \left(R_i = -\sum_{j=-\infty}^{\infty}[\ln p(x_{ij})]p(x_{ij}) \right)$$

Stone (1973) showed that virtually all commonly used risk measures can be viewed as special cases of the family of *three-parameter risk measures*. This rich and fairly general group of functions provides the research with an infinite variety of "risk measures" through different combinations of appropriate parameter values of c, α, and λ.

$$R_i = \int_{-\infty}^{\lambda}|c - x_i|^\alpha\, dF_i(x) \qquad \left(R_i = \sum_{j=-\infty}^{\lambda}|c - x_{ij}|^\alpha\, p(x_{ij}) \right)$$

In this general formula, c is a reference level of wealth from which deviations are measured. For example, c could represent $t\bar{x}_i$, zero, the initial wealth level, the mode, the median, etc. Parameter α is the power to which deviations are raised, and thus α reflects the relative importance of large and small deviations. For $\alpha = 1$ all deviations are weighted equally, for $0 < \alpha < 1$ small deviations become relatively more important than large deviations. Values $1 < \alpha \le \infty$ induce the opposite effect, with $\alpha = \infty$ taking only the largest deviation into consideration.

If $\alpha = 0$, we get an important special case, independent of c:

$$R_i = \int_{-\infty}^{\lambda} dF_i(x) = P(x \le \lambda) \qquad \left(R_i = \sum_{j=-\infty}^{\lambda} p(x_{ij}) \right)$$

that is, the probability of an outcome being smaller than some predetermined level λ. Parameter λ specifies what deviations are to be included in the risk measure $\alpha > 0$. Possible choices of the parameter λ include ∞, c, t_i, and some others.

Of course, one can introduce the "root mean deviation power" to obtain a more homogeneous family of measures:

$$R_i = \left[\int_{-\infty}^{\lambda} |c - x_i|^{\alpha} dF_i(x) \right]^{1/\alpha} \qquad\qquad \alpha > 0$$

These measures are now entirely analogous with so-called "L_p metrics," common measures of distance discussed in Appendix 6. All such measures of risk are still single-dimensional. Because they treat risk as a one-dimensional aggregate, they have been shown to be theoretically and empirically incompatible with risk-related *human* behavior.

It is characteristic of the problem that many researchers seem willing to recommend incorrect or even nonsensical measures "for the time being." Typical is the statement by Porter:

"The EV [mean-variance] rule implies violations of the assumptions of rational behavior and leads to decisions that are empirically unjustified. The use of semivariance around the mean as a measure of risk also leads to incorrect choices [italics mine], but with less frequency."

Porter 1974, p. 204

Stochastic Dominance

If we know cumulative distribution functions $F_i(x)$, then prospect x_1 *stochastically dominates* prospect x_2 if and only if either

$$F_1(x) \le F_2(x) \qquad \text{for all } x$$

(first-degree stochastic dominance [FSD]) or

$$\int_{-\infty}^{x} F_1(y)dy \le \int_{-\infty}^{x} F_2(y)dy \qquad \text{for all } x$$

(second-degree stochastic dominance [SSD]).

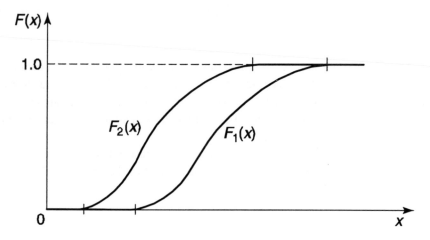

Figure 1 Prospect x_1 stochastically dominates prospect x_2.

Figure 1 represents first-degree stochastic dominance graphically. If x_1 dominates x_2, as in Figure 1, then x_1 will be preferred by any rational investor. That is, x_1 is less risky than x_2 – *regardless of their variances*. In Figure 2 we look at the problem of risk through the densities of stochastic returns.

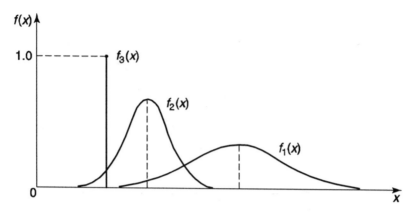

Figure 2 Prospects X_2 and X_3 are stochastically dominated by prospect X_1.

Any determined risk averter would choose x_1 even though it has the largest variance. Prospects x_2 and x_3 would not be chosen. Observe that the largest-variance distribution *stochastically dominates* the other two.

In Figure 3 we have concentrated all the relevant information, $\bar{x}_i$ and σ^2_i, on the horizontal axis of the traditional mean-variance space. Assuming normal distributions let us compare two prospects by drawing their densities and cumulative curves so that they correspond to the relative magnitudes of $\bar{x}_i$ and σ^2_i.

Both prospects, that is, points $(\bar{x}_1, \sigma^2_1)$, and $(\bar{x}_2, \sigma^2_2)$, are on the efficiency frontier (set of non-dominated solutions). But any investor would always choose $(\bar{x}_2, \sigma^2_2)$, which assures that the probability of getting less than a fixed return would always be smaller than if $(\bar{x}_1, \sigma^2_1)$ were chosen. Therefore, among the two "efficient" prospects, the one with larger variance is infinitely less risky. Why, then, should we measure risk by variance?

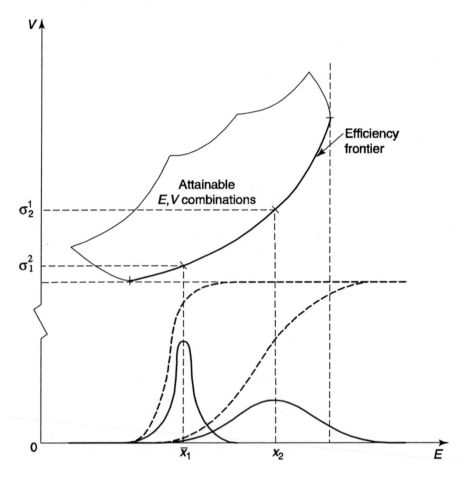

Figure 3 "Efficient portfolios" and stochastic dominance.

Prospect Ranking Vector

From the previous discussion it follows that "riskiness" is related to the *relative* positioning of the distributions, not to their variances.

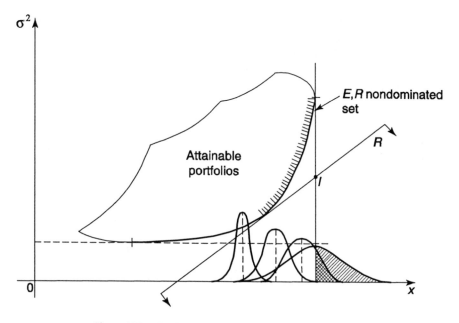

Figure 4 Non-dominated portfolios with respect to the ideal I.

Let us assume that a hypothetical measure of risk R_i decreases with smaller σ^2_i *and* with larger x_i. It is useful to display R_i in the traditional mean-variance space, as in Figure 4. Function R_i now decreases in the direction of the southeast corner. This reflects our previously discussed intuition that a smaller variance indicates less riskiness *only* if coupled with a larger return. In Figure 4 the heavily drawn boundary represents a traditional mean-variance efficiency frontier. Its shaded portion represents our new non-dominated set.

Note point I in Figure 4. This is another version of the well-known *ideal prospect*. It is characterized by the lowest achievable risk *and* the highest achievable expected return. It is, in general, nonattainable. Regardless of the form of a decision maker's utility function, the ideal prospect I would always be preferred by all investors who base their decisions on expected return and risk only

The current universe of available stocks and other investment possibilities determines the set of feasible prospects. The shape and location of this region defines the position of I. Each decision maker would prefer I to all other prospects or would like to move *as close as possible* to it.

In Figure 4 on the x axis are a few hypothetical density functions reflecting the relative magnitudes of variances taken from the σ^2 axis. Our next goal is actually to design R_i in such a way that all prospects in the non-dominated (shaded) set would satisfy the concept of stochastic dominance and also provide some protection against very low returns.

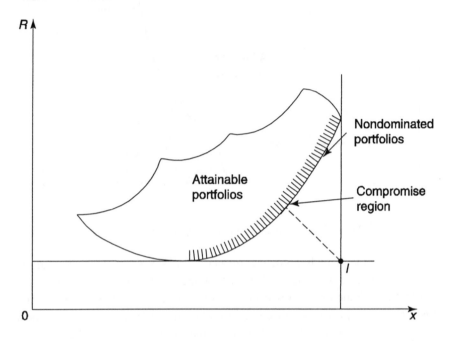

Figure 5 Compromise region of non-dominated portfolios.

Let us now assume that R_i replaces σ^2_i so that a proper picture can be drawn, as in Figure 5. Since we do not know the utility function, we have to use I as the point of reference. If both the expected return and the risk are equally important, then the small, heavily drawn boundary section in Figure 5 is the closest to the ideal. Changes in weights of importance would shift this *compromise region* along the non-dominated set.

The concept of stochastic dominance is preferable to the traditional concepts of portfolio selection. Its main shortcoming, however, is that a *complete knowledge* of the probability distribution is a necessary condition for its proper application.

From a purely practical viewpoint we cannot hope to measure and obtain anything more sophisticated than $\bar{x}$ and σ^2. We shall therefore develop the new risk measure under the conditions of such *partial information*. We shall express all relevant parameters in terms of the multiples of σ_i^2 from the $\bar{x}_i$, and thus most distribution-free inequalities of probability theory can be applied.

Formal Version of Prospect Ranking Vector

Consider a set of independent uncertain *returns* x_i associated with investment prospects i, $i = 1, 2 \ldots n$.

Each Xi can be defined on a given interval, say,

$$x_i \in \left[a_i, b_i\right] \subseteq \left[a, b\right]$$

where $[a, b]$ may extend over the entire line of real numbers x.

Let $f_i(x)$, $F_i(x)$, $\bar{x}_i$, and σ_i denote the density function, the cumulative distribution function, the mean, and the standard deviation of the ith uncertain return, respectively.

Given two random prospects 1 and 2, the *first stochastic dominance rule* can be summarized as follows (see also Figure 1):

$$1 \succ 2 \Leftrightarrow \begin{cases} F_2(x) \geq F_1(x) & \text{for all } x \in [a,b] \\ \text{and} \\ F_2(x) > F_1(x) & \text{for some } x \in [a,b] \end{cases} \qquad (1)$$

That is, prospect 1 stochastically dominates prospect 2 if and only if the above conditions are true. We can also state that:

$$1 \succ 2 \Leftrightarrow \begin{cases} \bar{u}(f_1) \geq \bar{u}(f_2) & \text{for all } u \in U \\ \text{and} \\ \bar{u}(f_1) > \bar{u}(f_2) & \text{for some } u \in U \end{cases} \qquad (2)$$

where U denotes a class of nondecreasing utility functions, continuous and with a first derivative, and $\bar{u}\,(f_i)$ denotes the expected value of a utility function defined on f_i. Symbol $\succ$ means "stochastically dominates," and symbol $\Leftrightarrow$ means "if and only if." Thus, any investor not wishing a decrease in wealth would prefer prospect 1 to prospect 2.

The FSD rule is very sensitive to low returns. Indeed, even a single intersection of the distribution functions F_i can be responsible for rejecting a prospect. Moreover, the lowest possible return, even if it has a very low probability of occurrence, can induce a prospect's rejection. Although protection against very low returns is generally desired, this safety requirement may vary from one individual to another and be situation-dependent as well. Taking this into account we propose a reasonable hypothesis of rational behavior, forming the *first decision rule*:

1. Prospect 1 will be preferred to prospect 2 if, *ceteris paribus*, the minimal return a_1 attainable by prospect 1 is greater than the minimal return a_2 attainable by prospect 2:

$$a_1 > a_2 \Rightarrow 1 \succ 2 \tag{3}$$

We would consider it unwise if an investor, all other things being equal, would not choose the prospect yielding *the highest possible minimal return*.

Investors often set a threshold on their required return: *a minimal acceptable return* r_m. Observe that r_m can be interpreted as a minimum threshold or as an *a priori* investment goal or aspiration level determined by the mth investor.

We may write the first objective function to be minimized as follows:

$$
\begin{aligned}
R_{im}^{(1)} &= P_i(x < t_m) = P_i(x < \max\{L; r_m\}) \\
&= P_i(x < \max_i\{\max a_i; r_m\})
\end{aligned}
\tag{4}
$$

Thus, in Equation (4) we have defined *the first component of risk* $R^{(1)}$. The least risky choice among all available investments is the one minimizing the probability P_i of realizing an outcome below the *individual effective threshold return* t_m. Observe that t_m is either the largest of all the smallest realizable returns (L) or the individually determined minimum acceptable return (r_m), whichever is larger.

Equation (4) can be viewed in terms of opportunity costs. Similarly, we can define opportunity costs with respect to high returns. We state our second hypothesis of rational behavior, the *second decision rule*, as follows:

2. Prospect 1 will be preferred to prospect 2 if, *ceteris paribus*, the maximum attainable return b_1 of prospect 1 is greater than the maximum return b_2 attainable by prospect 2:

$$b_1 > b_2 \Rightarrow 1 \succ 2 \tag{5}$$

It would be unwise if an investor seeking maximum returns, would not, all other things being equal, choose the prospect yielding *the highest possible maximum return*.

We can write the second objective function as follows:

$$1 - R_i^{(2)} = P_i(x \geq S) \; where \; S = \max_i b_i \tag{6}$$

and $(1 - R_i^{(2)})$ is to be maximized; or, minimize $R_i^{(2)}$, the complement to P_i.

$R_i^{(2)}$ represents the *second component of risk:* The least risky choice among all available investments is the one that minimizes the probability of not realizing the best outcome attainable.

As it is defined here, risk is *not* a single-dimensional concept, but it consists of *at least two* components $R_i^{(1)}$ and $R_i^{(2)}$. Thus, $R_i = [R_{im}^{(1)}, R_i^{(2)}]$ is a risk vector describing the riskiness of the ith prospect. Observe that the first component is more subjective, that is, more closely associated with an individual investor m and the specificity of that investor's position. Their simultaneous consideration is necessary to avoid a pessimistic view, $R_{im}^{(1)}$ alone, or an optimistic view, $R_i^{(2)}$ alone. These two components are consistent with both the habits of the practitioners[2] and the FSD rule.

The consistency of R_i with the FSD rule implies that an investor applying stochastic dominance is not allowed to make any choice which would be contradictory to the one implied by R_i.

---

[2] Practitioners scrutinize both the "upside potential" and the "downside risk" of an investment, in the language of Wall Street.

Next we present a *third rule* of rational behavior, which is based on the knowledge of the first moment (the expected value) of the probability distribution of returns:

3. Prospect 1 will be preferred to prospect 2 if, *ceteris paribus*, the expected return $\bar{x}_1$ of 1 is greater than the expected return $\bar{x}_2$ of 2:

$$\bar{x}_1 > \bar{x}_2 \Rightarrow 1 \succ 2 \tag{7}$$

Thus, under conditions of risk indifference, when we face linear utility functions, a reliance on expected returns is sufficient.

We shall compose a vector of the three objective functions, the *Prospect* (or portfolio) *Ranking Vector* (PRV). We adjust the components of PRV_{im}, so that the increases in their numerical values correspond to the increases in their desirability, namely:

$$PRV_{im} = (1 - R_{im}^{(1)}, \bar{x}_i, 1 - R_i^{(2)}) \tag{8}$$

We then define a *non-dominated prospect* as follows:

Definition. A *non-dominated prospect* is an attainable prospect for which an increase in value of anyone component of PRV_{im} can only be achieved at the expense of a decrease in value of at least one other component.

The set of all such prospects constitutes the *non-dominated set*. If we know the first two moments of the distributions (expected value E and variance V), then the non-dominated set would replace the traditional E-V efficiency frontier, except under two conditions:

1. When only E and V are known, and they are sufficient to describe the distribution completely – as is the case for the *normal distribution;* or
2. When the utility function is assumed to belong to the class of *quadratic functions*

We define the ideal prospect as the one which *simultaneously* maximizes all three components of the PRV vector. The ideal is thus the best with respect to the three stated hypotheses concerning rational behavior. Following the pessimistic hypothesis, one would choose the prospect which maximizes the first component. Following the risk-indifference hypothesis, one would choose the prospect which maximizes the second component. The prospect which maximizes the third component would be the choice of those following the optimistic hypothesis.

If this ideal prospect is unattainable – the usual case – the decision maker will attempt to move *as close as possible* to it. Only those non-dominated prospects which are the closest to the ideal would then be recommended. A discussion of how to measure "closeness" is found in Appendix 6.

Risk components in Equations (4) and (6) are only sufficient for comparisons between any two individual prospects. The ranking of *all* prospects, however, requires the knowledge of probabilities that the maximin L and the maximax S will be reached. Observe that according to Equation (6) the probability of reaching S would be zero for all prospects. Also, the search for the actual maximin and maximax might not be trivial from a practical viewpoint, and it is actually meaningless for unbounded distributions. We shall redefine L, S, and t_m in terms of available information.

If the first two moments are known for all distributions, one may compute the distance from the mean and express it as a multiple k of the standard deviation. The threshold L in Equation (4) will thus be determined as

$$L = \max_i (\bar{x}_i - k'\sigma_i) \tag{9}$$

and the threshold S in Equation (6) will be expressed as

$$S = \max_i (\bar{x}_i + k\sigma_i) \tag{10}$$

Observe that both k' and k may be set equal to zero. In principle, however, they could assume any positive value.

Thus we can summarize:

$$S = \max_i (\bar{x}_i + k\sigma_i)$$

$$L = \max_i (\bar{x}_i - k'\sigma_i) \tag{11}$$

$$t_m = \max(L; r_m)$$

PRV Under Partial Information

Under conditions of partial information, such as the knowledge of means and variances, an investor does not know the required probabilities. For the two components of risk one must estimate the probabilities $P(x_i \geq K)$ without the benefit of knowing the distribution function $F_i(x)$. Symbol K stands for t_m, L, or S, depending on the consideration of r_m and the PRV components.

We shall use the generalized forms of the *Tchebyshev inequality* to provide a solution to the problem, although there is a loss of reliability associated with it. We express K in terms of the multiples of σ_i from $\bar{x}_i$, according to Equations (9) and (10), and define k_i and k'_{im}:

$$k_i = \frac{S - \bar{x}_i}{\sigma_i} \qquad\qquad S = \max_i(\bar{x}_i + k\sigma_i) \tag{12}$$

and

$$k'_{im} = \frac{t_m - \bar{x}_i}{\sigma_i} \qquad\qquad \begin{aligned} L &= \max_i(\bar{x}_i - k'\sigma_i) \\ t_m &= \max(L; r_m) \end{aligned} \tag{13}$$

Since we are interested in the probability of deviations from the mean in only one direction, we can use the *Cramer inequality* of probability theory

$$1 - R_i^{(2)} = P(x_i \geq S) = P(x_i \geq \bar{x}_i + k_i\sigma_i) \leq \frac{1}{k_i^2 + 1} \tag{14}$$

for the third PRV component, and

$$R_{im}^{(1)} = P(x_i \leq \bar{x}_i + k'_{im}\sigma_i) \geq 1 - \frac{1}{k'^2_{im} + 1} \tag{15}$$

for the first component of risk. We can also express Equation (15) as follows:

$$1 - R_{im}^{(1)} = P(x_i \geq \bar{x}_i + k'_{im}\sigma_i) \leq 1 - \frac{1}{k_{im}'^2 + 1} \tag{16}$$

To summarize, for the ith prospect and the mth investor we obtain the *prospect ranking vector,* by taking the right-side limits from Equations (14) and (16), thus obtaining[3]

$$PRV_{im} \overset{P}{\Leftrightarrow} \left(\frac{1}{k_{im}'^2 + 1}, \bar{x}_i, \frac{1}{k_i^2 + 1} \right) * \tag{17}$$

Observe that Equations (12) to (17) can be used for the general class of probability distributions (discrete, mixed or continuous, unimodal and multimodal, skewed, symmetric, etc.).

We can now define, in analogy with stochastic dominance, decision rules designated as *PRV dominance* and based on partial information: Prospect j dominates prospect l in the PRV sense $\succ$ if and only if

$$(a) \ j \underset{PRV_1}{\succ} l \overset{P}{\Leftrightarrow} \frac{1}{k_{jm}'^2 + 1} \geq \frac{1}{k_{lm}'^2 + 1}$$

$$(b) \ j \underset{PRV_2}{\succ} l \Leftrightarrow \bar{x}_j \geq \bar{x}_l \qquad **$$

$$(c) \ j \underset{PRV_3}{\succ} l \overset{P}{\Leftrightarrow} \frac{1}{k_j^2 + 1} \geq \frac{1}{k_l^2 + 1}$$

with at least one strict inequality holding.

---

[3] $\overset{P}{\Leftrightarrow}$ denotes a probable implication.

* This formula is for $k'_{im} > 0$.

** For k'_{jm} and $k'_{lm} > 0$.

The probable implications $\overset{P}{\Leftrightarrow}$ are used because, strictly speaking, we should not call them necessary and/or sufficient conditions of partial information. Thus, the inequalities of the above definition are the best guide in cases of imperfect knowledge, but they would often supply misleading conclusions if perfect information about the distributions were available.

Observe that PRV dominance depends on the investor through coefficients r_m, k, and k'.

The assessment of k and k' depends on the investor's confidence in the occurrence of extreme values among different available prospects. The farther the extreme values are from the means, the larger are k and k'. Also, the more optimistic the investor, the larger will be the values for k and $1/k'$. The more pessimistic the investor, the larger will be the values of $1/k$ and k'. Hyperoptimistic is the investor who chooses $k = \infty$ and $k' = 0$, and hyperpessimistic the one who chooses $k' = \infty$ and $k = 0$. Thus, we can represent the whole spectrum of attitudes ranging from a great fear of low returns $(k'$ high) to a speculative liking of high returns $(k$ high).

Appendix 8

Formalism of Fuzziness

It is not our intention here to develop a full mathematical formalism for the contextual analysis of linguistic fuzziness.

Objects of human knowledge, things, events, situations, etc., are brought forth into an observer's focus, for the purposes of description, understanding and communicating, through identifying or invoking (or imparting upon them) a set of characteristics or *attributes*. (Humans are incapable of bringing objects forth holistically, as a whole, but only in terms of chosen attributes.)

The level of association of a given attribute with a given object is the subject of human perception, judgment, cognition and production of knowledge. For the set of attributes (or descriptors) $A = (A_1, ..., A_n)$, selected from all available attributes $\mathbf{A}$, the amount (or degree) of attribute A_i possessed by an object Ω, in the domain of discourse Ω *(empirical domain)*, is dependent on gauge (reference, ideal, bounding) elements Ω_m and Ω_M, possessing the minimum and maximum of A_i, respectively. Thus, $\Omega_M \geq_{A_i} \Omega$ and $\Omega \geq_{A_i} \Omega_m$, for all $\Omega \in \Omega$. The Ω_M has maximum ("most A_i") and Ω_m minimum ("least A_i") *membership* in the set representation of A_i. Observe that although Ω_M or Ω_m form the *referential domain* $\Omega_R = [\Omega_m, \Omega_M]$ for Ω, they are not necessarily elements of Ω (For example, existing men's heights can be related to those of mythical giants). Without establishing the gauges of Ω_R, no relational discourse could take place, no concepts could be constructed and no knowledge produced.

Any domain of discourse Ω can be represented in a chosen *numerical domain* $X(\Omega)$. The membership of Ω and $x(\Omega)$ in A_i then becomes continuous over $X(\Omega)$ rather than discrete over Ω.

For example, if $\Omega = \{$men of various heights$\}$ and $A_i = $ *tall,* then $X(\Omega) = [0, \infty]$ inches and the function $\mu_{Ai}(x(\Omega))$ is a membership function for objects $\Omega \in \Omega$ and $x(\Omega) \in X(\Omega)$ in the set representation of A_i. The *membership domain* contains the degree of membership of $\Omega \in \Omega_R$ in the attribute A_i.

413

The transformations from empirical to numerical, referential and membership domains cannot be reduced. That is, one cannot take an object and simply ask for its membership in a given set. The referential domain is pivotal and any membership domain must be referentially bounded.

Traditionally, a fuzzy *set* F_i in X was defined as a set of ordered pairs $F_i = \{x, \mu_{Ai}(x) \mid x \in X, \mu_{Ai}(x) \in [0, 1]\}$, F_i being an element of a fuzzy *structure* (complex or construct) F.

It is now asserted that genuine measurement structures of membership have not yet been developed[22], apart from the first insights of Norwich and Türksen[12]. It is clear that membership has to be measured on an *interval scale* and that the notions of difference or *distance* in the referential domain are crucial determinants of fuzziness.

The degree of fuzziness or membership of Ω in A_i must be related to its position in Ω_R, i.e., its distance from Ω_M, Ω_m, or both, or from other relevant referential values. To the extent humans can choose different referential gauges in different contexts and towards different purposes, the membership of Ω in A_i is a dynamic and complex construct which cannot be fixated through a context-free function.

Thus, a man 6'2" tall can be *tall* to degree 1 among midgets, to degree 0.6 among basketball players, and close to 0 in the world of Swift's giants. It is the referential domain that is being chosen, not the degree of fuzziness itself. It is the *distance* from referential value(s) that determines fuzziness. Human beings do not perform fuzzy operations on membership functions, but assess the ratios of distances between membership functions, so that:

$$\pi_{Ai}(\Omega) = [\mu_{Ai}(\Omega) - \mu_{Ai}(\Omega_m)] / [\mu_{Ai}(\Omega_M) - \mu_{Ai}(\Omega_m)],$$

where $\pi_{Ai}(\Omega) \in [0, 1]$ and $\pi_{Ai}(\Omega)$ is on an absolute scale. As Norwich and Türksen proposed, as a minimal initiatory step, we can substitute $\pi_{Ai}(\Omega)$ wherever $\mu_{Ai}(\Omega)$ occurs in the traditional fuzzy sets literature.

It is clear that operational characterization of context must enter the formalism of membership spaces or complexes (rather than functions). This can most likely be accomplished by introducing two or more reference points or "ideals," characterizing the context from which particular meaning is derived, and then measuring "membership" in terms of referential distance(s) from the reference points.

Changes in context are then reflected in the displacement of "ideals" or "reference points" and so the "degrees of membership" are directly and immediately affected and the meaning of a given fuzzy label correspondingly adjusted.

We can differentiate further and postulate the *degree of closeness* to the essential referential maximum as:

$$\prod_{Ai}(\Omega) = [\mu_{Ai}(\Omega_M) - \mu_{Ai}(\Omega)] / [\mu_{Ai}(\Omega_M) - \mu_{Ai}(\Omega_m)],$$

and the *degree of remoteness* from the essential referential minimum as:

$$\pi_{Ai}(\Omega) = [\mu_{Ai}(\Omega) - \mu_{Ai}(\Omega_m)] / [\mu_{Ai}(\Omega_M) - \mu_{Ai}(\Omega_m)].$$

Both the closeness and remoteness from the two essential and displaceable referential points can be measured in order to characterize the fuzziness of Ω in A_i as a *referential distance*.

If John is labeled *tall* in a group where Bill serves as a gauge or reference point, then the removal of Bill from the set will redefine the referential framework and John might be labeled as *very tall,* even if John height's remains unchanged and the observer is the same.

We now attempt to define fuzziness as a subject of scientific study:

"Humans bring forth the objects of reality as linguistically labeled concepts within the requisite referential domains. The fuzziness of any linguistic label reflects the "distance" of the labeled objects, either measured or perceived, from one or more referential points. The bounds of referential domains are chosen and adjusted for the purposes of contextual communication or negotiation. The degrees of fuzziness of linguistic labels are therefore context dependent and implied by the referential choice."

According to the above definition, fuzzifying and defuzzifying of objects of linguistic labeling is a function of the size of the referential domain. The broader the domain, the more fuzzy the labels, the narrower the domain, the crisper are the labels.

The degree of fuzziness of any linguistic label is not derived from the label itself, but only from specifying the circumstances surrounding it: from its chosen referential domain. There are no *a priori* fuzzy or crisp meanings of words *per se*. All is negotiated and renegotiated via social intercourse.

There are of course some habits, *habitual domains* and habitual meanings. Some referential domains are common to large numbers of humans or cultures for long periods of time.

We can consider even more specific, exponential function based models like:

$$\pi_{Ai}(\Omega) = \{\mu_{Ai}(\Omega_m) + [\mu_{Ai}(\Omega_M) - \mu_{Ai}(\Omega_m)/1 + e^{-a(\mu(\Omega)-b)}]\}.$$

The notions of "anchors" or "ideals" are being used here, as known from the theory of displaced ideal of decision making. Objects are not being compared one with another, as if comparing "bundles" of goods in classical economics, but with an anchor, ideal, reference point or gauge. Comparisons of objects are then indirect and derived from their measured or perceived "distances" from such comparisons.

Numerical Example

Let us introduce a simple database as a numerical example.

There are eleven firms, candidates for acquisition, described in terms of their size and profitability, as (the first three columns) in Table 1.

The database of Table 1 can be queried in a traditional *quantitative* fashion: precise cutoff points with respect to sales and margins are determined. For example, sales should be equal to or greater than $1000 and margin equal to or greater than 14%. This particular query would elicit a response of only two firms satisfying such goals: *F* and *G*. All other firms are passed over. This "approach" is totally inappropriate and unsuitable for decision making and judgment.

The fuzzy sets approach allows a more useful, *qualitative* evaluation of this inherently complex multi-criteria situation. For example, "sales should be *high* and margins *acceptable*." What do we mean by labels *high* and *acceptable*? Let us say that anything under $600 is definitely not high and thus can be assigned a degree of membership as zero. Anything above $1150 is definitely high, thus the degree of membership is equal to one. Similarly, let *acceptable* be defined by membership zero if below 12% and one if above 18%. All values between these limits are assigned numbers between zero and one.

In order to come up with the overall fuzzy sets response, one is arbitrarily advised to take *the smaller* of the membership levels for sales and margin. For example, firm K is 1 with respect to sales and 0 with respect to margin, thus 0 overall. Firm H is 1 with respect to sales and 0.10 with respect to margin, thus 0.10 overall. The results are summarized in the fifth column of Table 1.

It is easy to see that the qualitative or fuzzy sets inquiry is not much different from the traditional one: it is still fixed, context free and characterized by rigid cutoff points (Firms K, B, D, J, and A are all "cut off"). The world of human decision making and judgment just does not work this way.

The last column of Table 1 contains response to the referential or *intelligent* queries (proposed in this paper) that are neither quantitative nor "qualitative" in the above sense.

Table 1 Data and results for the numerical example.

Firm	Sales	Profit margin (%)	Classical	Response Fuzzy sets	Referential (% of the ideal)
E	900	18	0	0.80	92.0
C	800	17	0	0.52	85.8
F	1000	15	1	0.36	79.8
G	1100	14	1	0.19	77.0
I	1300	13	0	0.10	75.0
H	1200	13	0	0.10	73.6
K	1500	12	0	0	73.6
B	600	14	0	0	70.4
D	850	12	0	0	65.0
J	1400	6	0	0	45.0
A	500	7	0	0	37.8
Ideal	1500	18	–	–	100

First, firm K provides the largest sales level and E the largest margin level in the T group. The firm characterized by both $1500 and 18% would be an undisputed winner, an "ideal firm." Which firm approximates the ideal best? Which firm comes closest to the ideal? Any intelligent inquiry brings thus naturally forth the question of "distance."

For example, firm E represents 60% of the ideal sales and 100% of the ideal margin, while K is characterized by 100% and 67%, respectively.

The intelligent thing we can say is, given this set of eleven options, that if definitely acceptable is anything over 18% (100% of the ideal) and definitely high is anything over $1150 (77% of the ideal), then margin is considered to be far more important than sales in this context. Let us then use weights of importance $W_1 = 0.2$ and $W_2 = 0.8$ for sales and margin, respectively. Then the weighted average percentage of the ideal (referential distance) for firm E would be 0.2(60) + 0.8(100) = 92%. These referential distances are summarized in the last column of Table 1. The last column can of course be normalized into the [0, 1] interval by the purists, but such manipulations are now unnecessary and redundant. Also, humans do relate to the percentage measurement of referential distance (fuzziness) in a natural and easy fashion.

Observe that now there are no strict or crisp boundaries (like the [600, 1150] and [12, 18] in the fuzzy sets analysis). To see that fuzzy sets analysis is really a very crisp analysis in different clothing, ask simply: "What about numbers 559 and 1149? Or 11.99 and 17.999?" Can we say that anything above $1150 is definitely *high* and assign it membership degree I? Of course not. If we find that $1200 is the very best achievable, can $1150 still be the same *high* as compared to a situation where we find that $1500 is the best? Of course not. Nothing is *high per se*; anything can be *high* only with respect to something else.

The truly fuzzy (with no cutoff points) ranking in the last column of Table 1 is flexible and context dependent: any changes in the set of firms under consideration will imply changes in ideals, redefinition of *high* and *acceptable* and shifts in weights of importance W_1 and W_2. Each situation and its context are unique and must be handled as such.

Author's Biography

Milan Zeleny, Professor of Management Systems, Fordham University, New York City, recently published *Information Technology in Business* (Thomson International) and co-authored *New Frontiers of Decision Making for the Information Technology Era* (World Scientific). Current book, *Human Systems Management: Integrating Knowledge, Management and Systems*, is to be followed by *Roads to Success: Bata Management System* and by the works-in-progress, including *Knowledge of Enterprise, Social Autopoiesis, Organization as an Organism,* and *The Art of Asking Why: Foundations of Wisdom Systems.*

Previously published books include *Multiple Criteria Decision Making* (McGraw-Hill), *Linear Multiobjective Programming* (Springer-Verlag), *Autopoiesis, Dissipative Structures and Spontaneous Social Orders* (Westview Press), *MCDM-Past Decades and Future Trends* (JAI Press), *Autopoiesis: A Theory of Living Organization* (Elsevier North Holland), *Uncertain Prospects Ranking and Portfolio Analysis* (Verlag Anton Hain), *Multiple Criteria Decision Making* (University of South Carolina Press), *Multiple Criteria Decision Making: Kyoto 1975* (Springer-Verlag), among others.

He is the author of over 350 papers and articles, ranging from operations research, cybernetics and general systems, to economics, history of science, total quality management, and simulation of autopoiesis and artificial life (AL). Articles on Integrated Process Management (IPM), the Bata-System and Mass Customization were translated into Japanese, others into Chinese, French, Italian, Hungarian, Slovak, Czech, Russian and Polish (also wrote over 500 short stories, literary essays and political reviews in Czech, Slovak and English).

He has served as the Editor-in-Chief of *Human Systems Management*, the global journal, over the last twenty five years. He also served on editorial boards of *Operations and Quantitative Management, International Strategic Management, Operations Research, Computers and Operations Research, Future Generations Computer Systems, Fuzzy Sets and Systems, General Systems Yearbook* and *Prestige Journal of Management and Research.* Currently serves on editorial boards of *International Journal of Information Technology and Decision Making, International Journal of Mobile Learning and Organization, and International Journal of Innovation and Learning.*

419

Among his main awards are:

- Erskine Fellowship, University of Canterbury
- The Georg Cantor Award, International Society of MCDM
- USIA Fulbright Professor in Prague, Czechoslovakia
- Bernstein Memorial Lecturer, Tel-Aviv, Israel
- Alexander von Humboldt Award, Bonn, Germany
- Rockefeller Foundation Resident Scholar, Bellagio Study Center
- Norbert Wiener Award of *Kybernetes*

Zeleny holds Dipl.Ing. from the Prague School of Economics, M.S. and Ph.D. from the University of Rochester in Business Management. Previous academic appointments include Columbia University School of Business, University of South Carolina, Copenhagen School of Economics, the European Institute for Advanced Studies in Management (EIASM), School of Advanced Technology at SUNY in Binghamton and Irish Management Institute in Dublin; also, the Department of Architecture at the University of Naples, Centro Studi di Estimo e di Economia Territoriale in Florence, EPFL in Lausanne and the University of Padua. Currently he also serves as a Professor at the Tomas Bata University in Zlín, Moravia, Professor and Academic Vice Dean at Xidian University in Xi'an, the principal of ZET-Organization consultancy, president of the Central European Productivity Center (allied with Productivity International) and director of the Czech Productivity Center (CPC) in Prague.

Human Systems Management, the Journal

Human Systems Management (HSM), a global journal, has entered its 25th volume. There is an admirable longevity implied by such an anniversary: from its remarkable history unfolds a promise of a greater future...

The first issue of HSM appeared in February 1980. The journal was the brainchild of Milan Zeleny and the two co-founding editors: Manfred Kochen and Erik Johnsen. Both its title and message were quite ahead of its time: very few people knew or cared what "human systems" were about and the need for their management was not widely perceived. This has now changed significantly.

HSM covers and their texts were personally designed, and have not had to be changed, amended or adapted ever since. North-Holland Publishing Company was the first Publisher and Dr. Einar Fredriksson was the Publishing Editor.

The first issue started with Nobelists Joshua Lederberg as an author and Ilya Prigogine on the Editorial Board. First Board members also included R.M. Cyert,

M.M. Flood, D. Gerwin, K.R. Hammond, P.G.W. Keen, I.I. Mitroff, E. Rhenman, G.R. Salancik and others. The first HSM issue also carried papers by R.K. Mueller and J.F. Magee of Arthur D. Little, Eugen Loebl on "Humanomics" and Joshua Lederberg on EUGRAMS, among others.

The founding "Circle of Human Systems Management" listed its members also in the first HSM issue. Among the hundreds members of the Circle, we find names like Ackoff, Ansoff, Barankin, Bass, Bennis, Carlsson, Gaines, Hertz, Kuhn, Lewin, Pask, Prigogine, Roy, Shakun, Starr, Trappl, Turoff, Varela, Von Foerster, Weick, Zadeh, Zimmermann, Zionts, etc.

Among the better known authors publishing in HSM we find Karl W. Deutsch, Edgar Morin, L.A. Zadeh, Marvin Minsky, Myron Tribus, Magoroh Maruyama, Geert Hofstede, Sir Karl Popper, Peter Checkland, Allan H. Meltzer, Jaroslav Vanek, and C. West Churchman.

In 1980 Leonard Uhr proposed knowledge sharing through Computer network-based responsive self-organizing groups. Gorelik wrote on Bogdanov's Tektology, H.E. Daly introduced Ecological economics in 1981. In 1984 R.W. Blanning introduced Knowledge acquisition systems. In 1985 Marvin Minsky published his Remotely-Manned Systems, Holsapple and Whinston their Management Support through AI. In 1986 Zeleny published High Technology Management and in 1987 his Management Support Systems: Towards Integrated Knowledge Management, where the label of "knowledge management" was first introduced.

What about the future of HSM?

In recent years, HSM has redefined itself through incorporating information technology, knowledge and wisdom management, network organization and human issues of the New Economy among its areas of interest.

The scope of Human Systems Management has evolved and become better defined and established. Its three main components, Human – Systems – Management, have been meshed and integrated to form a unified organism of thought. Humans are the source of knowledge and systems interactions. Systems refer to an integrated whole rather than to separate functioning of specialized parts. Management refers to human coordination of human action in all their effective modes and forms. None of the three components can be reduced or omitted without "killing" the whole.

In the following table we list the typical concerns of each of the three HSM components:

HUMAN	**SYSTEMS**	**MANAGEMENT**
knowledge	information	goal setting
intelligence	data	coordination
creativity	optimization	teamwork
innovation	organization	strategy
brainware	structure	tradeoffs
decision making	communications	self-management
judgment	reengineering	knowledgement
intuition	resource allocation	leadership
human capital	info-technology	motivation

The above scheme is still evolving and provides an ongoing framework for HSM.

The journal of Human Systems Management is well positioned for the new millennium with greater drives towards better focused creativity, innovation and knowledge enhancement. Concerns with e-commerce, m-commerce and e-management are going to provide both human and technological embedding. Knowledge management and wisdom systems have become integrated and important subsets of human systems management.

SELECTED PUBLICATIONS OF THE AUTHOR
(Related to Human Systems Management)

1973

Multiple Criteria Decision Making, University of South Carolina Press, Columbia, S.C., 1973, p. 816. (Editor with J.L. Cochrane)

"Compromise Programming," in: *Multiple Criteria Decision Making,* edited by M. Zeleny and J.L. Cochrane, University of South Carolina Press, Columbia, S.C., 1973, pp. 262-301. Also: "A Priori and A Posteriori Goals in Macroeconomic Policy Making," pp. 373-391 (With J.L. Cochrane). "A Selected Bibliography of Works Related to the Multiple Criteria Decision Making," pp. 779-796.

1974

Linear Multiobjective Programminq, Springer-Verlag, New York, 1974, p. 220.

"The Techniques of Linear Multiobjective Programming," *Revue Française d'Automatique, d'Informatique et de Recherche Operationelle,* 8(1974) V-3, pp. 51-71. (With P.L. Yu)

"A Concept of Compromise Solutions and the Method of the Displaced Ideal," *Computers and Operations Research*, 1(1974) 4, pp. 479-496.

1975

"The Set of All Nondominated Solutions in Linear Cases and A Multicriteria Simplex Method," *Journal of Mathematical Analysis and Applications*, 49(1975) 2, pp. 430-468. (With P.L. Yu)

"Managers Without Management Science?" *Interfaces*, 5(1975) 4, pp. 35-42.

"New Vistas of Management Science," *Computers and Operations Research*, 2(1975) 2, pp. 121-125.

1976

"On the Inadequacy of the Regression Paradigm Used in the Study of Human Judgment," *Theory and Decision*, 7(1976) 1/2, pp. 57-65.

Multiple Criteria Decision Making: Kyoto 1975, Springer-Verlag, New York, 1976, p. 340. (Editor)

"The Theory of the Displaced Ideal," in: *Multiple Criteria Decision Making: Kyoto 1975*, Springer-Verlag, New York, 1976, pp. 287-317. Also: "MCDM Bibliography – 1975," pp. 318-340. "Multicriteria Simplex Method: A FORTRAN Routine," pp. 318-340.

"Games with Multiple Payoffs," *International Journal of Game Theory*, 4(1976) 4, pp. 179-191.

"Simulation of Self-Renewing Systems," in: *Evolution and Consciousness: Human Systems in Transition*, edited by E. Jantsch and C.H. Waddington, Addison-Wesley, Reading, Ma., 1976, pp. 150-165. (With N.A. Pierre)

Book review: A. Kaufmann, Introduction to the Theory of Fuzzy Subsets, Volume 1, *Interfaces*, 6(1976) 4, pp. 113-115.

"The Attribute-Dynamic Attitude Model (ADAM)," *Management Science*, 25(1976) 1, pp. 12-26.

"Linear Multiparametric Programming by Multicriteria Simplex Method," *Management Science,* 23(1976) 2, pp. 159-170. (With P.L. Yu)

"Conflict Dissolution," *General Systems Yearbook*, XXI, 1976, pp.131-136.

1977

"Intuition and Probability," *The Wharton Magazine*, 1(1977) 4, pp. 63-68.

Multiple Criteria Decision Making, TIMS Studies in the Management Sciences, Vol. 6, North-Holland Publishing Co., Amsterdam, 1977, p. 270. (Editor with M.K. Starr)

"MCDM – State end Future of the Arts," in: *Multiple Criteria Decision Making*, TIMS Studies in the Management Sciences, Vol. 6, North-Holland Publishing Co., Amsterdam, 1977, pp. 5-30. (With M.K. Starr). Also: "Adaptive Displacement of Preferences in Decision Making," pp.147-158.

"Self-Organization of Living Systems: A Formal Model of Autopoiesis," *Int. J. General Systems*, 4(1977) 1, pp. 13-28.

Columbia Journal of World Business, Focus: Decision Making, XII (1977) 3, p.136. (Editor with M.K. Starr)

"'Decision Making: An Overview," *Columbia Journal of World Business*, XII (1977) 3, pp. 5-8. (With M.K. Starr and R.L. Denosowicz)

"Membership Functions and Their Assessment," in: *Current Topics in Cybernetics and Systems*, edited by J. Rose, Springer-Verlag, Berlin, 1978, pp. 391-392.

1978

"APL-AUTOPOIESIS: Experiments in Self-Organization of Complexity," in: *Progress in Cybernetics and Systems Research*, vol. III, edited by R. Trappl et al., Hemisphere Publishing Corp., Washington, D.C., 1978, pp. 65-84.

"Multidimensional Measure of Risk: Prospect Ranking Vector (PRV)," in: *Multiple Criteria Problem Solving*, edited by S. Zionts, Springer-Verlag, New York, 1978, pp. 529-548.

1979

Book reviews: B. Trentowski, Stosunek Filozofii do Cybernetyki czyli sztuki rzadzenia narodem; A.A. Bogdanov, Tektologia: vseobschaia organizatsionaia nauka; J.Ch. Smuts, Holism and Evolution; S. Leduc, The Mechanism of Life, *Int. J. General Systems*, 5(1979) 1, pp. 63-71.

"Cybernetics and General Systems – A Unitary Science?" *Kybernetes*, 8(1979) 1, pp. 17-23.

"The Self-Service Society: A New Scenario of the Future," *Planning Review*, 7(1979) 3, pp. 3-7, 37-38.

"Intuition, Its Failures and Merits," in: *Surviving Failures*, edited by B. Persson, Humanities Press, Atlantic Highlands, N.J., 1979, pp. 172-183.

Uncertain Prospects Ranking and Portfolio Analysis Under the Conditions of Partial Information, Mathematical Systems in Economics 44, Oelschlager, Gunn & Hain Publishers, Cambridge, M.A. 1979/1980. (With G. Colson)

"The Last Mohicans of OR: Or, It Might Be in the 'Genes'," *Interfaces*, 9(1979) 5, pp. 135-141.

1980

Computers and Operations Research, Special Issue on Mathematical Programming with Multiple Objectives, 7(1980) 1/2. (Editor)

"Descriptive Decision Making and Its Applications," in: *Applications of Management Science*, Vol. 1, edited by R.L. Schultz, JAI Press, Greenwich, Conn., 1981, pp. 327-388.

"Multiple Objectives in Mathematical Programming: Letting the Man In," in *Computers and Operations Research*, Special Issue on Mathematical Programming with Multiple Objectives, 7(1980) 1/2, pp. 1-4. Also: "Multicriterion Concept of Risk Under Incomplete Information," pp. 125-143. (With G. Colson)

"Ellipsoid Algorithms in Mathematical Programming," *Human Systems Management*, 1(1980) 2, pp. 173-178.

Autopoiesis, Dissipative Structures, and Spontaneous Social Orders, AAAS Selected Symposium 55, Westview Press, Boulder, Co., 1980. (Editor)

"Autopoiesis: A Paradigm Lost?" in: *Autopoiesis, Dissipative Structures, and Spontaneous Social Orders*, AAAS Selected Symposium 55, edited by M. Zeleny, Westview Press, Boulder, Co., 1980, pp. 3-43.

"Towards a Self-Service Society," *Human Systems Management*, 1(1980) 1, pp. 1-3.

Book review: L.C. Thurow, The Zero-Sum Society, *Human Systems Management*, 1(1980) 3, pp. 276-277.

"Strategic Management within Human Systems Management," *Human Systems Management*, 1(1980) 2, p. 179-180.

Book review: P. Nijkamp end A. van Delft, Multi-criteria Analysis end Regional Decision-making, *Journal of American Statistical Association*, 75(1980) 372.

"Multiple Scenarios of Reindustrialization," *Human Systems Management*, 1 (1980) 4, pp. 281-282.

1981

"Satisficinq, Optimization and Risk in Portfolio Selection," in: *Readings in Strategy for Corporate Investment*, edited by F.G.J. Derkinderen and R.L. Crum, Pitman Publishing, Boston, 1981, pp. 200-219.

"Socio-Economic Foundations of a Self-Service Society," in: *Progress in Cybernetics and Systems Research*, vol. 10, Hemisphere Publishing, Washington, D.C., 1982, pp. 127-132.

Autopoiesis: A Theory of Living Organization, Elsevier North Holland, New York, NY, 1981. (Editor)

"What Is Autopoiesis?" in: *Autopoiesis: A Theory of Living Organization*, edited by M. Zeleny, Elsevier North Holland, New York, NY, 1981, pp. 4-17.

"Autogenesis: On the Self-Organization of Life," in: *Autopoiesis: A Theory of Living Organization*, edited by M. Zeleny, Elsevier North Holland, New York, NY, 1981, pp. 91-115.

"On the Squandering of Resources and Profits via Linear Programming," *Interfaces*, 11(1981) 5, pp. 101-107.

"The Pros and Cons of Goal Programming," *Computers and Operations Research*, 8(1981) 4, pp. 357-359.

"Self-Service Trends in the Society," in: *Applied Systems and Cybernetics*, Vol. 3, edited by G.E. Lasker, Pergamon Press, Elmsford, N.Y., 1981, pp. 1405-1411.

"Fuzzy Sets: Precision and Relevancy," in: *Applied Systems and Cybernetics*, Vol. 6, edited by G.E. Lasker, Pergamon Press, Elmsford, N.Y., 1981, pp. 2719-2721.

Cybernetics Forum, Special Issue Devoted to Autopoiesis, 10(1981) 2/3, Summer/Fall 1981. (Editor)

"Autopoiesis Today," in: *Cybernetics Forum*, Special Issue Devoted to Autopoiesis, edited by M. Zeleny, 10(1981) 2/3, Summer/Fall 1981, pp. 3-6. Also: "Self-Organization of Living Systems: A Formal Model of Autopoiesis," pp. 24-38.

"Self-Service Aspects of Health Maintenance: Assessment of Current Trends," *Human Systems Management*, 2(1981) 4, pp. 259-267. (With M. Kochen)

Book review: I. Kristol and N. Glaser (eds.), The Crisis in Economic Theory, Special Issue of "Public Interest," *Human Systems Management*, 2(1981) 3, pp. 228-230.

"A Case Study in Multiobjective Design: De Novo Programming," in: *Multiple Criteria Analysis: Operational Methods*, edited by P. Nijkamp and J. Spronk, Gower Publishing, Hampshire, 1981, pp. 37-52.

1982

Multiple Criteria Decision Making, McGraw-Hill, New York, 1982.

Multiple Criteria Decision Making: Selected Case Studies, McGraw-Hill, New York, 1982. (Editor with C. Carlsson and A. Törn)

"High Technology Management," *Human Systems Management* 3(1982) 2, pp. 57-59.

"New Vistas in Management Science," in: *Cases and Readings in Management Science*, edited by E.F. Turban and P. Loomba, Business Publications, Plano, Texas, 1982, pp. 319-325.

1983

"Holistic Aspects of Biological and Social Organizations: Can They Be Studied?" in: *Environment and Population: Problems of Adaptation*, edited by John B. Calhoun, Praeger Publishers, New York, 1983, pp. 150-153.

"Qualitative versus Quantitative Modeling in Decision Making," *Human Systems Management*, 4(1983) 1, pp. 39-42.

Book review: W. Lowen, Dichotomies of Mind, *Human Systems Management*, 4(1983) 1, pp. 52-54.

"The Social Progress of Nations," *Human Systems Management*, 4(1983) 1, pp. 1-2.

"Optimal System Design: Towards New Interpretation of Shadow Prices in Linear Programming," *Computers and Operations Research*, 14(1987) 4, pp. 265-271. (With M. Hessel)

"The Roots of Modern Management: Bat'a-System," (in Japanese, transl. Y. Kondo) *Standardization and Quality Control*, 40(1987) 1, pp. 50-53.

"Is Japan Reluctant To Go International?" *Human Systems Management*, 7(1987) 2, pp. 85-86.

"Management Support Systems: Towards Integrated Knowledge Management," *Human Systems Management*, 7(1987) 1, pp. 59-70.

"Cybernetyka," *Int. J. General Systems*, 13(1987) 3, pp. 289-294.

"Systems Approach to Multiple Criteria Decision Making: Metaoptimum," in: *Toward Interactive and Intelligent Decision Support Systems*, edited by Y. Sawaragi, K. Inoue and H. Nakayama, Springer-Verlag, New York, 1987, pp. 28-37.

1988

"Three-Men Talk on Bat'a-System," (In Japanese) *Standardization and Quality Control*, 41(1988) 1, pp. 15-24.

"La grande inversione: Corso e ricorso dei modi di vita umani," in: *Physis: abitare la terra*, edited by M. Ceruti and E. Laszlo, Feltrinelli, Milano, 1988, pp. 413-441.

"Bat'a System of Management: Managerial Excellence Found," *Human Systems Management*, 7(1988) 3, pp. 213-219.

Book review: The Tree of Knowledge: The Biological Roots of Human Understanding, by H.R. Maturana and F.J. Varela, *Human Systems Management*, 7(1988) 4, pp. 379-380.

"Tectology," *Int. J. General Systems*, 14(1988) 4, pp. 331-343.

"Beyond capitalism and socialism: Human manifesto," *Human Systems Management*, 7(1988) 3, pp. 185-188.

"Osmotic Growths: A Challenge to Systems Science," *Int. J. General Systems*, 14(1988) 1, pp. 1-17. (With G.J. Klir and K.D. Hufford)

"Integrated Process Management: A Management Technology for the New Competitive Era," in: *Global Competitiveness: Getting the U.S. Back on Track*, edited by M.K. Starr, W.W. Norton & Co., New York, 1988, pp. 121-158. (With M. Hessel and M. Mooney)

"Knowledge As Capital/Capital As Knowledge," *Human Systems Management*, 9(1990) 3, pp. 129-130.

"Management Wisdom of the West," Part 1 (in Japanese), *Standardization and Quality Control*, 43(1990) 11, pp. 41-48. Part 2, 43(1990) 12, pp. 43-48.

"Trentowski's Cybernetyka," in: *Systems & Control Encyclopedia*, Supplementary Volume 1, Pergamon Press, Elmsford, N.Y., 1990, pp. 587-589.

"Simulation Models of Autopoiesis: Variable Structure," in: *Systems & Control Encyclopedia*, Supplementary Volume 1, Pergamon Press, Elmsford, N.Y., 1990, pp. 543-547.

"Optimizing Given Systems vs. Designing Optimal Systems: The *De Novo* Programming Approach," *Int. J. General Systems*, 17(1990) 4, pp. 295-307.

"De Novo Programming," *Ekonomicko-matematicky obzor*, 26(1990) 4, pp. 406-413.

Book Review: "The Eternal Venture Spirit," by K. Tateisi, *Human Systems Management*, 9(1990) 2, pp. 127-128.

1991

"All Autopoietic Systems Must Be Social Systems," *Journal of Social and Biological Structures*, 14(1991) 3, pp. 311-332. (With K.D. Hufford)

"Gestalt System of Holistic Graphics: New Management Support View of MCDM," *Computers and Operations Research*, 18(1991) 2, pp. 233-239. (With E. Kasanen and R. Östermark)

"Management Challenges in the 1990s," in: *Managing Toward the Millennium*, edited by J.E. Hennessy and S. Robins, Fordham University Press, New York, 1991, pp. 3-65. (With R. Cornet and J.A.F. Stoner)

"Spontaneous Social Orders," in: *A Science of Goal Formulation: American and Soviet Discussions of Cybernetics and Systems Theory*, edited by S.A. Umpleby and V.N. Sadovsky, Hemisphere Publishing Corp., Washington, D.C., 1991, pp. 133-150.

"Knowledge As Capital: Integrated Quality Management," *Prometheus*, 9(1991) 1, pp. 93-101.

"Transition To Free Markets: The Dilemma of Being and Becoming," *Human Systems Management*, 10(1991) 1, pp. 1-5.

"Are Biological Systems Social Systems?" *Human Systems Management*, 10(1991) 2, pp. 79-81.

"Privatization," *Human Systems Management*, 10(1991) 3, pp. 161-163.

"Cognitive Equilibrium: A Knowledge-Based Theory of Fuzziness and Fuzzy Sets," *Int. J. General Systems*, 19(1991) 4, pp. 359-381.

"Fuzzifying the 'Precise' Is More Relevant Than Modeling the Fuzzy 'Crisply' (Rejoinder by M. Zeleny)," *Int. J. General Systems*, 19(1991) 4, pp. 435-440.

"Cognitive Equilibrium," *Ekonomicko-matematicky obzor*, 27(1991) 1, pp. 53-61.

"Measuring Criteria: Weights of Importance," *Human Systems Management*, 10(1991) 4, pp. 237-238.

1992

Foreword to *Knowledge in Action: The Bata System of Management*, (First English translation of T. Bata's "Uvahy a projevy"), IOS Press, Amsterdam, 1992, pp. v-vii.

"An Essay Into a Philosophy of MCDM: A Way of Thinking or Another Algorithm?" Invited Essay, *Computers and Operations Research*, 19(1992) 7, pp. 563-566.

"The Application of Autopoiesis in Systems Analysis: Are Autopoietic Systems Also Social Systems?" *Int. J. General Systems*, 21(1992) 2, pp. 145-160. (With K.D. Hufford)

"The Ordering of the Unknown by Causing It to Order Itself," *Int. J. General Systems*, 21(1992) 2, pp. 239-253. (With K.D. Hufford)

"Reforms in Czechoslovakia: Tradition or Cosmopolitanism?" in: *Management Reform in Eastern and Central Europe: Use of Pre-Communist Cultures*, ed. by M. Maruyama, Dartmouth Publishing Company (Dover), 1992, pp. 45-64.

"Structural Recession in the U.S.A.," *Human Systems Management*, 11(1992) 1, pp. 1-4.

"Beauty, Quality and Harmony," *Human Systems Management*, 11(1992) 3, pp. 115-118.

"Governments and Free Markets: Comparative or Strategic Advantage?" Editorial, *Human Systems Management*, 11(1992) 4, pp. 173-176.

1993

"Alla ricerca di un equilibrio cognitivo: bellezza, qualità e armonia," in: *Estimo ed economia ambientale: le nuove frontiere nel campo della valutazione*, edited by L. Fusco Girard, FrancoAngeli, Milano, 1993, pp. 113-131.

"Kenneth Boulding (1910-1993)," *Human Systems Management*, 12(1993) 2, pp. 159-161.

"Working at Home" *Human Systems Management*, 12(1993) 2, pp. 81-83.

"Economics, Business and Culture," *Human Systems Management*, 12(1993) 3, pp. 171-174.

"Eastern Europe: Quo Vadis?" *Human Systems Management*, 12(1993) 4, pp. 259-264.

1994

Book review: "Management & Employee Buy-Outs as a Technique of Privatization," by David P. Ellerman (Ed.), *Human Systems Management*, 13(1994) 1, pp. 79-81.

"W. Edwards Deming (1900-1993)," *Human Systems Management*, 13(1994) 1, pp. 75-78.

"Foreign Policy: A Human Systems View," *Human Systems Management*, 13(1994) 1, pp. 1-4.

"Fuzziness, Knowledge, and Optimization: New Optimality Concepts," in: *Fuzzy Optimization: Recent Advances*, edited by M. Delgado, J. Kacprzyk, J.-L. Verdegay and M.A. Vila, Physica-Verlag, Heidelberg, 1994, pp. 3-20.

"In Search of Cognitive Equilibrium: Beauty, Quality and Harmony," *Multi-Criteria Decision Analysis*, 3(1994), pp. 48.1-48.11.

"Nicholas Georgescu-Roegen (1906-1994)," *Human Systems Management*, 13(1994) 4, pp. 309-311.

"Towards Trade-Offs-Free Management," *Human Systems Management*, 13(1994) 4, pp. 241-243.

1995

"The Ideal-Degradation Procedure: Searching for Vector Equilibria," in: *Advances In Multicriteria Analysis*, edited by P.M. Pardalos, Y. Siskos, C. Zopounidis, Kluwer, 1995, pp. 117-127.

"Reengineering," *Human Systems Management*, 14(1995) 2, pp. 105-108.

"Trade-Offs-Free Management via De Novo Programming," *International Journal of Operations and Quantitative Management*, 1(1995) 1, pp. 3-13.

"Ecosocieties: Societal Aspects of Biological Self-Production," *Soziale Systeme*, 1(1995) 2, pp. 179-202.

"Global Management Paradigm," *Human Systems Management*, 14(1995) 3, pp. 191-194.

"Human and Social Capital: Prerequisites for Sustained Prosperity," *Human Systems Management*, 14(1995) 4, pp. 279-282.

1996

"Work and Leisure," in: *International Encyclopedia of Business & Management*, Routledge, London, 1996, pp. 5082-8. Also: "Multiple Criteria Decision Making," pp. 978-90. "Critical Path Analysis (CPA)," pp. 904-9. "Optimality and Optimization," pp. 3767-80. "Bata-System of Management," pp. 351-4.

"On Social Nature of Autopoietic Systems," in: *Evolution, Order and Complexity*, edited by E.L. Khalil and K.E. Boulding, Routledge, London, 1996, pp. 122-145.

"Rethinking Optimality: Eight Concepts," *Human Systems Management*, 15(1996) 1, pp. 1-4.

"Customer-Specific Value Chain: Beyond Mass Customization?" *Human Systems Management*, 15(1996) 2, pp. 93-97.

"Asset Optimization and Multi-Resource Planning" *Human Systems Management*, 15(1996) 3, pp. 153-155.

"Comparative Management Systems: Trade-Offs-Free Concept," in: *Dynamics of Japanese Organizations*, edited by F.-J. Richter, Routledge, London, 1996, pp. 167-177.

"Knowledge As Coordination of Action," *Human Systems Management*, 15(1996) 4, pp. 211-213.

"Tradeoffs-Free Management," in: *The Art and Science of Decision-Making*, edited by P. Walden et al., Åbo University Press, Åbo, 1996, pp. 276-283.

1997

"Eight Concepts of Optimality," in: *Multicriteria Analysis*, edited by J. Clímaco, Springer-Verlag, Berlin, 1997, pp. 191-200.

"Towards the Tradeoffs-Free Optimality in MCDM," in: *Multicriteria Analysis*, edited by J. Clímaco, Springer-Verlag, Berlin, 1997, pp. 596-601.

"From Maximization to Optimization: MCDM and the Eight Models of Optimality," in: *Essays in Decision Making*, edited by M.H. Karwan, J. Spronk and J. Wallenius, Springer-Verlag, 1997, pp. 107-119.

"Ecosocietà: aspetti sociali dell'auto-produzione biologica," in: *Teorie Evolutive e Transformazioni Economiche*, edited by E. Benedetti, M. Mistri and S. Solari, CEDAM-Padova, 1997, pp. 121-142.

"The Decline of Forecasting?" *Human Systems Management*, 16(1997) 1, pp. 1-3.

"The Fall of Strategic Planning," *Human Systems Management*, 16(1997) 2, pp. 77-79.

"Work and Leisure," in: *IEBM Handbook on Human Resources Management*, Thomson, London, 1997, pp. 333-339. Also: "Bata-System of Management," pp. 359-362.

"Autopoiesis and Self-Sustainability in Economic Systems," *Human Systems Management*, 16(1997) 4, pp. 251-262.

"Insider Ownership and LBO Performance," *Human Systems Management*, 16(1997) 4, pp. 243-245.

"Bata, Thomas (1876-1932)," in: *IEBM Handbook of Management Thinking*, Thomson, London, 1997, pp. 49-52.

1998

"National and Corporate Asset Optimization: From Macro- to Micro-Reengineering," in: *Economic Transformation & Integration: Problems, Arguments, Proposals*, edited by R. Kulikowski, Z. Nahorski and J. Owsinski, Systems Research Institute, Warsaw, 1998, pp. 103-118.

"Multiple Criteria Decision Making: Eight Concepts of Optimality," *Human Systems Management*, 17(1998) 2, pp. 97-107.

"Telework, Telecommuting and Telebusiness," *Human Systems Management*, 17(1998) 4, pp. 223-225.

1999

"Beyond the Network Organization: Self-Sustainable Web Enterprises," in: *Business Networks in Asia*, edited by F.-J. Richter, Quorum Books, Westport, CT, 1999, pp. 269-285.

"Global Management Paradigm," *Fordham Business Review*, 1(1999) 1, pp. 91-101.

"What is IT/S? Information Technology in Business," *Human Systems Management*, 18(1999) 1, pp. 1-4.

"Industrial Districts of Italy: Local-Network Economies in a Global-Market Web," *Human Systems Management*, 18(1999) 2, pp. 65-68.

"Strategy for Macro- and Micro-Reengineering in Knowledge-based Economies" in: *The Socio-Economic Transformation: Getting Closer to What?* edited by Z. Nahorski, J. Owsinski, and T. Szapiro, Macmillan, London, 1999, pp. 113-125.

2000

"New Economy of Networks," *Human Systems Management*, 19(2000) 1, pp. 1-5.

"Global E-MBA for the New Economy," *Human Systems Management*, 19(2000) 2, pp. 85-88.

IEBM Handbook of Information Technology in Business, Editor, Thomson, London, 2000, p. 870.

"Introduction: What Is IT/S?" in: *IEBM Handbook of Information Technology in Business*, edited by M. Zeleny, Thomson, London, 2000, pp. xv-xvii. Also: "High Technology Management," pp. 56-62. "Global Management Paradigm," pp. 48-55. "Mass Customization," pp. 200-207. "Autopoiesis (Self-Production)," pp. 283-290. "Business Process Reengineering (BPR)," pp. 14-22. "Knowledge vs. Information," pp. 162-168. "Integrated Process Management," pp. 110-118. "Self-Service Society," pp. 240-248. "Telepresence," pp. 821-827. "Kinetic Enterprise & Forecasting," pp. 134-141. "New Economy," pp. 208-217. "Tradeoffs Management," pp. 450-458. "Critical Path Analysis," pp. 308-314. "Decision Making, Multiple Criteria," pp. 315-329. "Optimality and Optimization," pp. 392-409.

New Frontiers of Decision Making for the Information Technology Era, Editor with Y. Shi, World Scientific Publishers, 2000, p.

"Elimination of Tradeoffs in Modern Business and Economics," in: *New Frontiers of Decision Making for the Information Technology Era*, edited by M. Zeleny and Y. Shi, World Scientific Publishers, 2000, pp.

"New Economy and the Cluetrain Manifesto," *Human Systems Management*, 19(2000) 4, pp. 151-156.

2001

IEBM Handbook of Information Technology in Business, Editor, Paperback edition, Thomson, London, 2001, p. 870.

"Knowledge and Self-Production Processes in Social Systems," *UNESCO Encyclopedia*

"Bat'a, Tomás (1876-1932)," *Biographical Dictionary of Management*

"Human Systems Management at 20," *Human Systems Management*, 20(2001)1, pp. 1-2.

"Herbert A. Simon (1916-2001)," *Human Systems Management*, 20(2001)1, pp. 3-4.

"Claude E. Shannon (1916-2001)," *Human Systems Management*, 20(2001)1, pp. 5-6.

"Autopoiesis (Self-production) in SME Networks," *Human Systems Management*, 20(2001)3, pp. 201-207.

2002

"Knowledge of Enterprise: Knowledge Management or Knowledge Technology?" *International Journal of Information Technology & Decision Making*, 1(2002)2, pp. 181-207.

2004

"Knowledge-Information Circulation through the Enterprise: Forward to the Roots of Knowledge Management," in: *Data Mining and Knowledge Management*, edited by Y. Shi, W. Xu, and Z. Chen, Springer-Verlag, Berlin-Heidelberg, 2004, pp. 22-33.

2005

"The Evolution of Optimality: De Novo Programming," in: *Evolutionary Multi-Criterion Optimization*, edited by C.A. Coello Coello *et al.*, Springer-Verlag, Berlin-Heidelberg, 2005, pp. 1-13.

Cesty k úspìchu (Roads to Success), Èintámani, Brno, 2005.

Human Systems Management: Integrating Knowledge, Management and Systems, World Scientific, 2005.

2006

"Knowledge-Information Autopoietic Cycle: Towards the Wisdom Systems," *Int. J. Management and Decision Making*, Vol. 7, No. 1, 2006, pp. 3-18.

Bibliography

Anderson, J.C. et al. (1988). Operations Strategy: A Literature Review, *Journal of Operations Management*, 8, 2, April, 137.

Anokhin, P.K. (1935). *Problem centra i periferii v fiziologii nervnoi deiatel'nosti* (The problem of the center and periphery in the physiology of nervous activity). Collected works, Gorkii.

Bata T. (1992). *Knowledge in Action: The Bata System of Management*, IOS Press, Amsterdam.

Baumol, W.J. (1963). An Expected Gain-Confidence Limit Criterion for Portfolio Selection, *Management Science*, Vol. 10, pp. 175-182.

Bawa, V.S. (1977). Mathematical Programming of Admissible Portfolios, *Management Science*, Vol. 23, no. 7, pp. 779-785.

Beach, L.R. (1967). Multiple Regression as a Model for Human Information Utilization, *Organizational Behavior and Human Performance*, Vol. 2, 276-289.

Beer, S and Casti, J. (1975). Investment against Disaster in Large Organizations, *IIASA Research Memorandum*, RM-75-t6, April.

Beer, S. (1975). Preface to Autopoietic Systems, in: H.R. Maturana, F.G. Varela, *Autopoietic Systems*. BCL Report No. 9.4, University of Illinois, Urbana, Ill., pp. 1-16.

Beer, S. (1975). *Platform for Change*, John Wiley & Sons, New York.

Blackwell, D. (1956). An Analog of the Minimax Theorem for Vector Payoffs, *Pacific Journal of Mathematics*, Vol. 6, No. 1, pp. 1-8.

Blin, J.-M. (1976). How Relevant are "Irrelevant" Alternatives? *Theory and Decision*, Vol. 7, *pp.* 95-105.

Bogdanov, A.A. (1901). *Poznaniye z istoricheskoi tochki zreniya* (Knowledge From the Historical Point of View), St. Petersburg.

Bogdanov, A.A. (1904). *Empirio-monism. Stati po filozofii,* Vols. I-III, St. Petersburg-Moscow.

Bogdanov, A.A. (1922). *Tektologiia: vseobschaia organizatsionnaia nauka*, Z. I. Grschebin Verlag, Berlin.

Bogdanov, A.A. (1927). *Bor'ba za zhizniesposobnost'* (The Struggle for Viability), Moscow.

Bogdanov, A.A. (1984). Essays *in Tektology*. Transl. by G. Gorelik, Intersystems, Seaside, C.A.

Bogdanov, A.A. (1984). *Red Star* (Includes: Red Star-A Utopia; Engineer Menni: A Novel of Fantasy; A Martian Stranded on Earth: A Poem), Indiana University Press, Bloomington.

Bogdanov, A.A. (1926-1928). *Allgemeine Organisationslehre (Tektologie)*. Bd. I & Bd. II, Alexander und Lang, Berlin.

Borgwardt, K.-H. (1982). Some distribution-independent results about the asymptotic order of the average number of pivot steps of the simplex method, *Mathematics and Operations Research*, 7, 441-462.

Brian, A. (1994). *Increasing Returns and Path Dependence in the Economy*. Ann Arbor, University of Michigan Press, pp. 2-10.

Brumelle, S.L., and Vickson, R.G. (1975). A Unified Approach to Stochastic Dominance, in W.T. Ziemba and R.G. Vickson (eds.), *Stochastic Optimization Models in Finance*, Academic, New York, pp. 101-113.

Bruner, R.F. et al. (1998). *The Portable MBA*, Wiley, New York.

Cairncross, F. (1997). *The Death of Distance*, Harvard Business School Press, Cambridge, M.A.

Castellan, N.L, Jr. (1973). Comments on the "Lens Model" Equation and the Analysis of Multiple-Cue Judgment Tasks, *Psychometrika*, Vol. 38, 87-100.

Champy, J. (1995). *Reengineering Management*, New York: Harper Business.

Chentler, A. (1990). *Scale and Scope*. Belknap Press, Cambridge, M.A.

Cochran, M. et al. (eds.), (1990). *Extending Families*, Cambridge University Press, Cambridge.

Cochrane, J.L. and Zeleny, M. (eds.). (1973). *Multiple Criteria Decision Making*, The University of South Carolina Press, Columbia, S.C., p. 816.

Coello Coello, C.A. (1999). A comprehensive survey of evolutionary-based multiobjective optimization techniques, *Knowledge and Information Systems*, vol. 1, no. 3, pp. 269-308.

Coello Coello, C.A. (2000). Treating constraints as objectives for single-objective evolutionary optimization, *Engineering Optimization*, vol. 32, no. 3, pp. 275-308.

Colson, G. and Zeleny, M. (1979). *Uncertain Prospects Ranking and Portfolio Analysis under the Conditions of Partial Information*, Mathematical Systems in Economics, no. 44, Verlag Anton Hain, Meisenheim.

Colson, G. and Zeleny, M. (1980). Multicriterion Concept of Risk under Incomplete Information, *Computers & Operations Research*, Vol. 7, no. 1-2, pp. 125-143.

Contini, B.M. (1966). A Decision Model under Uncertainty with Multiple Payoffs, In A. Mensch, ed., *Theory of Games: Techniques and Applications*, New York.

Coombs, C.H. (1958). On the use of inconsistency of preferences in psychological measurement, *Journal of Experimental Psychology*, Vol. 55, pp. 1-7.

Coyle, D. (1998). *The Weightless World*, Cambridge, MIT Press.

Cortaid, J.W. and Woods J.A. eds. (1999). *Knowledge Management Yearbook 1999-2000*, Butterworth-Heinemann, Woburn, M.A.

Davis, S.M. (1989). From Future Perfect: Mass Customizing, *Planning Review*, Vol. 17, 16-22.

Dawes, R.M. and Corrigan, B. (1974). Linear Models in Decision Making, *Psychological Bulletin*, Vol. 81, 95-106.

Dawes, R.M. (1973). "Objective Optimization under Multiple Subjective Functions," in J.L. Cochrane and M. Zeleny (eds.), *Multiple Criteria Decision Making*, University of South Carolina Press, Columbia S.C., pp. 9-17.

De Geus, A. (1997). *The Living Company*, Harvard Business School Press, Boston.

Dewey, J. and Bentley, A.F. (1949). *Knowing and the Known*, Beacon Press, Boston.

Edelman, G.M. (1988). *Topobiology*, Basic Books, New York.

Edelman, G.M. (1992). *Bright Air, Brilliant Fire*, Basic Books, New York.

Eigen, M. (1971). Self-Organization of Matter and the Organization of Biological Macromolecules, *Naturwissenschaften*, Vol. 10, pp. 466.

Eldredge, N. (1996). Ultra-Darwinian Explanation and the Biology of Social Systems, in: *Evolution, Order and Complexity*, edited by E.L. Khalil and K.E. Boulding, Routledge, London, pp. 89-103.

Festinger, L. (1964). *Conflict, Decision and Dissonance*, Tavistock Publications, London.

Fishburn, P.C. (1978). A Survey of Multiattribute/Multicriterion Evaluation Theories, in S. Zionts (ed.), *Multiple Criteria Problem Solving*, Springer-Verlag, New York, pp. 181-224.

Fradette, M., and Michaud, S. (1998). *Corporate Kinetics*, Simon & Schuster, New York.

Friedman, M. (1962). *Price Theory: A Provisional Text*, Aldine, Chicago, IL.

Fukuyama, F. (1995). *Trust: The Social Virtues and the Creation of Prosperity*, Free Press, New York.

Gardner, M. (1971). On Cellular Automata, Self-reproduction, the Garden of Eden, and the Game of Life, *Scientific American*, 224, 2.

Garfinkel, A. (1987). The Slime Mold Dictyostelium as a Model of Self-Organization in Social Systems, in: *Self-Organizing Systems: The Emergence of Order*, edited by F. Eugene Yates, Plenum Press, New York, pp. 181-212.

Gierer, A. (1974) Hydra as a Model for the Development of Biological Form, *Scientific American*, pp. 44 -54

Gilmore, J.H. (1995). Understanding the Market of One, *U.S. Distribution Journal*, 222, 6, p. 13.

Gold, T. (1971). Machines, not Men, in Space, *Times Magazine*. 22 August.

Gorelik, G. (1975). Principal Ideas of Bogdanov's 'Tectology': The Universal Science of Organization, *General Systems Yearbook*, 20, pp. 3-1 3.

Gorelik, G. (1975). Reemergence of Bogdanov's Tektology in Soviet Studies of Organization, *Academy of Management. Journal*, vol. 18.

Gorelik, G. (1987). Bogdanov's Tektologia, General Systems Theory, and Cybernetics, *Cybernetics and Systems*, Vol. 18, pp. 157-175.

Grossman, G. (1965). "Notes for a Theory of the Command Economy" in: M. Bornstein (ed.), *Comparative Economic Systems*, Richard D. Irwin, Homewood, Ill.

Grove, A.S. (1996). *Only the Paranoid Survive*, Bantam Dell Press.

Hadar, J. and Russell, W.R. (1969). Rules for Ordering Uncertain Prospects, *American Economic Review*, Vol. 59, 1969, pp. 25-34.

Haken, H. (1996). "Synergetics as a Bridge between the Social and Natural Sciences," in: *Evolution, Order and Complexity*, edited by E.L. Khalil and K.E. Boulding, Routledge, London, pp. 234-248.

Halal, W.E. et al. (1993). *Internal Markets*, John Wiley, New York.

Hamada K. and Monden Y. (1989) Profit Management at Kyocera Corporation: The Amoeba System, *Japanese Management Accounting*, ed. Y. Monden and M. Sakurai, Productivity Press, Cambridge, M.A., pp. 197-210.

Hammer, M. (1996) *Beyond Reengineering*, Harper Business, NewYork.

Hammer, M. and Champy J. (1994). *Reengineering the Corporation*, Harper Business, New York.

Hanoch, G., and Levy, H. (1969). The Efficiency Analysis of Choices Involving Risk, *Review of Economic Studies*, Vol. 36, pp. 335-346.

Hayek, F.A. (1937). Economics and Knowledge, *Economica*, February 1937, 33-45.

Hayek, F.A. (1945). The Use of Knowledge in Society, *American Economic Review*, 35, 519-530.

Hayek, F.A. (1973). *Law, Legislation and Liberty,* University of Chicago Press, Chicago.

Hayek, F.A. (1975). *Kinds of Order in Society,* Studies in Social Theory, No. *5,* Institute for Humane Studies, Menlo Park, Ca.

Hayek F.A. (1988). *The Fatal Conceit*, University of Chicago Press, Chicago.

Hayes, R.H. and Pisano, G.P. (1994). Beyond World-Class: The New Manufacturing Strategy, *Harvard Business Review*, 77.

Heer, E. (1973). *Remotely Manned Systems*, Caltech Press, Stanford.

Heery, E. and Salmon, J. (eds.) (1999). *The Insecure Workforce*, Routledge, London.

Heimann, S.R., and Lusk, E.J. (1976). Decision Flexibility: An Alternative Evaluation Criterion, *Accounting Review,* Vol. 51, January, pp. 51-64.

Hessel, M. and Zeleny, M. (1987). Optimal design: towards new interpretation of shadow prices in linear programming, *Computers and Operations Research,* 14, pp. 265–71.

Hessel, M, Mooney, M. and Zeleny, M (1988). Integrated Process Management: A Management Technology for the New Competitive Era, in: *Global Competitiveness: Keeping the United States on Track*, edited by M.K. Starr, W.W. Norton, New York, pp.121-158.

Hoebeke, L. (1988). From work ethics towards work esthetics: Work as art and technological choice, *Human Systems Management*, Vol. 7, pp. 333-340.

Huxley, J.S. (1912). *The Individual in the Animal Kingdom*, G.P. Putnam's Sons, New York.

Jackson, P.C. Jr. (1974). *Introduction to Artificial Intelligence.* Petrocelli Books, New York.

Jantsch, E. (1975). *Design for Evolution,* George Braziller, New York.

Johnson, E.G. and Corliss, W.R. (1971). *Human Factors Applications in Teleoperator Design and Operation*, Wiley, New York.

Katona, G. (1976). *Psychological Economics*, Elsevier, New York.

Keeney, R.L. and Raiffa, H. (1976). *Decisions with Multiple Objectives: Preferences and Value Tradeoffs*, Wiley, New York.

Kelly, K. (1998). *New Rules for the New Economy,* Viking, New York.

Khalil, E.L. (1990). Rationality and Social Labor in Marx, *Critical Review*, 4, 1-2, pp. 239-265.

Khalil, E.L. (1996). Networks and organizations, *International Encyclopedia of Business & Management*, Routledge, London, pp. 3629-3636.

Klir, G.J., Hufford, K.D. and Zeleny, M. (1988). Osmotic Growths: A Challenge to Systems Science, *International Journal of General Systems*, 14, 1, pp. 5-9.

Kochan, T.A. (1988). Adaptability of the U.S. Industrial Relations System, *Science*, Vol. 20, 15 April, pp. 287-292.

Kochen, M. and Zeleny, M. (1981). Self-service aspects of health maintenance: assessment of current trends, *Human Systems Management*, Vol. 2, 4, pp. 259–67.

Kotha, S. (1995). Mass Customization: Implementing the Emerging Paradigm for Competitive Advantage, *Strategic Management Journal*, 16, pp. 21-42.

Krogh, von G., Roos, J., and Slocum, K. (1994). An Essay on Corporate Epistemology, *Strategic Management Journal*, vol. 15, pp. 53-71.

Krugman, P. (1996). *The Self-Organizing Economy*, Blackwell Publishing, New York.

Langton, C.G. (1989). Artificial Life, in: *Artificial Life: The Proceedings of an Interdisciplinary Workshop on the Synthesis and Simulation of Living Systems*, Edited by C.G. Langton, Vol. VI, Santa Fe Institute Studies in the Sciences of Complexity Series, Addison-Wesley, pp. 1-47.

Leduc, S. (1911). *The Mechanics of Life*, Rebman Ltd., London.

Lee, E.S. (1994). On Fuzzy De Novo Programming, in: *Fuzzy Optimization: Recent Advances*, edited by M. Delgado, J. Kacprzyk, J.-L. Verdegay and M.A. Vila, *Physica-Verlag*, Heidelberg, pp. 33-44.

Lee, E.S. (1996). Optimal-design models. *International Encyclopedia of Business & Management*, Routledge, London, pp. 3758-3766.

Leibenstein, H. (1976). *Beyond Economic Man: A New Foundation for Microeconomics*, Harvard University Press, Cambridge, Mass.

Lerner, E. (1971). *Managerial Finance*, Harcourt Brace Jovanovich, New York.

Lewis, C.I. (1929). *Mind and the World-Order*, 2nd ed., Dover Publications, New York, 1956.

Lewontin, R. (1983). The Organism as the Subject and Object of Evolution, *Scientia*, 118, pp. 63-82.

Li, R-J. and Lee, E.S. (1990). Fuzzy Approaches to Multicriteria De Novo Programs, *Journal of Mathematical Analysis and Applications*, 153, 1, pp. 97-111.

Li, R-J. and Lee, E.S. (1990). Multicriteria De Novo Programming with Fuzzy Parameters, *Computers and Mathematics with Applications*, 19, 5, pp. 13-20.

Li, R-J. and Lee, E.S. (1993). De Novo Programming with Fuzzy Coefficients and Multiple Fuzzy Goals, *Journal of Mathematical Analysis and Applications*, 172, 1, pp. 212-220.

Locker, A. (1973). Systemogenesis as a Paradigm for Biogenesis, in: *Biogenesis-Evolution-Homeostasis*, edited by A. Locker, Springer-Verlag, New York, 1973, pp. 1-7.

Luce, R.D. and Raiffa, H. (1957). *Games and Decisions: Introduction and Critical Survey*, John Wiley, New York, pp. 23-31.

MacCrimmon, K.R. (1973). An Overview of Multiple Objective Decision Making, in: J.L. Cochrane and M. Zeleny (eds.), *Multiple Criteria Decision Making*, Columbia, S.C., USC Press, pp. 18-44.

Mackay, Ch. (1849). *Memoirs of Extraordinary Popular Delusions*, Richard Bentley, London.

Malone T.W. and R.J. Laubacher (1998). The Dawn of the E-Lance Economy, *Harvard Business Review*, Sept.-Oct., pp. 145-152.

Mann, C. (1991). Lynn Margulis: Science's Unruly Earth Mother, *Science*, Vol. 252, pp. 378-381.

Marais, E.N. (1970). *The Soul of the White Ant*, Human & Rousseau, Pretoria.

Markowitz, H. (1952). Portfolio Selection, *Journal of Finance*, Vol. 7, no. 1, pp. 77-91.

Markowitz, H. (1959). Portfolio Selection: Efficient Diversification of Investments, Wiley, New York.

Maruyama, M. (1992). Entropy and Beauty, *Human Systems Management*, Vol. 11, pp. 165-168.

Mathews, J., (1992). *TCG: Sustainable Economic Organization through Networking*. UNSW Studies in Organizational Analysis and Innovation, no. 7, July.

Maturana, H.R. (1970). Neurophysiology of Cognition, in: *Cognition: A Multiple View*, edited by P. Garvin, Spartan Books, New York, pp. 3-23.

Maturana, H.R. and Varela, F.J. (1973). *De Máquinas y Seros Vivos*. Editorial Universitaria, Santiago, Chile.

Maturana, H.R. and Varela, F.J, (1975). *Autopoietic Systems*, Biological Computer Laboratory, BCL Report No. 9.4, Department of Electrical Engineering, University of Illinois, Urbana, Illinois, September.

Maturana, H.R. and Varela, F.J. (1987). *The Tree of Knowledge*, Shambhala Publications, Boston.

Maturana, H.R. (1975). The Organization of the Living: a Theory of the Living Organization, *International Journal of Man-Machine Studies*, Vol. 7, pp. 313- 332.

Menger, C. (1883). *Untersuchungen uber die methode der Sozialwissenschaften und der Politischen Okonomie insbesondere*, Duncker & Humblot, Leipzig.

Miller, J.L. and Miller, J.G. (1992). The Boundary, *Behavioral Science*, Vol. 37, 1, pp. 23-38.

Minsky, M. (1985). Toward a remotely-manned energy and production economy, *Human System Management*, 5, 2, pp. 111-121.

Minsky, M. (1986). *The Society of Mind*, Simon and Schuster, New York.

Mintzberg, H. (1994). *The Rise and Fall of Strategic Planning*, Free Press, New York.

Moad, J. (1995). Let Customers Have It Their Way, *Datamation*, pp. 34-39.

Moiseev, Nikita N. (1982). *Chelovek-sreda-obshchestvo*, (Man-environment-society), Nauka, Moscow.

Moore, J.F. (1996) *Death of Competition: Leadership and Strategy in the Age of Business Ecosystems*, HarperCollins, New York.

Morgenstern, O. (1972). Thirteen critical points in contemporary economic theory: An interpretation, *Journal of Economic Literature*, Vol. 10, December, pp. 1163-1189.

Neumann, J. von and Morgenstern, O. (1953). *Theory of Games and Economic Behavior*, Princeton University Press, 3rd edition, Princeton, N.J.

Ohmae, K. (1995) *The End of Nation State*, Free Press, New York.

Papalambros, P.Y. and Wilde, D.J. (1988). *Principles of Optimal Design*, Cambridge University Press, New York.

Pask, G. (1971). Interaction between Individuals, Its Stability and Style, *Mathematical Biosciences*, Vol. 11, 59 - 84.

Pask, G. (1975). Conversation, *Cognition and Learning*. Elsevier, New York.

Pask, G. (1976). *Conversation Theory. Applications in Education and Epistemology*. Elsevier, New York.

Pask, G. (1976). Minds and Media in Education and Entertainment: Some Theoretical Comments Illustrated by the Design and Operation of a System for Exteriorising and Manipulating Individual Theses, *Proceedings of the Third European Meeting on Cybernetics and Systems Research*, Vienna, April 1976.

Pattee, H. (1973). Physical Problems of the Origin of Natural Controls, in: *Biogenesis-Evolution-Homeostasis*, edited by A. Locker, Springer-Verlag, New York, pp. 41-49.

Pekelman, D. and Sen, K.S. (1974). Mathematical Programming Models for the Determination of Attribute Weights, *Management Science*, Vol. 20, 8, pp. 1217-1229.

Peppers, D. and Rogers, M. (1997). *Enterprise One to One*, Doubleday, New York.

Perechuda, K. (1984). Rekonstrukcia tektologicznej teorii organizacii A. Bogdanowa, *Prakseologia*, 91-92, pp. 7-102.

Petzinger, Jr., T. (1999). *The New Pioneers*, Simon & Schuster, New York.

Philippatos, G.C., and Wilson, C.J. (1972). Entropy, Market Risk, and the Selection of Efficient Portfolios, *Applied Economics,* Vol. 4, pp. 209-220.

Pilzer, P.Z. (1990). *Unlimited Wealth*, Crown Publishers, New York.

Pine II, B.J. (1993). Making Mass Customization Happen: Strategies for the New Competitive Realities, *Planning Review*, Sept.-Oct., 2, 5, pp. 23-24.

Pine II, B.J. (1993). Mass Customizing Products and Services, *Planning Review*, pp. 6-15.

Pine II, B.J., Victor, B. and Boynton, A.C. (1993). Making Mass Customization Work, *Harvard Business Review*, September-October, p. 108.

Polanyi, M. (1983). *Tacit Dimension*, Peter Smith Publications.

Ponssard, L-P., and Zamir, Sh. (1973). Zero-Sum Sequential Games with Incomplete Information, *International Journal of Game Theory*, 2, pp. 99-107.

Porter, M.E. (1996). What Is Strategy? *Harvard Business Review*, pp. 61-78.

Porter, R.B. (1974). Semivariance and Stochastic Dominance: A Comparison, *American Economic Review,* Vol. 64, pp. 200-204.

Porter, R.B. and Gaumnitz, J.E. (1972). Stochastic Dominance vs. Mean-Variance Portfolio Analysis: An Empirical Evaluation, *American Economic Review,* Vol. 62, pp. 438-446.

Prusak, L. (1999). What's Up with Knowledge Management: A Personal View, *The Knowledge Management Yearbook 1999-2000*, eds. J.W. Cortada and J.A. Woods, Butterworth-Heinemann, Woburn, M.A., pp. 3-7.

Quinn, J.B. et al. (1997). *Innovation Explosion*, Free Press, New York.

Quirk, J.P. and Saposnik, R. (1962). Admissibility and Measurable Utility Functions, *Review of Economic Studies,* Vol. 29, pp. 140-146.

Raiffa, H. (1969). Preferences for Multi-Attributed Alternatives, *RAND Memorandum*, RM 5868-DOT/RC, April, p. 8.

Richta, R and collective. (1969). *Civilization at the Crossroads*, Prague.

Rodin, R. (1999). *Free, Perfect, and Now*, Simon & Schuster, New York.

Rome, B.K and Rome, S.C. (1971) *Organizational Growth through Decision-Making*, American Elsevier, New York.

Rothschild, M. (1990). *Bionomics: Economy as Ecosystem*, Henry Holt, New York.

Roy, B. (1973). How outranking relation helps multiple criteria decision making, in: J.L. Cochrane and M. Zeleny (eds.), *Multiple Criteria Decision Making*, University of South Carolina Press, Columbia, pp. 179-201.

Sabbagh, K. (1996). *Twenty-first-Century Jet*, Scribner, New York.

Samuelson, P.A. (1970). The Fundamental Approximation Theorem of Portfolio Analysis in Terms of Means, Variances and Higher Moments, *Review of Economic Studies,* Vol. 37, October, pp. 537-542.

Sanchez, R. (1997). Strategic Management at the Point of Inflection: Systems, Complexity and Competence Theory, *Long Range Planning*, Vol. 30, pp. 939-946.

Saxenian, A., (1994). *Regional Advantage: Culture and Competition in Silicon Valley and Route 128*, Harvard University Press, Cambridge, M.A.

Schelling, T.C. (1960). *The Strategy of Conflict*, Harvard University Press, Cambridge, M.A.

Schor, J.B. (1992). *The Overworked American: The Unexpected Decline of Leisure*, Harvard University Press, Cambridge, M.A.

Schrage, M. (1990). *Shared Minds: New Technologies of Collaboration*, Random House, New York.

Serageldin, I. (1995). Sustainability and the Wealth of Nations: First Steps in an Ongoing Journey, *Third Annual World Bank Conference on Environmentally Sustainable Development*, Washington, D.C., September 30, 1995.

Serageldin, I. (1995). Monitoring Environmental Progress: A Report on Work In Progress, *Environmentally Sustainable Development Series*, The World Bank.

Shapiro, C. and Varian, H.R. (1998). *Information Rules*, Harvard Business School Press, Cambridge, M.A.

Shepard, R.N. (1964). On Subjectively Optimum Selection among Multi-Attribute Alternatives, in: M.W. Shelly and G.L. Bryan (eds.), *Human Judgments and Optimality*, John Wiley and Sons, New York.

Shelly, M.W. and Bryan, C.L., eds. (1964). *Human Judgments and Optimality*, John Wiley and Sons, New York.

Sherali, H.D., Soyster, A.L. and Baines, S.G. (1983). Nonadjacent extreme point methods for solving linear programs, *Naval Research Logistics Quarterly*, 30, pp. 145-161.

Shi, Y. (1995). Studies on Optimum-Path Ratios in De Novo Programming Problems, *Computers and Mathematics with Applications*, vol. 29, pp. 43-50.

Shils, E. (1980). *The Calling of Sociology*, University of Chicago Press, Chicago.

Shils, E., (1985). Sociology, in: *The Social Science Encyclopedia*, Routledge & Kegan, London, pp. 799-811.

Shingo, S. and A. Robinson (1990). *Modern Approaches to Manufacturing Improvement: The Shingo System*, Productivity Press, Portland, O.R.

Shocker, A.D. and Srinivasan V. (1974). A Consumer-Based Methodology for the Identification of New Product Ideas, *Management Science*, 20, 6, February, pp. 92-137.

Slovic, P. and Liebtenstein, S. (1973). Comparison of Bayesian and Regression Approaches to the Study of Information Processing in Judgment, in: L. Rappoport and D.A. Summers (eds.), *Human Judgment and Social Interaction*, Holt, Rinehart and Winston, New York, pp. 16-108.

Slovic, P. (1969). Analyzing the Expert Judge: A Descriptive Study of a Stockbroker's Decision Processes, *Journal of Applied Psychology*, No. 53, pp. 255-263.

Smuts, J.Ch. (1973) *Holism and Evolution*, Greenwood Press, Westport, C.T.

Sowell, T. (1980). *Knowledge and Decisions*, Basic Books, New York.

Spencer-Brown, G. (1972). *Laws of Form*, Julian Press, New York.

Srinivasan, V. and Shocker, A.D. (1973). Linear Programming Techniques for Multidimensional Analysis of Preferences, *Psychometrika*, vol. 38, 3, pp. 337-369.

Starr, M.K and Zeleny, M., eds. (1977). North-Holland, Amsterdam.

Starr, M.K. and Greenwood, L.H. (1977). Normative generation of alternatives with multiple criteria evaluation, in: *Multiple Criteria Decision Making*, TIMS Studies in the Management Sciences, 6, pp. 111-127.

Steuer, R.E. (1986). *Multiple Criteria Optimization*, Wiley, New York.

Stock, G.B. and Campbell, J.H. (1996). Human Society as an Emerging Global Superorganism: A Biological Perspective, in: *Evolution, Order and Complexity*, edited by E.L. Khalil and K.E. Boulding, Routledge, London, pp. 181-198.

Stone, B.K. (1973). A General Class of Three-Parameter Risk Measures, *Journal of Finance,* Vol. 28, June, pp. 675-685.

Stonier, T. (1983). *The Wealth of Information*, Methuen, London.

Susiluoto, L (1982). *The Origins and Development of Systems Thinking in the Soviet Union.* Dissertationes Humanarum Litteratum, No. 30, Academia Scientarium Fennica, Helsinki.

Sveiby, K.E. (1999). Tacit Knowledge, in: *The Knowledge Management Yearbook 1999-2000*, eds. J.W. Cortada and J.A. Woods, Butterworth-Heinemann, Woburn, M.A., pp. 18-27.

Taylor, J.R. (1983). Conceptual impediments to productivity, *Optimum*, Vol. 14, pp. 19-42.

Tenner, A.R., DeToro, I.J. (1997). *Process Redesign*, Addison Wesley, Reading, Mass.

Toffler, A. (1980). *The Third Wave*, Bantam, New York.

Topoff, H. (ed.), (1981). *Animal Societies and Evolution*, W.H. Freeman & Co., San Francisco, C.A.

Trentowski, B. (1843) *Stosunek filozofii do Cybernetyki czyli sztuki rzadzenia narodom.* J.K. Zupanski, Poznan.

Utterback, J.M. (1994). *Mastering the Dynamics of Innovation*, Harvard Business School Press, Cambridge, M.A.

Varela, F.G. (1975). A Calculus for Self-Reference, *International Journal of General* Systems, 2, 5.

Varela, F.G. (1976). The Arithmetics of Closure, in: *Proceedings of the Third European Meeting on Cybernetics and Systems Research*, Vienna, April.

Varela F.J., Maturana H.R. and Uribe R. (1974). Autopoiesis: The Organization of Living Systems, Its Characterization and a Model, *Biosystems,* vol. 5, pp. 187-196.

Varela, F.J., Thompson, E. and Rosch, E. (1991). *The Embodied Mind*, MIT Press, Cambridge, M.A.

Venkataraman, N. and Henderson, J.C. (1998). Real Strategies for Virtual Organizing, *Sloan Management Review*, pp. 33-48.

Von Foerster, H. (1971). Computing in the Semantic Domain, *Annals of the New York Academy of Sciencies,* 184, June, pp. 239-241.

Von Foerster, H. (1972). *An Epistemology for Living Things*, Biological Computer Laboratory, BCL Report No, 9.3, Department of Electrical Engineering, University of Illinois, Urbana.

Von Foerster, S.C. (1971). Molecular Ethology, in: Molecular Mechanisms of Memory and Learning, edited by C. Jung, Plenum Press, New York.

Wallin, J. (1973). *Computer-Aided Multiattribute Profit Planning,* Skriftserie Utgiven av Handelshogskolan vid Abo Akademi, Abo, Finland.

Ward, B. (1972). *What's Wrong with Economics?* Basic Books, New York.

Warsh, D. (1984). *The Idea of Economic Complexity*, Viking Press, New York.

Weitzman, M.L. (1984). *The Share Economy*, Harvard University Press, Cambridge, M.A.

Whinston, A. et al. (1997). *The Economics of Electronic Commerce*, Macmillan Technical Publishing, New York.

Whitmore, G.A., and Findlay, M.C. (1977). (eds.): *Stochastic Dominance: An Approach to Decision Making Under Risk,* Heath, Lexington, Mass.

Wilkie, W.L. and Pessemier, E.A. (1973). Issues in Marketing's use of Multi-Attribute Models, *Journal of Marketing Research*, Vol. X, pp. 428-441.

Willcocks, L.P. and Lester, S., Editors (1999) *Beyond the IT Productivity Paradox*, Wiley, Chichester.

Wilson, E.O. (1998) *Consilience*, Alfred A. Knopf, New York.

Yu, P.L. (1985) *Multiple Criteria Decision Making*, Plenum, New York.

Yu, P.L. (1977). Decision dynamics with an application to persuasion and negotiation, *TIMS Studies in the Management Sciences,* vol. 6, pp. 159-177.

Zadeh, L.A. (1973). Outline of a New Approach to the Analysis of Complex Systems and Decision Processes, in: J.L. Cochrane and M. Zeleny (eds.), *Multiple Criteria Decision Making*, University of South Carolina Press, Columbia, S.C., pp. 686-725.

Zeleny, M. (1973). Compromise Programming, in: J.L. Cochrane and M. Zeleny (eds.), *Multiple Criteria Decision Making*, University of South Carolina Press, Columbia, S.C., pp. 261-301.

Zeleny, M. (1974). A Concept of Compromise Solutions and the Method of the Displaced Ideal, *Journal of Computers and Operations Research*, vol. 1, pp. 479-496.

Zeleny, M. (1974). *Linear Multi-objective Programming*, Springer-Verlag, New York.

Zeleny, M., ed. (1975). *Multiple Criteria Decision Making: Kyoto 1975*, Springer-Verlag, New York.

Zeleny, M. (1976). APL-AUTOPOIESIS: Experiments in Self-Organization of Complexity, in: *Proceedings of the Third European Meeting on Cybernetics and Systems Research,* Vienna.

Zeleny, M. (1976). Conflict dissolution, *General Systems Yearbook*, vol. XXI, pp. 131-136.

Zeleny, M. (1976). Multiobjective Design of High-Productivity Systems. *Proceedings of Joint Automatic Control Conference,* Purdue University, Paper APPL9-4, New York, pp. 297-300.

Zeleny, M. (1976). The theory of the displaced ideal, in M. Zeleny (ed.), *Multiple Criteria Decision Making: Kyoto 1975*, Springer-Verlag, New York, pp. 153-206.

Zeleny, M. (1977). The Decline of Forecasting, *Human System Management*, 16, 1, pp. 153-155.

Zeleny, M. (1977). Self-Organization of Living Systems: A Formal Model of Autopoiesis, *General Systems*, 4, 1, pp. 13-28.

Zeleny, M. (1978). Multidimensional Measure of Risk: Prospect Rating Vector (PRV), in: S. Zionts (ed.), *Multiple Criteria Problem Solving,* Springer-Verlag, New York, pp. 529-548.

Zeleny, M. (1979). Cybernetics and General Systems-A Unitary Science? *Kybernetes,* 8, pp. 17-23.

Zeleny, M. (1979). The Self-Service Society: A New Scenario of the Future, *Planning Review*, vol. 7, no. 3, pp. 3-7, 37-38.

Zeleny, M. (1979). Special book reviews, *International Journal of General Systems,* 5, pp. 63-71.

Zeleny M. (1980). *Autopoiesis, Dissipative Structures, and Spontaneous Social Orders*. Westview Press, Boulder, Co.

Zeleny, M. (1980). Towards a self-service society, *Human Systems Management,* 1, 1, p. 77.

Zeleny, M. (1981). *Autopoiesis: A Theory of Living Organization*, New York: North-Holland.

Zeleny, M. (1981). On the Squandering of Resources and Profits via Linear Programming. *Interfaces,* vol. 11, pp. 101-107.

Zeleny, M. (1981). Tektology. News item (including photo of Bogdanov with Lenin, Bazarov, Gorkii, Ladyzhnikov, wife and son A.A. Malinovskii), *Human Systems Management*, 2, pp. 234-235.

Zeleny, M. (1982). *Multiple Criteria Decision Making*, McGraw-Hill, New York.

Zeleny, M., ed. (1984). *MCDM: Past Decade and Future Trends*, JAI Press, Greenwich, C.T.

Zeleny, M. (1984). Multicriterion design of high-productivity systems, in: *MCDM: Past Decade and Future Trends* (ed. M. Zeleny), JAI Press, Greenwich, C.T, pp. 171-187.

Zeleny, M. (1984). De novo programming with single and multiple objective functions. Technical Report, TWISK 352, CSIR, Pretoria.

Zeleny, M. (1985). Multicriterion design of high-productivity systems: Extensions and applications, *Proceedings of the VI. International Conference on Multiple Criteria Decision Making (MCDM)*, Springer-Verlag, New York.

Zeleny, M. (1985). Spontaneous Social Orders, in: *Foundations of Cybernetics and General Systems Theory*, Proceedings of the USA-USSR Conference, May 17-19, 1985, Hemisphere Publishing Corp., Washington, D.C., 1988. Also in: *General Systems*, 112, pp.117-131.

Zeleny, M. (1985). Spontaneous Social Orders, in: *The Science and Praxis of Complexity*, The United Nations University, Tokyo, pp. 312-328; *International Journal of General Systems*, 11, 2, pp. 117-131; also as Les ordres sociaux spontanes, in: *Science et pratique de la complexite*, Actes du colloque de Montpellier, Mai 1984, IDATE/UNU, La Documentation Francaise, Paris, 1986, pp. 357-378.

Zeleny, M. (1986). At the End of the Division of Labor, *Human Systems Management*, vol. 6, no. 2, pp. 97-99.

Zeleny, M. (1986). High technology management, *Human System Management*, vol. 6, no. 2, pp. 109-120.

Zeleny, M. (1986). Management of human systems & human management of systems, *Erhvervs økonomisk Tidskrift*, 50, pp. 107-116.

Zeleny, M. (1986). Optimal System Design with Multiple Criteria: De Novo Programming Approach, *Engineering Costs and Production Economics*, 10, pp. 89-94.

Zeleny, M. (1986). The Law of Requisite Variety: Is It Applicable to Human Systems? *Human Systems Management*, 6, pp. 269-271.

Zeleny, M. (1986). The Roots of Modern Management: Bat'a-System, *Human Systems Management*, vol. 6, 1, pp. 4 -7.

Zeleny M. (1987). Cybernetyka, *International Journal of General Systems*, 13, pp. 289-294.

Zeleny, M. (1987). Management Support Systems: Towards Integrated Knowledge Management, *Human Systems Management*, vol. 7, no. 1, pp. 59-70.

Zeleny, M. (1987). Systems Approach to Multiple Criteria Decision Making: Metaoptimum, *Toward Interactive and Intelligent Decision Support Systems*, ed. by Y. Sawaragi, K. Inoue and H. Nakayama, Springer-Verlag, New York, pp. 28-37.

Zeleny, M. (1988). The Bata-System of Management: Managerial Excellence Found, *Human Systems Management*, 73, pp. 213-219.

Zeleny, M. (1988). Beyond capitalism and socialism: Human manifesto, *Human Systems Management*, vol. 7, no. 3, pp. 185-188.

Zeleny, M. (1998). Multiple Criteria Decision Making: Eight Concepts of Optimality, *Human Systems Management*, vol. 17, no. 2, pp. 97-107.

Zeleny, M, (1988). La grande inversione: Corso e ricorso dei modi di vita umani, in: *Physis: abitare la terra*, edited by M. Ceruti and E. Laszlo, Feltrinelli, Milano, pp. 413-441.

Zeleny, M. (1988). Parallelism, Integration, Autocoordination and Ambiguity in Human Support Systems, in: *Fuzzy Logic in Knowledge-Based Systems, Decision and Control*, edited by M.M. Gupta and T. Yamakawa, North-Holland, New York, pp. 107-122.

Zeleny, M. (1988). Tectology. *International Journal of General Systems*, 14, pp. 331-343.

Zeleny, M. (1988). What Is Integrated Process Management? *Human Systems Management*, vol. 7, no. 3, pp. 265-267.

Zeleny, M. (1989). The Grand Reversal: On the Corso and Ricorso of Human Way of Life, *World Futures*, 27, pp. 131-151.

Zeleny, M. (1989). Knowledge as a New Form of Capital, Part 1: Division and Reintegration, *Human Systems Management*, 8, 1, pp. 45-58. Knowledge as a New Form of Capital, Part 2: Knowledge-Based Management Systems, *Human Systems Management*, vol. 8, no. 2, pp. 129-143.

Zeleny, M. (1989). Stable patterns from decision-producing networks: new interfaces of DSS and MCDM, *MCDM WorldScan*, 3, pp. 6–7.

Zeleny, M. (1989). The Role of Fuzziness in the Construction of Knowledge, *The Interface between Artificial Intelligence and Operations Research in Fuzzy Environment*, eds. J.-L. Verdegay and M. Delgado, Interdisciplinary Systems Research Series no. 95, Verlag TÜV, Rheinland, pp. 233-252.

Zeleny M. (1990) Amoeba: The New Generation of Self-Managing Human Systems, *Human System Management*, 9, 2, pp. 57-59.

Zeleny, M. (1990). De Novo Programming. *Ekonomicko-matematicky obzor*, vol. 26, pp. 406-413.

Zeleny, M. (1990). Optimizing Given Systems vs. Designing Optimal Systems: The De Novo Programming Approach, *General Systems*, vol. 17, pp. 295-307.

Zeleny, M. (1991). Cognitive Equilibrium: A Knowledge-Based Theory of Fuzziness and Fuzzy Sets, *General Systems*, vol. 19, no. 4, pp. 359-381.

Zeleny, M. (1991). Knowledge as Capital: Integrated Quality Management, *Prometheus*, vol. 9, no. 1, pp. 93-101.

Zeleny, M. (1992). Foreword to *Knowledge in Action: The Bata System of Management*, (First English translation of T. Bata's *Úvahy a projevy*), IOS Press, Amsterdam, pp. v-vii.

Zeleny, M. (1995). Global Management Paradigm, *Human System Management*, 14, 3, pp. 191-194.

Zeleny, M. (1995). Reengineering, *Human System Management*, 14, 2, pp. 105-108.

Zeleny, M. (1995). Tradeoffs-Free Management via De Novo Programming, *International Journal of Operations and Quantitative Management*, 1, 1, pp. 3-13.

Zeleny, M. (1996). Bata system of management, *International Encyclopedia of Business & Management*, London: Routledge, pp. 351-354.

Zeleny, M. (1996). Optimality and optimization, *International Encyclopedia of Business & Management*, London: Routledge, pp. 3767-3781.

Zeleny, M. (1996). Work and leisure, *International Encyclopedia of Business & Management*, London: Routledge, pp. 5082-5088.

Zeleny, M. (1997) The Decline of Forecasting? *Human System Management*, 16, 1, pp. 153-155.

Zeleny, M. (2000). *IEBM Handbook of Information Technology in Business*, Thomson, London.

Zeleny, M (2000). Knowledge vs. Information, in: *IEBM Handbook of Information Technology in Business*, ed. M. Zeleny, Thomson, London, pp. 162-168.

Zeleny, M. (2000). Optimality and Optimization, in: *IEBM Handbook of Information Technology in Business*, ed. M. Zeleny, Thomson, London, pp. 392-409.

Zeleny, M., Cornet, R. and Stoner, J.A.F. (1990). Moving from the age of specialization to the era of integration, *Human Systems Management*, 9, 3, pp. 153–71.

Zeleny, M. and Hufford, K.D. (1991). All Autopoietic Systems Must Be Social Systems, *Journal of Social and Biological Structures*, 14, 3, pp. 311-332.

Zeleny M., Klir G.J. and Hufford K.D. (1989). Precipitation Membranes, Osmotic Growths and Synthetic Biology, in: *Artificial Life*, The Proceedings of an Interdisciplinary Workshop on the Synthesis and Simulation of Living Systems, Santa Fe Institute Studies in the Sciences of Complexity Series.vol. VI, ed. C. Langton, Addison-Wesley, pp.125-139.

Zeleny, M. and Pierre, N.A. (1975). Simulation Models of Autopoietic Systems, in: *Proceedings of the 1975 Summer Computer Simulation Conference*, Simulations Council, La Jolla, California, pp. 831-842.

Zeleny, M. and Pierre, N.A. (1976). Simulation of Self-renewing Systems, in: *Evolution and Consciousness,* edited by E. Jantsch and C.H. Waddington, Addison-Wesley, Reading, Mass.

Zuboff, S., *In the Age of the Smart Machine*, Basic Books, New York, 1988.

Index

DATE DUE

GAYLORD

PRINTED IN U.S.A.